# 101
# STUMBLES
# IN THE
# MARCH OF
# HISTORY

### What If the
### Great Mistakes in War,
### Government, Industry, and Economics
### Were Not Made?

## BILL FAWCETT

New American Library
New York

NEW AMERICAN LIBRARY
Published by Berkley
An imprint of Penguin Random House LLC
375 Hudson Street, New York, New York 10014

Library of Congress Cataloging-in-Publication Data

Names: Fawcett, Bill, author.
Title: 101 stumbles in the march of history: what if the great mistakes in war,
government, industry, and economics were not made?/Bill Fawcett.
Description: New York: NAL, New American Library, [2016]
Identifiers: LCCN 2016012531 | ISBN 9781101987049 | 9781101987056 (ebook)
Subjects: LCSH: World history—Miscellanea. | Errors—History. | Imaginary histories.
Classification: LCC D24 .F39 2016 | DDC 909—dc23
LC record available at https://lccn.loc.gov/2016012531

First Edition: September 2016

Printed in the United States of America
1   3   5   7   9   10   8   6   4   2

Jacket illustrations by Dave Hopkins

# INTRODUCTION

The march of history is really more like a drunkard's rambling walk. No matter what the wisest and most powerful leaders carefully plan, history has a habit of going its own way. Communism falls and Russia is on a vector for democracy with the West cheering; then Putin arrives. The US and allies invade Iraq, but stop short of Baghdad, then do it again and finish the job so that it seems all is well; then we pull out and it isn't, and ISIS rises. If history has a consistent theme, it might be that nothing goes as planned. One of the reasons for this is that people make history, and men and women make mistakes. Those miscalculations and omissions are the potholes that history stumbles in and that cause it to change direction as it lurches ahead into the unknown.

With the benefit of 20/20 hindsight, this book, in ninety-six articles, looks at 101 mistakes that were made in times and places ranging from ancient Persia to modern Washington, DC. A hundred and one blunders that in each case helped divert the course of history. Some errors created disasters, some changed how we all think or feel, and a few even benefited mankind. We end many of our looks at these world-changing blunders by speculating on what your life today might be like if those mistakes had not been made.

# 1

||||||||||||||||||||||||||||||||||||||||||||||||||||||||||||||||||||||||||||||||||||

# EARTH AND WATER,
# A MISUNDERSTANDING

## 490 BCE

### By Bill Fawcett

||||||||||||||||||||||||||||||||||||||||||||||||||||||||||||||||||||||||||||||||||||

*What we have here is a failure
to communicate.*

This book begins with a situation where a politician caused a war that changed the world. It ends with another example of the same thing. Both even deal with the spread of democracy.

Greece in the fifth century BCE was made up of dozens of independent city-states. Two of the greatest, Athens and Sparta, were close to war. Athens feared defeat from the much more warlike Spartans and searched for an ally that would discourage their enemy from even attacking. They soon realized that there was really only one power so great that even Sparta would have to hesitate. This was the Persian Empire, ruled by Darius.

Now, the Athenians already had a dubious relationship with Darius and his empire. Ten years earlier, they had sent an army to support a revolt by one of their former colonies that had been absorbed by Persia decades earlier. The revolt never had a chance, but the combined army of Athens and two other Greek cities did succeed in almost conquering the capital of the Persian state (known as a satrapy), the city of Sardis. They managed to capture all of the city except the central fortress, where the Persians were still resisting—when a large relief army approached. The Athenians burned Sardis before hurriedly withdrawing. It was an insult made even stronger by the fact that the ruler of the satrap of Sardis was Darius's brother-in-law.

So when these same Athenians appeared a decade later, looking for an alliance, they were informed that Persia would protect them only if an offering of "earth and water" was made to Darius and Persia. It seems that the Athenians, anxious for support, did not check out exactly what this meant. There were many ceremonies sealing alliances with pledges before the gods within Greece itself. They may have thought this was just another version of that. They probably did not realize that this particular offering involved a pledge of fealty and obedience to Persia *forever* by Athens and all her citizens. By doing this, Athens was, in the eyes of the Persians, joining the Persian Empire and acknowledging Darius as its emperor. Or perhaps the members of the Athenian delegation were so desperate that they accepted or ignored the meaning of the demand. So, through their ambassadors, Athens swore an oath of earth and water to Darius. Considering all the problems Athens had caused Darius before, it is not surprising he demanded a high price for his support.

The delegation had not even been back in Athens long enough for the promised Persian support to follow when the Spartans hurried to attack. To the amazement of both sides, Athens met them in battle outside the city and drove off the Spartans. The threat ended, Athens sent a message to the Persians that their aid was not needed and the deal was off. But you just did not pledge, then take away, your allegiance to a Persian emperor. You certainly did not do this if you were just a small city-state that was hundreds of times smaller than their empire. More so since you had already earned the emperor's enmity. It was by Persian standards a supreme insult. To them, Athens had agreed to be part of their empire and then was in revolt before the ink dried.

This misunderstanding initiated more than a century of warfare. Where the Greek cities had been basically ignored by the Persians, now their destruction and incorporation into the empire became an imperial priority. The resulting wars strained all the Greek city-states. The first battle resulting from the Persians sending an army to claim Athens, which they felt was theirs, led to a Persian defeat at the Battle of Marathon in 490 BCE. Darius's son Xerxes invaded with a massive army and fleet seeking revenge for the Athenian insult and perfidy, but was defeated finally at Salamis. That Greek victory came too late to save an evacuated Athens from being burned by the Persians, possibly in direct revenge for their burning of Sardis. The conflict was only settled a century later when a united Greece, in the form of Macedonia and Alexander the Great, turned the entire dynamic around and conquered Persia.

There is a good probability that, if the desperate Athenian embassy had just checked to see what they were agreeing to, war between Persia and Greece could have been delayed or even avoided. The repeated wars and invasions had to have distracted the Athens of Plato and Socrates from even greater development and advancement. How far would the arts, sciences, and thinking of the classic Greek thinkers have advanced with a century of peace with Persia? There would still have been intercity conflicts, though without Persian meddling even the destructive Peloponnesian War would have been shorter and less damaging. Science could have advanced, democracy spread, and distant colonies such as Rome might have been less independent. A golden age of Greek culture would have profoundly changed life today. It would barely be recognizable. Given time for Greece to unite, there might never have been a Roman Empire. Southern Europe might be speaking not a Romance language today (one based on the Latin of Rome) but a descendant language from the Greek. Democracy in some form might have been the rule for two thousand years, rather than kings and emperors. The trouble started when those sent to ask for Persian aid failed to understand, or reject, a price too high for something they eventually did not even need. If they had, there might well have been a very different and better world today. All the mistakes that follow in this book would not have been made, though it is safe to assume that humanity would have found new ones to replace them.

|||||||||||||||||||||||||||||||||||||||||||||||||||||||||||||||||||||||||||||||

## BAD OMEN

### 414 BCE

### By Bill Fawcett

|||||||||||||||||||||||||||||||||||||||||||||||||||||||||||||||||||||||||||||||

An unnecessary war.

I t took two mistakes, both classical in all senses of the word, to bring down the world's first democracy. There have been times when superstition in the form of omens and prophecies affected a battle, but there was one omen that lost Athens the entire Peloponnesian War. Athens had been winning a protracted war with Sparta and that city's allies. It appeared to almost everyone that Sparta was about to lose and just one more push was needed. But military actions were expensive, particularly for Athens, which traditionally paid the rowers and other sailors. This meant they had the best and most enthusiastic crews, but this was costly. Then one of the city's most ambitious and controversial figures, Alcibiades, began to push for Athens and its allies to invade Sicily and conquer Syracuse. The fabled treasury of Syracuse could then be used to finance the rest of the war.

No one, except the most conservative Athenians, cared that they were starting a second war with one of the other democratic cities on a distant island. They were defeating Sparta; how difficult could Syracuse be? Everyone expected to win quickly, long before a battered Sparta could react. Athens, as head of the Delian League, literally voted to open a second front against a powerful and rich enemy in the middle of war. This was so classic a mistake that, even then, there were already a thousand years full of examples of why it shouldn't be done. Then, to make sure the mistake was really serious, it was decided to double the expedition to Sicily and so jeopardize a large part of their army and navy. A good decision if the numbers led to victory, but a risk that Athens simply did not have to take. Another world-changing military disaster that did not need to happen that can be attributed to the heady and blinding optimism of "victory disease." No one considered what it meant if the invasion failed. So the first mistake was starting the war to begin with.

From the beginning things did not go well in Sicily. The reason for this was the choice of commanders. At first it looked like Athens was going to make the traditional mistake of splitting command. Both the impulsive Alcibiades and perhaps the most reverent and hesitant noble in the city, Nicias, were put in command of the invasion of Sicily. Likely the idea was for the two to balance out each other. What happened was that, due to a scandal involving the destruction of sacred statues of Hermes just before they left, Alcibiades was recalled shortly after arriving. Since it appeared that he was about to be railroaded on the charge, Alcibiades sailed not home, but to Sparta—and changed sides.

Alcibiades' defection left Nicias in charge of the entire invasion. But this meant that it was to be run by a hesitant commander who had originally opposed it. In the first months, the Athenians missed two chances to easily conquer Syracuse. One where they had quick access to the unready city and then another when Syracuse's army ventured off to a distant corner of Sicily and left the city virtually unprotected. But both times Nicias dithered, waiting or marching indirectly. Both opportunities for a quick victory were missed.

For the next two years neither of the two sides was able to strike a winning blow. Battles over walls that should have cut Syracuse off and fleet actions in their small harbor eventually tilted the victory against Athens. Nicias called for reinforcements and, just when Syracuse thought they were about to win, five thousand additional hoplites and sixty-five warships arrived, under the command of Demosthenes. The morale of the Athenians soared and that in Syracuse plummeted. Then Demosthenes, looking for a quick win, made a night attack on

Syracuse's allied city of Epipolae. At first things went well. Then the certain chaos caused by a night battle was increased by a counterattack that forced the Athenians to retreat in confusion. Athenian morale crashed and never recovered.

The fighting continued in bursts until it was finally decided, more than two years after landing and after another naval defeat, that the Athenian force needed to simply retreat back to Athens. There still remained forty thousand Athenian hoplites and sailors and enough ships for them, too, to leave. They were preparing to do this when there was an eclipse. Nicias, commanding with Demosthenes, announced that he needed to interpret the omen before they could leave. He retreated to his tent for twenty-seven days. By the time he emerged and announced they could finally retreat, it was too late. The situation was desperate. The army was almost out of food, had lost more ships, and was nearly surrounded. Finally, it managed to break out across Sicily in two columns. The one under Demosthenes was forced to surrender first; he tried to negotiate, but got only the assurance that his men would not be killed outright. At this point, only six thousand of his original twenty thousand still survived. Nicias was later surrounded by the entire might of Sicily and, after an intense battle, forced to surrender as well. He may have had fewer than five thousand of his original twenty thousand left. All the surviving Athenians were sold into slavery or worked to death in the local quarries. Demosthenes and Nicias were executed.

Making a military decision, or rather not making it, for twenty-seven days on the basis of one general's reverence for, and fear of, an omen was the second mistake. Between the two mistakes, the Delian League and Athens turned near-certain victory into defeat. It took ten more years to lose. Athens held on and raised fleets whenever it could. But the Delian League had lost tens of thousands of soldiers, citizens, and sailors, and nearly its entire fleet in an unnecessary war. The city of Athens and its League were literally and monetarily spent. Eventually, the Spartan side, helped by the defections of Athens' former allies, won the war and doomed the city. The Delian League was dissolved. Because of two mistakes—fighting a war on two fronts and allowing superstition to override military necessity—Athens was never again the center of Greece or its culture.

Your life would today be different had the Delian League prevailed, which it almost certainly would have if its ill-fated invasion of Syracuse had not happened. Greece might have united as a nation. Macedonia would not have been able to overwhelm a united Greece. Persia might well have hesitated to make its many invasions, or perhaps Alexander would have partnered with Greece to invade Persia and change the world. Or Philip of Macedon and his son Alexander might have been obscure footnotes in books about the Delian League's defeat of Persia. Or there might be chapters about Persia defeating Greece. If Athens had been dominant for more centuries, then would democracy in some form have become the conventional form of government, not the exception, for the next twenty-five hundred years? That surely would have changed everything.

# 4

## LOST VICTORY

### 387 BCE

### By Bill Fawcett

> When someone is an absolute ruler,
> his personal flaws can create
> an absolute disaster.

Before Alexander became Alexander the Great, conqueror of the known world, he had to defeat the most powerful and largest empire that had been formed up to his time. One whose scope would not again be matched for four hundred years. The Persian Empire was one of a kind. It was much bigger, much wealthier, and more powerful than any of its neighbors or predecessors. No other empire waited on its borders to compete with it. At seemingly no risk to itself, Persia meddled constantly and overtly with Greece, using the empire's wealth and power to play one city state against another. The ferocity and length of the ruinous Peloponnesian War can be partially attributed to Persian support shifting to whichever alliance of Greek cities was losing.

There was a great deal of difference between the two cultures. The Greek and neighboring peoples valued individualism, courage, and accomplishment. It was in the city state of Athens in Greece that democracy first arose. The key values of the Persian Empire were obedience to central authority, accepting your place in society, and generally being a good part of a very large machine.

In 336 BCE, the Emperor Darius III was installed as king of the Achaemenid Dynasty of Persia. He did not sit easily on the throne. Darius was, at best, a shirttail relative of the past emperors Artaxerxes III and Arses. Known as Codomannus before becoming emperor, Darius III was a proven general, but initially nothing but a pawn placed on the throne. He was put in power by a eunuch named Bagoas. This court officer virtually controlled the empire and had poisoned both previous emperors when they proved difficult to control. After becoming emperor, Darius III, too, had too much of a mind of his own for Bagoas to tolerate. But he proved better than his predecessors at court politics. When Bagoas turned up with a goblet of poison, the new emperor forced the eunuch to drink it himself.

So Darius III was an emperor with little, if any, royal blood who had to kill the man who had placed him on the throne. In the next few years, he handled himself well, quickly putting down a few revolts. But when he got word that the Greeks had invaded one of the distant satrapies (similar to states) in his empire, he ordered that it be handled locally. Unfortunately for him, this was not just an ordinary raid by Greeks (as he'd expected) but the beginning of an invasion by Alexander of Macedon.

The local governor and his Greek mercenaries were easily crushed by Alexander. In response, Darius began gathering an army from all the western satrapies and moved to meet the Macedonian army. When they converged, he had managed to maneuver his men into position behind Alexander and cut off all retreat. With an army twice the size of the Macedonians', this meant that any defeat would have resulted in the complete destruction of the Macedonian forces. Battling across the River Issus, Alexander managed to flank and defeat the larger force. Darius, when he saw that the battle was lost, rode back to his distant capital and began forming a much larger army by summoning troops from all parts of the empire.

Alexander then defeated the powerful Persian Mediterranean fleet—without a battle—by simply conquering all the ports they could be based in. This included taking all of the coastline down to Egypt, where he was hailed as a god. Alexander next moved toward Babylon and its capital. At this point, Darius III did everything correctly and by the book . . . er, tablet. But the massive Persian army always stayed near its supplies, was trained to be more effective and work together, and had added special units, such as elephants and scythed chariots. To ensure that his much more numerous mounted forces would be most effective, Darius III had the battlefield smoothed and cleared of even small obstructions.

On the last day of September 331 BCE, Alexander and his army arrived at the well-prepared battlefield. Across it was a Persian force that outnumbered them at least five to one. Alexander, knowing he had the initiative, ordered his army to rest. Darius, fearing a night attack, kept his standing at arms all night. The next morning the refreshed Macedonians marched to face the larger Persian army.

After both the chariots and the elephants struck early and proved less than decisive, the battle began in earnest. Soon the Macedonian left was attacked by a significantly larger force of Persian cavalry and infantry that, from the first contact, pushed the Greeks very slowly back. Alexander refused to react and instead began riding along with his best cavalry units in front of his right wing and across from the bulk of the Persians. This opened a hole in the Macedonian center. A portion of the Persian cavalry broke through and raided Alexander's baggage camp, but Alexander again refused to react. The Macedonian king continued to ride across the Persian front until, while trying to adjust to his movements, the Persian line had thinned at the center. Alexander turned and charged into this weak spot in the line of infantry. Riding at the tip of a triangle of horsemen, with thousands of pike-armed infantry following, he thundered directly toward the wagon containing Darius III, sitting on an ornate throne.

A look at the general situation when Alexander led this charge does not bode well for the Macedonians. On the left side, his best infantry is being pushed back and is in danger of being flanked and broken by a massive number of Persian horsemen. The Macedonian center has been split and Persian light horsemen are pillaging his baggage camp. The right side of his army is not engaged, but would soon be even more badly outnumbered than the left was. From Darius III's perspective, things were going as planned—before Alexander charged at him. His superior numbers were making a difference on the only flank currently engaged, the thinner Macedonian line had already been breached once, and most of his quarter of a million men were unengaged and ready to fight. His opponent was parading away from the only part of the field where there was any fighting, but had no real chance of flanking or riding around the much larger Persian army.

A few minutes later, everything had changed. It did not matter what was happening elsewhere in the battle. Alexander, at the head of that wedge formed with his heavy horsemen, was cutting his way through the infantry directly in front of the Persian emperor. The emperor's bodyguards, the Immortals, were hard-pressed. There was no question that he, personally, was the target of the thundering attack of thousands of Macedonian soldiers, led by a commander some thought to be the son of a god. And here is when Darius made the mistake. At this point, the Persians still greatly outnumbered Alexander's army, Darius had additional forces yet to commit, and his army was beginning to win on the one engaged flank. With Alexander bearing down on him, the imperiled Persian emperor chose not to move to one side, not to shift to where more units could protect him, not to order a general attack by all his forces. What he did was run. Darius III jumped off his throne, hopped into a chariot, and fled, abandoning his gigantic army and leaving it leaderless. He made the mistake of putting greater value on his immediate personal safety than on victory. By doing this, Darius lost everything, eventually even his life.

Darius III's army was still winning when he and his top commanders fled the battlefield. The young Macedonian wanted to follow Darius, but he was made aware that his left was near collapse. It shows just how close-run things still were that Alexander swung all of his troops to the left and hit the back of the tens of thousands of Persians who had been pressing his phalanxes back. That broke their attack, and as word spread that Darius III had fled, the rest of the massive Persian army collapsed.

All of the world's history could have been changed if this one man had shown some personal courage. Because Darius made the mistake of fleeing from the threat that Alexander might cut through to him, he lost his empire. The most powerful man in the ancient world became a footnote and Alexander of Macedon became Alexander the Great. Because the Persian emperor made this cowardly mistake, the dominance and almost inevitable expansion into Europe of Persian culture was stopped and Greek values instead spread across Alexander's empire. Greece and Europe were now safe to develop based upon their unique cultures. If Darius had not fled, there is a good chance he would have defeated Alexander or the two armies would have destroyed each other. We might all today be calling him Darius the Great, whose descendants continued the expansion of Persia across Europe. Rather than success or achievement, we might now all consider that obedience to authority and groupthink are the only way to go. There probably would be no democracy, no Bill of Rights or Magna Carta. Science and original thought would likely have been equally stifled. Then again, there might well have been the kind of peace only found for a number of decades a few centuries later under the next great Western empire, Rome. But the Greek culture of individualism was saved. So the Greek culture, not the authoritarian Persian model, became the basis of the European and American ways of life and how we live today, because Darius III fled.

# 5

|||||||||||||||||||||||||||||||||||||||||||||||||||||||||||||||||||||||||||||||||

# THE ALEXANDRIAN
# EMPIRE

## 323 BCE

### By Bill Fawcett

|||||||||||||||||||||||||||||||||||||||||||||||||||||||||||||||||||||||||||||||||

One mistake can undo the
accomplishments of even the
greatest of men.

There are many mistakes that have affected history. Mistakes made by kings, presidents, and corporate leaders, which have determined how we live, earn, and even think. Most of these mistakes did not have to happen. They were not inevitable. That is why they are called mistakes. So, if something had been a bit different, if a missing fact had been known, or the right thing had been said and a better decision made, what would our world, *our lives*, be like today? Some world-changing mistakes are recent; others still echo from the distant past. This Alexander-sized mistake occurred twenty-four centuries ago, and it reverberates in the way we live and think today.

Arguably the greatest military mind in history, Alexander the Great ended his amazing career with a mistake of omission that has echoed throughout history. After the defeat of Darius III, Alexander occupied the Persian capital and found himself in control of an empire, including lands he probably had not previously even been aware existed. The treasury he captured contained literally tons of gold and precious gems. He then went to great effort to get the Greeks to accept the Persian culture and to marry Persian women, and to introduce Greek values across the empire. He preached tolerance, trade, and education. This should have been the beginning of a golden age similar to that of Augustan Rome, the Pax Romana.

After settling things in the capital, he led his army first north into today's Afghanistan and then east into India. During the many battles and sieges this entailed, Alexander received more than thirty wounds. Eventually his many wounds and a fever began to debilitate the great conqueror. Only six years after he had crossed into Persia, Alexander, age thirty-six, was back in the palace and gravely ill.

As Alexander's condition worsened, his generals began to look to a future without him. They are said to have approached the weakened emperor several times asking about the succession. Alexander's only child was a son only a few years old. Generals offered to act as his guardian. Others offered to rule and preserve what Alexander the Great had created. Several of his generals later showed that they could have successfully succeeded him, but he refused to name anyone.

No one can be sure why Alexander failed to pick the man who could rule the empire after him. Perhaps he did not wish to acknowledge how ill he was. Or perhaps he was believing his own propaganda, and thought himself a god and, therefore, immortal. What *is* known is that, even the day before his death, Alexander refused his generals' pleas to choose one of them. The story, probably apocryphal, is that, when Alexander was asked to whom he would leave his empire, instead of naming someone, he looked at the powerful men gathered around him and responded with "to the strongest."

The effect of this nondecision was that each leader felt himself to be a worthy heir and the empire was divided up between over a dozen men. This led, not surprisingly, to constant warfare between the "successors," which continued until only three successor states remained. These were Macedonia (which included Greece), the Seleucid Empire (comprising most of Asia), and the Ptolemaic Empire (which had lasted for over two centuries in Egypt). The sister of the nineteenth (and last) pharaoh, Ptolemy, was Cleopatra (a good Greek name), of Caesar and Antony infamy. The lands of the empire Alexander had once united were plunged into wars that lasted for decades.

If, rather than two generations of war, there had been a peaceful and acceptable succession by a leader named by Alexander, prosperity could have replaced war. Generations would have been able to develop the sciences and the arts, and explore the rest of the world from a peaceful and secure base. There could have been a golden age in which the two cultures, Greek and Persian, merged gradually, where Alexander's view that all peoples be respected would be upheld. Hundreds of thousands who died violently would have lived and helped to produce a period of growth and scientific advancement. Without those centuries of warfare that were the Succession Wars, we today might be experiencing a world three hundred years more advanced. If there had been an Alexandrian Empire that replaced the Persian Empire, which had been relatively stable for two centuries, today you might even be reading this article in your Martian villa or flying car. Perhaps even reading it in a more peaceful and less bigoted world. Be it from false hope, pride, or delusions of godhood, Alexander's error of omission changed our world forever.

# 6

## ELECTED DICTATOR

### 44 BCE

### By Bill Fawcett

*Doing the wrong thing for
the right reason.*

One of the turning points in Roman history was the Roman Senate's vote to make Julius Caesar dictator for ten years, with no term limits. Despite the horrible legacy of earlier rulers, there were those in Rome who actually *wanted* the famous general to become the "king" of the Roman Empire. After the Romans managed to throw out the Tarquin kings, who, by comparison, made Stalin's paranoid rule look beneficent, the title had been banned permanently. Dictator was a position in Rome that was supposed to be temporary, and such a leader was normally appointed only if the empire or the city was threatened. He remained in office as long as the crisis lasted. Even then, under the republic, the reign of a dictator was limited to no more than two years, no matter what.

Still, if Rome had to make the mistake of picking a dictator, Gaius Julius Caesar was an excellent choice. He was popular, persuasive, and charismatic. This is shown by the simple fact that he got the Senate to basically vote itself into obsolescence. While Caesar's father had been the proconsul of Gallia Narbonensis, this relatively small province on the south coast of modern France, including Marseille, had become a booming trading area and a constant target for Germanic raiders. The rest of modern France and Germany, the real Gaul, was still ruled by a number of tribes. It had been assumed that Julius, as the son of a not-too-wealthy patrician, would go into politics, rising slowly through the ranks until he, too, could rule one of the small provinces, if he was lucky.

After his father, Gaius Caesar, died when Julius was sixteen, Julius revealed himself to be a young man of unbridled ambition. He began by marrying into a much more politically powerful (and wealthier) family. Caesar then began establishing a power base that included a number of factions. Unfortunately for him, one of these was the remaining supporters of the disgraced Gaius Marius. Marius had led what was effectively a peasants' revolt in Rome that nearly toppled the patrician class. Their reaction was to put Lucius Sulla in charge, and he went after all of Marius's supporters and their allies. This included young Julius Caesar, who found it expedient to join the army and leave Rome rather hurriedly.

With his connections and wealth, Julius Caesar started near the top in the legions. He began as the military assistant to a provincial governor. Then he served in combat in Cilicia and was honored for his courage. Caesar returned to Italy and may have aided in the campaigns that annihilated Spartacus's slave revolt. But finding Rome still controlled by Sulla (and therefore still dangerous), Caesar avoided politics, for the most part, and spent some time concentrating on rhetoric—the art of swaying others by verbal argument. He must have been well trained and had some talent, because Cicero himself later publicly observed, "Do you know any man who, even if he has concentrated on the art of oratory to the exclusion of all else, can speak better than Caesar?"

Deciding to spend part of the winter in the warmer Rhodes, Caesar sailed from Italy. He never arrived. His ship was captured by pirates and he was held for several months, until a substantial ransom was paid. Caesar himself later wrote about how, during his captivity, he constantly made a point to warn his captors that he would return and crucify them all—a warning he delivered with a smile. The Roman was still a young man. The pirates took it as a joke. When he was freed, he quickly raised a small fleet, returned to the place where he'd been imprisoned, and scoured the coastline for the men responsible, crucifying each and every one of them. By the time he was done, not only had he eliminated the pirates who had held him, but he had also substantially reduced piracy throughout the Mediterranean. This success led him to be appointed to organize and command the army and fleet that were needed to defend the coast of what is today Turkey. This, too, the young noble accomplished, thus enhancing his reputation.

Finally, Sulla's faction lost power and it was safe for Caesar to return to the Seven Hills of Rome. There his recent successes and connections got him appointed to the high position of quaestor in Spain. Most notable, when the twenty-six-year-old first arrived in Spain, were the words he spoke while standing before a statue of Alexander the Great. Caesar was said to have broken into tears when he compared what little he had achieved to the accomplishments of Alexander—who, by age thirty, had made himself emperor of the known world. Returning to Rome, Julius Caesar then bribed and cajoled himself into a series of higher and higher positions. He was elected aedile, which put him in charge of public buildings and festivals. He spent a large fortune throwing lavish festivals, using borrowed money, and even did a decent job of repairing many buildings. All this brought Caesar to the attention of those to whom his rise was a threat. So he wisely then took the job of pontifex maximus, which was the head priest for the city of Rome. This gave him prestige—and also protected him from his many enemies and creditors.

When his term as pontifex ended, the forty-one-year-old patrician was still deeply in debt, and still a target. There had been trouble with the tribes in Spain. So Julius Caesar pushed the Senate to send him back to that territory as the praetor, a military commander. He was expected to fail in that role, but instead showed real talent as a military leader. This shocked not only his opponents, but Caesar himself. The wealth gained from the spoils of that campaign paid off all of Caesar's debts, and his reputation was now so great that most of his enemies could only watch in frustration as he joined the ranks of the empire's most important citizens. He formed a three-way partnership, a triumvirate, with the older, politically stronger general Gnaeus Pompeius Magnus and the richest man in Rome, Marcus Licinius Crassus. They were both first consuls. Julius Caesar became (officially) one of two second consuls.

The other second consul quickly decided his best and healthiest move was to spend most of his time home with his family, leaving the administrative duties and power to Caesar alone. The triumvirate pushed through many reforms that had been resisted by the patricians in the Senate, most of which endeared them to the common men and the merchants. Caesar's daughter married Pompey, cementing their alliance.

When it was decided that Rome finally needed to tame the fringes of Gaul far north of Italy and the greater Gaul beyond, Caesar was tasked with raising one of the largest armies in the empire's history. Before that was completed, a barbarian tribe, the Helvetians, was pushed by other tribes into the Roman province of Transalpine Gaul. This was located in the north of Italy. Julius Caesar took what he had formed of his army so far and marched north. A few months later, he had decisively defeated the Helvetians and ended the threat. But within a few more months, two German tribes (the Swabians and Sueves) had invaded his father's old province. He again led his still-growing army to meet this threat and was again decisively victorious.

With all these invasions, some of Rome's neighbors saw an opportunity to attack—while Rome was distracted and her legions busy. One group, the Belgae, prepared to invade Roman territory. After being surprised by several Belgae ambushes, Caesar finally engaged the main tribe, the Nervii, whom he defeated in a very close-run battle. With their largest tribe broken, it was only a matter of weeks before the rest of the Belgae were suppressed.

Having conquered most of Gaul, Julius Caesar remained behind to govern the large and wealthy province. He defeated a German invasion and even marched into Germany. Then he returned to Britain, this time to stay, and again increased his power. The next year, 54 BCE, the Belgae again revolted and it took a year to ruthlessly end all resistance. Less than two years after that revolt, all Gaul rose against Rome under the charismatic Vercingetorix. All but three of the nearly three dozen tribes in Gaul joined this revolt. Always outnumbered, Caesar again prevailed. Eventually, he spent a total of nine years conquering and then stabilizing Gaul—and away from Rome.

By this point, things in the Roman Empire had changed. Crassus tried to prove himself as good a general as Pompey or Julius Caesar. His attempt ended in the Parthian desert, with the loss of two legions and his own life. When Julia, Caesar's daughter and Pompey's wife, died in childbirth, the tenuous bond that held the two highly ambitious Romans together was gone. Competition between the followers of the two generals became fierce and occasionally violent. The city of Rome and the empire were also in constant social upheaval. Unemployment in Rome may have been as great as 50 percent. The leading citizens lowered produce prices by using slave labor on their large estates. The result was that they impoverished the small landholders. Then, by raising taxes on land, they forced them off their property, which they added to their own estates. These small farmers, who once had been the backbone of both the legions and the electorate, now streamed into Rome, unemployed and unhappy. Riots in Rome were becoming too common, and conflicts between political factions ever more violent.

With Caesar away, Pompey changed sides and joined the aristocratic party, the Optimate. Caesar remained the darling of the people, but was far away in Gaul. For a while, he stayed out of Roman politics and in Gaul. But he remained a threat. When Pompey tried to remove him from his governorship, he really left Julius Caesar no choice. A few months later, Caesar had gathered up his legions, crossed the Rubicon, and marched his army on Rome itself.

With the general population supporting Caesar, Pompey found himself outnumbered and unable to hold Rome. He fled and was later defeated in Greece. It took more battles in Egypt, northern Africa, and, a few years later, Spain, but the Optimate faction was destroyed and no one was left to oppose Julius Caesar's supporters.

The republic had lasted for centuries, but many in the Senate agreed this was a time of crisis and a strong hand was needed. The once-jealous Senate was cowed by Caesar's public and military support and so voted to make him, as it had made Pompey earlier, sole consul. Julius Caesar then personally appointed all the magistrates (judges) and controlled every aspect of the government. He also spent lavishly the loot gained in his battles to sustain the support of the people. In 44 BCE, the Senate made its final mistake.

It voted to make Julius Caesar "dictator perpetuus"—dictator for life. He had the power of the long-detested Tarquin kings handed to him by the representatives of the people. The Senate, at the insistence of the masses living in Rome, chose to cede all power to an unquestionably capable and charismatic man. What they never considered was that, once that power was given, it could never be taken back. Caesar became, effectively, an unchecked dictator because his ten-year, rather than two-year, term meant no one really could countermand any of his decisions. Effectively Julius Caesar had become the very thing many Romans feared, a virtual king, accountable to no one. Caesar rapidly took advantage of this situation, using the position for his own gain. That one vote, which was made under pressure from the people and Caesar himself, ended the republic, and indirectly doomed the Roman Empire to extinction. One has to wonder what they expected would follow a lifetime of one-man rule.

A month later Julius Caesar was assassinated on that same Senate's steps by senators who feared he would become what they themselves had voted to make him. If the senators had continued to show the courage they had shown by assassinating Caesar, and reasserted the power of the Senate, there might have been a counterbalance to later Caesars. But by showing that it could be cowed by the mob and a powerful general, the Senate destroyed its own power. Rather than a return to a republic after the assassins were defeated, Caesar's adopted heir, Augustus, stepped into the role of "first consul"—effectively the same dictatorial position voted to his father. For a few decades under Augustus, Rome thrived. Then, with the Senate no longer able to remove incompetent or dishonest administrators, there was no check at all on the emperor, nothing to prevent the Caesar (or, later, his praetorian guards) from abusing his position. Some truly terrible and demonstrably insane men held the position. Rome lost its power, its ability to defend itself, and even split the empire. The last man declared emperor of Rome was not even a Roman, but a barbarian chief.

All this, perhaps, might also be a lesson even today: don't let immediate concerns and problems allow citizens to turn into dictators and demagogues, who will destroy people's freedom or way of life. If the Senate had somehow managed to resist the call to dictatorship, Caesar might have had his power limited. More importantly, there would have been a mechanism to elect the empire's leaders for their competence, and not simply for their Julian blood. Emperors who were (literally) insane might not have ruled and helped the empire destroy itself from within. Rome might have managed to recuperate its greatness, and the Pax Romana, the fleeting decades of peace during Augustus's reign, might have lasted for centuries. With barbarian tribes held at bay, there would have been no dark age, no era of church dominance and religious wars, or possibly even nationalism. The concept of an elected government might have not disappeared for over a thousand years. If instead of giving in to a soon-to-be assassinated Julius Caesar, the Senate could have found the courage it once had demonstrated and saved the republic, life today would be different and possibly much better.

‖‖‖‖‖‖‖‖‖‖‖‖‖‖‖‖‖‖‖‖‖‖‖‖‖‖‖‖‖‖‖‖‖‖‖‖‖‖‖‖‖‖‖‖‖‖‖‖‖‖‖‖‖‖‖‖‖‖‖

# 7

# GIVE ME BACK MY LEGIONS

## AD 9

### By Bill Fawcett

‖‖‖‖‖‖‖‖‖‖‖‖‖‖‖‖‖‖‖‖‖‖‖‖‖‖‖‖‖‖‖‖‖‖‖‖‖‖‖‖‖‖‖‖‖‖‖‖‖‖‖‖‖‖‖‖‖‖‖

Trusting the wrong person
can be a fatal mistake.

In AD 9, during the third decade of his reign as the first emperor of Rome, Augustus Caesar thought he had found the right man for a tough job. He needed a governor for the newly formed province of Germania. To the minds of most Romans, Germany had been pacified. Any tribe that revolted had been crushed and it appeared that the Germans were quickly being absorbed into the empire. German mercenaries were now in Roman employ across the empire. Some had fought so well they had been integrated into the legions and even made citizens. What Augustus now felt he needed was a competent governor who could begin turning what had been an expensive military occupation into a profitable province. The Roman Empire, like most governments, always needed more money.

The Emperor Augustus felt he had the right man in the imperial Roman legate—Publius Quinctilius Varus. Varus had already been the governor of Syria, which included many restive areas, including Israel. Along with suppressing a number of revolts, he had been very good at extracting taxes. This was, above all else, the measure of a good governor in the eyes of Rome and those who depended on those taxes to maintain the empire. Varus was also an in-law of the emperor, always an advantage. So the legate Varus was recalled from relatively peaceful and developed Syria, and sent to rule the wild and darkly forested Germania. In the beginning, all seemed to go well for him. With his fifteen thousand crack legionnaires in three legions, at first no one challenged him. But appearances were deceiving. Rome was used to conquering richer lands, such as Greece, Egypt, or even Gaul. The many tribes living in the German forests were relatively poor and had little in the way of gold or coins. This made the taxes Varus imposed a hard burden. Resentment of taxes, Roman arrogance, and being on the wrong side of most deals grew. When Gaul was conquered less than a century before, it had enough trade and industry that it benefited from its inclusion in the Roman Empire. Germany, though, was not in a position to gain much of anything from Rome. Roman rule was becoming universally resented and despised by the German tribesmen, but it appears Varus was unable to understand this. He assumed that Romanizing Germany was something the German tribes would welcome. He ruled just as he had in much different and long-conquered Syria, and expected the same results. It was a fatal misconception.

Perhaps Varus's real error was trusting one man, a German prince of the influential Cherusci tribe who used the name Arminius. Arminius had served in the Roman army, excelled in his duties, and was made a citizen and knight. He was expected to rise in Roman society and even served as a personal adviser to Varus. It was a prestigious, and often profitable, post. But Arminius had other ambitions.

It was the German's ambition to become the chief of his tribe and, perhaps, to unite all of the other German tribes under his rule as well. To do this, he had to impress the *German* warriors, not the Romans, in a dramatic way. Because he had convinced Varus to trust him, he found a way. A way that would give Rome her worst defeat since Hannibal.

It wasn't that Varus had not been warned. A chieftain friendly to Rome, Segestes, who was a Cheruscan noble of equal rank to that of Arminius's father, warned Varus not to trust Arminius. Varus rebuffed the warning. So, when it came time for all three legions, their auxiliaries, and thousands of camp followers to march south from their summer camp on the Weser River to their winter camp in southern Germany, he appointed Arminius to command the mounted auxiliaries. These were local horsemen in Roman hire, whose job was to make sure the way was clear. And to put down minor rebellions that could delay the march. Instead of carrying out Varus's orders, Arminius began immediately to incite the local tribes to revolt. He then reported back to Varus that there was a small uprising, but one too big for him to handle with his horsemen. He assured the governor that that revolt could be quashed if the legions simply marched back past the rebels. This would require only a two-day detour and would end the problem without the expense of a battle. Varus trusted Arminius, and turned off the main roads and into the forests and swamps.

With the traitorous Arminius as guide, the massive column was soon weaving its way through narrow trails and bog-filled paths. A storm occurred, slowing and further disorganizing the Romans. When they were strung out for several miles, with civilians and supply wagons pulled by slow-moving oxen tangled among the centuries, the Germans struck. At first, they simply threw javelins and ran. These legions had beaten them in battle after battle. But as the condition of the Roman army degenerated, the German warriors became bolder. Soon sections of the extended column were attacked by large numbers of German warriors from either side. If the attack went badly, the Germans just fled back into the forest. But too often these ambushes were devastating.

The Roman army's strength was fighting in formation. In open-field battles, these three legions had slaughtered any tribe that resisted them, often suffering few casualties in the effort. But on narrow trails through swamps and deep forests, there was no way for the army to form up. Instead, the fighting was man to man, with all the advantages to the Germans. When the first German attacks were successful, word spread and previously friendly tribes hurried to join in. In an area called the Great Bog, the only path was just over fifty feet wide and surrounded by swamp or dense forest. Strung out in a line, burdened with civilians, and unable to support one another, century after century was destroyed. The running battle lasted for days, but the result was inevitable. When it became apparent that all was lost, Varus and his top officers chose suicide—quite literally falling on their swords. Eventually, what little remained of three crack legions was broken up, surrounded, and leaderless. The cavalry at the front of the column got within sixty miles of the permanent Roman camp at Haltern, but only a few legionnaires managed to escape and report the defeat.

Rome and Augustus panicked at the loss. There were only twenty-eight legions in the entire empire, and three of the most elite and experienced were gone. Worse yet, their aura of being undefeatable was lost, too. All free Germans were driven out of Rome, and all of Italy waited tensely for an expected horde of Germans to sweep down on them. That never happened. What did result was that, after a few punitive expeditions, Rome never again tried to occupy Germany. The Rhine became a permanent boundary—until two centuries later, when the Germanic Teutons, beginning with the Goths, were pushed by the Huns into Gaul. By the time the Huns followed them, the part of the empire based in Rome was a hollow shell of its former self.

The historian Herbert W. Benario once wrote what might have been, if Varus had not trusted Arminius. "Almost all of modern Germany as well as much of the present-day Czech Republic would have come under Roman rule. All Europe west of the Elbe might well have remained Roman Catholic; Germans would be speaking a Romance language; the Thirty Years' War might never have occurred, and the long, bitter centuries of conflict between the French and the Germans might never have taken place.

"With a more Romanized Germany united as one country centuries earlier, there would be no World Wars, no Nazis, and no holocaust."

Just as importantly, Germany would have been a strong buffer, united under Rome against the later invasions of the Goths, Huns, and other barbarians. Western Rome need not have fallen. With the core of the empire, Italy and Gaul, shielded from the barbarian invasions, a significant portion of the social and economic strength of Rome might have remained intact. Society would not have broken down. England would not have lost its legions. There might well never have been any dark age. Five centuries of chaos, illiteracy, and ruin would have been avoided. The scientific life we live today might have evolved as soon as the fifteenth century and we might now be living in a world so advanced it currently only appears in science-fiction novels. One man, Varus, governor of Germania, trusted the wrong person and, if he had not, the world might have been spared immeasurable grief and the march of civilization would not have stumbled.

# 8

## EMPERORS SHOULDN'T SKIRMISH

### Julian the Apostate

354

**By Harry Turtledove**

Julian, often called the Apostate because he rejected Christianity, was Augustus (Roman emperor) from 360 to 363 and sole Augustus following the death of his foe and cousin, Constantius II (reigned 337–361). Constantius was the last surviving son of Constantine the Great (reigned 306–337), who made Christianity first a permitted and then the dominant faith of the empire. At the Council of Nicaea, which condemned the Arian heresy in 325, Constantine began a long tradition of imperial meddling in church affairs.

Although down, Arianism was not yet out. Constantius adhered to it and persecuted its opponents. Sandwiched between his illustrious father and spectacular cousin, Constantius gets short shrift nowadays. He was a grayly competent ruler and capable administrator with a gift for civil war—he handily disposed of Magnentius, the rebel who had overthrown his brother Constans (who had already crushed their other brother, Constantine II). Constantius might well have defeated Julian, too, if sickness hadn't killed him at only forty-four.

Julian was the son of Constantine's half brother, and thus Constantius's half first cousin. He spent his early years staying as inconspicuous as he could. Drawing too much notice from Constantius would have been hazardous to his life expectancy. He went to

Athens for the ancient equivalent of a university education. Many philosophers—professors—remained pagan. Julian seems to have cast off whatever attachment he had for Christianity while in Athens, though coming out and saying so at the time would have been fatal.

With Constantius's brothers deceased, he needed officials he could rely on. He named Julian's older half brother Gallus Caesar (a rank just below that of Augustus) in the east in 351, so he could fight Magnentius in the west. Gallus proved untrustworthy and alarming. Constantius gradually reduced his power, then had him arrested and executed in 354.

But troubles kept coming. Under Shapur II (309–379), the Sassanid Persians attacked Roman territory in the east, while the Alemanni, a German tribe, crossed the Rhine and began conquering Gaul. Desperate, in 355 Constantius appointed Julian Caesar to deal with the German invaders while he fought the Persians himself. Although trained as a philosopher, Julian proved a good general. He defeated the Alemanni and drove them back over the Rhine.

In 360, the Persians took the important Roman fortress of Nisibis. Constantius summoned many of Julian's soldiers to fight in the east. They refused, and proclaimed Julian Augustus in defiance. Constantius was on his way west to fight his cousin when he died. To avoid further strife, he named Julian his successor.

As soon as Julian became sole emperor, he disestablished Christianity. He stopped state subsidies for the religion. He started them for the elder faiths. He also tried to organize their priesthoods in a hierarchical system like the one the Christians used. And he gave the Jews permission to rebuild the Temple in Jerusalem, aiming to show Christian prophecy false (this failed, due to what the Christians called a miracle and what looks to an outsider uncommonly like arson) and to give Christianity another strong theological rival.

He also continued Constantius's war against Persia. His attack nearly reached Ctesiphon, the Persian capital (near modern Baghdad). But his opponents' scorched-earth policy forced the Romans to fall back. A Persian said he knew a good, well-supplied land route for the retreat. Julian made the mistake of believing him, and burned the Roman army's boats on the Tigris to leave his men no other choice.

But the Persian was a plant, as the Romans soon discovered. They were dogged by heat and hunger and thirst as they moved north and west. And Julian himself did not have the sense to stay out of a no-account cavalry skirmish. He was speared, probably (though not certainly) by a Saracen horseman on the Persian side, and died not long afterward. Any hope for a pagan revival died with him. His successor, an officer called Jovian, had to agree to a humiliating peace with Sassanid Persia as the price for extricating his army from its impossible position.

What if Julian had gotten back to the Roman Empire, though? What if he'd ruled for twenty-five or thirty years, as his two predecessors did? What would the world have looked like then?

Obviously, he wouldn't have destroyed Christianity. It was far too well established for that, after half a century in the saddle. But he might have managed to keep it from entrenching itself as the state religion—and less in the way of state interference (the fancy word is *caesaropapism*) might well have proved good for it. A temple rebuilt three centuries after its destruction would have had an enormous and incalculable effect on Judaism, too.

Constantine's Edict of Milan, promulgated in 313, allowed all religions, Christianity included, to be freely practiced on equal terms. Only gradually did Christianity become not just allowed but favored. Had something on the order of the original equality been restored, and had it had a generation or so to take hold, the world might have become a more tolerant one than it really did.

On the political-military front, Julian already had experience fighting German invaders in Gaul. He might well have done better against the Goths entering the Balkans in the 370s than the existing authorities did. He could hardly have done worse; at Adrianople in 378, the Goths destroyed a Roman army and killed the Emperor Valens. Their wanderings through the Roman Empire did much to weaken its grip. The Visigoths would end up ruling Spain and southern Gaul after sacking Rome itself in 410. After they left Italy, the Ostrogoths took control there in their place.

Had the Goths been either defeated or peaceably assimilated, the stress on the Roman Empire during the late fourth and early fifth centuries would have been greatly reduced. Rome might have remained a unified political and cultural entity stretching from the Atlantic all the way to Mesopotamia.

Most people then living in that part of the world would probably have adjudged it a better deal than the one they got. Whether the world now would be better or worse . . . well, who can say what 1,700 years of changes would have done? It would certainly be different. But Julian rode out to skirmish, and we have what we have.

# 9

## AN UNNECESSARY WAR

### 378 AD

**By Bill Fawcett**

Turning potential allies into enemies
has a long tradition.

The Battle of Adrianople doomed the Western Roman Empire (Rome) and crippled the Eastern Empire (Constantinople). The painful fact is that this was a battle that the Romans never needed to fight against an enemy that could well have become a valued ally.

The Goths were a people that lived north of the Eastern Empire. They were considered by the Romans to be barbarians and that image has come down through history so strongly that modern rebellious and black-clad youth identify themselves as "Goths." The reality was quite different. Before being displaced by the Huns, the Goths were a productive and relatively civilized people. They were unlike the Romans culturally, but were nonetheless accomplished in the arts, language, and commerce. Prosperous, the Visigoths actually had a higher literacy rate than did the western Romans. Still, they were also a military-oriented culture, with the heavily armored, mounted warrior typifying its upper classes. The Goths were a powerful, proud, and generally successful people. More so at this point than a few generations later when they completed their conquest of the Western Roman Empire and sacked Rome itself.

Goth tribes first fought against the Romans, not as invaders, but while taking sides in a dynastic battle for control of Constantinople. The Tervingi Goths sided with Procopius, whose claim to the throne was good enough to persuade many of the soldiers of the current emperor, Flavius Julius Valens Augustus, to defect to him. Eventually Procopius was defeated. After a short delay in 369, during which he solidified his control, Valens sought out and decisively defeated the Tervingi and the Greuthungi Goths, who had allied with the usurper.

Valens then turned east, trying to recover lost territory from the resurgent Persians and dealing with a number of local revolts. While he did this, in 375, another "barbarian" tribe began to drive the Goths westward and off their land. These true barbarians were the same Huns who would wreak destruction across both parts of Rome a century later. Evicted from their lands, as many as 200 thousand Visigoths (western Goths) were forced against the Roman border. Their leader, Fritigern, knew they needed a home, but did not want to fight the Huns on one side and the Romans on the other. Even then, two-front wars were a bad idea. He offered an alliance with Valens in exchange for land in Dacia and enough food for his people to survive until new crops could be harvested. The Roman emperor saw in them a new source of military power and agreed.

If only the Roman officials had seen the benefits of the Goths becoming part of the empire. Instead they saw only opportunity for personal gain. With Valens distracted by his own eastern wars, rather than welcome the Visigoths, the local commanders, Lupinicus and Maximus, began to exploit them and, by doing so, took away the Roman Empire's best chance of returning to glory and power. These corrupt Romans slowed the transfer of the lands, denied the promised food, and charged exorbitant rates for what food was available. They generally made life as miserable as possible for the Goths. It soon became apparent that the goal of the Romans was to weaken and (eventually) break the Visigoths—hammer at them until they were so desperate that the entire tribe would submit to slavery rather than allow their families to starve. The Romans would then sell them as slaves.

But the Visigoths soon realized what was happening. Since they had retained all of their weapons and warhorses, they reacted exactly as would be expected. First, there were small battles, as groups of Visigoths stole food. The Goths drove back the Romans, thrusting their way into the empire in search of food and other needs. Another tribe (the almost equally numerous eastern Goths, or Ostrogoths) was being harried by the Huns. They followed in the wake of the advancing Visigoths as they forced their way into Roman lands. The Roman army resisted, but in 377 was defeated by the Visigoths in a pitched battle. Valens finally had to take notice and march a large army to meet the threat his own generals had caused.

The final battle occurred near Adrianople in today's Bulgaria. Valens, a normally astute commander, made a number of mistakes. Fritigern agreed again to discuss peace and proper treatment of his followers. He needed a home for his people more than a war with Rome. But once the two armies faced each other, Valens seems to have decided to attack. There was the mutual hate created by the raids and battles already fought that, perhaps, the two wiser leaders could not overcome. There are some stories about Valens's ambassadors firing or being shot by arrows as they approached the wagon laager containing the Visigoths' women and children (and many thousands of infantry). But something started the battle at a time that seemed to have surprised both sides. It was particularly bad timing for Valens. Twenty thousand more Roman troops were marching toward the battlefield, but were several days away. Yet Valens choose to attack.

It appears the Roman emperor thought, incorrectly, that half of the Visigoths' army was away on a raid. This meant that he temporarily had the larger army and the only mounted forces. Valens ordered his cavalry to attack the laager. The Roman horsemen pressed it hard, but could not break through the circle of wagons. Then the Visigoth cavalry returned, having only been a few hours' ride away grazing their horses in fresh pastures. Their anger at *yet another* Roman betrayal and an attack on their families had to be extreme. Suddenly outnumbered two to one by the more heavily armored Visigoth horsemen, the Roman riders fled. This left the Roman infantry to face the enemy alone. The legions of Caesar could have stood and even won such a battle, but the Roman legions of this era were poorly trained and less well armed. With the Visigoth horsemen attacking them from every side and an equal number of Visigoth foot soldiers slamming into their front and pinning them, the Roman infantry fell apart. The result was a slaughter, with all forty thousand infantry either slain or enslaved. Rome never recovered militarily.

Instead of being sheltered and incorporated into the defense of the Roman Empire, the Goths were turned into enemies. Enemies that went on to sweep through the Western Roman Empire—and eventually a Visigoth chief was able to declare himself the emperor of Rome.

Valens made the mistakes that lost the battle of Adrianople, but the mistake that doomed all of Rome was that of Lupinicus and Maximus, and the other greedy Romans who could see the Visigoths only as a source of personal wealth. They made the mistake of mistreating and betraying the Visigoths, and forcing them into a war and battle against Constantinople that the Goths did not want. This changed the course of history, and not for the better. If they had just been honorable men or used sense when they saw how powerful an enemy the Goths could be, it would today be a better world. The possibilities for Rome, had they honored their agreement and formed a firm alliance with the two Goth peoples, would have been immeasurable—it would have changed the face of history. The Visigoth army as an ally would have nearly doubled the number of defenders protecting the bisected Roman Empire. The dynamic and strong character of the Goths, educated and relatively wealthy, could have revived Roman values and provided a new source of wealth and taxes. When the real barbarians struck, and the Huns were barbarians in every way conceivable, Rome might have been capable of holding them off without being crippled. In reality, a joint Visigoth and western Roman army did finally defeat and drive away Attila and his Huns in 451 at the Battle of Châlons. But it was only a temporary alliance. After another century of war and distrust, what could have been a civilization-preserving alliance was no longer really possible.

As in all the scenarios where the stability and culture that ancient Rome offered is preserved, the dark age might have never occurred. Society, science, medicine, and trade could have continued to progress and the centuries of the dark ages might instead have been more like those of the Enlightenment. The march of civilization would not have become a retreat if the Roman generals had just kept their word and made allies, instead of enemies, of the Goths. If the Visigoths had helped preserve rather than destroy Rome, today calling someone a Goth would have a far different meaning.

# 10

||||||||||||||||||||||||||||||||||||||||||||||||||||||||||||||||||||||||||||

# HAROLD, KING
# OF THE BRITONS

## 1066

## By Bill Fawcett

||||||||||||||||||||||||||||||||||||||||||||||||||||||||||||||||||||||||||||

How to turn victory into defeat
with one decision.

Edward the Confessor was a very religious man. He was so devout that he never managed to produce an heir. This is a problem when you are king of Britain. A later king, Henry VIII, was so concerned with producing a legitimate heir that he disrupted all of England and, eventually, Europe. When Edward died, there was no son to inherit the crown. Britain needed a king NOW. It was a nation under siege (think Viking invaders) and the country needed a strong leader. It was up to the *witan*, who normally served as the king's advisers, to find a replacement. For the witan (literally the "wise men"), there was no real precedent or authority for them to do this. Not surprisingly, most kings made sure that there was no tradition that allowed anyone to appoint a king. It made replacing them too easy.

It was a religious time and kings ruled by divine right. The question of who had the divine right was most often decided by determining who had royal blood. But there was no one related to the king who could rule Britain. This meant that many of the proud and independent British nobles could, *and would*, question whoever was chosen. The witan's choice was Harold Godwinson. Harold was one of the most powerful nobles in the kingdom. He was also the king's brother-in-law. He did not have even the slightest bit of royal blood. Still, Harold was grudgingly accepted by most of the nobles in Britain. This meant that Harold had to prove himself worthy to be king.

Before there was a chance for any real internal revolt, England was invaded. Two different groups looked to take advantage of Edward's death. Both were preparing to invade. Harold had a small navy. All the British king could do was wait. The first to actually invade were the Vikings from Norway, commanded by Harald Hardrada, commanding close to five thousand warriors in almost three hundred ships. Hardrada's excuse was an alliance with Tostig, Harold Godwinson's brother. Tostig felt he should have been chosen king instead of Harold, though he had no royal blood either. It wasn't much of an excuse, but Vikings didn't worry about such things. So, a few months into Godwinson's reign, word came that a Viking army had landed near York.

Harold had to defend the kingdom or lose his throne. Fortunately he had one asset. This was the Huscarls. These were about three thousand well-trained and professional warriors, armed with axes and shields. They were sworn to be his personal bodyguard—and they were also the only standing army on the island. The Huscarls were not cavalry, but would ride mounted to a battle. The ax is not a good mounted weapon. When they got to a battle, they would dismount to fight. Harold rushed north at the head of his Huscarls, gathering up nobles and the local militia, known as the fyrd, as he went. By the time he neared the invading army, he had about the same number of men as the opposition, though, man for man, the fierce Vikings were far superior to his yeoman militia.

Hardrada knew Harold had to meet him, but badly underestimated how long it would take for the new king to cover the two hundred miles to the place where the Viking army was camped. Doing this in an amazing five days, Godwinson was able to surprise Hardrada's troops. He caught them with their army split as they were crossing Stamford Bridge, for which the ensuing battle is named. With half their army on the either side of a narrow bridge, the half on the far side was unable to reinforce those who were attacked. Further, the arrival of the British was so unexpected that, according to some sources, many of the invading warriors were not wearing their armor and some had left it behind on the boats that were beached miles away. This put Hardrada's Vikings at a real disadvantage. Stamford Bridge was still a hard-fought battle. Finally, the Vikings were defeated and it was recorded that their losses were so great that they left behind dozens of ships, because there were no warriors to man the oars. But the cost to Harold was high; a full third of the Huscarls were dead or wounded. Many of the fyrd died as well. Still, Stamford Bridge was a brilliant victory and, if nothing else had happened that year, Harold Godwinson might be remembered as one of Britain's great kings.

In reality, Harold was given no time to savor his victory over his brother and Hardrada. Defeating a Viking army must have gone a long way to showing the other nobles he was worthy to be king, but another invader materialized. Within days of Stamford Bridge, word arrived that William of Normandy had landed near Hastings. Both the person and the place made this invasion unusually threatening to the new and insecure king.

The man who led this second invasion was William, Duke of Normandy. (Also known as William the Bastard, as he was, um, related to the king of France, but not in such a way that he could inherit that throne.) William actually had a sufficient blood and legal claim to being Edward's successor that the pope in Rome supported assertion. This was a real aid to William for the purpose of raising troops and, perhaps more importantly, loans. William had also landed at a very strategic, or at least sensitive, location near Hastings. Harold Godwinson had estates in that part of England. The king would lose his reputation if he was unable to protect his own lands. That was something a man placed on the throne by other men, and with no other right to rule, could not afford. Harold also would lose considerable income if his estates were destroyed by the Normans. Perhaps one, or both, of these considerations explains why Harold made the mistake that changed Britain forever.

Harold and his Huscarls were still near York when word arrived that William had landed. There were about two of the three thousand men still able to ride and fight. There were also thousands of fyrd and nobles with armed retinues spread throughout Britain. There was no question they would support even a new king against an invasion. Most began to gather. Harold Godwinson could have waited and gathered a massive army that was far larger than William's. But to do so would have taken weeks. Harold had surprised Hardrada and that had won him the battle, so perhaps he thought he could do it again against William. What we know for certain is that, for whatever reason, Harold chose to rush south toward Hastings almost as rapidly as he had on his trip north. The speed at which he rushed south had two effects. One was that some of his already exhausted or wounded Huscarls and nobles had to withdraw from the army. The second was that his rapid pace meant that a large number of the fyrd who would have joined his army were unable to reach it before the battle.

Having hurried down, Harold was soon near William and his army of mounted Norman knights and mercenaries. Again, the two forces were about equal in size. They did not have to be, but Harold did not wait for more fyrd to reach him. The British army, mostly Saxon by descent, formed up on what is today called Battle Hill and challenged William to attack. The Norman had no choice; he would have been unable to move or search for food with a hostile force nearby.

The Huscarls stood in the center of the line across the top of Battle Hill. Arrows did not discourage the defenders. Repeated attacks up the slopes by Norman infantry and mounted troops failed to dislodge the Saxons. But it did wear down the already tired defenders. For hours the Normans attacked time after time, but the English line held. Eventually, when those attacking the right side of Harold's army feigned withdrawal (or maybe even really did retreat in a panic), the Saxon warriors who had driven them off broke formation to pursue them. Once the British were out of formation and on level ground, the Norman armored horsemen slaughtered them. The losses caused by the pursuit turned the tide of battle. Their line weakened and with no men to reinforce it, the English were pushed by the Normans. The now-outnumbered fyrd were driven off or killed. The remaining Huscarls formed up to protect Harold, as they had sworn to. Arrows showered the ax-wielding Saxons as they were attacked from all sides. The Huscarls fought desperately, until an arrow killed Harold Godwinson. The battle was over and Duke William of Normandy became William the Conqueror.

What if Harold had paused to gather up the full strength of England? As the Battle of Hastings went, he would have had enough troops that even the losses from the disastrous pursuit would have not endangered his position. With William being on a hostile shore with an army that followed him on the pledge of loot, money, and other promises, he might well have had to retreat. Saxon England would not have become Norman England and that would have made a tremendous difference. In the last thousand years, Britain has played a major role in history. But if William had lost, it would not have been the same Britain.

To begin with, the Saxon system was less centralized. There were local gatherings that ruled villages and the king's rule was affected by their opinions. The nobles and the church had real influence on national policy. The witan was an established institution and a second council of military leaders was gaining in influence when Edward died. Norman England became an oligarchy, where everyone else but nobles and merchants were serfs bound to the land, virtual slaves subject to whims of the nobles. The Saxon model forbade the farmers from moving, but granted them a set portion of the harvest, and guaranteed they kept the land so long as their family could farm it. A Saxon king was subject to the law and Saxon laws granted individuals (who were not nobles) real rights. Norman England was an oligarchy, with all power concentrated in the hands of a few, mostly the king. Rule of law was lost; the law was whatever the lord said it was.

Saxon England was more akin to what England and the United States have become than the reality of Norman England. There is a chance that a Saxon England would have moved to some sort of representative government, like Parliament perhaps, much earlier. This does not guarantee that Saxon England would have become the industrial giant, a world-spanning empire, or created a Royal Navy, but it might have developed the idea of freedom and individual rights long before the American colonies and the French revolted. All history would be different. The concepts of individual rights and the rule of law could have proved as influential as they have in the last few hundred years and spread to the rest of Europe. If Harold had not made the mistake of rushing to Hastings, an argument can be made that democracy and the rights of man might have gotten several hundred years' head start.

||||||||||||||||||||||||||||||||||||||||||||||||||||||||||||||||||||||||||||||||||||||||

# 11

# HOW BYZANTINE CAN YOU GET?

## 1071

### By William Terdoslavich

||||||||||||||||||||||||||||||||||||||||||||||||||||||||||||||||||||||||||||||||||||||||

There are some people you just don't
turn your back on.

The funny thing about decline is that you never can spot it when it happens. The Byzantine Empire found itself in that fix in 1071, when it lost a battle.

That clash happened at Manzikert, an obscure frontier fortress south of Lake Van, near Turkey's present-day border with Iran and Iraq. But a thousand years ago, it was a rough neighborhood, where Byzantines and Seljuq Turks pushed the border back and forth in a series of skirmishes and sieges. This was par for the course in the long-running dogfight between Christians and Muslims. But why would the loss of one battle set up Byzantium for a downward slide lasting almost four hundred years?

## Politics as Usual

An empire is only as good as its emperor—like Basil II, who ruled Byzantium at its zenith. He won a decisive victory over the Bulgars, so ridding the empire of an ever-present threat, then died in 1025. He bequeathed a strong empire to his successors.

But in the following fifty years, Byzantium blew that inheritance. The capital of Constantinople was a snake pit of office politics. Weak emperors, stubborn patriarchs, and cunning bureaucrats played a never-ending game of political musical chairs, promoting favorites to various offices and punishing reformers. Any focus on strategy and diplomacy was lost in a swirl of embezzlement and venality.

Out of this mess emerged Emperor Romanus IV. Formerly Romanus Diogenes, the future emperor was a general posted in Eastern Europe. Accused of plotting against his predecessor, Constantine X, Romanus was stripped of his command and sentenced to death. But Constantine expired instead. The death sentence was dropped. Romanus was politically "rehabilitated." The widowed Empress Eudocia chose him to wed in 1068. And so he was crowned Romanus IV.

Romanus was competent at first. He sized up the growing "Seljuq threat" to his east and began raising an army. His Seljuq counterpart, Sultan Alp Arslan, did not spot the "Byzantine threat" to his west. Ensconced in Baghdad, Alp Arslan had his eye on the heretical Ismaili sect of Shi'ism ruling Egypt, Palestine, and Syria. To the Sunni Seljuqs, this was the real war. They preferred to maintain peace with the Byzantines.

Alp Arslan was busy besieging Aleppo, Syria, when he got word that Romanus was coming after him with an army of about forty thousand. Breaking the siege, Alp Arslan hustled his army back across the upper Euphrates, now in spring flood. That move cost Alp Arslan almost half his army. But having *some* forces to face the Byzantines was better than having none at all.

## Split Decision

As the Byzantines approached Lake Van in the Armenian region (now northwest Turkey), Romanus divided his army, sending roughly half his force to besiege the Seljuqs at Ahlat, approximately thirty miles south, on Van's western shore.

History is unclear if this force was defeated in battle outside of Ahlat, or deliberately withdrawn by its commander as an act of political sabotage to hinder Romanus. Either way, the detachment was not around to answer Romanus's eventual call for reinforcement.

Hearing of Manzikert's fall, Alp Arslan moved his army to about a day's march away from the Byzantines and encamped. It was late August. Both forces were evenly matched in number, but differed in composition. The Seljuqs relied on light cavalry; the Byzantines had a mixed force of infantry and heavy cavalry.

Romanus failed to use his cavalry for reconnaissance, so he did not have a precise idea where the Turkish main force was. He found out the hard way when Seljuq horsemen harried the Byzantine foraging parties sent out to gather supplies. Romanus reinforced his foragers with a small detachment, only to have them sucked into a bigger battle with the Seljuq cavalry. Romanus then led an even larger relief force to save the foragers and their reinforcement.

He pursued the skirmishing Turks away from his camp toward some distant foothills. As evening approached, Romanus had to make a decision. Should he pursue the Turks into the foothills and risk a night battle, or march back to camp while there was enough daylight left? Romanus was prudent. He broke off the action and marched back to camp.

## Let Battle Decide

On the night before battle, Alp Arslan sent a delegation to make a deal with Romanus, rather than risking a battle. But Romanus was deaf to the pleas of the Seljuqs. He sought decisive victory while he had an army big enough to win it. Going back to Constantinople without a victory was out of the question for Romanus. His political enemies would carve him up.

So it was on a Friday morning in late August that Romanus arrayed his army for battle. Cavalry was posted on the flanks, infantry in the center under Romanus's control, with a reserve body to the rear. The Seljuqs arrayed themselves into a crescent formation that enveloped both wings of the Byzantine army, but the Turks kept their distance. Mounted archers harried the Byzantine cavalry, provoking them to charge into preset ambushes away from the main force. Romanus marched onward, failing to bring the Turks to blows. He then found himself with the same dilemma as the day shortened: press on to risk a night action, or return to camp while there was still enough daylight?

Romanus ordered his standard turned around, the signal for his army to march back. The Byzantines turned about-face in some disorder. And that is when Alp Arslan ordered his cavalry to charge. Byzantine mercenary units, seeing the royal standard reversed while the Turks attacked, took flight, believing that Romanus had been killed. The Byzantine reserve, instead of aiding the stricken line, ran away. Historians are again unsure if this was an act of cowardice, incompetence, or treachery. Romanus held the center with a rear guard. But the rest of the army had broken and fled.

Eventually Romanus was captured and brought to Alp Arslan. He spared the Byzantine emperor and sent him back. The Seljuqs now owned the border region. Romanus managed to raise another army, this time to march on his own capital. He was twice vanquished by those who were never on his side. Blinded and disgraced, Romanus died at the island of Prota in 1072.

## No Second Chance

Emperor Michael VII Ducas succeeded Romanus, but the new emperor lacked strategic aptitude. He could have raised another army and marched back to recapture the frontier. Court intrigue and more marginal troubles in Italy distracted the foolish emperor from focusing on the real threat. Within ten years, Turkish raiders faced no Byzantine deterrent. Raids into the Anatolian heartland turned into an occupation, depriving Byzantium of one of its richest provinces. From that point, decline was irreversible.

It would have been a hundred times better if the Byzantine emperors who ruled after Basil II, and their rivals and colleagues, had all shared a sense of duty that was greater than their self-interest. This would have given the Byzantines the strength to hold out as a Greco-Christian bulwark against a rising Turko-Muslim tide.

The Byzantine hold on Anatolia also would have changed another trajectory in history. The Ottoman Empire never would have gotten its start. Osman I was born in north-central Anatolia in the 1200s, his people finding refuge there after fleeing the Mongol conquest to the east. Without that starter sanctuary, the rise of the Ottomans might never have occurred. Instead, they grew to eventually conquer Constantinople in 1451. No Ottoman Empire would have meant the frontier with Islam would have been drawn along the Taurus Mountains and not in the Balkans.

No ruler can be expected to know how well his country will do against future enemies. But every ruler can maintain a strong foundation for the next to build on. Romanus IV inherited a state in decline, and could not reverse its direction. Neither could his successors. It would have been a hundred times better if they could have.

# 12

## RICHARD LIONHEART

### 1192

### By Bill Fawcett

Lionhearted but thickheaded.

Being a king in the Middle Ages meant you had to act like a king. A humble, retiring king often found his cousin on the throne. But sometimes, acting with noble dignity can cause a problem. This is particularly true if the king is trying to sneak across all of Europe.

Saladin had hard-pressed the Crusaders under the leadership of Richard, king of England and duke of Normandy, but was unable to defeat them. By 1192, he had managed to push them back into a strip of land along the coast and into a number of massive castles. Both armies were exhausted and finances were dwindling, so a truce that allowed both leaders, Richard and Saladin, not to lose face was agreed to. Basically both kept what they held, making Saladin the real winner, but Christian pilgrims were to be allowed to travel freely and safely to Jerusalem. This provision allowed Richard to also claim victory and fulfillment of his Crusader vow.

Things in Richard's own kingdom had gotten out of hand during the years he had spent in the Holy Land. Philip of France had been gradually stripping castles and cities away from Richard's holdings in Normandy. Worse yet, in England, his younger brother John had replaced most of the officials Richard had appointed with his own men. John's power would soon threaten the king's. It was definitely time for Richard to go home.

The problem the Lionheart had with going home was that he had to travel across Europe to get there. Richard was opinionated, outspoken, critical, and demanding. Something lesser men tolerated in a king, but his fellow rulers did not. During his crusading years, the English king seems to have managed to antagonize most of the crowned heads on the continent. He had managed to sour his youthful friendship with Philip of France, publicly insult Duke Leopold of Austria, and then support the king of Sicily against Henry VI, the Holy Roman emperor who controlled most of the German states.

To return home, Richard had a choice of two routes. One required travel by ship. This was risky in the extreme. Pirates from what was later known as the Barbary Coast were already common. Worse yet, southern Spain was still in Muslim hands and anyone attempting the difficult transit against the currents flowing into the Strait of Gibraltar would have been sure prey. The other route required riding across Europe, where most of the leaders had become his enemy. According to some accounts, Richard chose to disguise himself as a more common Templar Knight and use the land route.

First, he put his wife on a ship and sent her off to the pope in Rome. Next, he sailed for Greece and then made for the head of the Adriatic, traveling in three new galleys, which he had reportedly acquired at Corfu (possibly to better conceal his movements or indulge his desire to travel in style) before finally landing at Zara in Slavonia. He was hundreds of miles from the nearest friendly ruler, the duke of Savoy. Now, here is a hint: if you are sneaking across Europe, try not to act like you are a king. Opinions vary, but one source of Richard's undoing might have been his demand for fine meals, something a Templar would not have done, including the then-exotic dish of roast chicken. Or perhaps the fact that his few escorts continued to call him Sire gave away the ploy. What *is* known is that men serving his enemy Duke Leopold captured the English king near Vienna, possibly in a brothel.

Crusaders were supposed to be protected, so the pope excommunicated both Leopold and Henry VI over the capture. This made no difference, since excommunications could be rescinded by the proper act—and a large contribution to the Church. Richard of

England was paraded around the German states, a well-kept prisoner. His captors made no secret of their holding him and, eventually, two abbots from England caught up with him and negotiated his ransom. The ransom was to be the enormous amount of 150,000 marks. This was far greater than the total annual income of his entire kingdom. Hostages were also required, to ensure there would be no English reprisals. It took a very long time for the English to gather the money and Richard finally returned to England in 1194. England was impoverished from paying the ransom and Richard spent most of his time in Normandy, so his country was still being ruled by an absentee king.

Richard died five years later, having spent most of his time trying to regain his possessions in Normandy rather than clearing up the problems in England. Richard had no heir. It is possible that personal factors precluded his having any children. Upon Richard's death, his brother John assumed the throne he had so obviously coveted.

Richard's ego seems to have caused his capture. What if he had used more common, as opposed to noble, sense and managed to sneak back to England? The immediate effect would be that his nation would not have been impoverished by his ransom. England was, however, impoverished, and this hindered future kings and the nation's power. There is a good chance that the English could have held on to Normandy, if they'd held on to the ransom money. Today's Europe would look very different if half of France were ruled by England. On the darker side, John might never have taken the throne. Those living under his rule, including the nobles, might have considered that a benefit. The loss in the long run was that, because of the poverty caused by the ransom, King John was forced to push harder and tax more, but had much less power. A king without money can only push so hard on his rich nobles who have their own troops. John was also much less popular than the charismatic Richard. If Richard had returned, there likely would have been no Magna Carta. The document that led to the growth of modern democracy, rule of law, and individual rights might not have been written.

Would the world be better today? Not if the movement started by the Magna Carta had never happened. Would we still be living in the age of kings and divine right? Possibly. Or perhaps a stronger England would have spread the idea of rights earlier and farther.

# 13

‖‖‖‖‖‖‖‖‖‖‖‖‖‖‖‖‖‖‖‖‖‖‖‖‖‖‖‖‖‖‖‖‖‖‖‖‖‖‖‖‖‖‖‖‖‖‖‖‖‖‖‖‖‖‖

## DIVINE CALM

### 1274

### By Charles E. Gannon

‖‖‖‖‖‖‖‖‖‖‖‖‖‖‖‖‖‖‖‖‖‖‖‖‖‖‖‖‖‖‖‖‖‖‖‖‖‖‖‖‖‖‖‖‖‖‖‖‖‖‖‖‖‖‖

Here is a fictionalized version of how a mistake that changed the history of Korea and China may have happened. The facts are accurate.

*November 20, 1274, Hakata Bay,*
*Island of Kyushu, Nippon*

Admiral Hong Dagu nodded; the captains of his mostly Korean landing force rose from their obeisant prostrations on the deck. "Report," he ordered.

The tallest of the officers stepped forward. "Honored Hong Dagu, sea lord of Goryeo—"

Dagu made a chopping gesture with his hand. "The sky darkens behind us. There is no time for titles and ritual. How went the battle on the beaches?"

The captain swallowed. "We have carried the day, Admiral. The samurai who engaged us were brave, but fought more as individuals than as soldiers. I am told it is their fashion, and that they often resolve battles through one or more individual combats."

"Uncivilized savages," sniffed Dagu's adjutant and childhood compatriot Ja-o dismissively. "Too stupid even to respond to Kublai Khan's repeated, explicit commands that they recognize him, in title and tithe, as their suzerain. So the samurai of their leading shoguns make their impossible stand here in Hakata Bay, choosing a desperate defense over thralldom."

Dagu shrugged. "I cannot say I blame them. And they die well."

Ja-o's voice lowered. "Do you respect them so much?"

"Respect them?" Dagu raised an eyebrow. "I observe they do what they think they must bravely. That does not make them any less stupid, any less a horde of vermin. Do you not agree, Captain?"

The tall Korean to whom he addressed this question snapped to attention. "Sir, they are vermin—but tenacious, even so. They suffered great casualties from our bow fire, and I do not believe they had prior experience with our flaming or gunpowder arrows. And after advancing through that fire, they had no organized tactics for breaching our shield wall. But despite their losses, they did not relent."

"Did you take many casualties?"

The captain's gaze wavered. "Fewer than they did."

"Hmm. I see. So, if we were to face five times their number tomorrow?"

The captain grew pale. He paused long enough to choose his words carefully. "With your leadership, great Dagu, we would, of course, prevail. But I suspect that they would inflict even more casualties upon us with their strange, long swords and their—tenacity."

Dagu frowned. "Yes. Of course. So what have your scouts reported? Are their forces massing inland, behind the rises and brush that hem in the shore?"

The captain licked his lips. "Our first two scouts did not return. We have sent another two. We await their return." He shrank slightly before Dagu's glower. "I shall send more," he offered uncertainly.

Dagu frowned, turned away. "No. We have few enough men who have any familiarity with these people, their ways, their language, their coastline. We cannot spend them too freely. Besides, if the second pair of scouts does not return, that partially settles a measure of our present uncertainty: whether control of the beach means control of the coast. If these Japanese are picking off our scouts, denying us the ability to see what lies farther inland, it stands to reason that they wish to conceal a force from us, that our control may very well be limited to what we can see. So if we allow the army to camp on the beach, where it would be vulnerable to a much larger counterattack at night—" Dagu broke off, straightened formally. "Jo-a, pass the word: ready the landing barges to bring our men back to the ships."

"Jun-gi," Jo-a whispered, using Dagu's given name, the one from their shared childhood, "is that wise?"

Dagu leaned closer to him, kept his own voice equally low. "Old friend, we know there is a literal tempest approaching from the sea. We have reason to fear there is a figurative Japanese tempest waiting just beyond the ridges lining this bay. We have two choices: leave or stay. We may gamble that the Japanese are not there and allow our army to bivouac on the beach. But that also means that we must keep our vessels here, where we may support and resupply them. Yet the masters of our ships tell me that our best chance to avoid their destruction is to escape this bay before the storm makes landfall. So, even if there is no Japanese army waiting beyond those ridges, our fleet might be wrecked if we remain here."

Jo-a made a deferential bow as he offered an alternate perspective. "An almost equal number of the shipmasters are urging you to draw in closer behind the headland and weather the storm as best we might, that it is approaching too swiftly to avoid it."

"A chance I would take, *if* we knew the soundings and rocks of this bay and *if* I knew there was no Japanese army beyond that ridge," Dagu replied, jabbing a finger toward the open window of his cabin and at the body-littered beaches and the bluffs beyond. "If we receive a report from one of these scouts that the inland plains are clear, then we shall leave our men on the beach and our ships will weather the storm here as best as they may. But if we hear nothing, I must presume that destruction is bearing down on us from the sea *and* the land. In that event, our army might be slaughtered in the surf before the sun comes up. In that event, we must take them aboard and listen to our foremost shipmasters: that in order to save this fleet and the army that it will be carrying, we must flee this bay with all haste."

Ja-o shrugged. "Then let us hope we hear from one of those scouts."

Dagu stared back out the window. "If the gods are kind, we shall."

. . .

Gwan crept through the unfamiliar undergrowth that dominated the floor of the small defile between the ridges hemming
in Hakata Bay. He had already found one of the prior two scouts
slumped in the bushes, an arrow through his back. He hoped that
discovery was not a harbinger of his own imminent fate.

Flinching as an incautious step snapped a twig, Gwan crouched
down, his upper teeth set upon his lower lip. The slightest sound
could kill him, if a Japanese archer was still nearby, was still—

Gwan saw the edge of a sandal, its sole turned perpendicular to
the ground, beneath a bush on the other side of the game trail.
Leaning down even farther, he peered between the leaves that concealed him and saw, quite clearly, the scout that had been sent out
with him—a Mongol named Tughur—sprawled beneath the foli-
age, the snapped shaft of an arrow protruding from this left temple.

*I am the accursed of the gods,* Gwan thought, offering a quick
devotional word to those same gods in the hope that it would pro-
pitiate them enough to grant him deliverance. If only they would
give him some sign of assurance—

Gwan caught a glimpse of movement to his left, glanced swiftly
in that direction—but what he had at first imagined was the feathered
fletching of a Japanese archer's arrow was, in fact, the wing of a butterfly, or perhaps a moth, which had alighted upon a nearby branch.
*Late in the season for you,* Gwan thought. *It puts you in at least as
much peril as I am.* Curious that such an insect was still flitting
around in November, he reflexively moved closer to examine it.

In another reality, in an alternate world, Gwan's typically cautious habits of thought might have caused him to pause just long
enough to worry about the sound he could make while moving in
that direction, and could have instead propelled him back out onto
the game trail to die at the hand of a hidden Japanese archer. But
instead, before he could think the better of it, Gwan had moved
deeper into the bushes to get a better view of the butterfly and so
startled it into flight again.

Disappointed, having come within a foot of its simple, white
wings, Gwan stared up after it, then lowered his eyes—

And discovered that he had stumbled upon a perfect vantage point that showed him the plains that lay behind the ridges around Hakata Bay. He inched forward, pushing a stray bough out of his way.

The plains were empty. There was no Japanese army, not even patrol encampments or pickets. The path inland, and to Kyushu's administrative capital at Dazaifu, was clear.

And best of all, Gwan reflected as he began to carefully and quietly retrace his steps, he would live to make that report.

### August 18, 1853, War Department, Washington, DC

Secretary of the Navy James Cochran Dobbin glanced up from fortress assessment reports as Lieutenant Billings ran in, breathless. "Sir, today's mail pouch. A letter from the *Susquehanna*."

Dobbin stuck out a hand that was at once forceful in motion but patrician in form. "About time." Not bothering with the saber-shaped letter opener in the top drawer of his immense desk, he tore off the sealing flap, pulled out the folded papers within, and read:

> *Commodore M. C. Perry*
> *to the Secretary of the Navy, the Hon. James C. Dobbin*
> *United States Steam Frigate* Susquehanna,
>
> *Yedo Bay, July 14, 1853*
>
> *Sir:*
>
> *I have the pleasure of informing you I have now commenced my mission to open relations with the islands of Nippon, which the Chinese call by the pejorative title Dongyang.*
>
> *The flotilla arrived in Yedo harbor on July 8. As the reports of Siebold led us to anticipate, the ruling classes of these islands affect Chinese or Korean names. However, the great majority of these administrators and bureaucrats trace very little if any of their personal heritage back to the invaders who*

*secured a foothold on Kyushu for the Yuan Dynasty in 1274, which enabled the larger and decisive landing in June of 1275.*

*Although Siebold's accounts had readied us to expect an initial rebuff, we were instead met with guarded interest by a legation of officials from China's Qing Dynasty, attended by an almost equal number of native notables. The circumstances, dress, and titles of the former were as opulent as those of the latter were unassuming. These profound distinctions in authority and class were repeatedly observed during our initial visit to the city itself, there to provision the ships under the direct supervision of the imperial Chinese authorities.*

*The condition of the majority of the population is reminiscent of a country that remains under strict occupation, although Chinese military forces are not commonly in evidence. However, imperial officials and bureaucrats are omnipresent, maintaining close watch on almost all transactions of any political or economic import. Furthermore, it soon became apparent that this autocratic power was maintained through the exercise of severe punishments—including torture and execution—for the slightest of infractions. The unremitting fear that is the daily diet of the indigenous Japanese is matched only by the suppressed hatred with which they regard their foreign rulers.*

*We were at a loss to understand why the famed isolation of these islands was so readily relaxed upon our arrival, but this became evident when the local prefect's exchequer entertained us with a light lunch in his own secluded garden. It seems that with the increasing chaos arising from the Opium Wars on the Chinese mainland, Dongyang has become a poor relative in the greater family of Peking's satrapies. The resident imperial authorities, holding their offices by familial inheritance and sinecure, are mindful of their need to maintain control through harsh measures. But with China spending lavishly to both quell the Taiping Rebellion and restore authority lost in its Opium Wars, Nippon's imperial factotums are painfully aware that their reduced coffers are insufficient to the costs of ensuring their own protection and continuance. Through tor-*

tuously indirect insinuations, the exchequer let it be known that if our flotilla had arrived with the purpose of opening Nippon for trade in opium, this could be effected, but surreptitiously, and only if the local imperial authorities were properly compensated for their carefully averted attention.

I am happy to report that none of our shore party expressed their resentment at this assumption that their oath, uniform, and flag were presumed to be nothing more than facades behind which we concealed profiteering ambitions and the intent to trade in substances that are not only contraband but patently unwholesome and unholy in their effects. (I suspect the youngest of our party held his tongue more out of shock than circumspection.)

These initial encounters also served to bring us into contact with various Japanese who revealed that the truth of their nation's sad durance beneath its Chinese masters was even worse than we had thus far conceived. Whereas we projected that Peking kept Nippon inviolate from foreign contact because it wished to maintain a monopoly over the resources and clever craftsmen of these islands (and then later, to protect them from the scourges of opium), we learned that the real reason was far different.

In the nearly six centuries since the Japanese were conquered by the Chinese (or, more precisely, Mongols and Koreans), there have been at least five rebellions which stretched from the northernmost islands down to their southernmost extent at Yakushima. There may have been further rebellions almost as expansive, but since local histories are forbidden (all chronicles are kept by the Chinese bureaucrats; the writing or possession of rival accounts carries a capital sentence), there is no reliable consensus on just how many full-scale revolts have occurred. What a matter of both record and recent memory are the bloody reprisals, in which whole families or towns have been put to the sword on the faintest of suspicions. The fashion in which these reprisals have been carried out rivals the most savage and extreme to be found in the an-

*nals of human history. The veracity of these claims is not to be readily doubted: the diverse accounts of Japanese from every social station varied little on the bloody particulars of these atrocities.*

*In consequence, we have come to learn that there is a very large number among the indigenous Japanese that trace their traditions and influence back to pre-invasion Nippon. Although stripped of their lands and official titles, the descendants of the shoguns and samurai are remembered through secret names and shown great (albeit covert) deference and honor by the overwhelming majority of the population. Similarly, although native Buddhism has been uniformly suppressed for the last five hundred years (insofar as it was deemed a refuge for cultural intransigence and insolence), its undisclosed practitioners still roam the land, often working as itinerant healers, scribes, or storytellers. Members of both these now-secret societies are avidly sought by imperial intelligencers, who routinely seize, torture, and slay their suspected members on the thinnest of pretexts.*

*Through channels which I shall not endanger by sharing either names or places of contact (not being able to ensure the fate of the contents of this mail pouch), I and several of my officers have been approached by well-situated members of this diffuse cabal who are committed to tossing off the yoke of their oppressors. Specifically, they have made it quite clear that, were we to use our new presence on Nippon to surreptitiously aid them, they would remember our United States with deathless gratitude at such time as they might free themselves from the shackles of more than half a millennium of bondage. While I refused to vouchsafe them an immediate answer, I vigorously commend their request to both the State Department and the Executive for long and careful consideration.*

*In closing, I do not possess the arrogance, nor presume the competence, to discourse upon the issues of farsighted statecraft or implicit moral responsibility that are raised by this request from a long-oppressed people whose industry and courtesy have been beyond compare. What I may speak to with reasonable competence are the military practicalities inherent in embracing the relationship they propose.*

*To wit:*

*We live in the era of steam as the decisive naval innovation of this moment and of the foreseeable future. This means that safe harbors and far-flung coaling stations populated by loyal populations are necessities if our burgeoning Republic, barely seventy-five years old as I pen these words, is to stand as a strategic equal among its globe-spanning peers. The location of Nippon alone, convenient to the Chinese coast and furnished with numerous well-developed ports, makes it ideal to those purposes. We would also possess the deathless gratitude of its people, while conversely resting assured in their enduring enmity toward the only regional power large enough to warrant our military concern: China. The iron foundries and steel products of the Japanese are superior to Chinese manufactures in almost all regards, and their attention to detail and innovation promises that they shall more readily and successfully adopt the principles of industrialization.*

*It is said that no force may project itself into new regions without first securing a steady ally therein. I submit we may have just found that ally.*

> *With Great Respect,*
> *I am, sir, your obedient servant,*
> *Commodore M. C. Perry,*
> *Commander, Pacific Squadron*

Billings was standing on the balls of his feet, having watched Dobbin digest the contents of the letter in that precarious posture. "Sir, what does it say? Has Commodore Perry done it?"

Dobbin smiled—not an entirely benign expression—and carefully folded the letter. "Yes, Billings, he has done it. As for what it says—well, I suppose you could summarize it this way:

"Now things will be different."

‖‖‖‖‖‖‖‖‖‖‖‖‖‖‖‖‖‖‖‖‖‖‖‖‖‖‖‖‖‖‖‖‖‖‖‖‖‖‖‖‖‖‖‖‖‖‖‖‖‖‖‖‖‖‖‖‖‖‖‖

# 14

# BAD MATH

### 1492

### By Bill Fawcett

‖‖‖‖‖‖‖‖‖‖‖‖‖‖‖‖‖‖‖‖‖‖‖‖‖‖‖‖‖‖‖‖‖‖‖‖‖‖‖‖‖‖‖‖‖‖‖‖‖‖‖‖‖‖‖‖‖‖‖‖

What is a mile or two?

According to a popular myth, Christopher Columbus won the support of Queen Isabella by demonstrating to her that the world was round. Actually, every scholar in Europe had already known this for about two thousand years. But the part of the myth that concerns the scholars and other explorers in the Spanish court who opposed Columbus is more accurate. They did this because they saw that the sailor's math was wrong, and they were correct.

Columbus had correctly interpreted the Moorish texts that specified the circumference of the earth. The problem was that he read the distance in the familiar, European miles, when the texts were referring to the much longer Moorish mile. One Moorish mile equaled 1.6 of the Spanish miles. By overlooking this difference, Columbus determined that the earth was only fifteen thousand modern miles around at the Equator. But when you convert this to Moorish miles, the result is twenty-five thousand miles. So the scholars advised against trusting Columbus because he was quite simply and demonstrably wrong in his basic assumption. Considering this, one has to wonder just how Columbus succeeded in persuading the queen to give him three ships for his initial voyage.

Then the Indies turned out not to be where he expected them to be. Being off ten thousand miles will have that effect. This was such a concern that Columbus actually hid from his sailors the distance they had really sailed. He kept a second, false log showing that the three small ships had traveled a much shorter distance than they really had.

Perhaps Columbus's most serious mistake was that he refused to admit he was wrong. Even years later, when he was the Admiral of the Ocean Seas, the explorer referred to the land he found as part of the Indies. He never acknowledged that he had discovered a new continent, two actually. This is why Native Americans were referred to as Indians. Perhaps had Columbus been more willing to accept the truth, we would all be living in North and South Columbia rather than America. But since he was stubborn until his death, the New World was named for another explorer, Amerigo Vespucci, who correctly recognized what had been found.

What if someone had simply shown Columbus his error and the seaman believed him? It is almost a sure thing that he would not have sailed west. Columbus was not exploring for its own sake; he was in search of the wealth that would be his when he reached the "Indies": Asia, China, and Japan. But if Columbus had never sailed, it might well have been another century or more before Europe "discovered" the Americas. The greatest effect this would likely have had would be that Spain, not a rich nation to begin with, would have been two centuries' worth of American plunder the poorer and probably remained a second-rate power. A weak Spain might well have meant a much more peaceful Europe, and the religious wars of the seventeenth century might not have happened or they might have been less destructive. The people living in the often-pillaged or contested princedoms of Germany might have been spared immense grief. Germany, less damaged, could have united earlier.

Portugal, whose explorers may have already touched on Brazil, a surprisingly short sail west and a bit south of the coastal nation, might well have taken the lead in settling or conquering the Americas. Bolstered by American wealth, Portugal might have played the same role that Denmark later played—a small and very wealthy nation with a strong navy and many foreign interests. So, in a world without Columbus's voyages and the interest they generated,

South America would most likely have been the first area settled. If the trade-oriented Portuguese had been the first to encounter the Aztecs, instead the greedy and religiously fanatic Spanish, that American people might have well survived long enough to maintain some degree of independence, or even find moderation. Or perhaps not. The culture of most American tribes, even the Aztecs, was not one that encouraged innovation. Only in a scenario in which the Portuguese drastically slowed the invasion of Europeans into the Americas would there be a chance for the American tribes to gain enough technology, and understanding of what they faced, to adjust to and meet the invasion effectively. But then, Portugal managed to keep its trade routes to Japan secret for decades. Could they have done so with the Americas? On the other hand, a delay in the surge west by Europeans could have been even more disastrous for the tribes they met than it was. Even then, most Native American cultures were fairly static and lagged far behind, when compared to the scientific and technological growth occurring during this time in Europe. When the white man finally did land in the Americas, the difference in culture and knowledge, and perhaps the abuse, might have been even greater.

Certainly, if the Europeans had come later to the Americas, the industrial revolution might have been slower to occur, without the support of the wealth and raw materials that the western colonies provided. Also, one wonders if the Northern Europeans might have also discovered North America independently. There is some evidence that the British and fishermen from other nations were already working near the shores of Canada not long after Columbus sailed. What if the English, instead of the Spanish, had pillaged the wealth of the Aztecs? What would the map of Europe look like today if England had been able to enforce its claims on France? Or if England could have dominated the Atlantic from the beginning? Would English be the language of the entire hemisphere?

So how would the world be today if Christopher Columbus had gotten his computations right? The settlement of the Americas would have been different. Europe would have industrialized more slowly with less colonial wealth to spend. The natives might have been spared the horrors brought on by the religious fanaticism of the

Spanish. The tribes in North America might have benefited from a more gradual settlement by the Europeans. Or it might simply have delayed the inevitable for a while. Indian language (this author lives in Chicago, in the state of Illinois, both Native American words) and culture might have had an even greater influence. There might even have been a greater appreciation of nature and much earlier concern for ecology. And the map of the Americas might well contain American Indian lands never taken or conquered. Then again, there is no reason to think that wisdom or a concern for others would suddenly overwhelm European society, given an extra century or two. They didn't in the real world. The bloody tale might not have been that different from the way it was. But the dates we had to memorize would be different. Perhaps all we would have learned about the discovery of America was that "in 1581, Drake got the job done."

# 15

## YOU WANT OUR GOLD, OUR WOMEN, AND NO MORE SACRIFICES, TOO?

### 1519

### By Dr. Paul A. Thomsen

|||||||||||||||||||||||||||||||||||||||||||||||||||||||||||||||||||||||||||||

> Ray, when someone asks if you're a god, you say yes.
>
> —DR. EGON SPENGLER, IN *GHOSTBUSTERS*

Leaders are often called upon to make life-or-death decisions based on insufficient information. In 1519, Aztec emperor Montezuma II learned from his scouts that a group of strangers had landed on the shores of his empire, but were they the prophesied return of minor gods or a rumored lethal band of foreigners from distant shores? His scouts didn't know. Faced with two prospects, each of them dangerous, the Aztec emperor chose poorly and the Americas suffered as a result.

Earlier troubling news had reached the Aztec Empire of the Spanish imperial expansion into Central America. Traders told them of men who were pale of skin, rode strange creatures, and were, apparently, from distant lands. In time, terrifying stories were also told of their decimating battlefields, and of entire nations with new kinds of weapons. Eventually, Montezuma's men reported that a small party of these strangers had just arrived on the shores of his empire, looking for a way to meet the emperor.

Although the emperor sent a warmly received welcoming committee in April 1517, the Spanish conquistador Hernán Cortés and his men unnerved the Aztec leader. The Spanish were afflicted, they said, with an illness, which could only be cured by gold. Their swords were far sharper than his own warriors' famed obsidian blades, which shattered against Spanish armor. As time passed, Montezuma's men noted that Cortés's men were also given to drink and had a fondness for local women. Some of his men believed the Spaniards were just superb warriors, but others considered that Cortés might be the ancient Aztec god of rain, Quetzalcoatl, returned from his ages-long travels.

Likewise, Montezuma found the ease with which Cortés and his men managed to ingratiate themselves with the most distant of Aztec vassals extremely alarming. Worse, the strangers set up a colony (Veracruz) on Aztec land. Worse still, they wanted the Aztecs to discontinue their central religious ritual: human sacrifice. Whether these strangers were godlike or just plain strange, the mounting data indicated to Montezuma II that they would be trouble for the Aztec leader. Only proper study and time, he believed, would reveal the truth about the Spanish and how to best treat them.

The Aztec Empire and Central America would have stood a fighting chance if Montezuma II had just chosen between the godlike and the lethal options early in their encounter. His empire had, in fact, arisen through the conquest and absorption of numerous, smaller neighbors. Many of the conquered cities never liked the Aztecs, because of the regular tithes and sacrificial victims they demanded. Others detested the hierarchical caste system the emperor had recently imposed. Some would have even joined Cortés, if asked. Yet most would have remained with Montezuma II out of fear of the Spanish. With fear as a unifier, Montezuma could have played the safe bet of considering the Spanish as "possibly" gods until his people's disappointment intensified, and then joined them in warlike action. Alternately, the Aztecs could have attacked the Spanish outright. According to period narratives of Cortés's expedition, the Aztecs were capable of summoning two hundred thousand trained warriors for battle and possibly even larger forces, given sufficient time. Unlike Cortés, Montezuma II knew the terrain and the people of his region. Unlike Spain, Aztec culture literally lived for bloody combat. Montezuma's only concern would have been that the fear engendered by the strangers and their weapons might paralyze his men in battle.

Cortés might have had more advanced weapons technology, such as mounts, swords, and armor, and recourse to unorthodox tactics, such as mounted charges into infantry lines, but he also faced many strategic disadvantages. The Spaniard had only a limited complement of five hundred troops under his command. The Spanish were also terrified of the Aztecs, and unknown to Montezuma II, they were incapable of summoning reinforcements. In a few early skirmishes, Cortés's expedition had nearly been destroyed. A concerted effort by Montezuma II's united front would have annihilated the Spanish force, leaving the jungle to swallow their remains and Spain to wonder whatever happened to that man called Hernán Cortés.

Furthermore, either course of action would have afforded the Aztec Empire the necessary resource of time. With even a mild reprieve of a few months or a year, Montezuma could have adequately prepared his nation for war against a second Spanish expedition/invasion. Likewise, the Aztecs' neighbors could have augmented the native force, costing Spain more time, money. Who would have made a more fearsome foe for the Spanish Empire than a people that reveled in the regular practice of human sacrifice, sometimes wearing the skin of captives killed in battle? Under Aztec leadership, the regional powers might have managed to hold off the Spanish Empire indefinitely.

Instead, Montezuma II made the worst choice available to him: he chose not to choose until he had proof. By then, it was already too late for the Aztecs and American history. Because Montezuma repeatedly stalled Cortés and his men with gifts of gold and finery befitting gods, the Spanish inferred that much more gold lay inland just waiting for the taking. By conducting them on a circuitous journey to test their divinity, the Aztec leader inadvertently showed the Spanish his domain's strategic resources, weaknesses, and strengths. The route also allowed Cortés to mislead more Aztecs and turn some of Montezuma II's shaky vassals against him. By the time there was a consensus that Cortés and his men were not gods, the point of no return had long since passed. The Spanish were inside the capital of the empire, Tenochtitlán. Sadly, the Aztec emperor paid for his indecisiveness with his life. On June 30, 1520, Montezuma II was killed by the stones and arrows of his own subjects. Although Cortés and his surviving men were driven off in an uprising, they were saved by some dissident natives they had befriended along the way. In time, they returned and completed the conquest of Central America with their new friends.

Without all that easily gained Aztec gold, the Spanish Empire would never have had enough money to threaten England with invasion in 1588. It would have left the papacy without a puppet to challenge the rise to power of England's queen Elizabeth I. Likewise, in the event of a shooting war in the Caribbean, North America would have been targeted for Spanish colonization to supply material and money to offset the cost of the Aztec war. The Pacific would have remained an uncontested ocean for Asiatic exploitation. And judging by Spain's Aztec situation, the few English, Dutch, and French North American colonies would have had to seriously reconsider their passive-aggressive relationships with the continent's native populace. If only Montezuma II had made a choice, the dominant native culture of the Americas might have survived. Today, Texas and even California might be part of a Pan-American Aztec Empire.

# 16

## HENRY GETS HIS ANNULMENT

### 1530

**By Mike Resnick**

Shorter than a Hollywood marriage?

Henry VIII was the king of England from April 1509 until his death in January of 1547. He put a lot of living into that time span, as well as a lot of planning and plotting and scheming and loving. Even American schoolkids have heard of Henry VIII five centuries later, and the one thing they know is that his wives didn't last very long.

He had six of them: in chronological order, they were Catherine of Aragon, Anne Boleyn, Jane Seymour, Anne of Cleves, Catherine Howard, and Catherine Parr. Two were beheaded, three were divorced, one died from complications of childbirth, and one outlived both all the other wives and the king himself.

Why is that important?

Because when Henry ascended to the throne, England was a Catholic country.

Henry wanted an heir, and in his mind—and the minds of a lot of his subjects and advisers—that meant a son. It became pretty clear that Catherine of Aragon, his brother's widow, whom he had married in 1509, was nearing the end of her childbearing years around 1530. Consequently, Henry decided he wanted an annulment so he could marry someone younger, better connected politically, and above all, capable of giving him his male heir.

Now, Henry knew that the problem of a male heir didn't lie

with him. He'd already produced a couple of bastard sons (and a daughter), but of course they couldn't inherit the throne. He'd been having an affair with Mary Boleyn, who is said to have been the mother of two of the kids (though Henry denied it). In the normal course of events, he met her younger, smarter, prettier sister, Anne, and decided that she would make the perfect queen and mother to his not-yet-conceived male heir.

There was a little problem, though. As I mentioned, England was a Catholic country, and the Catholic Church does not condone divorce. He appealed to Pope Clement VII for an annulment, assuming that there would be no difficulty, given his position—and Clement said no. It was just as simple as that.

What happened next was a little more complicated. After having his representatives try two more times, Henry decided to cut his ties with Clement and the Catholic Church, a decision that eventually cost him his best adviser, Sir Thomas More. By 1533, the Reformation Parliament had stripped Catherine of Aragon of her title, banished her from the court, and given her rooms to Anne Boleyn. Thomas Cranmer, who then became the archbishop of Canterbury, declared Henry's marriage to Catherine annulled, and five days later he declared the marriage between Henry and Anne Boleyn legal and binding.

And that was the first major shot fired at the Vatican by the Church of England. Everything followed from that. It might be interesting to speculate on what would and would not have transpired had Clement decided to grant Henry's annulment. Obviously, the major change would be that England would not have broken away from the Catholic Church.

What does that mean?

Well, for one thing, the Reformation would be without its most powerful player, England.

For another, almost all of the United States would be Catholic, since the original thirteen American colonies were governed by British law.

The constitution of the United States would make more than one or two mentions of God, and nowhere would it, or our subsequent code of laws, be in any way contradictory to the Church's teachings.

Most of the Protestant nations and areas, after being totally surrounded by Catholic powers and superpowers for half a millennium, would have reverted to Catholicism.

Divorce would be infinitely rarer than it is today. Many of the things we take for granted in our daily lives would no longer exist. Which things? I hear you ask. Cremation. Abortion. Hamburgers on Friday. Give it some thought. You'll come up with double digits' worth.

And unlike some of the major historical changes that can fill a book like this—Abe Lincoln isn't elected, JFK isn't assassinated, and others—this significant alteration of history hinges on just one little thing: one particular man cannot get an annulment from the woman he's been married to for twenty-four years, and it affects the belief system of some twenty billion people over the next few centuries.

‖‖‖‖‖‖‖‖‖‖‖‖‖‖‖‖‖‖‖‖‖‖‖‖‖‖‖‖‖‖‖‖‖‖‖‖‖‖‖‖‖‖‖‖‖‖‖‖

# 17

# THAT OTHER KOREAN WAR

### 1592

## By William Terdoslavich

‖‖‖‖‖‖‖‖‖‖‖‖‖‖‖‖‖‖‖‖‖‖‖‖‖‖‖‖‖‖‖‖‖‖‖‖‖‖‖‖‖‖‖‖‖‖‖‖

Korea and Poland must be the world's
two most invaded nations.

Hideyoshi Toyotomi was Japan's ultimate badass in the early 1590s. He had just vanquished lesser rivals to unify Japan after a century of civil war. But he needed respect. With it, he could rule Japan as shogun, with the emperor sidelined as political window dressing, as usual.

But how do you get respect?

Invade Korea.

This may sound harebrained, until you realize that brute force has its own logic. The more wars you win, the more powerful you become. No one challenges a winner.

Conquering Korea was something Hideyoshi pondered for several decades as he fought under Oda Nobunaga to knock the other *daimyos*—or lords—into line. Winning that civil war left thousands of samurai with nothing to do, but still under arms and answering to their provincial masters. Moving Japan's war to Korea would give them purpose, cement Japanese unification, and most importantly, keep war's destruction on foreign soil and away from home. If Hideyoshi could conquer Korea, *it might also be possible for him to conquer China!*

Diplomatic overtures to get Korea to submit to Japan proved fruitless. A vassal of China, Choson Dynasty Korea believed it deserved Japan's submission. Hideyoshi chose to end the farce, dispatching an army of 158,000 from Japan's southernmost home island of Kyushu to teach the Koreans a lesson.

## Same War, Different Century

The Imjin War began with the Japanese army landing in Busan (Pusan) in 1592. Nine divisions were sent to the Korean peninsula, taking Seoul and Pyongyang with ease. The Korean army really sucked, breaking under the charge of sword-wielding samurai and Japanese infantry armed with muskets and spears. The Japanese met with little resistance as they approached the Yalu River, which marked the border with China. This looked like the Korean War the US once fought, *only it was happening centuries earlier!*

While the Korean army was hopeless, the Korean navy proved deadly. Tucked away in southwestern Korea was a fleet under the command of Yi Sun-Shin. He understood strategy. All he had to do was vanquish the Japanese fleet in Korean waters, thus cutting off the invading army from resupply and reinforcement. He also understood tactics and sought to match the strengths of his fleet against the weakness of his enemy's ships.

This was shown to great effect at the Battle of Hansan Do, an island about twenty miles southwest of Busan. Here the coast is rocky and irregular. Numerous offshore islands bracket local waters into narrow straits. Yi knew a Japanese fleet of eighty-two warships was anchored nearby. The Koreans had between sixty and eighty ships, so it looked like an even match. Yi ordered six war galleys to advance within sight of the Japanese. Headstrong admiral Wakizaka Yasuharu took the bait and gave chase with about sixty ships. His fleet pursued the fleeing Korean squadron through a narrow passage into the wider waters beyond.

That is when Yi sprang his trap. Galleys tucked behind smaller islands rushed out, surrounding the Japanese. The squat Korean vessels stood off at a distance, using their superior cannons to bash the Japanese galleys into splinters. Three Korean "turtle boats"— armored galleys covered in iron sheets—rowed into the Japanese formation, firing their cannons at close range. The Japanese depended on closing with the enemy, grappling and boarding with their superior infantry, but the turtle boats could not be boarded. And the Japanese could not close with the distant Korean galleys firing from afar. Admiral Yi destroyed more than sixty Japanese vessels that day. This was his sixth naval victory. He would win seventeen more.

With the Choson Dynasty on the ropes, China intervened. The Ming army crossed the Yalu and besieged Pyongyang, driving the Japanese southward to Seoul. (The Americans would make the same retreat, centuries later.) The Japanese eventually abandoned Seoul, retreating to Busan. A cease-fire was declared as diplomatic talks resumed.

## Talk, Followed by Action

From 1594 to 1596, Japanese and Chinese envoys tried to hammer out a peace treaty, to no effect. The Chinese treated Japan as a suppliant, offering recognition of Hideyoshi as Japan's king, provided he became a vassal. Conversely, Hideyoshi's representatives believed China was asking for peace. Hideyoshi issued demands as a victor, which the Ming emperor dismissed.

War resumed in 1597, when Hideyoshi dispatched a second army to Busan. Only now the campaign was aimed at controlling the southern quarter of the Korean peninsula, with one force invading southwestern Korea to deprive Admiral Yi of his much-needed naval bases.

Also aiding the Japanese was political infighting in the court of Korean king Seonjo. Admiral Yi had a bad habit of disobeying orders from the court, even though he usually won battles by doing so. But Yi fell into disfavor with the king, who fired and jailed him. Command of the fleet went to the more impulsive Won Gyun.

With a hundred ships, Won attacked the Japanese fleet near Busan. This time the Japanese won, safeguarding their supply line back to Japan. However, thanks to a disobedient Korean captain, thirteen galleys broke off from the action and retreated. Yi was released from prison and restored to command, but these thirteen war galleys were all that was left of Korea's navy. And there were no turtle boats handy.

In 1597, in the narrow waters of the Myeongnyang strait in southwestern Korea, Admiral Yi lined up his galleys from shore to shore so that they blocked the passage of an oncoming Japanese war fleet. Crossing the Japanese T, the Korean ships poured gunfire into the advancing Japanese warships, forcing them to retreat.

The following year, Yi commanded a combined Chinese-Korean fleet. At Noryang Point, he attacked the remaining Japanese warships *at night*. The enemy either fled or was sunk. At sunrise, Yi ordered one last charge at the remaining Japanese galleys, only to be shot on deck while closing with the enemy. Yi knew his wound was mortal and ordered his officers to keep secret the news of his demise, lest it undermine morale. Like Nelson at Trafalgar, Yi did not live to see his last victory.

## The Outcome

Hideyoshi died of natural causes in 1598, though some chroniclers claim it was due to a broken heart after his Korean scheme was defeated. The war weakened the Toyotomi clan and its surrounding allies. By default, the eastern faction headed by Tokugawa Ieyasu strengthened, as he was wise enough to give Korea a pass. In 1600, at Sekigahara, Tokugawa won the last battle in Japan's century-long civil war, becoming shogun and closing the country to all outsiders. Japan became backward as a result.

It would have been a hundred times better if Hideyoshi had kept his eyes on the real prize—control of Japan—rather than gambling on foreign conquest and glory. Hideyoshi could have kept Japan open to outsiders, able to absorb Western technology. Japan would have become a regional power sooner rather than later. And it would have had mastery over a different map of East Asia, perhaps conquering other islands and states before any European power had a chance to colonize in the region.

Win or lose, Korea is still a prisoner of its geography, caught between a rock (China) and Japan (a hard place). But as a vassal of China, Korea was able to keep its language and culture. Winning the Imjin War brought Korea some breathing space under Chinese protection, but not much else.

As for China, the Ming Dynasty limped along for another fifty years until it was overthrown by the Manchurians. A Japanese invasion might have weakened Manchuria to the point of preventing this. But Chinese dynasties always succumb to the passage of time. The Ming would fall sooner or later.

# 18

## CHARLES THE MAD VS. PETER THE GREAT

### 1708

### By William Terdoslavich

*Talk about biting off more
than you can chew.*

Back when armies were the playthings of kings, European nations tried to expand at each other's expense. It gets a little complicated when a smaller state tries to punch above its weight.

Take Sweden. Today we view this nation as a socialist utopia. Go back three hundred years and it was a major player in European geopolitics. And like any nation thinking big, Sweden only wanted one thing: total control of the Baltic Sea. To get it, Sweden would have to conquer or control every state along the Baltic's shores. For a nation of only 1.2 million people, this was going to be a tall order.

That was the goal Charles XII inherited when he became king of Sweden in 1697. A young king, Charles was spoiling for a fight. As Sweden was surrounded by unfriendly states, this was probably a reasonable posture. Charles, though, did not temper this outlook with good judgment.

### The Great Northern War Begins

Eager to make gains at Sweden's expense were Denmark-Norway, Saxony, and Russia. Together they started the Great Northern War in 1700. Saxony's king Augustus II wanted Riga and access to the Baltic. Denmark-Norway's Frederick IV sought to conquer Holstein-

Gottorp. And Russia's Peter the Great would march westward into Swedish Ingria. All Peter wanted was a sliver of Baltic beachfront so he could build a port to export resources and import technology. That was not going to happen with Sweden in the way.

Charles handily defeated Denmark-Norway and checked Saxony. The Swedish army, though small, was well trained, well led, and always attacked, even when outnumbered. This penchant for action was seen in 1704 at Narva, when Sweden first clashed with Russia.

Peter the Great entrusted his army of forty thousand to his generals. Charles XII led his ten-thousand-man army from the front. Despite the odds, the Swedes executed a night attack, driving the Russians off the field by midmorning the next day. The Russian army sucked.

Charles based all future strategy on this first impression. But he had to whip Saxony and Poland first, before turning east. Peter the Great was safe, for now.

During the next few years, Peter rebuilt his army along Swedish lines. But Peter also had three things going for him that Sweden lacked: more space, more time, and more men. Peter could afford to replace losses, surrender territory, and drag out any campaign from months to years. So long as Russia could field an army and fight, the war was not over.

Sweden's strategic predicament was that its singular army was excellent but brittle. Lose one major battle and this fine weapon could not be replaced. Charles XII, while an aggressive battlefield commander, never saw this. Sweden always won. What could go wrong?

## Invading Russia Is Always a Mistake

In 1708, Charles turned his attention eastward. He would not be the first, or the last, to do so. On January 28, he assembled about thirty-five thousand men in Gardinas, Poland (now Grodno in western Belarus). Charles assigned fourteen thousand to attack St. Petersburg. An additional thirteen thousand became an "army of reinforcement" based in Riga under his trusty lieutenant Lewenhaupt. This force would march east with supplies to join Charles later in the year. Charles would take the remaining troops and march on to . . . *Moscow!*

Later in July, Charles would try to pick off a Russian army at Holowczyn that was barring his advance on Mohylew, near Smolensk. The Russians had set up camp in two halves. Charles decided to advance into the gap and attack. The divided Russian army failed to unite, as one wing was driven off before being supported by the other. But the Russians did not fold like they did at Narva. They were badly handled by their generals, but they did fight. And the Russians retreated as an army, burning pastures and farms to deny the Swedes any supplies and forage.

The Swedes finally made it to Mohylew to await Lewenhaupt's arrival. It was here that Charles changed his mind. Cossack Hetman Mazepa arrived at the camp, seeking an alliance with Sweden. He promised thirty thousand horsemen if Charles would only advance south into Ukraine and help throw the Russians out.

Strategy was not exactly Charles's strong suit. But he often seized an opportunity wherever he could. He needed allies. What made this promise sweeter was the possibility that the Crimean Tatars would also join in.

Charles marched south. Eventually, Lewenhaupt caught up with the Swedish main force, but only brought seven thousand men, no artillery, and no supplies. Peter the Great's army had mauled Lewenhaupt's force at Lesnaya as it marched eastward to join Charles.

The Swedish army finally arrived at Sivershchyna. But all it found was ruin. Peter's Russians got there first, sacking the Cossack capital at Baturyn and burning any food or forage for miles around. And Hetman Mazepa showed up with only several thousand Cossacks, maybe a tenth of what he promised.

But what about the Crimean Tatars? The Ottoman Empire had just wrapped up a war with Austria in the preceding decade and was in no mood to start another fight somewhere else. The Crimean Tatars were told by their Ottoman overlords to sit this one out.

Charles and his Swedes would now have to go into winter quarters with few supplies in the middle of Ukraine. The winter proved to be a harsh one.

## Poltava and Worse

Peter the Great was now ensconced in the fortress of Poltava, an army of eighty thousand at his command. Charles limped into the neighborhood that summer with only seventeen thousand Swedes, now depleted after a long march through a countryside short on forage. Only four guns could be brought to bear in the upcoming battle. Undeterred, a bedridden Charles ordered his generals to attack.

The Swedes were supposed to bypass a series of Russian field fortifications, but instead assaulted them. One detachment of Swedes became separated from the main body. Peter attacked and crushed them.

By the time the Swedes made it through the enemy screen to attack the Russian main line, only 4,000 men remained. Peter deployed ten times their number and attacked, sweeping the Swedes away. The Swedish cavalry, still intact, covered the retreat. Charles had lost more than half his army. Peter's losses amounted to only 4,500. The retreating Swedes lacked the means to recross the Dneiper River. Charles fled with a small force to seek sanctuary in Ottoman territory, while the remainder of the Swedish army surrendered to Peter.

## Unhappy Ending

Charles spent years trying to persuade the Ottoman sultan to attack Russia, all for naught. The Russian steamroller had no trouble ousting Sweden from the Baltic states. With Russian access to the Baltic secured, Peter began building Russia's new capital, St. Petersburg.

Charles eventually made it back to his home country and managed to raise forces to attack Norway. This effort became a dead end, as Charles died in combat while leading an attack on a fortress. The war ended with a whimper in 1721, a generation after it started. By invading Russia and losing all, Charles the Mad certainly earned his nickname.

There was no way Sweden could stop Russian expansion with

only one-twentieth of Russia's population. Russian access to the Baltic was possibly a question of when, not if. Victory over Sweden allowed Russia to emerge as a great power in European geopolitics. Sweden was cut down to the level of a secondary power, never to play a great role again.

It would have been a hundred times better if Charles XII had limited his ambition to vanquishing Saxony and Denmark-Norway, perhaps persuading his foes to become allies. This would have preserved Swedish power for another generation or two. But that would have required a cooler head. Charles XII lacked that temperament.

But more importantly, Swedish victory in a defensive war could have changed the trajectory of Russian history. Peter the Great had undertaken a forceful plan to modernize Russia, which his nobles resisted. Defeat would have undermined this program and opened Peter to overthrow.

Russia would still have been a big nation. But if it was hobbled by backwardness, its role in shaping European history would have been muted. Perhaps a more powerful Poland could have survived. Perhaps a stronger Ottoman Empire could have checked Russia's ambition. Perhaps a Russia more focused on expanding eastward would have been somebody else's problem. Perhaps today's Russia would be messing around in Mongolia instead of in Ukraine.

Perhaps . . .

# 19

|||||||||||||||||||||||||||||||||||||||||||||||||||||||||||||||||||||||

## WE *WANT*
## TO LIKE YOU,
## KING GEORGE . . .
## BUT COME ON!

### 1763

### By Douglas Niles

|||||||||||||||||||||||||||||||||||||||||||||||||||||||||||||||||||||||

Once vigorous measures appear to
be the only means left of bringing
the Americans to a due submission
to the mother country, the
colonies will submit.

—KING GEORGE III TO PARLIAMENT, 1775

With the conclusion of the Seven Years' War in 1763, Great Britain stood alone as the most powerful empire in the world, possessor of profitable colonies in North America, Africa, and Asia. The defeat of France in that conflict—which in the American colonies was known as the French and Indian War—had eliminated French power on the American continent, with the French ceding Canada, most of Florida, several Caribbean Islands, and much of the middle of what would become the United States to the British Crown.

In 1763, that crown rested on the bewigged and obstinate head of King George III, who had ascended to the throne only three years earlier. Stubborn and insecure, George distrusted some of the advisers who had guided England to victory in the war against France. He had detested his late grandfather, George II, and when the old king died, the new king determined to chart a new path. He was a man of strong passions, George III, but his intellect was not a match for those impulses of emotion.

In particular, George III determined to cast out the lords and advisers who had served his predecessor so well. Most notably, he disliked William Pitt the Elder, aka "the Great Commoner," who was a gifted politician and diplomat, with keen insight into the affairs of the British Empire, and a particular understanding of her relationship with her colonies. Pitt was the brain behind the strategy that had resulted in England's triumph during the Seven Years' War.

But George III had forced Pitt to resign in 1761, and instead placed his trust in the Earl of Bute, John Stuart, employing Bute as a mentor and adviser. Sensing a mistake, the king recalled Pitt to service in 1763, but by that time the Great Commoner's health had begun to fail, and he would be unable to make his mark on the history that would play out so violently and catastrophically over the next two decades. Furthermore, Bute proved to be every bit as stubborn, shortsighted, and abrasive as his king, and together the two men held firm against the counsels of wiser men.

Beyond the vast increase in territorial holdings, the other legacy left to England in the wake of the Seven Years' War was a mountain of debt. Britain's expenditures had more than doubled as the nation borrowed heavily to pay for the far-flung conflict. Some in England, including the king and a number of powerful mercantile interests and lords, felt that it was only fair that the colonies be taxed to help make up the deficit. After all, they had surely been beneficiaries of the British victory, had they not?

However, the colonists took a different view. They regarded themselves as loyal subjects of the king, but distrusted a Parliament from whose ranks they were sternly excluded. Feeling themselves to be English citizens, they expected, and soon demanded, the rights of other Englishmen. These grievances swelled in the late 1760s as Pitt the Elder's former underling Charles Townshend took over for the great man and began to mercilessly squeeze the colonies for every farthing he could extract.

The Stamp Act, in 1765, imposed a tax on the colonies that was protested so strongly that it was repealed a year later, only to be followed by the Townshend Acts in 1767, which imposed a whole series of import and export taxes on the American colonies. These decrees increased colonial resentment and also hampered trade, as the Americans began to boycott (taxed) English imports. British troops were dispatched to New England and New York to keep order, and the colonists were often required to billet these soldiers in their homes, a fact that contributed to growing American resentment.

Still, the colonists remained mostly loyal to the king, and a few symbolic olive branches extended by the Crown could have defused the rebellion before it began. Though most of the Townshend taxes were soon suspended, the tax on tea remained, and it would become an extraordinary flash point. In 1770, the king appointed Lord North as his prime minister, and that nobleman was more determined than even George III to put the rambunctious Americans in their place. In that same year, British soldiers fired on an angry group of Massachusetts citizens, killing five of them in the so-called Boston Massacre. The Boston Tea Party, in December of 1773, further derailed relations, as the king imposed more punitive measures and the colonists grew more restive.

By 1775, when battle erupted at Lexington and Concord, it was too late to heal the relationship. But there had been plenty of opportunities during the 1760s, when a ruler with a more long-term view could have worked out a compromise that would have allowed the Crown's richest and most vibrant colony to remain as a reasonably content partner in the empire—much as happened later with Canada and Australia, after England had been forced to come to terms with the mistakes that led to the American Revolution.

And how might the future have played out, if the United States of America had not declared and fought for independence? In many ways, a lot of future bloodshed could have been avoided. Well before the end of the eighteenth century, England would have stood alone as the great power in the world, supported by her robust American colony that spanned the North American coast from Georgia to Hudson Bay. Neither France nor the dying Spanish Empire would have been any match for the United Kingdom economically or militarily.

Almost certainly there would have been no French Revolution—or only a significantly less effective rebellion, since that event was heavily inspired by the American revolt across the ocean—and that would mean no Reign of Terror, no Emperor Napoleon, and an avoidance of the countless wars and deaths that were the result of the emperor's ambitions. The Pax Brittanica, which historically began after Waterloo in 1815, might have commenced forty or fifty years earlier.

And consider the effect on American history as well. The American Civil War would probably not have been fought. Great Britain outlawed the buying and selling of slaves in 1807, and banned slavery altogether in 1833. The southern American economy would have been forced to adjust to abolition sooner than it did historically, and it is unlikely that the Confederate states would have even tried to stand against the force of a British Empire that also included the populous, industrial northern colonies. Also, the genocidal removal of Native Americans from their ancestral homes would have been considerably diminished by English restraint. In fact, the Crown's ban on westward expansion past the Appalachians played at least a small part in stirring up colonial resentment of the mother country, but that in and of itself would not have been sufficient to provoke revolution.

It is well-known that disease rendered King George III almost completely insane by the time of his death in 1820. But it is just possible that the greatest manifestations of the "Mad King's" effect on history occurred before he became ill, when he was merely a stubborn and prideful young man who held the future of the world in his hands, and let it slip away.

# 20

A YOUNG GEORGE
WASHINGTON
STARTS A WAR

## 1754

### By Bill Fawcett

Ambushing the French, young George
Washington starts a war.

Tensions were high in the Ohio River Valley. The French and British both claimed the rich and fertile area. Both nations had sent soldiers to occupy and control it. In March 1754, Lieutenant Governor Dinwiddie of Virginia ordered 140 men of the Virginia militia into Ohio with orders to "make prisoner of or kill or destroy" any Frenchmen they encountered. Most of the militia he sent were experienced woodsmen. Newly promoted to lieutenant colonel and anxious to enhance his growing reputation, a young George Washington was appointed to lead the expedition.

On May 27, Washington and forty of his militia marched all night toward where their scouts had discovered a French camp. They crept up on the sleeping French at dawn and were able to surround them without being discovered. In the camp were about 34 French soldiers and 12 Seneca warriors and their chief. Just after dawn Washington's militia was spotted and a fierce firefight followed. Firing from cover and with surprise, the militia soon overwhelmed the French, killing 13 and capturing 21. The Seneca were able to escape. It seemed to be a victory, and word of it helped launch George Washington's political career. He made the most of his success and published an account of the fight including an account of his own courage.

> I fortunately escaped without any wound, for the right wing, where I stood, was exposed to and received all the enemy's fire, and it was the part where the man was killed, and the rest wounded. I heard the bullets whistle, and, believe me, there is something charming in the sound.

There was a real problem with the battle. It should not have happened. The French soldiers were not invading or occupying the area. A year earlier the British had sent to the French a formal note claiming the Midwest and warning them to stay out of it. The patrol Washington ambushed was a diplomatic party carrying the reply to this note and a counterclaim. Had he not attacked them, those same French soldiers would have marched openly into Virginia to deliver the missive. By the law and standards of the time, diplomatic parties were immune from attack.

George Washington gained a good deal of recognition in Virginia for leading the attack. The reactions in Quebec and Europe were very different. The French were irate and angry that the rules of diplomacy had been ignored. In Paris the French court saw the attack as a demonstration of why the lawless British had to be driven from North America, or at least taught that they had no claim to the Ohio River Valley. Formal complaints were sent, and notes were exchanged between London and Paris. What was an already tense situation began to degenerate further. Washington's attack on the diplomatic party, combined with other tensions within Europe, soon led to what is now called the French and Indian War (North America) / Seven Years' War (European), which ran from 1754 to 1763.

Had Washington asked the French to surrender that dawn, they would have quickly explained their mission and no fighting would have occurred. But to do so would have given up the element of surprise. So to surprise the enemy, George Washington helped trigger a war.

Had Washington not attacked the diplomatic party, it is possible the French and Indian War might have been avoided or at least been delayed and less costly. The results of that would have been dramatic. The British might not have captured Canada in 1759, so it would all have remained French. More importantly, a less costly war would have meant that England would not have had to try to recoup the cost of that war from the American colonies. The reviled Stamp Act and tea taxes were partly an attempt to recover the military costs of the French and Indian War, along with paying to support British Army troops that remained in the colonies. A shorter war or no war at all would likely have meant that the cash-strapped British government would not have tried to tax their colonists so heavily. Without those taxes, it is very possible that there would have been no American Revolution. The irony of this whole situation is that in effect George Washington's actions in 1754 began or greatly pushed forward the chain of events that twenty-two years later would put him in command of the rebelling Continental Army. If he had not encountered that French patrol, or had asked for their surrender and talked to the men, the entire American Revolution might never have happened.

# 21 and 22

||||||||||||||||||||||||||||||||||||||||||||||||||||||||||||||||||||||||||||||

## TWO MEN WHO
## LOST AMERICA

1781

**By Bill Fawcett**

||||||||||||||||||||||||||||||||||||||||||||||||||||||||||||||||||||||||||||||

The British Royal Navy was so good,
it took two admirals to lose the
American colonies.

I t took two mistakes by leaders of arguably the most competent
military force on the planet to cause the American Revolution to
be won at Yorktown. By 1781, the revolutionary forces controlled
most of the colonies, but were unable to actually win the war. They
were in rather desperate straits, with the economy collapsing under
the strain of war and their currency, the Continental, being value-
less. A victory was needed—soon. As it was, the Crown could simply wait until it inevitably outlasted the rebels. Even with the newly
arrived assistance of several thousand veteran French infantry,
they had no way to drive the British from New York, or any of
a number of other coastal cities the British occupied, including
Savannah and Charleston.

At this time, there were several British garrisons holding coastal
cities, including the largest, New York City, but the British had only
one significant field army. This one army was that of General Cornwallis and it had been subduing the Southern colonies with some
success. By October of 1781, that army had settled into a fortified
camp on the shores of Chesapeake Bay in the small city of Yorktown. This type of location was considered ideal for any British
force, as it could be supported at sea by the Royal Navy. But because

of the mistakes made by two men, both British admirals, this proved not to be the case.

Normally, the much larger, more aggressive, and better-trained Royal Navy dominated the Atlantic. But Louis XVI's France had been building up its navy. In March of 1781, it was able to dispatch to the West Indies a fleet of twenty ships of the line and three frigates. This fleet, plus the nine more already in the Indies, convoyed 156 merchant ships. They were under the control of recently appointed rear admiral François Joseph Paul, comte de Grasse. This fifty-eight-year-old nobleman had a drive and willingness to take chances that were uncommon in the French navy. In addition, the French had sent five thousand soldiers to Rhode Island to join Washington's Continentals.

When George Washington heard that Cornwallis had withdrawn to Yorktown, he deferred plans for what was likely a very costly and dubious attempt to retake New York City, and hurried to Yorktown with his army and the newly arrived French. A token force was able to maintain the illusion of preparation for attack outside New York City, fooling the British for some weeks. Soon Washington was able to place Yorktown under siege. The problem was that it would mean nothing if Cornwallis could be resupplied or evacuated by the Royal Navy. The war would go on, the Continental Congress was already having trouble raising any funds, and the revolution might well have simply fizzled out.

While Washington was moving on Yorktown, de Grasse made a courageous decision. Rather than use his entire fleet to escort the now fully laden 126 merchant ships back to France, as ordered, he decided instead to reduce their escort to a single sixty-four-gun ship of the line. This was a pitifully small escort for what was basically a treasure fleet carrying goods, silver, and gold worth more than his government's entire annual budget. If it had been attacked, even by just a handful of British frigates, he would probably have been executed and France would have been in dire financial straits. But his gamble paid off and the merchant fleet arrived unmolested. This left the French fleet of twenty-eight ships of the line able to act independently.

De Grasse was not under the command of the French army commander, or anyone else in the same hemisphere. But when, in mid-July 1781, he received a letter hinting about the plan to corner the British in Yorktown, the French admiral sailed for the Chesapeake Bay. His orders were to sail to New York City to assist in the now canceled assault. However, the French minister in America soon made Admiral de Grasse aware that his fleet could make the difference between American independence or, at best, a continuing stalemate in North America. So the bold French commander sailed for the Chesapeake. He also sent a letter to the commander of another small fleet operating out of Newport (it had been directly supporting the French infantry) and asked its admiral to join him there with his nine ships of the line.

The British, too, had a fleet along the American coast and it also sailed to the Chesapeake. It was commanded by Rear Admiral Samuel Hood. But the British ships arrived before the French and found the bay empty. Correctly guessing that the original French orders involved New York City, he had the fourteen British ships change destinations. In New York Harbor, they joined up with another five ships under Vice Admiral Thomas Graves. At the end of August, the nineteen British ships sailed again for Chesapeake Bay looking for de Grasse.

The French had arrived in the bay outside Yorktown a few days earlier. They were still in the process of unloading cannons and supplies when the British were sighted. Once the tide allowed, de Grasse's ships cut their cables and struggled against the wind to sail out of the channel and into open waters. This process took several hours and meant the French fleet was badly disorganized as the British approached.

The British, commanded by Admiral Graves, had been sailing under the order of "line ahead." This basically told the ships to follow his flagship in a single line. As they approached the more numerous, but still disorganized French fleet, everyone waited for Graves to raise the signal flags for "close action." This would have sent his fleet plunging into the French with likely a similar result as later occurred at Trafalgar. But rather than do this, Graves stuck to the standard fighting instructions. He ordered line ahead for his leading ship squadrons and a reversal of their course. This maneuver would allow room for the nineteen British ships to eventually sail against the still-forming French line of battle, in the traditional manner. Graves played it by the book. It took the British ninety minutes to go farther out to sea, reverse direction, and return in a line of battle. During this time, the French finally managed to maneuver their twenty-eight ships into formation. Then Graves made a second mistake. Instead of engaging de Grasse's ships, he ordered his fleet to "heave to" and wait for the French to sail to them. Both sides crept toward each other.

It took six long, mostly wasted hours from the first sighting of the British to the moment the battle actually began. Time wasted as Graves hesitated and maneuvered, rather than just going at the still-forming French. Even outnumbered, the more experienced Royal Navy, with its superior gunners, might have at least damaged Admiral de Grasse's fleet badly enough that the French would have had to withdraw. Since their objective was to support Cornwallis's army, that would have been a victory. But then Graves made another mistake that further crippled his fleet. His signal flags currently read "Close Action"—but his flagship still displayed the flags for "Line Ahead." This led to some (understandable) confusion and an additional error—one that lost the battle and the war. This was Admiral Hood's mistake. Rather than close with the enemy, Admiral Hood and his five ships "followed orders," even as the rest of the British ships fought. His five ships continued to try to sail behind Graves's flagship, the *London*. They barely fired at all and only did so after the battle was lost.

With Hood's ships failing to attack, Graves's fleet was outnumbered two to one in the line of battle. The British were good, even exceptional by any other nation's standards, but not that good. The normally dominant Royal Navy found itself outgunned and taking more damage than it could dish out. When the fighting finally ended that evening, the French had four ships that were badly damaged and unable to continue in the line of battle. The British had five ships no longer able to fight. This left de Grasse with twenty-four ships and Graves with only fourteen, including Hood's. Only two French ships reported sustaining any significant damage from enemy fire. As the day ended, both sides maneuvered, with Graves hoping (but failing) to slip into Chesapeake Bay behind the French. When de Grasse and his independent fleet arrived late in the day, the odds were thirty-six French ships, most in good repair or undamaged, against fourteen British ships, several in poor condition. Graves felt he had no choice but to return to New York City. Never before had the Royal Navy failed the British army so badly. Cornwallis found himself outnumbered and under siege on land and sea. His surrender did not end the British efforts to retain their colonies in North America, but guaranteed Britain's failure and destroyed Parliament's faith that any victory was possible.

The British defeat in Chesapeake Bay need not have happened. Ship for ship and cannon for cannon, the Royal Navy had shown it was superior to the French. But Graves and Hood made two mistakes and lost the American Revolution. Had the British attacked when they first sighted the French and while the French were in disarray, a victory would have been more than likely. But Graves hesitated and stuck to the standing orders, which were designed to minimize casualties, not win battles. If the British had charged, as Nelson did so successfully in later years, they could have, at the very least, battered the French fleet badly enough that the French admiral would have had to abandon the Chesapeake Bay. Admiral de Grasse was commanding more than a third of the French ships of the line in the French navy and could not afford to lose too many. Then, protected by the guns of Graves's ships, General Cornwallis and the last mobile British army could have easily escaped to New York.

But Graves played it by the book, and badly at that. He tried to form his fleet into a line of battle parallel to the French. This maneuver was poorly handled, and literally took hours and a return to the high seas to accomplish. When he finished the maneuver, rather than leading his line of ships, Graves found himself at the very rear of the formation, with his slowest and most vulnerable ships leading it. Fighting in a line of battle also guaranteed at best an incomplete victory or at worst (as in this case) a defeat. He then commanded badly, flying conflicting instructions even during the battle. Had Graves been braver, and more competent, the overextended French might have seen their best chance to thwart England and free the colonies fail. A financially strained King Louis could have lost faith and withdrawn. The already bankrupt American Revolution would likely have collapsed. If one of Graves's officers had just pointed out and corrected the problem with the signal flags, nearly a third of the British ships would not have missed most of the battle. With much greater damage, the French again might have had to withdraw or even have lost a rematch the next day.

Had Graves not dithered and signaled contradictory orders to Hood, Cornwallis and his army would have been freed. Even reinforced by the French, Washington would have likely been unable to produce a defeat dramatic enough for the royal government to lose faith that any victory in the colonies was possible. Even with French aid, which was limited by the poor condition of Louis XVI's finances, the revolution might have been halted. The forefathers of the United States would be known to history as a pack of traitors to be vilified for the damage they did and the deaths they caused for no purpose. The eastern coast would have remained a collection of separate British colonies. Napoleon would certainly not have offered them the Louisiana Purchase, and the Midwest might well today be part of Canada or even Mexico. The United States, stillborn, would be nothing and we might all be singing "God Save the Queen" at our sporting events. North America might have ended up divided between many areas controlled by different European powers, and the Russians might have even colonized California. If the colonies did expand west, and there is no guarantee an untrusting Parliament would have allowed this, there likely would still have come a day when the wealth of the New World made the colonies more important than the home islands. Finally, our accents would likely be very different as well, old chap.

# 23

## LOUIS XVI FLEES PARIS

### 1791

**By Bill Fawcett**

*He may have lost his head,
but he did it in style.*

n 1791, the city of Paris was in revolt. The king had lost control of the city and most of France. But the king was a rallying point for the many who still supported his rule. Realizing that their lives were in danger, the king and his wife, Marie Antoinette, decided to flee the palace. The idea was for them to head to one of the many areas that still strongly supported them. The plan was supposed to be secret—only a few knew of it. The couple were to make their escape covertly, with virtually no guards or protection. That was the plan, but not what happened.

The failure of the escape has to be put on Marie Antoinette. Rather than sneak away separately, at the last minute she insisted that they travel with their children. That meant a delay. It also meant that the carriage they planned to flee in was too small. So Marie demanded they take one of the massive royal carriages covered in gilt and rich woods. Loyal staff rushed in the darkness to change the arrangements and word was sent for Marie and Louis to each make their way to the carriage. Evidently, Marie chose to sneak out through the ornamental maze on the palace grounds. She then proceeded to get lost in it and took an extra half hour to arrive. Rather than making their entire journey at night, the royal couple were still on the road near Paris when the sun rose. Within a few hours, revolutionaries in one of the villages they passed through recognized the ornate carriage. They were stopped at the next village and forced to return to the palace.

Upon his return, the beleaguered Louis XVI accepted a constitution that limited his power. Under the new document, all laws would come from a newly formed legislative assembly. One of the first actions of the assembly was to order the hundreds of nobles (who had fled France in fear) to return. The king vetoed this decree. Within the next few weeks, there was a food shortage in the city as transport and control had been disrupted by the riots and émigrés had shut down their companies and fled with much of their wealth. Food riots followed. In response, the assembly ignored the king's veto and began confiscating the lands and businesses of the émigrés. The Jacobin extremists used the city's problems, general discontent, and a defeat of the army by the Austrians to whip up the masses. As neighboring nations threatened to invade France, a mob, supported by national guard units, attacked the palace. Louis XVI ordered his personal bodyguard, the Swiss Guard, not to fire, but eventually they did anyway. The Swiss Guard was slaughtered and the king taken prisoner. On January 21, 1793, Louis was executed. Nine months later, on obviously bogus charges, Marie also lost her head.

If Louis XVI had managed to successfully reach the Vendée or any other area of France that was still fiercely loyal to him, the revolution might well have been limited to Paris. At the time that Marie Antoinette's unrealistic behavior thwarted their escape, much of the army outside of Paris was either loyal or neutral. The Vendée and Brittany remained so royalist that, even two years after Louis XVI's death, the revolutionary leaders were dispatching whole armies to pacify them. With the French Revolution limited, the history of Europe would have changed drastically. Free, Louis could have once more attempted to negotiate the constitutional monarchy he desired. Executions, the atrocities under Robespierre, and twenty years of war against the rest of Europe might have been avoided. Even if Louis had eventually been forced to flee, his living presence would have acted as a counterbalance and alternative choice to the extremely radical and unpopular Robespierre or, later, the Directorate.

Napoleon Bonaparte was brought to a high rank at a young age by the acts of the Committee of Public Safety, which bungled the provisional government and caused the further militarization of France. If Louis had provided that other center for France, there would have been no committee and no "whiff of grapeshot" needed to save it. Without the Napoleonic Wars, France would not have needed to sell Louisiana (named after an earlier Louis) to the young United States. America would be smaller and the North American continent divided between many nations, rather than just three. If Britain had not had to tax the colonies for the cost of the French and Indian War, she might well have retained control of the thirteen colonies. But because Marie Antoinette was pampered, unrealistic, and demanding at the wrong time, Europe suffered from fifteen years of war and the age of kings soon came to an end.

# 24

# GEORGE WASHINGTON'S DEATH

1794

### By Bill Fawcett

The doctors knew best?

In December of 1799, about thirty months after he retired from being president, George Washington was killed by his own physicians. His death was not a murder, and his doctors were among the best in the new nation. He was treated vigorously in a time-honored and accepted manner, and he likely died from it.

On December 13, the former president had been riding on a windy, cold, and rainy day. He returned home to Mount Vernon feeling ill. Washington soon had a cough and runny sinuses, and he was very hoarse. The next morning, when he seemed worse and his throat was raw and swollen, Martha Washington sent for his aide, who summoned two physicians. In the next two days they literally treated George Washington to death.

The reason for their fatal actions was what was then accepted medical practice. It was a practice that had not changed in almost two millennia and had its roots in the treatments created by no less than Galen of Pergamon (AD 129 to 210), renowned as the world's first true physician. Galen was perhaps the first person to medically dissect a human body and he changed how a number of things about it were perceived. Among the revelations he offered was the concept that the arteries and veins carried blood and not air, as was commonly believed. Galen also got a few things very wrong, and because he was so right on others, these too were accepted as fact for the next fifteen hundred years.

The basis of Galen's errors was his conclusion that while blood was stored in the arteries, it did not move. He assumed that like other organs, such as the liver or the kidney, it just sat there and worked. His second mistake was that he accepted and reinforced the common belief that health was the result of a balance of the "four humors" within a body and all illness came when this balance was lost. The four humors were blood, phlegm, yellow bile, and black bile. Of these, too much blood was often thought to be the major problem, perhaps just because the body has so much of it. So Galen determined that the best way to cure anything from the common cold to kidney failure was to remove blood from those different parts of the body where there was an imbalance. This is to "bleed" the patient. Bleeding was so widespread a practice that when doctors were not available, the town barber would bleed his customers for a fee, which is what inspired the barber pole advertising the service. Yes, that red stripe represents blood. Bleeding was so entrenched that it was not until the nineteenth century that it finally stopped being used. This was a century too late to save the first president.

One of the two doctors Martha summoned was in attendance when at about six a.m. on December 14 Washington awoke with a serious fever and his raw throat very swollen. At seven thirty a.m., George Rawlins used approved medical devices to drain twelve or so ounces of blood out of Washington's throat. The president, accepting the treatment, even encouraged him to take more. Rawlins then gave Washington a mixture of molasses, butter, and vinegar, on which he nearly choked. At nine thirty a.m., the doctor decided that another bloodletting was needed. This time eighteen ounces of blood was drained. At noon, to clear out the imbalance in other humors, an enema was performed. For a while Washington seemed to recover and even walked around his bedroom, but then he weakened.

A physician, Dr. Craik, then had the former president drink a potion that forced him to vomit for some minutes. At five p.m., after some debate with a newly arrived physician, it was decided that Washington needed yet another and even more massive blood-letting. This time thirty-two ounces were drained from his weakened body. For a time Washington seemed to be somewhat better, though he was just well enough to take a final look at his will with Martha.

By eight p.m., Washington was fading and another treatment that involved raising blisters on his skin was tried. That did no good. By ten p.m., George Washington was dead, suffering from a severe sore throat and the best treatment medicine of his day had to offer. They had bled more than eighty ounces of blood from the sick leader (the average human body holds about 150 ounces), along with subjecting him to diarrhea and vomiting.

If George Washington had lived, it is likely that some of the bitter battles between the Western populists like Andrew Jackson and the leaders in the more settled states might have been mitigated. He might even have lived long enough to remind the nation of his warning that it should avoid "foreign entanglements" and the new nation might not have fought the meaningless and costly War of 1812. But with such a prestigious patient, his doctors aggressively used every accepted treatment they had. So, thanks to the mistakes of a second-century Roman doctor, the United States' first president died with raw blisters, purged, anemic, and weak.

# 25

# ONE MORE CONQUEST

## 1812

### By Bill Fawcett

Some people cannot stop eating chips.
Others are the same way about
conquering nations.

Napoleon Bonaparte did not lose his empire at Waterloo. That battle just prevented his return to power. He lost it at Moscow four years earlier. Invading Russia in 1812 was the single decision that doomed his reign and his dream of a unified Europe. In 1811, Napoleon Bonaparte ruled Europe. His armies controlled everywhere from Spain to Poland. Only two nations still challenged his supremacy. These were Russia and Britain. Russia was a massive nation in both population and size, but with a weak economy and high rate of illiteracy. Napoleon's real opponent was the British Empire. For the previous two decades, the wealth of that empire had financed the other European nations' resistance to French conquest. The Royal Navy still controlled the seas, blockading most French ports and allowing the English to threaten any part of Napoleon's empire.

Since the Battle of Trafalgar, the British domination of the seas was complete. What remained of the navies under Napoleon's control was all trapped in their ports. The British were even supporting a revolt in Spain—with growing success. Without a way to cross the Channel, there was no direct action that could be taken to punish Britain, but Bonaparte could attack them economically. Much of the wealth of Britain was the direct result of its merchants' success. A good part of that success and wealth was generated by trading with the various nations of Europe. The taxes on this trade went directly into the royal treasury, supporting those who opposed France and paying for the world's largest navy, plus Wellington's army in Spain. To stop this trade, Napoleon tried to force all the nations he controlled into his "Continental System," the main goal of which was to exclude British goods and British ships. In retaliation, the British tried to ban the import of French products, but that tactic failed due to massive smuggling. They made no real effort to control exports.

Smuggling was common; small European ports became rich catering to British smugglers. (So did some English ports, for the same reason.) The largest hole in the Continental System was Russia, which had been neither conquered by nor allied with Napoleon and which imposed no restriction on the British landing their cargoes in St. Petersburg and other Russian ports. With the Royal Navy so dominant, the English merchants faced little risk doing this. By 1810, the flow of British goods into Europe by way of Russia had partially undermined Napoleon's efforts at economic control. This gave an incentive for the greatest general of his age to strike at Russia and eliminate the last continental military threat to his complete authority and remove the last means by which British goods could enter Europe.

There are possibly other reasons Napoleon chose to invade Russia. Even after fighting for almost twenty years, he had never really lost a battle—there had to be a good part of hubris in the decision. He would go, defeat the Russian armies as he always had, and accept their surrender. Russia had been part of several alliances against him and its continued independence encouraged its former allies, Prussia and Austria, to repeatedly attempt to throw off French control. Once defeated, it would join those nations in Napoleon's continent-spanning empire. The kings, dukes, and czars would be gone. The egalitarian philosophy of the French Revolution would spread across all the lands, uniting them. Uniting them, that is, under Napoleon's rule.

Finally, Napoleon had always had a stated goal. Since the fall of Rome, Europe had been nearly constantly engaged in a war or preparing for one. They had fought for a millennium. The horrific effects of the Thirty Years' War and the Wars of Succession were still recent. He felt that, if he could bring all of the nations under one banner, as one empire, it would mean an end to wars within Europe. He literally intended to conquer and occupy his way to peace, a peace that would exist because there would be no one left to fight with. But so long as Russia and Britain remained independent, this high-flown goal was unachieved.

So, in 1812, the greatest army ever seen in Europe gathered along hundreds of miles of the Russian border. Six hundred thousand men, primarily French, but also including contingents from every nation Bonaparte controlled, marched into Russia or secured the flanks. Napoleon continued his unbeaten record. His first encounter with a Russian army at Eylau was a draw. A blinding snowstorm and misunderstood orders hampered his army. The Russians retreated. The invading Grand Army marched east toward one of the two capitals of Russia: Moscow. Napoleon defeated the Russian army at Borodino, though at a high cost. Days later, he marched into the nearly deserted (and soon burning) city of Moscow. There he expected the czar of the Russians, in his other capital at St. Petersburg, to accept his nation's defeat and surrender. So Napoleon rested his army and waited. And waited. And waited—for an embassy that never arrived. He waited too long. By the time he accepted his strategic failure and ordered his almost two hundred thousand remaining soldiers to march back to Poland, it was too late. An early and harsh winter, combined with constant harassment, depleted and demoralized his retreating army. Always in the distance was the Russian army. To stop or break into separate columns guaranteed defeat. The temperature dropped to below zero and stayed there. Snow slowed wagons and hid what little grass remained. Horses, the main transport of the army, died daily in droves. A true disaster followed when Bonaparte's retreating army was forced to follow the same route out of Russia as they took in. The already hungry and frozen men crossed deserted countryside that they had already stripped of all food and fodder on their way into Russia. The Russian resistance grew, and the dreaded Cossacks killed anyone who strayed from the main column, but to not search for food meant starvation.

Of the main body of the Grand Army, once numbering over a quarter million of the best French troops, fewer than ten thousand effective combat soldiers eventually crossed the Vistula into Poland and safety.

The Grand Army was effectively gone. Napoleon returned to France, and called up and trained more groups of conscripts. It was not enough. Too many veterans and too many officers and noncommissioned officers had been lost. Even horses were in short supply. The heart of his highly polished and professional fighting machine died on the wastes of Russia. France and its army never recovered. Within a year, Prussia, Russia, and even Sweden would defeat what remained of the Grand Army in the Battle of Nations. A few months after that, Napoleon Bonaparte went from ruler of Europe to exile on Elba.

Many of Napoleon Bonaparte's generals and marshals had advised him not to invade Russia. It was too backward a nation to really threaten the rest of Europe by itself. It was also very much an unknown land that was far different from the Europe they had conquered. Invading it was, some pointed out, an unnecessary risk. What if Napoleon had listened? Despite the generally successful propaganda spread by the British, Napoleon was a fairly enlightened ruler. He believed in a united Europe, though preferably under his rule. He encouraged science, literacy, and a social safety net. His homes for wounded soldiers, pensions for widows, and scientifically advanced medical corps were the models for all the armies that have followed, even to this day. The Veterans Administration today is the direct descendant of the French hospital Les Invalides. When a young Napoleon led an army to Egypt, it was accompanied by over four hundred scientists from many fields. Many of today's advancements started under his rule. Canning was actually invented in a contest to find the best way to preserve food for storage in the depots of the Grand Army invading Russia. Bonaparte believed in the rule of law and the sanctity of the contract. The Code Napoleon is still the basis of most continental European law.

So, the continuation of the Napoleonic Empire might have been good for parts of Europe, except possibly for the British. Germany would have been united fifty years earlier, though possibly in a Greater Europe. Wars that followed would not have happened. Certainly Germany, France, and all of the continent would not have gone through the traumas of two world wars. Science was advancing and would continue to do so. If a peace had been found with the British, then trade would have boomed and the economies soared as the new manufacturing methods already used in France were introduced generally. Certainly, there might have been a darker side as Bonaparte's family retained so much power. A bad emperor would have had little to counterbalance his actions and, like the mad emperors of Rome, would have damaged that empire. But if Napoleon had listened to his marshals and avoided the destruction of the army on which his power was based, the next two centuries of European history would have had a good chance of being a great deal more peaceful.

‖‖‖‖‖‖‖‖‖‖‖‖‖‖‖‖‖‖‖‖‖‖‖‖‖‖‖‖‖‖‖‖‖‖‖‖‖‖‖‖‖‖‖‖‖‖‖‖‖‖

# 26

# NEY AT
# QUATRE BRAS

### 1815

## By Bill Fawcett

‖‖‖‖‖‖‖‖‖‖‖‖‖‖‖‖‖‖‖‖‖‖‖‖‖‖‖‖‖‖‖‖‖‖‖‖‖‖‖‖‖‖‖‖‖‖‖‖‖‖‖‖‖‖

Maybe Napoleon should have assigned
the corps to the Brightest of the Bright
rather than to the Bravest of the Brave.

Here is a thought to wrap your mind around: Napoleon Bonaparte did not lose the Battle of Waterloo. The French lost the battle, but the man who lost it was Marshal Michel Ney. This noted French officer had unquestioned courage. In France, he was often called the Bravest of the Brave. Marshal Ney commanded the rear guard on the disastrous march out of Russia. He started that duty commanding twenty-five thousand men and, when they marched over the Vistula into Poland and safety, only five hundred remained. Yet behind Ney they formed up and crossed the bridge in good order. It was during that tour of duty that his famous red hair turned completely gray. Napoleon trusted Ney and there was no question that men would follow him into battle. Bonaparte could normally count on him to be his most aggressive corps commander. Ney loved to lead his men into a battle, preferring to be at the head of his troops in a charge to remaining in his headquarters. It took Michel Ney three major mistakes in two days of battle to guarantee a French defeat.

In 1815, Napoleon Bonaparte returned from exile on Elba to an enthusiastic welcome in France. Every unit sent by the king of France to arrest him joined his ranks instead. The marshals from Napoleon's regime had retained their positions under the reinstated king. One of the royal army's units was commanded by Ney, who boasted to the king that he would bring Napoleon back in a cage. When Ney faced his former emperor, he was at the head of an army of soldiers who had already changed sides and joined Napoleon, and there was a tense moment or two. Some said that Ney even ordered the line of infantry to fire, but no one obeyed. What is certain is that, within minutes, Ney approached Napoleon, who greeted him with great enthusiasm. Ney saluted—and rejoined his emperor. To a man, his fifteen hundred soldiers formed up behind the two of them and began to march to Paris. A few days later, the king fled France. In short order, Bonaparte had regained control of the country and was emperor again.

The allies, primarily England, Prussia, Austria, and Russia, had spent twenty years fighting against or being occupied by Bonaparte's armies. With his return to power, each immediately called up their armies and marched on France. But the allied armies were setting out from locations hundreds of miles away from each other. The Austrian and Russian armies would take weeks to reach France. But two of the allies were closer to France and soon were within a few days' march of each other. These were the English-Dutch army under the Duke of Wellington and the Prussian army commanded by Marshal Blücher. Blücher had been fighting the French for more than twenty years and was old, fat, and infirm enough that he often commanded in the field from a wagon rather than from horseback. Still, he had lost none of his fire. Wellington's army was located near Brussels and Blücher's was marching toward it from Germany. Wellington had about seventy thousand men and fewer than half of these were his veterans from Spain. In addition, there was the worrisome fact that many of the Dutch troops he led had served under Napoleon only a few years earlier. On the other hand, Blücher had eighty thousand men, but nearly all of them were new recruits and inexperienced. Napoleon had about a hundred and ten thousand men following him north to meet these two armies. In typical Napoleonic manner, he managed to surprise both opponents and place himself between them.

Napoleon led seventy-one thousand of his troops toward Blücher and the Prussians on his right. To his left was the vital crossroads of

Quatre Bras. He sent Ney, leading twenty-five thousand soldiers, to take Quatre Bras. He also sent orders for a second corps, that of the comte d'Erlon, to move to support the advance. If Napoleon held that junction, no matter what happened, it was unlikely that the British and Germans could join together without leaving Brussels open. On the night of June 16, he gave Ney verbal orders to take the town. That was when Ney made what was his first mistake. Returning to his command, he went to sleep without issuing any orders. It took a few hours just to form up camped troops to move, so this guaranteed that the morning would be lost before Ney's troops could reach their objective. In fact, it was not until about eleven a.m. the next day that his first divisions were on the march toward Quatre Bras. That morning, the Dutch generals Jean Victor de Constant Rebecque (actually a Swiss officer in service to the Dutch) and Hendrik George, count de Perponcher Sedinitzky, had realized the location's strategic value and rushed their lone division to defend the crossroads. Other British and Dutch units were ordered to reinforce the position, but all were hours away.

For his part, Napoleon spent the day fighting the entire German army with his other corps. The battle had degenerated into a slugging match, which Blücher's army was taking the worst of.

When his division finally reached Quatre Bras, Ney discovered it was already held. At two p.m., the allies had only eight thousand men and twelve guns. Ney's lead division had twenty thousand men and sixty guns, so he should have been able to push the British out with a single strong attack. But Ney made the mistake of hesitating. While he saw only about eight thousand British supported by fifty cavalry and twelve guns, all French marshals had learned on the peninsula that what you could see was often not all Wellington had nearby. For that reason, even though the attack started at two p.m., the advance was cautious and slow-moving. Ney sent a messenger asking that d'Erlon and his corps hurry to the battlefield, then pressed slowly forward. When they approached a wooded area on one side, the entire advance slowed until it could be determined that the trees did not hold hidden Englishmen waiting to jump on their flank. At two p.m., the French marshal received a written order from Napoleon stressing the importance of seizing the crossroads. Ney pushed the attack forward and began to drive into the thin British line. Wellington arrived at three p.m. and saw his line splintering. Then an entire Belgian-Dutch cavalry brigade arrived to aid the British, and the line held. Even when the brigade was lost, through inept leadership by the Prince of Orange, it bought enough time for eight thousand more men under Picton to reach the battle at about three thirty. When the French next attacked, they were met by a second line of fresh, veteran infantry and thrown back.

Ney then pulled back and waited for d'Erlon's corps, which was following his, to arrive. With them, he would again greatly outnumber Wellington, and be able to overwhelm and outflank the town. Unfortunately, this, too, was a mistake. D'Erlon had encountered one of Napoleon's aides, General de la Bédoyère, who knew of the situation at Ligny and ordered d'Erlon to turn about and march to attack the Prussian flank. D'Erlon had no choice but to obey someone speaking with Bonaparte's authority. So he marched away from Quatre Bras to Ligny.

When d'Erlon did not appear, Ney, rather than press the attack, sent an aide to d'Erlon with specific orders to hurry to Quatre Bras. Then he made his second mistake. He still had more men and many more guns than Wellington, but he waited for d'Erlon. A few hours later, d'Erlon did arrive at Ligny—but in the wrong place. Instead of appearing on the German flank, he arrived at the end of the French line. Fearing the large force appearing in the distance on their left, General Dominique Vandamme's Third Corps reacted with panic, and a vital attack by the guard was delayed for over an hour, until it could be determined that the troops were French and not Wellington's Brits. As a result, d'Erlon's corps did not fight at Ligny, even though they were in sight of the enemy.

At Quatre Bras, the English mounted a counterattack. This, combined with an order arriving from Napoleon reminding him how important the crossroads was, sent Ney into a fit of temper. He immediately sent riders to inform d'Erlon that, no matter where he was, his corps was to hurry to Quatre Bras. So the French army at Ligny saw an entire corps arrive at the battle, then saw it march away, without firing a single shot. Then the French marshal waited for d'Erlon to arrive. By the time orders from Napoleon arrived demanding he take the crossroads, it was six p.m.—too late. Before the French could strike, the British (now reinforced to thirty-six thousand to Ney's twenty thousand) counterattacked. In the next three hours, the outnumbered French were driven back beyond Perponcher's original lines. With more than eight thousand casualties split evenly between both sides, the result was a draw.

Had Ney moved on the morning of June 16 with speed in the face of the enemy, perhaps actually getting his corps moving three hours after dawn, he would have arrived at Quatre Bras first. Even if he had just dithered that morning long enough to have his lead elements arrive before noon, there would have been so few British in the vital town that they could have been thrown out easily. But Ney moved with no sense of urgency, even with the enemy nearby, and missed the opportunity for a nearly bloodless and decisive victory. The mistake he made in a fit of temper—ordering d'Erlon to countermarch, yet again—meant that Napoleon had no fresh troops with which he could press the retreating Prussians. Ney's waiting two hours for d'Erlon's troops to arrive before attacking again that day meant he lost his numerical superiority. The vital town and its roads remained in British hands. Two mistakes on the first of two days of battle. One, a failure to act with a reasonable sense of urgency when about to face the enemy. The second, an order to d'Erlon's corps demanding their return to Quatre Bras, without enough information and in contradiction to Napoleon's orders—because he was angry. Ordering the corps to countermarch, with no regard for why it was marching, toward Napoleon and to a major battle. Yet both these battle-losing mistakes were to be overshadowed by the one that Ney made the next day at the Battle of Waterloo itself.

Had Ney taken Quatre Bras, the British would have had to fall farther back, toward Brussels. If the Prussians, who arrived only in the nick of time, had arrived later or not come at all, knowing Wellington's Anglo-Dutch army was retreating, the Battle of Waterloo would be known by whatever name Bonaparte chose to give it. Battles are named by the victors and it would have been not a "near-run thing" but a French victory.

The Battle of Waterloo wasn't actually fought in Waterloo. The names Quatre Bras and Hougoumont were deemed by Wellington to be too difficult for Englishmen to pronounce, so he instead used the name of a nearby town, Waterloo.

Despite his failure to capture Quatre Bras, Napoleon kept his faith in the Bravest of the Brave. As the day progressed, the emperor became ill. Unable to ride among the troops, he placed Marshal Ney in direct command during the second day of the battle, the Battle of Waterloo.

# 27

## NEY AT WATERLOO

### 1815

**By Bill Fawcett**

Compared to his performance
at Waterloo, Ney was brilliant
at Quatre Bras.

After defeating the Prussians at Ligny, Napoleon moved the bulk of his corps the next day to face Wellington's Anglo-Dutch army. Ney again started the day slowly, and along with an unfortunate (for the French) thunderstorm, Wellington was able to retreat with some difficulty. The Prussians chose to retreat to Wavre, not Liège, which allowed them to move toward the Waterloo battlefield. Their movement was aided by a mishandled pursuit by Grouchy and the thirty-three thousand men in his corps.

On the second day after Quatre Bras and Ligny, Wellington faced Napoleon. Napoleon had with him seventy-one thousand mostly reliable soldiers, including almost sixteen thousand cavalry and 246 cannon. The French artillery was still the best in Europe—or in the world, for that matter. Wellington had about the same number of infantry, but only 156 guns and twelve thousand cavalry. His army was a mix of British battalions and the newly mustered Dutch regiments commanded by the Prince of Orange, who was in charge of the center of Wellington's line. About half the men in the British units were veterans of the Peninsular Campaign and the rest were new recruits. Although Wellington had some doubts about the Dutch units before the battle, many showed amazing courage and sacrifice.

The battlefield across which the two armies faced each other in the final great conflict of the Napoleonic Wars was only about three miles across. Napoleon formed up his battalions in plain sight of the British-Dutch. The reason for this was to intimidate those facing him, particularly the dubious Dutch units that composed almost 40 percent of the duke's army. Wellington, as was his habit, formed up many of his battalions on the backs of hills, protecting them from artillery fire. The night had been rainy and Napoleon chose to delay starting the battle until the ground had a chance to dry. So it was not until late morning that the Battle of Waterloo began with a barrage from a mass battery. Those British battalions on the reverse slopes suffered few casualties from the cannon fire. A Dutch battalion exposed to the cannon fire was mauled. The French artillery did real damage all through the first hours of the battle. Then the French infantry advanced. Twice in the next hours of battle, Napoleon felt he had a victory. Wellington's army held, but at a high price. Cavalry charges by the British regiments saved the army at least once. The Anglo-Dutch army was beginning to waver and Wellington was running out of reserves. In contrast, Napoleon Bonaparte had substantial reserves remaining. Two French forces—the Guard and over half of his cavalry—had not been engaged and could prove decisive.

Ney was already commanding the actual attacks. Bonaparte's health had limited the time he could spend rushing about the field on a horse. With the battle in the balance, the emperor sent Ney an order to take a fortified position that protected the British left: La Haie Sainte. The reason for this urgent order was that Prussians were beginning to appear near the French right flank. They had to win fast or face two armies at once. Ney led two brigades in a desperate attack, but was repulsed. When leading this attack, the marshal saw soldiers falling back on the road to Brussels. Closer to him, Marshal Ney saw a cavalry unit fleeing at high speed. The reality was that the road was crowded with ambulances, empty ammunition wagons, and the walking wounded. At this point, Ney jumped to a wrong conclusion and saw what he wanted to see. He became convinced that the British had broken and were retreating. Only one more push was needed to change that retreat into a rout.

Hurrying to the nearest cavalry formation, Milhaud's cuirassiers (a type of shock cavalry that wore chest armor and were mounted on the largest horses), Ney ordered them to follow him in a charge. To Ney this was simply the traditional tactic of using cavalry to break and scatter a defeated enemy. He did not even notify the emperor of his intentions. Seeing Ney lead the cuirassiers toward the British caused other heavy cavalry units to join in. Then, as this mass of heavy horsemen passed by, other officers took it on themselves to order the light cavalry to follow behind them. Within minutes, over five thousand horsemen were moving toward the British battalions that stood in the center of Wellington's thinning line.

The Anglo-Dutch officers could see the charge coming. Normally, such a charge was followed by infantry and supported by guns. This tactic wreaked havoc on the closely spaced squares that were the only way for infantry to survive a heavy cavalry charge. But Ney had not bothered to order any infantry or artillery into position. The marshal just charged, and most of Napoleon's remaining cavalry followed him. One of the French generals, Gourgaud, said in his memoirs that Ney was "carried away by an excess of ardor." Without any artillery to threaten them, the British and Dutch formed squares that Ney's horsemen were unable to penetrate. Time after time, Ney led the best of Napoleon's horsemen and most of the emperor's reserve against the squares. British gunners would man their cannon, firing until the last minute, and then run for shelter behind the infantry. The eighth and last time Ney's horsemen attacked the squares, their horses were so worn-out that they walked, not ran. Finally, Lord Uxbridge led a charge of British cavalry against the exhausted French. This drove them off, but the courageous French horsemen re-formed and tried to walk up to the squares for one more attack. More cannon had been brought up and it wreaked havoc on the slowly approaching riders. That attack failed and what remained of Napoleon's cavalry reserve was broken and useless for hours. Almost nothing had been achieved by their sacrifice.

Bonaparte rode forward and rallied his troops. Even with the Prussians approaching, he could see it was still a close battle. Wellington's center was still wavering. If they were to win the battle, they would have to do so *now*. The Prussians would have to halt and re-form before taking on the French army alone. So, on Napoleon's orders, Ney led yet another attack on La Haie Sainte, the key position in the Anglo-Dutch line. This attack finally succeeded. A grand battery moved forward into the captured ground that punished the now-exposed Dutch battalions. The survivors of d'Erlon's corps, who had been trying to take the position, re-formed and attacked the weakening British center as well. Ney sent an urgent message asking for Napoleon to send him the last reserve, the Old Guard. After so many mistakes, the emperor ignored the request. But by this point, the Prussians had begun to press on the French right. More than thirty thousand men were marching toward the weak French flank. To buy time, the middle Guard and eight battalions of the Old Guard counterattacked the front of the approaching Prussians and drove them back. Several battalions of the Old Guard then returned to re-form a last reserve. The irony here is that for the first time in the three days, Ney made the right decision. If the Guard had attacked when he asked, Wellington's army would have been split and forced to retreat, at best.

The Battle of Waterloo occurred at a decisive moment. The grand battery at La Haie Sainte had virtually destroyed two battalions in front of the farmhouse. After the battle, hundreds of bodies were laid out there in perfect formations. Wellington was out of reserves and forced to strip units from his right to reinforce his center and left. Some arrived just in time to prevent a collapse. There were few intact British battalions left for him to move.

Napoleon, too, was facing defeat. Prussians were arriving in large numbers and beginning to reinforce the end of Wellington's line. He had to win *then* or lose everything. The problem was he had only one reserve remaining. This was composed of nine battalions of the Old Guard. All the other infantry was committed, and the cavalry that would have smashed easily through the weakening British line had been wasted by Ney in his mistaken charges. The Old Guard formed up into a massive column and marched toward Wellington's center. The column split in two and came up to the one remaining line of British infantry. The attack did not have enough strength. They were fired upon from the front and flank, and repulsed.

What with the retreat of the "invincible" Old Guard and word that the Prussians were arriving in force, French morale broke. Napoleon's army collapsed. A few days later, Napoleon Bonaparte, just one hundred days after becoming emperor of France for the second time, surrendered to the captain of a British ship.

Had Ney not wasted the five thousand cavalry in the mistaken idea that the British were retreating, or had he at least handled the attack correctly by adding infantry and cannon, it seems likely Napoleon would have won the battle before the Prussians could intervene. With Wellington broken and fleeing to Brussels, the most the Prussians could have done was slow Napoleon's pursuit. This was Britain's only active field army and the bulk of Prussia's. With those nations out of the war, it is unlikely the Austrians, with the Russians weeks away, would have risked taking on Napoleon by themselves. At best, they would have retreated back to Austria. More likely, all of Europe would have had to accept Napoleon as the leader of France.

Even if Napoleon Bonaparte had consolidated his power without further conflict, today would be different in many ways. The Benelux nations would be part of France. So would parts of northern Italy. France and the American colonies would have continued to be close allies, with Britain as a mutual enemy. Britain and Russia would be natural allies with the Germans, while France would count on support from America in any war. Marshal Ney made at the Battle of Waterloo his third and worst mistake. There were many reasons why Wellington won and Napoleon lost the Battle of Waterloo. Three of them were the result of Ney's mistakes at Quatre Bras and Waterloo. Napoleon lost his throne and died a prisoner on a desolate island in the South Atlantic. Ney was executed (maybe) by the French king when the latter returned to his throne in Paris.

||||||||||||||||||||||||||||||||||||||||||||||||||||||||||||||||||||||||||||

# 28

# OFF BY A DECADE

## 1850

### By Bill Fawcett

||||||||||||||||||||||||||||||||||||||||||||||||||||||||||||||||||||||||||||

The first reason why the South lost
the American Civil War.

P erhaps the most important reason that the South lost the
American Civil War was that they started it ten years too
late. Yes, the mistake that nullified all the courage, determination, and sacrifice of the Confederate states was made in 1850,
not during the war. It was the timing of secession that doomed the
Southern war effort. It could have happened. Tensions were very
high in 1850 and many states were already threatening secession
over the issue of slavery, which included states' rights.

The reason that the delay from 1850 to 1861 doomed the Confederacy is that, during this period, the Northern states changed
dramatically, while the Southern states didn't. For example, the
population of the Northern states, those that eventually composed
the Union, grew dramatically due to immigration. Between 1850
and 1860, the population of the USA grew from 23 to 31 million—
8 million people. Most of the growth coming from immigration
was in the North. People came for the job opportunities available
in the expanding northern factories, and were welcomed. There
was relatively little immigration into the Southern states, as slave
labor meant that new workers were not needed. For example, the
population of Virginia grew from 1,119,000 to 1,209,000 during
this decade, while that of Ohio went from 1,900,000 to 2,340,000.
A gain of 8 percent versus 20 percent. The difference in population

was much less in 1850 than when the war actually started, and this proved a decisive advantage for the Union. The South constantly had to choose whether their able-bodied men would be workers or soldiers. The immigration into the Northern states continued even during the war. Union soldiers manned recruiting stations that literally were among the first things that many new immigrants saw when they walked into America. Had the Southern states chosen to withdraw in 1850, both sides would have found their losses as crippling as did the Confederacy in 1860.

Manufacturing was another difference. In 1850, the industrialization of the Midwest had just begun and the Eastern states were already developed. One of the big advantages that the Union had in 1860 was the ability to manufacture large quantities of ammunition, rifles, and artillery. They could replace their matériel losses or expand their army easily. This would not have been the case in 1850.

Finally, there were the railroads. These were the backbone of the Union offensives. The North's extensive railroad network allowed it to move large numbers of troops and keep them supplied. When the American Civil War started, there were 22,000 miles of rails in the Union, all the same gauge. This meant every engine and train car could go anywhere in the system. Furthermore, all the Union railroads were connected to each other in one big net. The Confederacy had about 9,500 miles of rails, mostly concentrated in the cotton-producing states, and these were laid in different gauges. This meant that a Confederate force often had to ride to the end of one railroad's track and then march some distance to get onto trains running on track of a different width, and forces sometimes had to do this more than once. The railroad tracks in Texas, Louisiana, and parts of Tennessee and Florida were not yet connected to the rest of the Confederate tracks in 1861. From 1850 to 1861, the Union states laid almost 15,000 miles of new tracks, all interconnecting. During this same period, the Southern states laid just over half that much, not all interconnected. Simply put, in 1850, the railroads would not have given the Union the advantage they did in 1861.

So, why did the South hesitate a decade? In 1850, feelings were almost as strong as in 1861. That year, a Southern senator, believing his family insulted by a comment about breeding with slaves, beat another senator unconscious with his cane on the floor of the Senate. The North was outraged, but the Southern politicians took to wearing cane pins on their coats. The real issue was the balance between slave and free states, which was being disrupted by the new states and territories from New Mexico to California being carved from land captured from Mexico. If the new states, and the territories that would eventually become states, were free, the slave states would be outnumbered. Considering the strong opposition of most of those living in free states, this would have guaranteed the end of the "peculiar institution." Seeing their way of life endangered, the Southerners were adamant and prepared to act. But events that year defused the situation.

In January of 1850, Henry Clay introduced a series of legislative remedies to the crisis in what is known as the Compromise of 1850. It gave some things to the North. These included California, entering the US as a free state, and simply ending slave auctions in Washington, DC. For the slave states, the benefits included changing the Fugitive Slave Act and allowing many of the territories to determine slave or free for themselves. The debate continued for months. Finally, with tensions high, Senator Daniel Webster delivered a stirring speech and eventually the compromise was passed. As is the case with all compromises, no one was happy with it. The disputed territories soon were the scenes of sectarian violence as each side tried to drive out the other's supporters. The slave states saw the antislave states grow more quickly and control more of the federal government. A decade later they did secede. But it was a decade too late.

Had the slave states seceded in 1850, as they had threatened, there is a good chance they would have worn the Union down and succeeded in leaving the Union. The Southern states did not need to defeat the Union states; they needed only to wear them out and demonstrate that they could not force the South to return. Without the industry, the railroads, and the population it had ten years later, there is good reason to believe the Union could not have prevailed. Even with all the advantages, it took five years of hard fighting.

The seceding states also might have included Kentucky, Tennessee, and Maryland. There were anti-Union riots in Maryland so severe that armed troops were called in. It is likely that the USA would have been able to maintain control of the Western territories, but in 1850, the Confederacy would have extended from Texas to Virginia (or Maryland). Slavery was already proving economically unsustainable when the American Civil War began. Some farsighted Southerners were already looking at ways to phase it out. A split nation would have meant a very different history. Which side would the Southern states have sided with in WWI? Would the war have spread to America, if they had supported Germany? If they supported Germany, could the latter have won or forced an advantageous peace, rather than the punitive Versailles Treaty? Certainly the boom that made the USA an economic leader would have been stifled. Was there the possibility then of a *Spanish and Confederate War*, perhaps one in which Cuba would be a Confederate state? The history of the Philippines would be drastically different if Spanish rule had continued. If the Southern states had acted in 1850, the world today would be unrecognizable.

III

# LARD

**1857**

**By Bill Fawcett**

IIIIIIIIIIIIIIIIIIIIIIIIIIIIIIIIIIIIIIIIIIIIIIIIIIIIIIIIIIIIIIIIIIIIIIIIIIIII

*Not being socially aware can
make a difference.*

This is one time when sensitivity training would have paid off. The mistake that changed the Indian subcontinent was not made by a general or a rajah; it was made by a clerk and bureaucrat somewhere in England. The British Empire spanned the world, and the boast that the sun never set on the empire was true. At any time, the sun shone on Britain or one of her colonies. The largest, the richest, and the most important of these colonies was India.

The British ruled India through the East India Company. Having conquered or bought off almost all of the local rulers, the company controlled the entire subcontinent. The backbone of their rule was the Company Army. This consisted of a limited number of actual British units on loan to the company and a much larger number of "sepoy" units. These were composed of native soldiers who served under European officers. The sepoy divisions were armed as well as the British troops with modern weapons. They were trained in the same tactics as the Royal Army and many were known for their skill and courage. For many years, there was a strong bond between the Indian soldiers and their British officers. A mistake by the supply office back in England managed to destroy this bond in a matter of weeks.

It was decided to equip all of the units in India with the Pattern

1853 Enfield, which was the most modern weapon of its day. The Enfield rifle had a ladder rear sight that allowed for dramatically more accurate fire at longer ranges. Until a short time before, to load a weapon you put a pinch of powder on the firing mechanism, then poured a quantity of powder down the muzzle and covered the loose powder by inserting a piece of cloth or paper (a wad) with your ramrod to hold it in place. The next step was to drop in a musket ball, which you then tamped down on top of the paper with your ramrod. An elite rifleman could load and fire three, occasionally four times a minute. One of the innovations of the Enfield design was that it used a cartridge. This put all the elements in one piece and greatly simplified loading. The cartridge was a paper container with powder in one end and the bullet in the other. To load a rifle using the Enfield's cartridge, you simply bit off and spat out the end of the cartridge and then poured the powder down the barrel. Since the ball was wrapped in the paper, its wad was built in. You inserted both the wad and the ball at the same time, saving one complete step in the process. This cartridge could almost double the rate of fire and guaranteed that each shot used the same amount of powder.

The only real drawback to the new cartridge was that it was harder to push down into the barrel. This problem was solved by covering the cartridge in lard. Lard lubricated the barrel as the cartridge was pushed down and simplified loading. The heat of the weapon's firing burned away any remnants of the lard, keeping the barrel clean. The lard coating had the added advantage of weatherproofing the cartridges by keeping the powder dry. Issuing the new Enfield rifled muskets to the Indian troops would allow them to fire more quickly and more accurately.

The new rifles were issued in March of 1857. There was only one problem with this great improvement. Lard is composed of a mixture of cow and pig fat. The population of India was either Hindu or Muslim. In the Hindu religion, cows are sacred beasts. To slaughter one is a serious sin. To use the fat that came from a slaughtered cow was sacrilege. Even today, in India the meat patties in a McDonald's burger are mutton, not beef. To make matters worse, the Koran says, "Forbidden to you [for food] are: dead meat, blood, the flesh of swine, and that on which hath been invoked the name of other than Allah." Any Muslim sepoy who bit off the end of an Enfield cartridge was putting his soul in danger. No one in England had thought of this.

Discipline in any British army unit was harsh in 1857. With just a few officers controlling hundreds of sepoys, the British felt that any disobedience had to be severely punished. So when the soldiers were unwilling to even touch the new cartridges, much less bite the ends off of them, they were punished. This often involved flogging or worse. Rather than use the new cartridges, entire units revolted. The sepoy mutiny spread quickly. Those who were not soldiers, but resented company rule, joined in. Atrocities followed on both sides as rebelling sepoys killed any Europeans they encountered, even women and children. In response, the revolt was put down by the English units and others who remained loyal (yes, using the new Enfield rifles to great effect). Those considered to have led or commanded rebels, when captured, were often tied across the front of a cannon and the gun fired. The mutineers even captured Delhi. Desperate battles in which each side knew the other would offer no mercy occurred at Delhi, Lucknow, and Kanpur. By the time peace was officially declared in July of 1858, tens of thousands had died.

The Indian people never forgot the ferocity with which the mutiny was suppressed. Nor could they forget that the sepoys were forced to revolt by a demand that they perform an act of sacrilege. Muslim and Hindu shared a great sense of betrayal and bitterness.

If the Enfield cartridge had not been coated with something anathema to virtually every person in India, the introduction of the rifle would have gone smoothly. The independence movement that culminated with Gandhi was rooted in the injustice of the mutiny and its suppression. If the men most loyal to the company and Britain had not been forced to mutiny, the next century would likely have seen a closer bond between England and India, and greater Indian participation in WWI and WWII.

# 30

# COTTON IS KING

1861

**By William Terdoslavich**

Old times that should have been
forgotten.

The United States is the land of freedom and opportunity, unless you are a slave. And it is a democracy, except when it comes to cotton, which is king. That is the state of the Union in 1861. And the Union is about to be torn asunder by these contradictions.

The economics of cotton were brutal and compelling. It was the world's first vital commodity, predating oil by a century. Textile mills in Lancashire, Lyon, and Lowell, employing tens of thousands, would grind to a halt for lack of cotton. And no one produced more of it than the Southern states of the USA. Halt cotton production and the world economy would collapse.

## Economically Speaking . . .

Cotton can be grown anywhere in the world except Europe. It is a subtropical plant. Temperatures have to stay above fifty degrees Fahrenheit during the growing season, which has to be no more than two hundred days for the crop to mature. Subsistence farmers grew cotton in the same fields as food crops.

European demand for cotton was strong in the late 1700s, resulting in high prices, but US growers could not cash in on this. The upland cotton grown here had a pretty tough boll, making seed removal by hand difficult. A slave could process about one pound of cotton a day, making American exports uncompetitive with the more easily hand-processed cotton grown in India and the Ottoman Empire. That should have condemned American slavery to a slow economic death.

Yankee ingenuity solved Dixie's problem when Eli Whitney invented a machine to remove the seeds. The so-called cotton gin improved processing fiftyfold. Now more slaves could work the fields to grow more cotton. Other suppliers were priced out, as no laborer could be paid less than a slave. And no soil produced better cotton than that found in the American South. Up until the Civil War, the volume and value of cotton doubled every decade.

There were some downsides. Cotton sucked fertility out of the soil quickly. You could start with yields of a thousand pounds per acre, which would dwindle to four hundred pounds in a few years. Cotton planters found it easier to go west into the new, more fertile lands recently taken by force from Native Americans. And slave labor was portable.

Corresponding changes took place in Great Britain and, to a lesser extent, France. The industrial revolution mechanized cloth manufacture, fueled by cotton, as well as by coal and steam. By the 1860s, two-thirds of all the cotton spindles in the world were in Great Britain, with about one-fifth to one-fourth of all workers there employed in the textile industry.

By the American Civil War, cotton would make up 60 percent of US exports, and about 70 percent of cotton imports to Britain and the rest of Europe. Globally, twenty million people—about one out of sixty-five—labored in the cotton industry.

## A Nervous Prosperity

By the 1850s, the British cotton barons were getting a tad nervous. They began to notice their singular dependence on the United States for their raw material. They also noticed that their wealth rested on the backs of three to four million Negro slaves. Slave rebellions had occurred before in the Americas. If it happened again, what would become of cotton?

Britain tried to develop alternate suppliers. The lack of railroads in India made it impossible to get cotton from field to port. Egypt was not yet a supplier. South America was too far away. And none could produce cotton as cheaply as the US. Economists have a term for this: comparative advantage. The US was better at growing cotton than anyone else.

The Southern planters also noticed odd things happening with their economy during the same decade. Slavery and cotton together crowded out other investments. Railroad and canal construction increased far faster in the Northern states than in the South. Dixie could not attract much manufacturing, so it exported 70 percent of its cotton crop. And while the price of cotton doubled from a nickel a pound to a dime, about 20 percent of this income was lost to brokerage and transportation costs. More people also chose to migrate or immigrate to the Northern states as well. Economic advantage shifted decisively to the free states.

Other Southern planters and politicians seemed blind to this. Take Senator James Hammond of South Carolina, speaking to the US Senate in 1858. "What would happen if no cotton was furnished for three years? I will not stop to depict what everyone can imagine, but this is certain: England would topple headlong and carry the whole civilized world with her, save the South. No, you dare not make war on cotton. No power on earth dares to make war upon it. Cotton is king."

Three years later, King Cotton's global rule would be sorely tested.

## The Other Shot Heard Around the World

In April 1861, the guns of the Confederate States of America opened fire on Fort Sumter, starting the American Civil War. The CSA needed allies if it was going to win. France and Britain were the likeliest allies, given how economically dependent they were on Southern cotton. To compel their friendship and aid, the CSA ended cotton exports, figuring the threat of economic collapse would yield some cooperation. France and Britain did not feel the pain right away. Existing inventories were sufficient to guarantee cotton manufacture for another year at current capacity.

The embargo backfired on the Confederacy. In one stroke, they deprived themselves of export earnings, which could have been spent purchasing arms. The cotton ban also played into the hands of the United States, as the Lincoln administration declared all Southern ports closed to commerce. The Union's blockade was unusually effective. No ships hauled cotton out of Charleston, Wilmington, Savannah, or New Orleans.

By the end of 1862, economic pain set in. Textile workers in Lyon and Lancashire saw their hours cut or were laid off. Charity and welfare put a bandage on this problem, but only long enough for other suppliers to be found. Egypt, India, and Brazil increased cotton production starting in 1863. Substitution did not happen overnight, but by war's end, French and British textile production was just fine. The cotton barons of Lyon and Lancashire could not care less where cotton came from, so long as their factories got plenty of it. The world economy wobbled, but did not crash.

### The Happier Ending?

Overthrowing King Cotton was bloody and expensive. The Civil War cost the lives of more than 650,000 Americans out of a population of 30 million. It would have been cheaper for the US to spend $3 billion buying and freeing the slaves, compared to paying $6 billion for the war.

Finding a peaceful way to uncouple slavery from cotton would have been a hundred times better. That would have required "civil war by other means." Even a difficult political solution, like the civil rights movement of the 1960s, would have been preferable in the 1860s. Any progress on race would have come a century earlier. Not only would ex-slaves have moved up the economic ladder faster, but the Southern states could have handled the transition from slavery to free enterprise without the impoverishment that comes with losing a war. Rich planters would still be rich, but they would not own people.

If the United States had gone down this different path, Barack Obama would not have been the first black president of the United States. Perhaps that honor would have gone to Booker T. Washington or another black American, whose name never emerged in history because racial discrimination by law would not allow it. Martin Luther King Jr. would have been a church pastor in Atlanta, not a civil rights martyr. Scott Joplin would have been a major classical composer instead of a ragtime songwriter. Satchel Paige would have played in Major League Baseball far sooner than he actually did. Maybe today the Republican Party would still enjoy the unqualified support of black voters. Maybe racism would finally be dead and buried.

Maybe.

# 31

# LEE'S LUCK FAILS, BUT McCLELLAN HELPS OUT

### 1862

### By Harry Turtledove

"If I cannot whip Bobbie Lee . . ."
—GENERAL GEORGE McCLELLAN

A s the summer of 1862 slid toward fall, Robert E. Lee took the Army of Northern Virginia across the Potomac to invade the United States. He hoped to force a decisive battle against George McClellan and the Army of the Potomac. He trusted that he could win the fight and compel the United States—and, perhaps even more important, England and France as well—to recognize the Confederacy's independence.

Confident that McClellan would not move against him, Lee broke his army into several pieces and separated them from one another by miles as he moved north. Despite all evidence to the contrary, McClellan was always convinced that the Army of Northern Virginia outnumbered the Army of the Potomac. He had been extremely cautious and slow in the Peninsular Campaign earlier in the year. Lee had every reason to believe he wouldn't change his tactics.

But fate proceeded to deal Lee the most unkind blow of all. One of his couriers lost a copy of Special Order 191, which detailed how his army was divided. Two Union soldiers from the 27th Indiana, Corporal Barton W. Mitchell and First Sergeant John McKnight Bloss, found the orders wrapped around three cigars. They handed them to Captain Kopp, their company commander. Kopp brought them to regimental headquarters. Colonel Silas Colgrove, the senior officer of the 27th Indiana, gave the orders to his adjutant, who took them to the headquarters of the Army of the Potomac. General McClellan was excited, but suspicious—were they real or a trick? In the days before secession, though, one of his staff officers had served with Confederate colonel Chilton, who wrote orders for Lee. The man knew Chilton well enough to recognize his handwriting, and said the orders were undoubtedly genuine.

McClellan was jubilant. "Here is a paper with which, if I cannot whip Bobbie Lee, I will be willing to go home," he exulted.

He had to get west of South Mountain before Lee's army could reassemble, smash the pieces one by one with his united force, and then the Civil War in the East would be as good as won. He had to, and he intended to . . . but he was George McClellan, and driving urgency simply was not in him. He and Lee met at the Battle of Antietam.

McClellan did win the battle—barely. He had twice as many men as Lee—about eighty thousand to forty thousand—and a bigger edge at the start of the fight, because A. P. Hill's Confederates came in late, at the end of a seventeen-mile forced march, to save the day for Lee one last time. But McClellan (when he did attack, a day or two later than he should have) attacked in piecemeal fashion, and never got the full weight of his army into any one assault.

Tactically, the fight was a draw. Lee pulled back into Virginia with his army still a going concern. McClellan pursued slowly and halfheartedly. But he did gain an important strategic victory. The win at Antietam let Lincoln issue the Emancipation Proclamation (which McClellan heartily despised). Making the war about ending slavery changed its moral nature, and ensured that the European powers would not recognize the Confederacy without its winning an overwhelming military victory it was in no position to do.

But suppose McClellan had done very well, not just well enough. Supposed he'd whipped Bobbie Lee and smashed the Army of Northern Virginia. What would the world have looked like, then? It seems likely that the CSA would have quickly fallen. With Virginia overrun by Union forces, the Confederacy would have had trouble maintaining its war effort, which says nothing about the devastating blow Southern morale would have taken. Peace might well have come in 1863, not 1865. It could have come with far less destruction and far fewer casualties than real history saw.

What sort of peace would it have been? It would have included the end of slavery. If Lincoln felt able to emancipate Southern slaves after a skin-of-the-teeth victory at Antietam, he surely would have done so after a more decisive win. It might have been less punitive. The fight would have been shorter and less bitter, and its end probably would not have included Lincoln's assassination, which naturally raised resentments of its own.

Would it have included better relations between whites and blacks? Not to any great degree, chances are. Military defeat would have left Southern whites no choice but to accept emancipation. Equality would have been another story. A century and a half after the end of the Civil War, we're still working through the consequences of slavery based on race. The altered world wouldn't have changed much in that regard.

What would have happened to George McClellan himself, had he gained the great triumph he dreamed of? In the real world, he waited seven weeks before making a serious move south against Lee. Lincoln finally dismissed him from his command on November 2, 1862. His immediate successors, Ambrose Burnside and Joe Hooker, enjoyed even less luck against the Army of Northern Virginia than he had. George Meade stopped a second Confederate invasion of the USA at Gettysburg. Then Ulysses S. Grant took charge of the Army of the Potomac, and proceeded to grind Lee's force to death.

By the time McClellan ran for president in 1864, the war was nearly won, though he had to campaign as if it were nearly lost. Lincoln had little trouble beating him. With McClellan the hero of an already won war, he surely would have run against Lincoln that year. He might well have won. Americans have often liked electing successful generals: Andrew Jackson, William Henry Harrison, Zachary Taylor, Grant, and Dwight Eisenhower. McClellan might have been softer on the South than Union authorities were in real history. In the long run, it probably wouldn't have mattered much. Views about what each race was entitled to would have changed only slowly, over generations, any which way.

But in the real world, George McClellan gained and then failed to live up to the nickname of "The Little Napoleon." If he could have transcended himself just once, he might well be remembered right alongside the emperor of France instead of just as the man with a bad case of the slows.

# 32

||||||||||||||||||||||||||||||||||||||||||||||||||||||||||||||||||||||||||||||||||||

# MEADE DAWDLES

### 1863

### By Bill Fawcett

||||||||||||||||||||||||||||||||||||||||||||||||||||||||||||||||||||||||||||||||||||

The American Civil War could have
ended in 1863.

T here is no question that the Army of Northern Virginia lost
the Battle of Gettysburg. By any standard—casualties, retaining the field, achieving objectives—the Union prevailed.
Union losses were 23,049 (3,155 dead, 14,529 wounded, 5,365 missing) of almost 98,000 soldiers. Lee's army lost 28,063 (3,903 dead,
18,735 injured, and 5,425 missing) of just 73,000. The Confederate
casualties were spread almost evenly through the three large corps
that composed the Army of Northern Virginia. After the disaster
of Pickett's Charge, it was an army no longer capable of any offensive actions. Incidentally, Lee accepted responsibility for ordering that infamous charge, but never admitted it was an error. He
commented regularly that if the supporting attacks had gone as
planned, Pickett's and Pettigrew's divisions would have broken
through and split the Army of the Potomac. But they did not and,
by the time the last of Pickett's men had retreated to safety, one in
three was dead or wounded. But much of what was bought with the
Army of the Potomac's losses was lost by a continuing mistake, one
of omission, made by the commander of the Army of the Potomac,
General George Meade.

Meade was a West Point graduate who had served in Mexico
and the Seminole Wars. He was an engineer and had built a number of lighthouses along the US coast before the war. George Meade

was not Lincoln's first choice to command the Army of the Potomac. He wasn't even the fourth. To say that President Lincoln had a problem finding a competent commander for the Union's largest and most strategically important army would be an understatement. Winfield Scott had commanded before the war, but was considered too old for a field command. Then McDowell was followed by George McClellan. McClellan was given command more than twice, to be replaced by Burnside, then Hooker, and finally, just three days before the Battle of Gettysburg began, George G. Meade.

The condition of the Army of Northern Virginia after the failure of Pickett's Charge was pitiful.

It was divided into three corps and all had taken severe casualties. These were:

I Corps: 7575 of 20,700 men or over 35 percent

II Corps: 5935 of 29,700 men or 20 percent

III Corps: 6935 of 22,100 men or 31 percent

Cavalry and artillery losses were lighter, but significant.

The modern practice is to pull a larger unit out and restore it after 10 percent casualties, so it is apparent just how badly the condition of Lee's army was. Worse yet, his losses in officers was proportionally even higher.

The Union army had been divided into seven smaller corps that were from half to 60 percent the size of Lee's. Four corps of the Army of the Potomac (I, II, III, XI) took proportional losses to those of the Army of Northern Virginia, but three (V, VI, XII) were relatively better off with the largest, the Union VI Corps, losing only a few hundred men.

After the failed charge, General Lee struggled to form some sort of line to repel an expected Union counterattack. For much of that day, Lee was unable to form a contiguous line even with the reserves behind it. General Hancock, commander of the Union II Corps, even though wounded, sent Meade a note saying that if the VI and V Corps attacked, the Army of Northern Virginia would be destroyed. In the first step of his mistake, which extended the war for over a year, General Meade ignored his field commander and, in effect, did nothing but re-form and rearm.

The victorious Army of the Potomac continued to reorganize all through the next day, July 4, 1863. Robert E. Lee still expected an attack and spent that day refining his defensive lines while preparing his army to retreat and sending off his wounded. The next morning, July 5, Meade wrote his wife a letter. The message, written even as Lee had begun to pull back his entire army, showed the Union general's unwillingness to risk his partial victory in order to make it complete.

> It was a grand battle, and is in my judgment a most decided victory, though I did not annihilate or bag the Confederate Army. This morning they retreated in great haste into the mountains, leaving their dead unburied and their wounded on the field. They awaited one day, expecting that flushed with success, I would attack them, when they would play their old game of shooting us from behind breastworks.

When he should have been pushing Lee or later pursuing him, Meade instead issued his General Orders No. 68:

> The Commanding General, in behalf of the country, thanks the Army of the Potomac for the glorious result of the recent operations.
>
> An enemy, superior in numbers, and flushed with the pride of a successful invasion, attempted to overcome and destroy this Army. Utterly baffled and defeated, he has now withdrawn from the contest. The privations and fatigue the Army has endured, and the heroic courage and gallantry it has displayed will be matters of history to be remembered.
>
> Our task is not yet accomplished, and the commanding general looks to the army for greater efforts to drive from our soil every vestige of the presence of the invader.

*It is right and proper that we should, on all suitable occasions, return our grateful thanks to the Almighty Disposer of events, that in the goodness of His Providence He has thought fit to give victory to the cause of the just.*

*By command of Major-General Meade . . .*

Missing from both documents was the mention of any intent to trap or destroy the crippled and discouraged Army of Northern Virginia. Even Lincoln and his secretary of war noticed this omission. After reading the order, President Lincoln wrote to General Halleck in Washington that he was "a good deal dissatisfied. You know, I did not like Meade's phrase 'Drive the invaders from our soil.'" Lincoln was right to be concerned. In the days after the battle, Meade managed to squander what had been the Union's first real potentially war-ending victory. It was not until a full day after Lee pulled his army out that General Meade finally sent his army, led by the V and VI Corps, after him. Even then, he did not follow Lee directly or as quickly as possible. Instead, he split the army and they used three routes to Williamsburg. Along the way the Southerners would have to cross rivers including the Potomac and the James. This meant he could only attack once his army was united again—a further delay.

Lee's column was seventeen miles long and moving slowly. Meade managed to move even slower. Only a few Union cavalry units pecked on the edges of the retreating Confederate column, with little effect. There was no real contact between the two armies for three days. On July 7, General Halleck in Washington telegraphed Meade:

*You have given the enemy a stunning blow at Gettysburg. Follow it up and give him another before he can cross the Potomac. When he crosses, circumstances will determine whether it will be best to pursue him by the Shenandoah Valley on this side of the Blue Ridge. There is strong evidence that he is short of artillery ammunition, and if vigorously pressed he must suffer.*

The secretary was correct. Lee's army was short many important supplies. But Meade continued to advance only slowly behind the fleeing Confederates. Even they noticed how hesitant this pursuit was. The artillery commander of Longstreet's I Corps compared Meade's pursuit to a mule chasing a grizzly bear. It was apparent that General Meade, for whatever reason, was not anxious to catch up to his defeated foe. The retreating Confederate soldiers later commented on what a relief this was, knowing how vulnerable they had been. As they marched unopposed, the Army of Northern Virginia's morale began to return.

When Lee finally arrived at Williamsburg, he was unable to cross the river. The rainy weather had swollen it dramatically and the only pontoon bridge he had was destroyed by Union cavalry before his own arrived. On July 9, Halleck telegraphed Meade that Lee was crossing and he should hurry to catch his army while it was split on both banks. Meade responded that Lee would be crossing very slowly and he had plenty of time. He also complained that the bad weather and poor roads were hampering him in his task of concentrating his forces for an attack. The Army of the Potomac continued to sit only eight miles from where the entire Army of Northern Virginia was still trapped north of the James River.

For the next three days, the Army of the Potomac crept slowly toward Lee and his Virginians. On the morning of July 13, the James was low enough that a pontoon bridge constructed from lumber taken from the buildings of Williamsburg could be emplaced. Soon Lee's corps began to stream across the James to the relative safety of Virginia. Meade knew of the crossing at three a.m., but waited until dawn to have his cavalry attack. The first attack on Williamsburg was led by the horsemen, commanded by General George Armstrong Custer. The Union mounted regiments captured several hundred Confederates, but it was too late. The Army of Northern Virginia had crossed. Nine vulnerable days without an attack by Mead had allowed what remained of Lee's army to escape.

Even though General Meade failed to pursue Lee's defeated army, the Union politicians needed a hero and they had won the battle. Meade was honored for his success. There were not a lot of Union generals who had defeated Robert E. Lee for them to honor. But Lincoln never forgot the missed opportunity and, eventually, replaced George Meade with the more aggressive Ulysses S. Grant. Because Lee escaped, the war continued, and while it was crippled so badly it never tried another offensive, the Army of Northern Virginia held on until April of 1865.

Meade failed to follow up the Union's greatest victory to date and lost his chance to end the Civil War almost two years and tens of thousands of casualties sooner. Even if the Army of the Potomac had not completely destroyed the Army of Northern Virginia, a strong pursuit would have crippled it further. This would have made the Confederate capital, Richmond, vulnerable and, perhaps, encouraged the Southern politicians to question their chances of victory.

If Meade had not waited an entire day after Lee's withdrawal to begin his pursuit, he could have maintained pressure on the demoralized Confederates with just his intact V and VI Corps. If he had moved to Williamsburg and arrived a day after Lee, the Army of Northern Virginia would have been trapped against the flooding James River for days. Union attacks might not have broken Lee's army, but they certainly would have lowered its already diminished numbers and complicated any crossing. All General Meade had to do was obey Halleck's order to advance on the ninth of July and he would have had at least two days to confront the Confederates in Williamsburg. The American Civil War might have ended much sooner, with less loss of life and bitterness on both sides. Lincoln might not have been assassinated. The decades of resentment in the South and spiteful punishment by the Union could have been avoided. The economy of the South would have recovered less slowly and William T. Sherman would not have marched to burn Atlanta.

||||||||||||||||||||||||||||||||||||||||||||||||||||||||||||||||||||||||||||||||

# 33

# VICTORY DENIED

### 1864

### By Bill Fawcett

||||||||||||||||||||||||||||||||||||||||||||||||||||||||||||||||||||||||||||||||

*The cause of the problem
was the solution.*

I n 1864, the Confederate States of America was losing the war. Their cause had suffered from a lack of manufacturing, the Union blockade, and a lack of political unity. But there was one problem that was doing the Southern cause more harm than any other. This was a lack of manpower. The more populous Union was able to replace soldiers or increase the size of its armies, even after a defeat. In the South, the limited pool of men capable of serving had been exhausted. So few men were available that those who did enter often hurt the war effort because they left important jobs unfilled at home. If Grant lost five thousand men, it was a problem and caused bad press. Three months later, they were all replaced. If Lee lost three thousand men, they were gone and he could not replace them. The Confederacy was being ground down by superior numbers and a lack of reinforcements.

General Cleburne, who had commanded a division in the Army of Tennessee, approached his commanding officer, Braxton Bragg, with a plan to enlist slaves as soldiers. Of the nine million people living in the South, a full third were free or enslaved blacks. None had been allowed to actually serve as combat troops. Early in the war, a fully trained and armed, but also black, regiment of the Louisiana militia volunteered to fight in the Confederate army. It was refused military status and the men were used as laborers. Cleburne's plan was rejected.

Later that year, the South remained desperate for manpower and one man thought he had a solution. This was Judah Philip Benjamin. At the time, he was the Confederate secretary of state. He had previously been both attorney general and then secretary of war for Jefferson Davis. Before that, he had started life as a lawyer. Next, he was elected first as a representative in the Louisiana legislature, and then as a US senator. Many called this Sephardic Jew "Davis's brain," and he was most certainly the Southern president's trusted adviser. Judah Benjamin's advice was almost always valued and often acted upon by the Confederate legislature. Benjamin was also a slave owner and had over 140 on his plantation. An early secessionist, he was a strong supporter of states' rights, which meant institutional slavery—which shows how desperate the situation was that a lifelong advocate of slavery would suggest what he did.

The secretary of state, early in 1864, revived the idea of turning slaves into soldiers. If they joined, they became freemen and so did their families. Their former owners were compensated by the government. Since he was a slave owner himself, this made a lot of sense. There were at least twenty thousand black men serving as support staff or servants for officers in combat. Many had actually fought. Benjamin brought the idea to Jefferson Davis, who felt that allowing slaves to enlist would destroy the morale of the army. The Emancipation Proclamation basically made the same offer of freedom to all the slaves in areas still resisting the Union army. By the end of the American Civil War, more than two hundred thousand black men had enlisted in the Union army. Most fought with courage and determination. Had the Confederate secretary of state's plan been accepted, that number might have been matched in the Confederacy. Even if only fifty thousand enlisted and were trained, it would have been enough men to double the Army of Northern Virginia's numbers in 1865. What could Robert E. Lee have done with such a surge of volunteers?

Finally, when it was too late, Benjamin persuaded the Confederate congress to approve his plan. Any slave enlisting in the army would become free, as would his family. The secretary of state estimated that there were 680,000 black men who would fight for the Confederacy in exchange for becoming freemen on the day they enlisted. If only a third of these accepted the offer, it would more than double the size of the remaining army. Benjamin was quoted in his speech instructing army recruiters to say, "Fight for your masters, and you shall have your freedom."

The plan even made economic sense. There was a practice on both sides of granting a substantial enlistment bonus. This would be used to reimburse the slave owner for his loss. Several thousand slaves did eventually enlist in 1865 under this plan and some may have seen combat against the Union army. But, before most could be trained or more added, the war was over. It was too little too late.

Davis still publicly hated the idea, but accepted it as necessary. Had he done so a year earlier, the history of the war would be quite different. Given more Confederate manpower, Grant's army might have been checked. The siege of Richmond could have become untenable as significant Confederate armies threatened it from the outside. The rallying cry that the North was fighting a war against slavery would have lost much of its power and the European nations, with their repulsion to slavery rendered moot, might even have intervened. What if Bragg or Davis had been farsighted enough to accept Cleburne's suggestion almost two years earlier? The Confederacy might not have fallen. Slavery was certain to end, anyhow. It would have been impossible to enslave a handful of men, when tens of thousands of armed black veterans returned home. Things today would be as they are, except there would still be a Confederacy. Reconstruction, even if the South lost the war, might have been kinder and perhaps racist hatred would be less strong. And racial bigotry would have had to compete with the valor black soldiers showed in fighting, and maybe even stopping, the Union armies.

# 34

# JOHN WILKES BOOTH ASSASSINATES ABRAHAM LINCOLN

## 1865

### By Jim Werbaneth

Sic semper tyrannis.

I t is rare for the effects of a mistake, an act of a moment, to be felt over decades, even more than a century; rarer still when that act is committed by a single person. The most glaring example of this is the shooting of Abraham Lincoln and his subsequent death on the morning of April 15, 1865. Admittedly, John Wilkes Booth's actions were part of a conspiracy. But at the moment of decision, it was his finger on the trigger.

Booth's motivations were to avenge his beloved South, recently laid low by its defeat in the Civil War, and deep-seated racism. Witnessing an impromptu speech by President Lincoln, in which he promised the vote for some, but not all, black men, Booth pithily said, "That means nigger citizenship. Now by God I'll put him through. That is the last speech he will ever make." Then he made good on that promise.

If Booth wanted to save the South from further destruction, he failed. Instead, the former Confederacy was subjected to Reconstruction, during which black people were enfranchised and admitted to the halls of power, at least for a while. At the same time, the region was occupied by Northern troops, sent to protect freed slaves from a resurgence of Confederate loyalists. All of this took place in an environment of violence and vengeance, with night riders of the Ku Klux Klan terrorizing black people and demonstrating that military occupation was perhaps not such a bad idea after all.

What amounted to a war after the Civil War was waged by multiple combatants. There were the former Confederates, usually Democrats, who could not accept that slavery had been replaced by freedom, and even a degree of empowerment, for African-Americans. Then there was the army and agencies such as the Freedmen's Bureau. There were also "carpetbaggers," Northerners who moved south to take advantage of business opportunities created by victory, and the Southern "scalawags" who sided with them. And there were the former slaves, caught in the middle and largely without protection, except that provided by the federal government.

Eventually, it was the former Confederates who won. With the end of Reconstruction in 1877, the clock turned back. While legalizing slavery was out of the question, segregation was not. Furthermore, black people were increasingly denied the rights of full suffrage. They had a hard enough time getting *into* the polling places to cast their votes, let alone taking office in legislatures. This would last into the 1960s, at last overturned by the civil rights movement, Supreme Court decisions hostile to segregation, and a reengaged federal government. This time, ironically, the charge would be led by Democrats, especially Presidents John Kennedy and Lyndon Baines Johnson.

All of this can be traced to Abraham Lincoln's assassination at the hands of John Wilkes Booth. The next chief executive was a much-less-impressive figure, Andrew Johnson. His selection as the Republican vice-presidential nominee was a gesture of unity. Johnson was from Tennessee, and the only senator from a seceding state not to resign his seat. He was also a Democrat, and his presence was not only a bid to reconcile with the South; it was also meant to ensure that in his second term, Lincoln would not be dominated by radical "Black Republicans," the most adamant enemies of both the Confederacy and slavery.

Unfortunately Johnson was not nearly the man that Lincoln had been. While Lincoln struggled with issues of race, Johnson accepted the inferiority of black people as a matter of course. He was also an alcoholic who was alleged to have been drunk at his

1864 inauguration as vice president (Johnson, recovering from typhoid fever, may have been "self-medicating"). Finally, Lincoln was an astute politician, skilled at balancing competing interests and mediating conflict, and Johnson was not.

By assassinating Lincoln, Booth removed the South's best hope after its defeat. He heard Lincoln's call for "nigger citizenship," but apparently missed the part in his second inaugural address about "malice toward none" and "charity for all." Lincoln had the political skills to successfully reintegrate the South into the Union while preserving the emancipation of the slaves that was achieved on the battlefield. Johnson, on the other hand, lacked both the vision of Lincoln and his skills. Reconstruction ended with a return to the past and second-class citizenship for blacks. If anyone could have forestalled the strife of Reconstruction, and its disappointing outcome, it was Lincoln, given a full second term. It was a job wholly beyond Andrew Johnson's abilities. A continued Lincoln presidency would have added a powerful, compelling voice against the growth of the "lost cause" mythology, while extending more charity than malice to the defeated South. If Booth wanted to save the South's soul, he couldn't have made a poorer decision.

# 35

SELLING SEWARD
HIS ICEBOX

1867

By Bill Fawcett

Going-out-of-business sales are costly
for nations as well as for store owners.

For most of the century before it was sold to the United States, Alaska was actually owned and run by a corporation. This was the Russian-American Company, whose stockholders included the elite of Russia, among them the czar and his family. Under the very capable administrator Alexander Baranov, the RAC controlled everything from fishing to mining from its offices in the port of Novo Arkhangelsk. Today we call the city Sitka. Trade was robust. Not only were minerals and fish traded, but a fortune was made buying sea otter pelts from the Inuit. Fortresses, schools, and shipyards were built and extended. Profits some years were 1,000 percent of investment. The RAC even began using its own currency—strangely enough, some was made from leather.

Baranov felt a deep attachment to Alaska and its people. He even married an Inuit princess. His trading was always fair, and he always showed consideration for the land and the life it supported. For years, the RAC delivered high profits and the czar benefited. But then Baranov died in 1819 and everything changed. According to the charter of the RAC, only ranking military officers could serve as head of the company. In contrast to the reasonable salaries Baranov had paid his administrators, the officers working for the RAC paid themselves a salary of 1,500 rubles—the equivalent of what was earned by the top officials in the czar's court. The new president of the RAC paid himself 150,000 rubles per year. This was an unheard-of sum, and the massive salaries began immediately to strain the formerly profitable company.

In a desperate effort to maintain their salaries and still make some profit, the new officers cut in half the amount they paid the Inuit for otter hides, furs, and everything else. In order to survive, the Inuit had to double their harvest of otters. Over the next two decades, fur-bearing animals became scarce and the profit from them disappeared. Without money for repairs, the RAC buildings and forts decayed. There were no rubles to invest in new mines, even when silver and gold were discovered. Desperate for any profit, the new officers turned Novo Arkhangelsk into a trading center for tea and ice to be shipped to California and Vancouver. But even this failed to save the company.

By 1850, the RAC was losing money and had to be subsidized by up to 200,000 rubles a year. The sky-high salaries also ended. Further complicating the situation was the British Royal Navy, which was beginning to dominate trade across the Pacific. This discouraged the tea trade. While the British never actually tried to do it, nothing the Russians could do would have prevented them from sailing up the coast from Canada and seizing the entire territory if they had so desired. It was at this point that Grand Prince Konstantin Nikolayevich decided that the best course was to sell Alaska. The Russians approached the Americans and a price of $7.2 million was agreed to. But before the deal could be finalized, the American Civil War erupted. When it ended, American secretary of state William H. Seward was able to complete the deal. Unfortunately, the czar, with an annual budget of more than a billion rubles, wanted far more than $7 million, some of which he had already spent on paying off US administrators and senators in order to get the transaction approved. Yet Prince Konstantin Nikolayevich maintained that the deal was a good one and the czar agreed.

At first, many in the United States scoffed at "Seward's Icebox," but this quickly changed when prospectors struck gold in the Klondike. Within a few years, Alaska was adding a hundred times the $7 million to the American economy every year. Hundreds of millions of dollars in gold were extracted, gold that helped build the USA into an industrial giant.

The sale of Alaska was a mistake that cost Russia dearly. Had the czar not sold the land for a pittance, the Klondike gold strike alone would have greatly increased his wealth. With that extra money, his plans for modernization and reform might well have succeeded. A less fragile and more industrial Russia would have been a far greater factor in WWI. A more powerful Russia with a foothold in North America would also have greatly changed the political situation. If the czarist government had been richer and stronger, would it have been able to put down Lenin's revolution? Would it have allied so quickly with France and England if allying with Germany in either war would have opened the door to moving south from Alaskan bases into Canada? With bases on the border of Canada, could a different Russia even have seen all of North America as vulnerable? Would one front in WWII have been located in the suburbs of Seattle? Alaska would have been a sword of Damocles poised over the head of America all through the Cold War. Russian missiles and bombers that were impossible to intercept would have been waiting to launch only a few minutes of flight time from the USA. Even today, a Russian Alaska would change the economic dynamics of the world. Most of the Arctic could be validly claimed by Russia. All that North Slope oil would be Russian oil. But, for no good reason, the czar listened to the grand prince and Alaska was sold for about two cents per acre—a trivial sum that changed history.

‖‖‖‖‖‖‖‖‖‖‖‖‖‖‖‖‖‖‖‖‖‖‖‖‖‖‖‖‖‖‖‖‖‖‖‖‖‖‖‖‖‖‖‖‖‖‖‖‖‖‖‖‖‖‖‖‖‖

# 36

# THE AMERICAN ACCLIMATIZATION SOCIETY

## 1890

### By Bill Fawcett

‖‖‖‖‖‖‖‖‖‖‖‖‖‖‖‖‖‖‖‖‖‖‖‖‖‖‖‖‖‖‖‖‖‖‖‖‖‖‖‖‖‖‖‖‖‖‖‖‖‖‖‖‖‖‖‖‖‖

Destroying the American
ecology since 1890.

One man in New York City did more damage to the ecology of North America than every Exxon oil spill ever did. That man was Eugene Schieffelin, a very successful drug manufacturer, who lived near New York City at the end of the nineteenth century. The pharmaceutical business was booming and it made him very rich. One of the New Yorker's interests was William Shakespeare. Schieffelin was also a member of the American Acclimatization Society, which sounds like an innocuous group, but today they would be described as ecoterrorists. The American Acclimatization Society showed, even for those living in 1890, an amazing lack of knowledge of how ecology worked and what damaged it. Their purpose was to introduce new species into North America. That's correct: the hobby of this group of rich New Yorkers was bringing animals and plants from other parts of the world and releasing them in America. Today this is a crime, punishable by imprisonment. This is because of the Lacey Act, passed in 1900—ten years too late.

On March 6, 1890, society member Eugene Schieffelin appeared in Central Park with cages full of starlings. This large, speckled brown bird native to the British Isles. The starling is featured in *Henry IV*,

*Part 1*, where the Bard refers to the bird's ability to make sounds that mimic the human voice.

> *[The king] forbade my tongue to speak of Mortimer. But I will find him when he lies asleep, and in his ear I'll holla "Mortimer!" Nay, I'll have a starling shall be taught to speak nothing but "Mortimer," and give it him to keep his anger still in motion.* (Henry IV, Part 1, Act 1, Scene 3)

This is the only time the Bard mentions starlings, but it was enough to inspire Schieffelin to go to great expense to import the birds from England. On a rather cold morning in early March, he released sixty of the birds into the park. He probably intended them to thrive in their new abode, though in March in New York City, the weather is hardly welcoming. Most of the attempts by the American Acclimatization Society failed. But the starlings found a refuge under the eaves of the Museum of Natural History that sits on one side of Central Park. This provided warmth and places to nest. Today, there are 200,000,000—yep, an estimated *two hundred million*—starlings spread from Alaska and Canada to Mexico and Central America.

Starlings are a serious menace and a danger to native American birds. For one thing, they do not migrate. This means that the starlings are in the best nesting places when migrating birds return. They also compete for food, and are large enough to harass and drive off most species native to America. Starlings will commonly drive woodpeckers, bluebirds, and flickers from their nests and take them for their own. The starling alone has driven the eastern bluebird to near extinction.

Starlings are also now so numerous as to be a hazard and pest. Their droppings are infected with histoplasmosis, which is spread by inhalation of spores. If starlings nest near humans, the possibility of contracting the fungus, which can kill or blind, is much higher. Some towns in New England have been trying to drive them away for a century, with little success. The US Capitol building had a starling infestation and had to outfit its columns with electrified wires to keep them from nesting at their tops.

North America would look quite different if Eugene Schieffelin had not attacked its ecology. Cardinals, blue jays, and many other species of bird that we value would be more common. The songs of our forest would be more diverse. And, incidentally, the sidewalks near the Museum of Natural History would be much cleaner. When you combine the total number of imported pigeons and English sparrows with that of the starlings, the total could be half a billion birds. Some estimate that there are more of these three intrusive species now on the North American continent than there are native birds of all other species. Ecoterrorism indeed.

‖‖‖‖‖‖‖‖‖‖‖‖‖‖‖‖‖‖‖‖‖‖‖‖‖‖‖‖‖‖‖‖‖‖‖‖‖‖‖‖‖‖‖‖‖‖‖‖‖‖‖‖‖‖‖‖‖

# 37

# SAFETY GLASS

## 1903

### By Bill Fawcett

‖‖‖‖‖‖‖‖‖‖‖‖‖‖‖‖‖‖‖‖‖‖‖‖‖‖‖‖‖‖‖‖‖‖‖‖‖‖‖‖‖‖‖‖‖‖‖‖‖‖‖‖‖‖‖‖‖

A mistake that meant greater safety
for your family and you.

Moving from unmitigated disasters and toward politicians blundering into WWI, let us take a few moments to look at a mistake that had a positive result. There are actually many of these. They range from vulcanization to saccharin. This particular mistake has likely benefited you or a family member directly. Everyone has been in a car accident.

Édouard Bénédictus was working in his lab in 1903 when he had an accident. Bénédictus was a chemist and he was, not surprisingly, working with chemicals. Glass, which reacts to only a few chemicals, is the near-ideal medium for storing or working with almost any concoction. As he worked, Bénédictus accidentally knocked a glass flask off a shelf. A common, everyday mistake that is made more often than scientists will admit. This was long before Pyrex, so Bénédictus was amazed to notice that, rather than shattering, the glass mostly cracked in a spiderweb-like pattern. Investigating, he found that the dropped flask had contained cellulose nitrate. The chemical was adhesive and bonded to the glass, once dry. The cellulose nitrate had left a clear, nearly invisible, coating inside the flask and this caused the glass to crack rather than shatter. He was able to re-create the effect and applied for a patent for laminated glass in 1909.

While shattering windshields were a serious hazard, auto manufacturers did not adopt laminated windshields at first. But Bénédictus's safety glass did find an immediate use. The eyepieces in gas masks during WWI were made of glass. To prevent them from shattering and blinding soldiers when shells landed nearby, the new lenses were made of laminated glass. Bénédictus's "mistake" prevented tens of thousands of casualties. By 1927, all auto manufacturers were using laminated windshields and advertised them as a sales point. Gangsters and bank clerks soon also benefited from the chemist's mistake, as laminated glass in many layers was found to be bulletproof. If you have ever been in a serious auto accident and seen the spiderweb break of a window, remember: if it had not been for Édouard Bénédictus knocking just the right flask off his desk, and being smart enough to see the implications of what he found, you might well have been injured by flying glass shards.

Lamination made auto windows and many other uses for glass safer. It allowed windows on cars to be larger and the styling of automotive vehicles changed dramatically. Because Bénédictus made a mistake and learned from it, when you drive your car, you are safer and can see the world all around you.

# 38

# NOT ALWAYS A TWO-HORSE RACE

## 1912

### By William Terdoslavich

*Not in a century . . .*

Every four years, Americans by the tens of millions walk into voting booths and choose the lesser of two evils. The winner gets to sit in the White House for the next four years.

Voting is a public right, discharged more with reluctance than enthusiasm. But what if there was a third way?

Yes! Third-party candidates sometimes enliven presidential elections. They garner a lot of media coverage, as they do not fit the conventional narrative. Sometimes they propose programs beyond the reach of conventional wisdom.

But they never win.

Worse, they can siphon votes away from the expected winner, tossing the election to the expected loser.

This fact of life doesn't stop the damn fools from trying, because someone nearly did win and, in the process, mistakenly spoiled both the third-party option and several presidential elections.

## No Hope of Winning—or Making a Difference

Ex-president Theodore Roosevelt led the charge of the Bull Moose Party to notch the best performance of a third-party candidate in American history in 1912. No one has ever come close to equaling this as of 2012, a century later.

Roosevelt felt that his chosen replacement, President William Howard Taft, was backsliding on TR's progressive agenda. Taft was returning the GOP to its big business/small government center of gravity. He also had full control of the Republican Party, securing nomination even though Roosevelt had proven to be the more popular candidate during the primaries.

Denied the nomination, Roosevelt took his delegates out of the Chicago convention to a nearby auditorium and started the Progressive Party. It is better known by its nickname, the "Bull Moose" Party, after Roosevelt quipped to reporters that he was as fit as a "bull moose." *And he proved it by surviving an assassination attempt during the campaign.*

On election night, the damage became apparent. Roosevelt came in second, with just eighty-eight electoral votes. Taft came in third, with just eight. Roosevelt failed to attract enough Democrats to offset the loss of Republicans to Taft. The steadfast Democrats put Governor Woodrow Wilson (D-NJ) into office.

This was the high-water mark for third-party candidacies in the twentieth century. Since 1912, third-party candidates have run either as extreme liberals or extreme conservatives, trying to capture enough regional or ideological votes to finish like Roosevelt or, better yet, *win.*

In 1924, Senator Robert La Follette Sr. (R-WI) took his turn, forming the Independent Progressive Party and running on a very liberal platform. His ideology, however, drew only limited voter support. La Follette came in second in seventeen Western states, losing to President Calvin Coolidge, a Republican. While La Follette reaped nearly 17 percent of the popular vote, he only won his home state of Wisconsin (13 electoral votes). Coolidge won decisively with 382 electoral votes, snaring 54 percent of the popular vote. Democrat John W. Davis placed second with 136 electoral votes and nearly 29 percent of the popular vote.

Where La Follette tried ideology, others thought they could capture Roosevelt's appeal by focusing on regional issues. In 1948, Senator Strom Thurmond (D-SC) mounted his presidential bid as an extreme conservative, in reaction to President Harry Truman's executive order desegregating the military. It did not matter for the

"Dixiecrat." Truman took 49.5 percent of the popular vote, yielding 303 electoral votes. New York Governor Thomas E. Dewey came in second with 189 electoral votes and 45 percent of the vote. Thurmond took 2.4 percent of the popular vote and 39 electoral votes. He carried only Louisiana, Mississippi, Alabama, and his home state of South Carolina. *Truman won, despite Thurmond's drag.*

In 1968, Governor George Wallace (D-AL) followed in Thurmond's footsteps and ran against civil rights, ex–vice president Richard Nixon (R), and Vice President Hubert Humphrey (D). Nixon did about as well as Truman, gaining 43.4 percent of the popular vote and a decisive 301 electoral votes. But Wallace still did damage, winning 13.5 percent of the popular vote and depriving Humphrey of 45 electoral votes from the Deep South. Wallace's attraction to socially conservative white voters did not stop Nixon from winning. Four years later, Nixon reaped their support by abandoning the GOP's traditional campaign for the black vote, decisively trouncing liberal senator George McGovern (D-SD).

## Spoilers Become Meaningful Again

Like Roosevelt, the wacky H. Ross Perot, former CEO of Electronic Data Systems, ran as an independent in 1992. Governor Bill Clinton (D-AR) won with 370 electoral votes, but only 43 percent of the popular vote. Add Perot's 18.9 percent finish to President George H. W. Bush's share of the popular vote (37.4 percent), and Bush could have won reelection. This affected 324 electoral votes in thirty states, presuming that most of the voters in each state would have gone for Bush had Perot not been on the ballot.

Perot ran again in 1996, siphoning off 8.4 percent of the popular vote from Senator Bob Dole (R-KS) to allow President Clinton's reelection. Without Perot, Dole could have had 49.1 percent of the popular vote, along with Dole's already 159 electoral-vote finish against Clinton's 49.2 percent popular and 379 electoral votes. Perot's presence affected the outcome in twelve states for 138 electoral votes, again assuming that most of the votes would have gone to Dole in Perot's absence.

The prize for most consequential spoiler, however, must go to radical consumer advocate Ralph Nader. Running as a liberal Green Party nominee in 2000, Nader carried no states. He only picked up 2.7 percent of the popular vote, compared to 48.4 percent for Vice President Al Gore (D) and Governor George W. Bush (R-TX), son of the previous President Bush, who *won* the election with 47.9 percent of the popular vote.

Wait a second. *Bush came in second and won?*

It came down to Florida, which had 25 electoral votes. Gore and Bush finished with 48.8 percent each, and Nader trailed with 1.6 percent. Had Nader not run, many of his votes would have gone to Gore, yielding a final electoral vote result of 291 for Gore, 244 for Bush. A candidate needs 270 electoral votes to win.

## To the Winner Go the Spoils

Aside from Theodore Roosevelt, it has been the fate of every third-party candidate to be forgotten by American history. No one has replicated Roosevelt's results. Instead, we have third-party spoilers.

One of the vagaries of presidential elections is that candidates really run in fifty state races, plus the District of Columbia, getting all the electoral votes of a state on a winner-take-all basis (with two minor exceptions). A winner can beat a loser by 5 to 10 percent of the popular vote, but still win an outsized majority of electoral votes. Or the winner can lose the popular vote, and by winning the right combination of states, win the electoral vote and the presidency. *It has happened four times.*

Would it be a hundred times better if the US had a parliamentary system? Then those third-party candidates *would be* consequential. No longer would we be sending someone to the White House with less than 50 percent of the popular vote.

Wilson, Truman, Nixon, Clinton, and Gore would all have had to seek out the leaders of minor parties to form coalitions and gain a parliamentary majority, which is at least half of all seats, plus one. Forming a government would require compromise, perhaps allotting a number of cabinet positions to the smaller coalition partners, or adopting some planks from their party platforms.

The downside of coalition government is political fragility. If the larger partner overreaches, smaller partners can pull out, depriving the government of its needed majority. That would result in another round of elections.

How this would affect the Republicans and Democrats would be interesting, as both parties are collections of factions and their pet issues. In a parliamentary system, we could see the GOP split up between a religious conservative party, a rural party, a populist party, and a pro-business party. Split the Democrats and you would get separate parties for labor, women, centrists, liberals, socialists, blacks, and Latinos.

The majority coalition becomes the government of the day. The losing party becomes the loyal opposition, powerless but for the power to complain. But most importantly, the majority would rule, unhindered by gridlock and stalemate.

When you look at gridlock in Washington today, parliamentary government starts looking mighty attractive.

||||||||||||||||||||||||||||||||||||||||||||||||||||||||||||||||

## THE *TITANIC*

### 1912

**By Bill Fawcett**

||||||||||||||||||||||||||||||||||||||||||||||||||||||||||||||||

A tragedy of errors.

So many mistakes and failures were involved in the sinking of the *Titanic* that picking just one seems unfair. However, if we count them all separately, the total would equal a quarter of the book's 101, and the book would be twice as long. So, to compromise, we will count the *Titanic*'s many design errors, command errors, and incidental problems as just one big, continuing technical mistake followed by a second, seemingly trivial mistake made before the ship even sailed. A small mistake without which there would have been no disaster.

The White Star Line's *Titanic* was a technological wonder: a four-stacker passenger ship capable of speeds most of the era's battleships could not match. The *Titanic* was the largest passenger liner ever built, the most luxurious (if you were in first class), and the most highly promoted. It was the sensation of its day. Even before it launched, you could buy *Titanic* soap, *Titanic* tea, *Titanic* towels, *Titanic* candy, and just about anything else you could think of. Expectations were high and anything less than a record sailing time from Southampton to New York City would have been a disappointment. So it sailed at its best speed, without slowing. The risk was minimal because the ads all said the liner was unsinkable.

There were a number of engineering flaws in the design of the *Titanic*. To begin with, the hull was made up of a type of mild steel that tended to become brittle when chilled. Not really a good decision for a ship that was going to sail the frigid waters of the North Atlantic. But the rivets were iron, and their difference from the metal in the plates created a microcurrent that degraded and loosened them from the hull plates they held on. But beyond a weak hull, there was a built-in failure point. Worried that the ship was too big and would be damaged by rolling on the high seas, the designers decided to allow it to flex in rough waters. To do this a "flex panel"—basically, a separate part of the hull that would bend when needed—was added. But this flex point was, by its very nature, a weak spot in the hull. And so it proved. The *Titanic* actually split completely in half at the flex point, and so it sits on the bottom of the North Atlantic, in two pieces.

Furthermore, the allegedly unsinkable ship was really very vulnerable. Any military ship's watertight hulls extended from the top deck to the bottom of the ship. Most were also sealed or could be closed off at various levels by watertight doors. The watertight holds on the *Titanic* only extended up partway from the bottom of the hull. Worse yet, these were open on top, allowing water to pour in and fill them. A way to picture what this meant to the *Titanic* is to take out an empty ice cube tray and put it in a sink full of water. Sitting flat, the tray stays afloat. Now take one end of the tray and push it down until the first couple sets of ice cube compartments are filled up. As each one fills, it pulls that end of the tray down lower, which allows the third and fourth compartments to start filling. This will continue until enough ice cube compartments are filled and the tray sinks. That is exactly what happened to the *Titanic* when the iceberg opened a number of its forward compartments. As the nose of the ship plunged lower and lower, each watertight but open-topped compartment filled, one after another.

Having managed to create a ship that was highly vulnerable, the White Star Line then made arrangements to ensure that any sinking would be a disaster. Or, perhaps a more accurate description would be that they failed to make proper arrangements, just in case it did sink. Toward the end of construction (to save money and keep the appearance of the hull clean), it was decided to place only enough lifeboats on the ship to hold fewer than half of the passengers booked aboard. And never mind the crew. After all, this was the UNSINKABLE *Titanic*. But the passengers were unaware of the lack of lifeboats, because no lifeboat or emergency drills were ever held, even just among the crew.

Knowing that their ship was unsinkable, no one bothered to build into it a public-address system. The only way to communicate with passengers or the crew was to send crew members to walk down the corridors and announce any problems. But that was itself a problem, since many of the crew were from non-English-speaking countries, and were unable to communicate with the passengers—or many of the other crewmen.

There have been questions about the steering of the *Titanic* and why it slid along the iceberg rather than turn away, but the entire bridge crew perished, and knowledge of who did what perished with them. But one minor mistake, one really trivial oversight, contributed as much to the *Titanic*'s sinking as any of the mistakes mentioned above. This was recounted by one of the few surviving crew members, Fred Fleet. His job was to stand on the high mast and watch for hazards, including icebergs. He did this, but on the inaugural voyage of the *Titanic*, he could only use his naked eyes. There were binoculars on board, but they were locked in a cabinet that could not be opened. At the last minute, the first officer was changed to a different seaman. The original first officer had the key to the locker and failed to pass it on to his replacement. It seems there was only one key, so the lookout was limited to what he could see without magnification. We know this to be true, as both men attested to it at the congressional hearings subsequent to the disaster, and, in 2014, the missing key was actually sold at auction. No one was concerned enough to break into the shiny, new locker and take the binoculars out. After all, the *Titanic* was unsinkable, and what could possibly threaten such a great ship? With the special binoculars, any lookout would have seen the fatal iceberg much sooner—soon enough for the liner to avoid a collision. Without a collision, all the other flaws in the design and construction would not have mattered. So, for lack of a key, the *Titanic* was lost.

||||||||||||||||||||||||||||||||||||||||||||||||||||||||||||||||||||||||||||

# RUMOR

1914

**By Bill Fawcett**

||||||||||||||||||||||||||||||||||||||||||||||||||||||||||||||||||||||||||||

*The Russians Are Coming, the Russians
Are Coming* may have been a Cold
War comedy in 1966, but it was a
world-changing cry in Britain
fifty years earlier.

t took a while to figure out how the rumor had started. In wartime England, rumors were common, but this one persisted and spread until it was even being reported in the American newspapers. Initially, the story was that tens of thousands—some later said there were a million—Russian Cossacks had landed in Scotland and were traversing Britain on their way to fight on the Western Front. It first appeared in August, when the kaiser's armies were pressing the French back across northern France. Those were dark times for the Allies; perhaps that is why the story spread so rapidly. This one rumor, or rather the Germans' mistaken belief in it, may even have stopped them from winning WWI in its first months.

A careful study written after the war by Dr. David Clarke, of Sheffield Hallam University, traced the origin of the Russian tale. It appears to have started because the British government was gathering and transporting large numbers of reservists by train to the southeast coast. From there, the reservists were carried by whatever ships could be found to fight with the British Expeditionary Force in France. The mass of unscheduled trains clogged the routes and brought the normally efficient train system to a near halt. As a security precaution, the soldiers were ordered to keep the window shades down, even at night. Eventually, the railroad staff went out with lanterns and helped sort out the mess, but some trains sat for hours in the centers of English towns, with no one getting on or off, and the curtains blocking any view inside.

One of the battalions being rushed to the front was the 4th Seaforth Highlanders. They came from a Gaelic-speaking part of Scotland. Since few people in England had ever heard Scots Gaelic spoken, it sounded like a distantly foreign language to the people in hearing distance of the trains. The confusion increased when a porter, at a station where one of the mystery trains was waiting, managed to ask one of the soldiers where he and his fellow soldiers were from. He was answered with "Ross Shire," which is one of the northernmost of the Scottish shires and one that was hardly well-known to the average Englishman. Between the soldier's accent and other confusion, the porter went on to announce that the train was full of men from "Russia."

Adding to the confusion was the fact that there really were a few hundred Russian soldiers who had landed in Scotland and were traveling to London. No attempt was made to hide them and their presence gave credence to the rumors of trainloads of Cossacks. In reality, they were commissary staff, army clerks, whose job was to coordinate the aid being given the Russians.

Once the newspapers got onto the story, every effort was made to find these phantom Russians. The shipping agent for an import company was handling a large shipment of eggs from Russia. Easy to transport if kept chilled, eggs were a common import commodity. But in the terse, pay-by-the-word world of telegrams, the agent notified his home office only that one hundred thousand Russians were already in transit from Aberdeen to London. This was taken by some of the newspapers as proof that the Cossack stories were accurate.

MI5 soon got into the game. They had identified and were screening the mail from a number of German spies in their country. When one, a certain Carl Lody, sent to Berlin a report about trains filled with Russians who were ready to land in France, they let it pass unchanged. They even added to the rumor when possible. Any queries were answered with the reply that all information on the topic was top secret.

Soon the English were seeing, and telling reporters about, Russians everywhere. One man swore he had watched 10,000 fully armed Russian soldiers marching along the Embankment in London. Another claimed he had been on a ship from Archangel with 2,500 Cossacks, but that the army had confiscated his pictures of them. Another train porter in the city of Durham notified the press when a chocolate dispenser was jammed by someone's inserting a ruble into it. In Carlisle, stories of shouts of "vodka" were heard from trains passing through and foreigners ordering three hundred "lunchsky baskets" from a shop lady in Malvern were also immediately reported. It is not surprising that the story spread so widely and quickly. The war in France was not going well and anything that hinted at good news was welcome.

American newspapers, not censored or limited by fact-checking, jumped on the story with enthusiasm. The *New York Times* reported that seventy-two thousand Russian soldiers had arrived in Aberdeen and been hurried through Grimsby, Harwich, and Dover to the coast. The Russians were said to be in hidden camps near Ostend, waiting to make a flank attack on the advancing Germans. Copies of these newspapers, unrestricted since the USA was neutral, were shipped directly to the German general staff and intelligence bureaus.

In September, the general staff and the kaiser left their forward headquarters, which were located in a coastal area. One of the reasons news reporters gave for this action was the vulnerability of the area if the Russians landed. The Germans ordered two full divisions, more than thirty-five thousand men, and all their artillery and machine guns to wait near the coast. The only reason to do this was the fear of a landing in numbers large enough to threaten the main war effort. But it was a war-losing mistake. There they sat, apparently waiting for the Cossacks to come—for a vital month.

The German army had pushed the French back and were approaching Paris. Most of northeastern France was occupied. The capital was preparing for another siege like the one it had suffered in

1870. The French army had been making a fighting retreat before two German armies, both pushing south for weeks, and was exhausted and discouraged. General Joseph Joffre, commander of all the French forces, decided to make a bold move: he would counterattack. On September 6, 1914, the French 6th Army attacked the flank of the German 1st Army as it fought to cross the Marne only thirty miles from Paris. The German commander, von Kluck, changed his army's front with professional skill in order to face this new danger. But by doing this, with no further divisions available, he was forced to allow a gap of almost thirty miles to open between the 1st and the 2nd German Armies. On the Channel coast, the thirty-five thousand soldiers who could have filled that gap waited because of a rumor.

Another French army then charged with great élan into the gap on September 6. On the next day, six hundred Paris taxis carried six thousand reinforcements to the front and earned themselves immortal fame. This allowed the French 5th Army, now in the gap between both German armies, to attack east against the German 2nd Army and thereby widen the gap. The German 1st Army now faced an enemy on two sides. The French 5th was pressing it on one flank, while it faced increased resistance from those units on another. The gap that opened between the two advancing German armies changed the war. Before it opened, the Germans had pushed relentlessly forward, without a pause. That was never to happen again; out of position and in danger of being divided and defeated in detail, both German armies began a retreat beyond the Aisne River on September 10. There they dug in and a war of movement became one of trench warfare.

There is no questioning the courage, and desperation, that led to the French rallying and winning the Battle of the Marne. It takes nothing from that heroic event to speculate that, if those two divisions of Germans sitting idle on the coast (probably waiting for the Russians to attack during what proved to be the most important battle of WWI) had been available to von Kluck, there would have been no gap between the kaiser's 1st and 2nd Armies. With no gap, the Germans could have continued their advance to Paris, or beyond. The collapse of France that occurred in 1940 would have happened twenty-six years earlier. The unquestioned power in Europe in 1915 would have been an aggressive and colony-hungry Germany. France would have been merely the abused loser and any treaty would likely have been just as punitive as the Versailles Treaty was, but it would have been to the detriment of France. What would that peace have cost Britain? If the thorough and ruthless Germans had limited French arms in the way the Allies tried to limit Germany's, then WWII would have been impossible. An expansionist Germany, under a popular kaiser and expert military leadership, might well have redrawn the map of Europe with no one to oppose them. Who knows how large "greater Germany" would have become? But men who should have known better wasted two divisions protecting their flank coast against nothing more than a very silly rumor. It was a mistake that may well have cost them the war.

# 42

## MOURNING GLORY

### 1916

**By William Terdoslavich**

> The best-laid schemes o' mice an'
> men gang aft agley.
> —ROBERT BURNS

Battles define nations. For Americans, that battle is Gettysburg, the dramatic climax of the Civil War. Freedom was won there. For the British, it is the Battle of the Somme, a tragic bloodletting that evokes sorrow, not pride.

What happened on July 1, 1916, still draws British tourists to the battlefield, which stretched over twenty miles in length and up to eight miles in depth. They seek out the graves of family members among the twenty thousand soldiers buried long ago in the military cemeteries that now trace the former lines.

The disaster also colored the British military's outlook toward Germany's rearmament in the years before the Second World War. An aversion to mass casualties led to reluctance in war planning, while the hiring pool for general officers was pretty shallow, given the number of losses of lieutenants and captains in the First World War. Anyone exhibiting courage and leadership had a good chance of getting killed. Many were.

## Taking the King's Shilling

The Battle of the Somme did not just happen. It took planning, as well as a convergence of events.

You have to go back to August 1914. Britain had just declared war on Germany. Six hundred thousand volunteers overran the enlistment offices. Secretary of State for War Lord Kitchener now had to turn this mob into an army.

Five "New Armies" were formed, each of six divisions, a total of one hundred thousand men per army. Turning these civilians into soldiers was a challenge. The Territorial Divisions, much like our National Guard in national crises and war, had already been dispatched to France to help the British Expeditionary Force hold the line against the invading Germans. These divisions would help the old regulars in the BEF maintain position until the New Armies arrived.

Regular officers were in short supply, and with many at the front doing their duty, the responsibility of training devolved onto a small pool of retired officers and NCOs—perhaps not Britain's best. Three officers and three NCOs would be allotted to each battalion of volunteers, with junior officers being raised from the ranks by necessity. There simply weren't enough "gentlemen" to go around.

To maintain patriotic enthusiasm, the incoming men were told they could serve with their neighbors and coworkers. This gave rise to the so-called Pals Battalions, men from the same workplaces, cities, towns, and counties who were grouped together as units. Liverpool raised four Pals Battalions in the first month of the war alone. Many towns turned out single battalions. Many cities turned out brigades.

By the end of 1915, they would all be equipped and shipped to France. They knew how to march. They knew how to drill. They did not know how to fight. Their combat training was dangerously lacking.

## Best-Laid Plans . . .

The Allies—France, Britain, Italy, and Russia—had to fashion a plan to defeat Germany and Austria-Hungary. There was no supreme commander yet, but the Allies agreed that they had to attack the Axis from all sides to produce a German defeat.

General Sir Douglas Haig was the first among those equals. Commanding all British forces in France, Haig had to do his part in cooperation with French field marshal Joseph Joffre.

That timetable for joint planning was messed up by the German offensive aimed at taking Verdun, beginning in February of 1916. (By December 1916, it ended with a strategic withdrawal by a now chagrined German offensive force.) Defending that fortress sucked in French units like a bloody vacuum cleaner. Divisions were rotated into and out of that sector, which had to be held.

That pretty much scotched the original French plan to attack the Somme sector in early July with three armies. The original plan called for using sixty-seven French divisions and twenty-five British divisions. On July 1, a much smaller plan went into action, with fourteen British divisions (and four in reserve), plus another five French divisions with six in reserve.

Haig was looking to score a decisive victory at the Somme. Clear, flat ground beyond the German lines would be ideal for a breakout. He held three British cavalry divisions in reserve, ready to ride through the gap he expected to blast in the German lines. The objectives were very optimistic—attacking British units had to make it to the second line of the German defense belt, which was three lines deep.

The northern half of the attack was entrusted to General Sir Henry Rawlinson, commanding the 4th Army, while General M. E. Fayolle commanded the French 6th Army for the southern half. The Somme River neatly divided the two sectors. Facing these troops were low-rising hills held by the German 2nd Army. They had burrowed deeply into the chalky ground, their first-line troops well protected in dugouts thirty feet deep, virtually bombproof against the seven-day artillery bombardment that preceded the attack.

## Over the Top

To start the attack on July 1, the British set off eight mines that had been dug beneath the German lines, each packed with tons of high explosives. Once the British artillery fire stopped, the officers blew their whistles and the men deep in the trenches went over the top into "no-man's-land."

Each division attacked on a front two brigades wide, with the third brigade held in reserve. Each brigade sent two battalions forward. Each battalion advanced with each of its four companies in line, each line fifty paces apart. And they advanced at a walk, with every soldier burdened by his rifle, two hundred rounds of ammunition, two days of food, and an assortment of barbed wire, stakes, mortar ammunition, grenades—everything they would need to establish a defense once they took the German first line.

All that British artillery fire failed to cut the barbed wire that laced no-man's-land—the deadly space between the lines. Many of the shells used during the prep fire were shrapnel, not high explosives. Shell splinters simply whizzed past the wire with each explosion. Many shells were duds, the product of rush orders and poor quality control.

And the bombardment did not soften up German defenses. Troops emerged from their dugouts, thirty feet below the surface, set up their machine guns, and opened fire. With each belt of ammo fired, the Germans reaped a bloody harvest, sometimes catching advancing companies in their flanks. Some were little more than platoons by the time they captured a stretch of German trench.

Not every sector along the twenty-six-mile line saw failure. The regulars in British XIII Corps made the greatest advance—about two miles. But other attacks were well shredded by the time any troops made it to the first German line. Sometimes none made it at all.

The worst disaster of the day fell upon the 1st Newfoundland Battalion, losing 710 men, about 91 percent of its initial strength, in killed and wounded. They had to advance across open ground with zero support from artillery or neighboring units. Many Pals Battalions lost half their strength, as attacks made minimal gains up and down the line. Some were annihilated in the first hour of battle.

By the time the sun set, close to twenty thousand British troops lay dead and nearly another forty thousand were wounded. When news of the fallen reached home, entire towns, villages, and neighborhoods were plunged into mourning. Many who grew up and worked together, who enlisted together, died together, too.

## C'est la Guerre

French losses that day were fewer than two thousand killed and wounded. And *they* made their first-day objectives.

*What?!*

Why were French losses only one-thirtieth those of the British? The French had learned their tactical lessons the hard way two years before. They had once thought that bayonet charges could overcome machine-gun fire as they tried to retake their lost provinces of Alsace and Lorraine from the Germans. Heavy French casualties proved this was a bloody mistake.

After seeing how the Germans fought, the French army changed its tactics, emphasizing effective artillery fire that would precede a slow advance across no-man's-land, followed closely by minimal infantry in small groups, one group advancing while the other provided support fire. This was beyond the capability of the ill-trained Pals Battalions.

Haig wanted a breakthrough. Had he listened to his subordinate, Rawlinson, the 4th Army's attack would have aimed for more modest objectives, what Rawlinson called "bite and hold." Just take the first line of trenches and dig in. Let the Germans counterattack to retake their trenches. Mow them down with rifle and machine-gun fire as they cross the open ground. Yet even this would have depended on improving the skills of the Pals Battalions, which, sadly, lacked the tactical finesse to attack forward in small groups practicing bounding overwatch.

The British army would learn how to fight as well as the French and the Germans. They would change their tactics, and substitute tanks and artillery for flesh and blood. That took time. The British army of 1918 was much more competent than its predecessor in 1916.

All of this would have lessened the body count, but not the battle. Fighting on the Somme ground on for another four months.

By its conclusion in November, casualties numbered an estimated 195,000 for the French and about 650,000 for the Germans. British casualties numbered more than 415,000.

Such was the price paid by the British and the French to take eight miles of ground.

# 43

# TEACHING THE IRISH A LESSON . . . OR NOT

### 1916

**By Dr. Paul A. Thomsen**

Even the Vikings found Ireland
hard to hold.

Since the dark ages, residents of Great Britain have sought to control and consolidate the neighboring island of Ireland. In the early twentieth century, the rulers of the British Empire thought they had finally succeeded. On April 24, 1916, a small group of dissident Irishmen seized control of key points around the Irish city of Dublin. The British army's poor response invalidated their presumptions and changed the course of history.

Throughout modern European history, Irish nationalists have fought English/Irish Protestants for control of Ireland. In ages past, England attempted colonization and the confiscation of land. These didn't work. During the reign of Cromwell, England tried extermination. That also failed. Later, in the nineteenth century, elements of the British Parliament tried another tactic: deference to British royal heritage in exchange for "Home Rule." This legislation scared many groups among the populace—the minority Protestant hard-liners, the firebrand Irish nationalists, and the more traditional House of Lords—equally. It twice failed to pass Parliament. In 1914, a third Home Rule bill, milder in tone and aided by the cost of occupation with a war in Europe looming, narrowly passed Parliament with a proviso that it would not be enacted until after the war. It seemed like peace would finally be had in Ireland.

On the contrary, the delay in the law's enactment gave the extremists just enough time to test the limits of Britain's tolerance. The Protestant minority, fearing a soon-to-be Irish-Catholic regional government, formed a paramilitary organization called the Ulster Volunteers. In response, a band of Irish intellectuals and professionals organized a sixteen-thousand-strong island counterforce of civilians, called the Irish Volunteers, to oppose Ulster. The challenges were symbolic and ineffective. However, unknown to most participants, a third secret group was in charge of the nonpartisan Irish Volunteers, the very independence-minded Irish Republican Brotherhood (IRB). While Ulster was a problem, the IRB saw the new Home Rule law as the real threat, believing that under its authority they would never be rid of British influence. They also had a plan to achieve independence, hinging on the traditional British mistake of using overt force when facing any real or imagined resistance. If their long-shot plan worked, everyone, they hoped, would rapidly assume that the British army never intended to protect the Irish unless doing so was in its own interests; Home Rule would become a moot point, and Ireland would soon be a free and independent state.

On April 24, 1916, the clandestine IRB leaders hatched their plan and marched 1,500 Irish Volunteers into Dublin, detailing them to seize strategic points throughout the city. Shortly thereafter, Patrick Pearse, an IRB spokesman and the operation's leader, ordered two Irish republican flags raised over the general post office as he read a proclamation declaring the island an independent republican state. By occupying British property, the act could not have been more provocative to the Dublin-garrisoned British army. General John Maxwell, commander of Dublin's three battalions of 2,400 British soldiers, responded by making the worst mistake he could make. He immediately declared martial law and mobilized the soldiers in four city barracks to quash the insurgency, turning the puppet Irish Volunteers instantly into martyrs for the cause of Irish independence. There would be blood in the streets, just as the IRB had planned.

Although the notion might have seemed like folly to General John Maxwell in 1916, the British army could have foiled the IRB's plans with a defter hand and a longer view. Centuries of British military tradition dictated that riots and insurrections were best handled by the well-trained and well-equipped British army. Swift and strong responses were also key to preventing further acts of aggression. Although Ireland was still legally an occupied territory until war's end, the IRB's martyrs were not, however, a mob and should have fallen under the purview of local civilian governance. Their initial acts were orderly, deferential to civilians, and decidedly nonviolent until they were fired upon by their opposite numbers.

Yet, as a career officer, Maxwell saw his position through experience gained in the Boer War, the Western Front of the First World War, and in the 1914–1915 defense of the Suez Canal from Ottoman raids. The green of the IRB's flags and uniforms made him see red and act rashly. After all, the insurgents did eventually surrender because of the siege's drain on their resources—and the belief that the uprising would continue elsewhere. Furthermore, Maxwell's eventual offering of fair terms to the Irish prisoners, later reneged on, shows that he was capable of attaining a larger perspective. Had he acted more wisely, the Easter Rising, like so many other Irish revolutionary plans, would have failed and Ireland would have become an island dominion akin in status to Canada.

Instead, the Irish Republic, paradoxically, owes General Maxwell a debt of gratitude for his part in the execution of the IRB's plans by making things worse for the Dublin occupiers. Initially, the British army surrounded the Irish pickets and fired on the enemy. When that failed to move the resistance, the British charged the Dublin positions in repeated waves, attempting to dislodge their recalcitrant foes through the application of cold steel. When this, too, failed, they fired artillery to bring the British-owned buildings down around the Volunteers' heads. The rebels simply stood their ground as each violent British act, chronicled over several days by international newspaper coverage, showed the British army as first impotent, then incompetent, and finally, mad. The army demonstrated that England was willing to destroy British infrastructure in order to save it. As a result, on April 29, 1916, the Irish surrendered the Dublin Post Office, victorious.

The debacle was, indeed, a public relations nightmare for the British Empire. When the dust settled, the Volunteers who surrendered were discovered to be a cross section of Ireland's populace. Instead of hardened criminals and foreign fighters, the defenders were revealed to be led by schoolteachers, laborers, and poets who had withstood four days of attacks by the most lethal infantry in the world. Moreover, there was no promised fair public trial for those who surrendered. Most of the ringleaders were imprisoned, given summary military trials, and executed at Kilmainham Gaol by a British army firing squad. For many Irish, the aftermath strengthened the feelings stirred up by the Dublin siege. The British, they believed, would never change. Thanks to General John Maxwell's ill-thought-out actions, the British had to go.

Without an Easter Rising, Ireland and English history would have been fundamentally different. Initially, the third Home Rule bill would have been grudgingly accepted by the Irish people. There would have been no Irish Free State or republic. There would have been more money and more seasoned British veterans to fight both world wars. In World War II, Irish ports would have grown in influence, handling much of the international shipping trade and American military matériel used to defeat Nazi Germany. Conversely, Germany would have made the island suffer, targeting those same facilities. And the British Empire would have felt more willing to handle India and refuse the partition of Pakistan in 1947 and the 1948 divestment of Burma, preferring to "settle" matters as they had in Ireland. America's Irish communities would also have grown as important fund-raisers for a much longer and more violent IRB-inspired guerrilla war. Two-thirds of the island of Ireland would likely still be gripped by bombings and mass shootings from continued extremist attempts to bleed each other into submission. Today, Ireland would be as much red in color as emerald green.

||||||||||||||||||||||||||||||||||||||||||||||||||||||||||||||||||||

# 44

# STALIN, MY
# DEAR COMRADE

## 1917

### By Dr. Paul A. Thomsen

||||||||||||||||||||||||||||||||||||||||||||||||||||||||||||||||||||

> Comradeship can have a
> different meaning.

In the revolutionary Russia of 1917, Vladimir Lenin and Joseph Stalin were perfect complements. Both were strong in mind and body. Both were criminals in the eyes of the European powers. Although from different backgrounds, they shared common friends and enemies. Where one concentrated on matters of philosophy and policy, the other handled the administration of government and the military, both working to transform Russia into a Marxist utopia. Both men even spent time in Siberia and in exile from their homeland. In the 1910s, Lenin implicitly trusted Stalin completely. As he lay dying under de facto house arrest in 1922, however, Lenin finally realized that his belief in Stalin was mistaken and how Russia would suffer for it.

As the son of a schoolteacher and brother of a rebel, Vladimir Lenin dedicated his life to finding a means by which his country could escape poverty and brutal oppression. In 1887, his eldest brother was hanged for conspiring to assassinate Czar Alexander III. While dealing with an expulsion from school for leading an illegal assembly, Lenin became enamored of Karl Marx and Friedrich Engels's 1848 *Communist Manifesto*. The pamphlet articulated a theory of perpetual class struggle with capitalism, which was the cause of many of the modern world's ills, and declared communism as the remedy. The pamphlet, he thought, fit his image of Russian life. Eventually, Lenin found other like-minded Communists, and in 1917, they all rejoiced in the overthrow of the czar, knowing their time had come. Vladimir Lenin rapidly rose to the top of the Bolshevik Revolution's leadership. With his fellow Communists co-opted or neutralized by Stalin and others, his parliamentary manner and persuasiveness carried him to the leadership of the provisional government. Shortly thereafter, he supplanted that government with a new Marxist-Leninist one, which venerated the liberated serfs and industrial workers.

The Communist leader's protégés, Joseph Stalin and Leon Trotsky, had made the Soviet victory possible by shouldering the more mundane and problematic work of the Bolshevik Revolution. For example, between April 1902 and March 1913, Stalin had been arrested seven times for revolutionary activities, sent to Siberia, and eventually exiled for robbing banks, inciting mobs, spreading propaganda, and conducting counterintelligence operations with the Communist community for Lenin. Trotsky had a similar arrest record. He worked as a war correspondent, ambassador-at-large for the cause, and leader of the Military Revolutionary Committee. Together, Lenin, Stalin, and Trotsky formed a trifecta of support, advice, and management.

Vladimir Lenin believed that if the right conditions could be created, the Russian people would rush to construct a utopia. Unlike the later Stalin, he believed government should merely set up the conditions for success by a Communist revolution and spend the remainder of its time keeping a watchful eyes so that the system would be maintained while also fomenting the revolution abroad. Like Stalin, Lenin saw the need to industrialize Russia. Rather than resolve problems by unilateral dictatorial acts (except in emergencies), Lenin believed the people would naturally select the best course. For example, during the 1917 Revolution, Lenin appropriated surplus grain to feed the Red Army, without remuneration to its producers, to stave off starvation; once the crisis passed, the farmers' protests became the dominant concern and the practice was ended. He believed Russia should assume a hard outward-looking posture to coerce and incite other nations' workers and farmers to join the Communist fold. Eventually the capitalist imperialist leadership of the West would crumble before their Russian utopia.

The new Soviet leader should have seen the monster in Joseph Stalin. While many early comrades of the Bolshevik Revolution would later claim to have seen the man as nothing more than the ill-educated son of Georgian peasants, Lenin knew him to be an intellectual, encouraging him to write papers and manage publicity for the revolution. Time and again, Stalin proved himself to be cunning, ruthless, and an adroit manager in the civil war. Lenin, however, didn't care about Stalin's methods, because they achieved the goals Lenin wanted. Hence Lenin chose to believe that what Lenin taught, Stalin would believe and carry to his grave. The Soviet leader was at least partly correct. Stalin did carry Lenin's work to a grave—Lenin's.

In 1921, Vladimir Lenin's attempts to realize his vision of the new Soviet state suffered a series of blows. After his doctors removed an old would-be assassin's bullet from his neck in May 1922, he inexplicably became partially paralyzed and briefly lost his ability to speak. For a time afterward, he rallied and returned to work, but there he found equally disheartening news: Stalin had tampered with many of his policies, including foreign trade policies and the disposition of republics and colonies. And he discovered a transfer of overt power from the Soviet and Lenin's supporters to Stalin's loyal supporters. In 1923, Lenin, feeling sufficiently duped and in failing health, enlisted Leon Trotsky to try to stop Stalin, but it was already too late. Stalin's recently constructed power bloc of supporters, composed of anti-Trotsky Communists, interceded. They neutralized Trotsky, ordered Lenin to bed until he felt better, and confined the Soviet leader in a de facto state of house arrest. Although Lenin urged Trotsky to publicly attack Stalin, Trotsky, likely fearing a fatal reprisal, remained publicly silent. With no other recourse, Lenin penned a "testament" of his political will, hoping others would learn of Stalin's betrayal and take action after his own demise. Instead, in January 1924, Vladimir Lenin died and Stalin made certain that the manuscript was not published in his lifetime. The government subsequently underwent purge after purge by Stalin, removing anyone who could or would contradict the new leader's view of the events.

Whereas his old mentor had wanted to conquer the world through Communist philosophy, in the years that followed, Joseph Stalin set about conquering the Soviet people. He dispossessed millions of their homes and starved millions more. He crushed resistance in the Soviet republics and at home with equal vigor. He also directed the rewriting of his people's history, sent many to imprisonment in Siberia, and assassinated even minor vassals for the sheer joy of the act. As a result, Stalin's, not Lenin's, Soviet Russia is still the model that other, lesser totalitarian regimes follow.

By all accounts, Stalin murdered more of his own people than Adolf Hitler to maintain his rule. If Lenin had lived, the Russian people would have been safe—and the world would have suffered as Lenin's revolution was brought to every shore. With Lenin as a long-term Soviet leader, the Soviet Union would have reordered the world. Leon Trotsky would have lived to bring the Communist revolution to Africa, South America, and the British Empire. The Soviet intelligence services would have succeeded in their programs to lure rich Russian expatriates home from France and Britain. The post–First World War American occupation of Germany would not have been enough to stem growing anti-Communist fears. Subsequently, Germany would have rapidly rearmed, with likely assistance from the West, sensing the greater Soviet threat. The now-aged Lenin, although reluctant to directly face imperial Japan at the same time, would have probably reinforced Communist resistance in China and Southeast Asia against the Japanese. World War II, therefore, could have seen a Nazi-Allied fight against Soviet Russia, and western China against eastern China and Japan. In such a hotly contested world, there would never have been a Cold War. There would only have been fire, destruction, and death.

# 45

# THE AMERICAN INVASION OF RUSSIA

## 1918

### By Bill Fawcett

Maybe the Russians aren't as
paranoid as they seem.

Throughout its history, the Soviet Union prepared for an invasion from the West. In the case of Nazi Germany, Stalin was correct, and it took millions of Soviet lives to drive off the Wehrmacht. Once that war ended, the Soviets and Stalin prepared just as hard for invasion by the United States and its allies. More than any other reason, this is why Russia occupied half of Europe at the end of WWII. Stalin wanted a buffer zone. This expectation was always why he worked constantly to build up the Soviet army and degrade those of the West. Based on what most have read in their high school history books, this seems paranoid. After all, the United States would never invade Russia. But the reality is that Communist Russia had good reason to be concerned. A reason based on history, not philosophy or paranoia. This is because, in 1918, the United States and its WWI allies did actually invade Russia—twice.

At the start of 1918, Russia was in the middle of a civil war. Those loyal to the czar, or just opposed to the Bolsheviks, were battling Lenin's Red Army for control of the country. Lenin and the Communist Party had already gained enough control to pull Russia out of the war. This had allowed the kaiser's Germany to move a massive number of troops from the Eastern Front to battle the Allies in France. The intent of the American and other invasions was to put pressure on the Communists or replace them, so that Russia would rejoin the war against Germany. To accomplish this, tens of thousands of Allied troops landed in northern and western Russia. American divisions from Michigan and San Francisco took part.

*Where* the Allies chose to invade the giant country was one of many mistakes made in what turned out to be a meaningless and confused operation. The two locations in Russia that tens of thousands of Allied troops occupied could not have been more distant from the fighting or the centers of Russian power. The locations alone guaranteed that the invading troops would be safe from attack, but also would be unable to significantly affect events elsewhere in Russia.

One landing was at Archangel and Murmansk, two ports near each other in the frigid Barents Sea. In 1918, they were barely connected to the rest of Russia. Neither northern city was of any strategic or tactical significance in the civil war. Having landed there, thousands of Allied soldiers just sat. Promises were made to the White Russian leaders, but never kept. The frozen tundra was patrolled, but few enemies were ever encountered.

The second invasion included a large force that had originally been National Guard units stationed around San Francisco. The Americans, and a much greater number of Japanese and other allies, landed in Vladivostok. Now, if Archangel was isolated and unimportant, it was at least within a few hundred miles of the Russian capitals of St. Petersburg and Moscow. Vladivostok was on the far side of Russia, on the tip of the Kamchatka Peninsula. It was at the far end of the Trans-Siberian Railroad and five thousand miles from Moscow. The soldiers who were stationed there were barely able to get news from the main fronts of the distant civil war.

So, the thirteen thousand American soldiers and forty thousand of their allies, having landed in Russia, were content to simply do nothing. The troops in Vladivostok were able to assist almost fifty thousand Czechs who had been stranded in Russia to eventually get home. Otherwise, they basically fought the occasional Cossack, small and rare Red Army patrols, and larger groups of bandits.

From the unofficial accounts, what they mostly fought was boredom and venereal disease.

Within months after the troops had landed, Germany surrendered and the war was over. The original purpose for the invasions was gone. Yet it was not until 1919 that the last of the American soldiers left Russia. The two expeditions succeeded in invading Russia and then accomplished nothing further. They saw so little combat that only 174 men were lost to all causes, mostly disease and the cold. By the time they left, the White Russian armies had been broken. What the invaders did leave behind was suspicion and the certainty that the United States and its allies were most willing to invade Russia. After all they already had.

The allied intervention and invasion accomplished nothing. The real question is just how to define this obvious strategic and tactical failure. The White Russians were fighting to establish a Western-style democracy. It seems likely that if the two beachheads in Archangel and Vladivostok had been used to bring in weapons, trucks, and ammunition, they might have won the civil war. Russia would have been ruled by an elected parliament or legislature and not the dictator Stalin. But those making the decisions hesitated while their potential allies fought unassisted. By the time the Western governments awoke to what a Communist Russia meant to them, it was too late. This is a mistake that some contend the Western democracies continue to make.

Then again, the mistake can easily be said to be staging the invasions at all. They accomplished nothing. There never was a real reason for either landing. Both expeditions were a waste of resources and men. If they had never happened, perhaps Soviet Russia would have been less paranoid—though in the case of Stalin, this seems dubious. The Russian people would not be so willing to see the West as a threat, an enemy willing even today to see this threat to attack and invade their nation. The fact that they are so willing shows the American invasion was one lesson of history that the Russians learned well.

# 46

||||||||||||||||||||||||||||||||||||||||||||||||||||||||||||||||||||||||||||

## AMERICA VOTES
## AGAINST BOOZE

### 1919

### By Mike Resnick

||||||||||||||||||||||||||||||||||||||||||||||||||||||||||||||||||||||||||||

The only constitutional amendment
ever repealed.

There was a lot of drinking going on in the first couple of decades of the twentieth century. And after all, why not? We had entered the industrial age, an age of mass-market production and distribution of most products—including liquor, wine, and beer.

But at the same time, there were a lot of people campaigning against "demon rum." There was Billy Sunday, who used his fame as a baseball player to enhance his career as an evangelist. There were Wayne Wheeler of the Anti-Saloon League and Carrie Nation and the large and powerful Women's Temperance Crusade and dozens of others.

At first, the campaign didn't have much effect. Woodrow Wilson and his opponent, Charles Evans Hughes, both ignored the issue in the 1916 presidential election, and neither the Democrats nor the Republicans addressed it, even in passing, in their platforms.

But they were merely shutting their eyes to the growing movement to ban all liquor. Indeed, by 1916, some twenty-three states had passed antisaloon legislation. Finally, even Wilson had to pay attention. In 1919, Congress passed the Eighteenth Amendment to the Constitution: the one banning liquor. It still had to win two-thirds of the states, but when the dust had cleared, forty-six states—all of them except Connecticut and Rhode Island—had voted for the amendment, and the United States officially became a dry country on January 17, 1920.

The immediate results could have been predicted by any science-fiction writer.

First, consumption of alcohol went *up*, not down. (After all, the Eighteenth Amendment prohibited the manufacture, distribution, and sale of alcoholic beverages—but *not* the possession or drinking of them.)

Second, Canada's liquor manufacturers more than doubled their production and profits.

Third, more than a few people died from the effects of what we now call bathtub gin.

Fourth, the Mafia multiplied its clout and power tenfold, and not just in its headquarters in New York. Al Capone alone made more than $60 million annually, and criminals like Bugs Moran, Machine Gun Kelly, and Lucky Luciano became household names (and, to a certain impressionable element, heroes).

They had a lucrative, blood-soaked run of it. Then, on December 5, 1933, during the first year of Franklin Delano Roosevelt's first term, Congress passed the Twenty-first Amendment to the Constitution, the only one that negated a prior amendment.

The immediate result? The sale and consumption of alcohol was here to stay, the term *speakeasy* became a part of the American language, and major brewing companies returned to the United States, never to leave again.

Of course, there was another result. The Mafia wrapped its tentacles around dozens of other businesses, some legitimate, some borderline, most illegal (especially prostitution and gambling), and it gave up none of the power it had accumulated during Prohibition.

It's all there in the history books in black and white, and in the Hollywood films of the 1930s that glamorized both sides, the criminals and the lawmen. And a guess is that, even today, most people know a lot more about Al Capone than they know about Eliot Ness.

But what if Billy Sunday and Carrie Nation and their ilk had been a little less effective spreading the word, and Prohibition had gone down to defeat?

The most important single change would not be the absence of the Mafia, but a huge diminution of their power. The country was turning against booze just as the Mafia, composed mostly of Italian immigrants, was coalescing, and the liquor business was wide-open territory for a well-managed gang. But this doesn't mean there weren't Jewish and Irish and every other kind of gang, and they all knew how to protect their territory. In fact, America wouldn't see such organized violence until the drug wars of the mid-twentieth century and beyond.

Certain Hollywood actors who specialized in criminal types would have had a harder time making the kind of living they were able to make. Imports like Peter Lorre, Conrad Veidt, and others would have fared all right once the studios became aware of the Third Reich, but homegrown gangster types like James Cagney and Humphrey Bogart would have fared far less well.

Nothing would have prevented the stock-market crash of 1929, but the records show an enormous boost in illegal alcohol consumption from 1929 through 1933, and it would have helped the economy had the tax on all those hundreds of millions of bottles gone to the government.

The defeat of the Eighteenth Amendment would even have affected popular literature. Thorne Smith, a humorous fantasist (or perhaps a fantastic humorist), wrote nine bestsellers. Can anyone imagine a Thorne Smith book in which damn near every character *doesn't* drink booze to the exclusion of almost everything else, and act exactly the way you'd expect them to act after consuming all that booze?

By 1940, accountants had doped out exactly how much Prohibition had cost the government. In a much smaller, less vigorous economy than today's, the government lost $11 billion in tax revenues, and another half billion futilely trying to enforce the damned thing.

So . . . we'd have had a far better economy, the Mafia and other criminal classes would have grown far more slowly, and popular entertainment would not have made heroes out of villains. And one more thing: More than a million jobs would have been saved, which would have been very useful during the first four years of the Depression.

What jobs? I hear you ask.

Anyone who worked for a brewery, for starters. Or a saloon. Or a distillery. And let's not forget barrel makers, and waiters, and truckers, and truck manufacturers, and the fact that there was no such thing as Social Security, and . . . well, you get the picture. Compared to what actually transpired, that picture gets nicer and nicer the more you look at it.

‖‖‖‖‖‖‖‖‖‖‖‖‖‖‖‖‖‖‖‖‖‖‖‖‖‖‖‖‖‖‖‖‖‖‖‖‖‖‖‖‖‖‖‖‖‖‖‖‖‖‖‖‖‖‖‖‖‖

# 47

# STALIN'S RISE
# TO POWER

### 1920

### By Eric Flint

‖‖‖‖‖‖‖‖‖‖‖‖‖‖‖‖‖‖‖‖‖‖‖‖‖‖‖‖‖‖‖‖‖‖‖‖‖‖‖‖‖‖‖‖‖‖‖‖‖‖‖‖‖‖‖‖‖‖

Let's be glad he was born in Russia
and not here in the USA.

Stalin's rise to power in the Soviet Union was the product of many factors, some of them deeply rooted in the historical dynamics at work in the USSR in the 1920s, and some of them the product of his own political skills combined with his ruthless drive for dominance.

But two of the factors were contingent and completely outside his control—and if either of those factors had been different, Stalin would never have risen to the position he held and would not have unleashed the disasters he was responsible for.

The first of these two factors is simple and straightforward. Lenin died prematurely of a stroke at the age of fifty-three. By way of comparison, other world leaders of that era lived to the following ages:

Stalin, 74

Kerensky, 89

Roosevelt, 63

Churchill, 90

Poincaré, 74

Clemenceau, 88

Pétain, 95

Chiang Kai-shek, 87

Even Hitler, Mussolini, and Tojo outlived Lenin, despite all dying violent deaths—Hitler at the age of fifty-six, Mussolini at sixty-one, and Tojo at sixty-three.

What would have happened if Lenin had lived even as comparatively short a life span as Franklin Roosevelt? What would he have done or not done in that additional decade of life that might have thwarted Stalin?

The first thing to understand about Stalin is that, until the death of Yakob Sverdlov, whom we will discuss later, Stalin's position in the Bolshevik Party was not especially prominent. Unlike such leaders as Lenin himself, Trotsky, Bukharin, and Zinoviev, Stalin was not considered a theoretician—always prestigious in the socialist movement. He did write a book on the national question, but it was widely known that Lenin had worked closely with him on the project and was primarily responsible for its content.

Unlike Trotsky, Stalin had not played an overtly public role in either the 1905 Revolution or the October Revolution of 1917. Unlike Zinoviev, he was not viewed as an expert on foreign affairs. Unlike both Trotsky and Zinoviev, he was not a noted orator. His real claims to fame were as a modest contributor to the Bolshevik stance on the national question and as a capable organizer.

It was only with the death of Sverdlov (officially claimed to have been from influenza) in 1919 that Stalin's rise to power began. Sverdlov had been the recognized (albeit informal) organizer of the Bolsheviks. He was the man everyone, including Lenin, went to in order to get something done. Sverdlov, like Stalin, was neither a theoretician nor an orator. He was the consummate "inside man"— and, in that capacity, even more skilled and talented than Stalin, but with none of Stalin's overweening ambition.

And that was the second contingent factor—Sverdlov's death. He was only thirty-three years old. It was the death of Sverdlov that opened the way for Stalin to succeed him as the Bolshevik Party's central organizer. (The official title of the post changed over time until becoming that of "general secretary" when Stalin assumed the position. While Sverdlov was alive, he was known as "the chairman of the secretariat.")

Without Sverdlov's death, Stalin would have remained in relative obscurity. And without Lenin's series of incapacitating strokes that began in May of 1922—he had just turned fifty-two years old—and ended with his death in January of 1924, Stalin could never have transformed the position of general secretary from its initially administrative nature to the hub of power in the USSR.

What would the Soviet Union—indeed, the world—have looked like, had Stalin never come to power? It is impossible to know for certain, of course, but some broad outcomes seem fairly well assured:

First, while the USSR's political regime would have remained autocratic to some degree or another, it never would have descended into the bloodthirsty madness of Stalin's great purges. For this there are two reasons, one of which was personal and the other of what might be called an institutional nature.

The personal difference was simple. While Lenin was quite capable of being ruthless, as he demonstrated during the course of the Russian Civil War, which followed the October Revolution, he was not given to ruthlessness for its own sake. Nor was he, personally, autocratic.

Lenin is often referred to by historians as a dictator, but the term is flimsy at best when applied to him. It's really more of a cussword than a descriptive term. Throughout his time in power, he always abided by decisions made according to majority vote by the Politburo and the Central Committee. That was true even when he strongly disagreed with those decisions—as he did, for instance, over the issue of the Brest-Litovsk Treaty.

Perhaps even more indicative of Lenin's temperament is the nature of his writings after he came to power. Some of those writings consist of public speeches and a few consist of theoretical tracts. Most of them, however, contain polemics. As he had done throughout his life, Lenin argued constantly, not only with his opponents, but often with his own followers and allies.

Dictators do not write polemics. They dictate—and they imprison or execute their opponents. They do not *argue.*

But Lenin argued constantly, during his time in power as much as he had in coming to power. He argued with Trotsky and Bukharin over the so-called trade union question, for instance. After the revolution, Trotsky and Bukharin came to the conclusion that, since Russia was now a workers' state and the government had nationalized all major industry, the working class no longer needed independent trade unions. Lenin disagreed, arguing that Trotsky and Bukharin's logic was schematic and failed to account for concrete realities. Specifically, he argued that the Soviet workers' state was seriously distorted, both by Russia's social and economic backwardness, as well as by the devastation caused by World War I and the civil war. That meant that, as puzzling as the notion might be to logicians, the Russian working class did indeed still need institutions to defend themselves against their own state, since that state often behaved bureaucratically and dictatorially.

Incidentally, this is another indicator of the sharp personal difference between Lenin and Stalin. Of all the major Bolshevik leaders, Lenin was the one who was most acutely sensitive to abuses committed by the regime against workers and the one who most strenuously attempted to place checks on those abuses. The last two major campaigns of his life were to create a "Workers' and Peasants' Inspection"—essentially, a general ombudsman with some teeth—and to have Stalin removed from his post because Lenin had become convinced Stalin had the wrong temperament for the job of general secretary.

But the personal difference between Lenin and Stalin was not as important as the institutional one. Stalin's almost maniacal bloodthirstiness stemmed only in part from his personality. It also stemmed from the fact that, given his modest position within the Communist Party—and it was still modest even after he became general secretary—he could only have risen to power by destroying the Bolshevik core of the party. So long as the men who had formed and shaped the Bolshevik Party, and led both the 1905 and 1917 revolutions, remained in positions of power and authority after Lenin's death, Stalin's rise to power would be stymied, stultified even, if not completely prevented.

Everything Stalin did, from his accession to the position of general secretary until the conclusion of the Great Purges and his final consolidation of power in the mid-1930s, was driven by that factional imperative. He would change alliances overnight, shift and even completely transform his political opinions—whatever he needed to do in order to increase his power at any given stage of the factional struggle.

He blocked with Zinoviev and Kamenev in the mid-1920s against Trotsky; then, when Zinoviev and Kamenev became dismayed at the resulting developments and formed the United Opposition with Trotsky, Stalin allied with Bukharin against them. He adopted Bukharin's extension of Lenin's New Economic Policy, not from any theoretical conviction, but simply as a matter of factional convenience. And when factional convenience later led him to attack Bukharin, he did so by flipping his position around and advocating the extreme Ultra-Left policies known as the "Third Period." (More on that in a moment.)

All of this culminated, first, in driving Trotsky into exile; and then, a few years later, in the Great Purges, during the course of which Zinoviev, Kamenev, and Bukharin were executed.

The point being that, even if Lenin had been personally inclined toward factional ruthlessness, there would have been no need for him to behave the way Stalin did. Unlike Stalin, Lenin did not have to "rise" to power. *He was already there*—and would have remained there, so long as he was not incapacitated. Stalin was certainly a capable factionalist. But, as he had proved many times over the years, *nobody* was Lenin's equal in faction fighting, when he chose to do it. Had Stalin ever tried to challenge him, he would have been crushed. Even as it was, with Lenin incapacitated by strokes and almost completely isolated, he was able to mount a significant campaign to oust Stalin. Had he been healthy, he would easily have succeeded.

Stalin's subordination of everything to his factional needs had disastrous consequences both in the USSR and in the world.

In the USSR, it was the factional logic of what Stalin called the Third Period—which was essentially a meaningless label that he assigned to his Ultra-Left factional tactics in order to give them some "theoretical" heft—that led to the forced collectivization of agriculture and the headlong industrialization of the Soviet Union beginning in the late 1920s.

Leaving aside the horrendous number of casualties they caused, these policies were disastrous for the USSR in the long term. Stalin did succeed in bringing mass industrialization to Russia, but that could have been accomplished by other means, which we will discuss in a moment. But he did so only by crippling Soviet agriculture, from which Russia has still not recovered to this day.

And none of this was necessary. The policy Lenin advocated after the civil war, the so-called New Economic Policy, is similar to the policy that the Chinese Communist Party has followed for the past third of a century, since Deng Xiaoping took control in China. And it has proven enormously successful in carrying out everything Stalin claimed for his policies, with very little of the accompanying internal governmental chaos or loss of momentum.

Lenin's *New Economic Policy* is an umbrella term. There are many possible variations on the theme, one of which was Bukharin's policies—which are actually closer to what the Chinese have done than what Lenin himself initially proposed. The essential elements of the policy are:

Political power remains monopolized by the Communist Party. (Lenin proposed various checks and balances to restrain bureaucratic excesses and corruption. The Chinese leadership pays lip service to similar goals but, at least so far, has not shown much inclination to pursue them.)

The state retains ownership and/or control of what Lenin often called the "commanding heights" of the economy, leaving aside room for the peasantry to cultivate their own land and pay taxes from their earnings. Especially critical is control of banking and finance. The purpose is to allow capitalism a lot of room to function, but to keep it on an economic, as well as financial, leash.

Foreign corporations are allowed to invest, but under some restrictions. The same is done with domestic investment, leaving only domestic concerns to control heavy industry, transport, and foreign trade. And the population, as a whole, is given wide latitude in terms of what is usually called free enterprise.

Such a system is not, contrary to what a lot of people think, a "restoration of capitalism." It constitutes a mixed economy, true, in much the same way that the economies of many European countries can be called mixed (i.e., part capitalist, part socialist). But it's a mixed economy in which, unlike in Western Europe, it is the socialist and not capitalist elements that are politically predominant.

There are any number of problems with such a system, of which corruption is perhaps the most obvious. But whatever its failings, it is vastly superior to the destruction and sheer savagery that went along with Stalin's methods.

But Stalin's Third Period factionalism caused a disaster that was even worse than what was done to the Soviet Union itself. Because Stalin extended those Ultra-Left policies across the entire world, forcing them onto foreign Communist parties in his relentless determination to destroy any source of strength in his domestic opponents. (Who were, initially, far more highly regarded outside of Russia than Stalin himself—indeed, in the beginning, Stalin was almost a complete nonentity to foreign Communists.)

The result in Germany was a catastrophe. During the crucial years of Hitler's rise to power in the late 1920s and early 1930s, Stalin paralyzed the German working-class movement—which was immensely powerful at the time—by insisting that the real enemy of the German Communists were the so-called social-fascists, that is to say, the German Social Democratic Party. Hitler was given the luxury of an almost unimpeded consolidation of the Nazis' political position because Stalin ignored the fascist threat in favor of continually attacking the Social Democrats. He made a united front of the working class and all progressive forces in Germany impossible.

It was as if, to use an American football analogy, a member of one team tackled another who was in position to block the opponent's ball carrier . . . allowing the ball carrier to saunter almost unopposed across the goal line.

At no time, ever, until he came to power and used the state

apparatus to crush all opposition, did Hitler and the Nazis have the support of the majority of the German population. Even as late as the elections of November 1932, after years of Stalinist factionalism—driven entirely by Stalin's domestic concerns, not the needs of the German people—had demoralized many people on the left, the two great parties of the left in Germany still got more votes than the Nazis.

True, the Nazis were the single largest party, having gotten 33 percent of the vote. But between them, the Social Democrats (20 percent) and the Communists (16 percent) still outvoted them. Had they formed a united front against the Nazis, even at that late stage of the game, they could probably have forestalled the coming coup d'état.

But it was not to be. Stalin pursued his disastrous policies until Hitler's consolidation of power and the growing fascist menace—coupled with his own now-complete victory over his domestic opponents—led Stalin to carry out another of his many volte-faces. He jettisoned his Third Period policies and announced the adoption of the policy of "Popular Front," wherein all progressive forces and parties were to unite against the fascists.

As the old saying goes, he was a day late and a dollar short. And, in June of 1941, the Soviet Union would pay another horrendous price for Stalin's rise to power when the Wehrmacht launched Operation Barbarossa.

If Lenin lives to a normal age . . . if Sverdlov does not die of influenza at the age of thirty-three . . .

Two of history's "great ifs."

What would have happened instead? Most likely the following:

Whether under Lenin or, if he still dies at the age of fifty-three but Sverdlov survives, some collective body of leadership—most likely Zinoviev, Kamenev, and Bukharin, with Trotsky on the outs but not driven into exile or murdered—implements one or another variety of the New Economic Policy. The USSR experiences the sort of growth experienced in post-Mao China.

Foreign relations with Western Europe and America remain tense and unfriendly, for the most part. But those antagonisms never rise to the level of the Cold War.

Hitler does not come to power in Germany. World War II never happens—not, at least, in the form of an all-encompassing global war. No doubt a number of smaller wars would have erupted, of course. For one thing, Japan would almost certainly still have invaded China.

The Holocaust would not have happened. Israel would probably not have come into existence, and certainly not in 1948.

A very alternate history, indeed. If only two men—or either one of the two—had not died prematurely.

# 48

||||||||||||||||||||||||||||||||||||||||||||||||||||||||||||||||||||||||||

## THE FÜHRER
## SELLS A PAINTING

1920

**By Mike Resnick**

||||||||||||||||||||||||||||||||||||||||||||||||||||||||||||||||||||||||||

Just a little more talent . . .

Adolf Hitler was considered a brilliant student and a wildly popular class leader when he was in primary school in Braunau, Austria, the town where he was born. Secondary school was a little harder. In fact, at fifteen, he flunked his exams and was told that he'd have to repeat the year. His response was to quit school.

His greatest interest at that point in his life was painting, and after his father's death in 1903, he drifted down to Vienna, hoping to be discovered. Didn't happen. So he figured he'd go to the Vienna Academy of Art, find out what few things his enormous talent was lacking, and fix them. That didn't happen either. He flunked the entrance exams.

So okay, he decided, maybe the world wasn't ready for the next da Vinci or Michelangelo. He'd take his talent and go into architecture instead. He applied to the Vienna School of Architecture, and (you guessed it) he was turned down.

As it turned out, he was a lot better at destroying than creating.

You know the rest. He became enamored of the anti-Semitic Christian Social Party and joined it. He fought in World War I, ran dispatches for superiors, rose one rank to corporal, got mustard-gassed, and survived, a very bitter young man.

In 1919, Hitler joined the German Workers' Party and learned how to manipulate crowds while making dozens of speeches condemning the Treaty of Versailles. Within a couple of years, he was speaking to crowds of fifty thousand or more, he'd helped rename the party the National Socialist German Workers' Party (which the world came to know as the Nazi Party), and, in 1923, he staged the Beer Hall Putsch. It didn't work; he was jailed (with an exceptionally, almost ludicrously, light sentence for the charge of treason), and while in jail he wrote *Mein Kampf,* which told a mostly unbelieving world exactly what he planned to do when he got out.

And the rest is history. He took over the government in 1933, remilitarized the Rhineland in 1936, signed a nonaggression pact with Russia in 1939 (which he broke in 1941, when he invaded that country), began creating and filling concentration camps, which killed literally millions, tried to exterminate the Jews, conquered Poland and France, began bombing England, and declared war on the United States of America.

By 1944, the Allies had the Nazi army in trouble and, in 1945, with an absolutely certain defeat on the horizon, Hitler committed suicide.

When the dust had cleared, he was responsible for more than twelve million deaths (and that total includes his own soldiers, because Hitler was not inclined to listen to his generals when they spoke to him of the Russian winter or other hazards to his army). There is no question that he has gone down as, and will remain, the greatest villain of the twentieth century—worse than all the competition, including Stalin, including Pol Pot, including all of them.

So of course, as one looks back over Hitler's life, the question presents itself: At what turning point might he have gone a different direction? At what point in time might something have occurred that could have saved most of those twelve million lives?

And the answer is obvious, because Hitler remained a hobby painter throughout his life. In fact, a watercolor he did of Munich Hall sold for $161,000 as recently as 2014; another watercolor, this one of a flower, had a minimum bid of $30,000 and was auctioned off after this article was written.

All right, a lot of those prices were caused by who he was and not how the paintings looked, but there is nonetheless some basic talent on display in them. Had the Vienna Academy of Art not rejected him but allowed him to study there for four years, there's every chance he would have chosen a totally different career, either as an artist or in one of many related fields.

Let's say that he sold a painting, not for the kind of money they bring today, but enough to encourage him to think that he might actually be able to make a living at it.

How might that have affected history?

Well, if he was studying books on the creation of art rather than tracts on anti-Semitism, there's every likelihood that he would have become, at worst, a follower of the German Workers' Party and later the Nazi Party. Even had he wished to be more active, he would—in this future—be without the background of giving speeches to larger and larger crowds, and learning how to manipulate them.

Would there still be anti-Semitism in Germany?

Of course. The Nazis didn't invent it; they merely *used* it to unite the people against what Hitler had them believing was a common enemy (before he created a world full of common enemies). They wouldn't have been any better loved by the German people—after all, there's still anti-Semitism in Europe and, indeed, all over the world today—but six million more Jews would have been around in 1946.

The Russian pact? There was probably a need for it, since popular German thought was that Stalin wasn't any more inclined toward peace or respecting borders than Hitler was; but without Hitler trying to run an army based on his incredibly limited corporal's knowledge, the German generals would have convinced whoever was in charge to honor the treaty and never to invade Russia by land until winters were a thing of the past.

As for declaring war on the United States, it was a blunder above all others. We were already at war on the other side of the world after Pearl Harbor was bombed. There was every reason to assume we'd leave any European wars to the Europeans, given how Congress, until then, had defeated or ignored every attempt by the Roosevelt administration to enter the European war. And the outcome of World War II ceased to be in doubt the day the Americans entered the war. Most rulers and generals would have been once burned, twice shy.

So the young Hitler sells a painting and . . .

- He stays out of politics.
- He never writes *Mein Kampf*. He may paint the equivalent, but it will have an effect on a *far* smaller audience, possibly as few as half a dozen.
- Germany does not attempt to exterminate all the Jews.
- The term *concentration camp* never becomes synonymous with German death camps.
- Germany does not invade Russia.
- The United States does not enter the European conflict, and probably defeats Japan a year sooner because of that.

So . . . you think the best way to stop the Führer is by assassinating him?

Forget it. Been tried by his own generals and his own citizenry. Didn't work.

You *really* want to stop him?

Go back a little more than a century and buy his first few paintings. That'll do the trick.

||||||||||||||||||||||||||||||||||||||||||||||||||||||||||||||||||||||||

# 49

# STALIN'S BIG MISTAKE

## 1921

### By Bill Fawcett

||||||||||||||||||||||||||||||||||||||||||||||||||||||||||||||||||||||||

A mutual-destruction pact.

Despite what his own propaganda and, recently, some Russian revisionists have said, Joseph Stalin made a lot of mistakes. His greatest mistake was not Lysenkoism, which destroyed Soviet science and agriculture. It wasn't ignoring his own intelligence service's warning that Hitler was about to attack in 1941. Nor was it panicking and hiding when the Nazis did attack, though his mental collapse at that time cost hundreds of thousands of soldiers their lives. The Russian dictator Joseph Stalin's greatest mistake was a deal he made with Germany—long before the Nazis even took control.

The Treaty of Versailles was forced upon a defeated Germany after WWI. Many of the provisions in the treaty were designed to prevent any resurgence of the German army. Among the things explicitly forbidden to Germany were doing any tactical training, developing new doctrines, researching new weapon systems, and training in modern aircraft and tanks. Their officer corps and the entire army were limited to a size that was much smaller than those of any of their neighbors. Other treaty terms, particularly the economic ones, were also designed to keep Germany poor and unprepared for war. The resentment of this treaty by the German people and their elected government (which was closely tied to what remained of their army) was intense, and the German government made every effort to get around the restrictions. They found a strange ally, who proved vital in the revival of the Reichswehr.

Stalin's Soviet Union had its own problems. In 1918 and 1919, parts of Russia were still controlled by the White Russian armies. His military technology was primitive, compared to that of the rest of Europe, and his officers were experienced only in fighting equally badly armed and trained Russians. The dictator had long coveted the skill and technology of the German army. When a neutral observer, Enver Pasha, suggested that Germany and Russia share information on the Polish army and defenses, it opened a door. A joint committee was formed in 1921 to identify other ways they could cooperate and it found many. Under the cover of offices whose purpose was purportedly to help repatriate Russian and German POWs from WWI, the two nations began to cooperate on a number of levels. In 1922, the Rapallo Treaty was signed. The key element of this agreement concerned the cooperation between the two armies.

The German army needed two things: military equipment that was forbidden to them by the Versailles Treaty and a place to train and rebuild their army in secret. They also needed the raw materials of war: oil, steel, minerals, and chemicals. The Soviet army needed German technology, weapons designs, and the much superior German machine tools. Both armies quickly saw the benefits of cooperation. The Germans got all they needed: military bases suitable for training officers and men, air bases, and large areas in which to develop their armored doctrines and even experiment with chemical weapons. Both sides agreed to exchange the ideas and techniques as they developed. This arrangement allowed the Reichswehr not only to accomplish its goals, but to do so in near-complete secrecy. Great efforts were made to disguise what officers and men were going east to train for on Russian-built armored vehicles and airplanes. Some German technology was transferred to Russia, but much was withheld. Germany developed everything from tanks and aircraft to better artillery and machine guns in Russia, though trust between the two nations was never complete. As much as the Soviet officers admired the German armored fighting vehicles, the panzers, they never mentioned they were developing, and then beginning to build, their own less sophisticated (but far hardier) T-34 tanks.

The first time anyone in the rest of Europe learned about this cooperation was in 1925, when the liberal German government announced it. But details were lacking and the Allies did not press the issue. By 1926, the Germans had their own panzer training school at Kama in Kazan, and by 1924, they had established their own air base at Lipetsk. Such officers as Guderian, Model, and Thoma were trained to command a modern, armored German army on bases in Russia. Such close cooperation continued into the early 1930s, but faded quickly after Adolf Hitler became reich chancellor. There is no question that the German Army benefited much more greatly than did the Russian. Worse for Russia was that the many well-trained officers who had studied in Germany were considered later to be politically unreliable and most died in Stalin's 1938 officers' purge, simply because they had trained there.

Stalin literally allowed the revival and development of the Wehrmacht. He did this, and then squandered most of what the Red Army gained from that cooperation. There were doubters. Neither side ever trusted the other. Both were right not to. Had Joseph Stalin listened to those who remembered fighting the Germans in WWI, and not agreed to the joint cooperation or signed the Rapallo Treaty, there might never have been a WWII. The Reichswehr would never have been able to develop the panzer corps within Germany. There would have been no Luftwaffe, because the hundreds of pilots trained on the Lipetsk field would not have been ready to step into Willy Messerschmitt's new designs. Germany would have remained starved for raw materials as well, which would have further slowed its return to militarism. Stalin, to gain some technology and training for men he later killed, allowed the recovery of the German army that the Treaty of Versailles tried to prevent. Had he not done so, there would have been no Blitzkrieg, no London Blitz, no German army to threaten Austria and then Czechoslovakia. More directly, in 1941, the Wehrmacht would have been in no position to invade Russia. Without the war, communism would have been limited to industrially and economically back-ward Russia and never have become the world-threatening power that the looting of Eastern Europe allowed it to become. No World War II, probably no Hitler as Führer, and at least twenty million lives saved, if Stalin had not helped train the army of his nation's traditional and worst enemy.

# 50

||||||||||||||||||||||||||||||||||||||||||||||||||||||||||||||||||||||

# RETAINING
# J. EDGAR HOOVER

### 1924

### By Jim Werbaneth

||||||||||||||||||||||||||||||||||||||||||||||||||||||||||||||||||||||

> There is something addictive
> about a secret.
>
> —J. EDGAR HOOVER

John Edgar Hoover was one of the most enduring and power-ful unelected officials in American history—perhaps *the* most powerful. That he was permitted to remain in office for forty-eight years, amassing power for himself as well as for his agency, amounts to one of the worst long-term mistakes of modern times. It was the fault of every president under whom he served, all of whom kept him in office due to various combinations of respect and fear.

Hoover was appointed to head the relatively obscure Bureau of Investigation by Calvin Coolidge on May 10, 1924, at the age of twen-ty-nine. He would remain in this post until 1935, when Franklin D. Roosevelt named him to the newly upgraded and renamed Federal Bureau of Investigation. Little could either president have realized that Hoover would remain in office until his death on May 2, 1972.

Hoover's goal was to build a fundamentally professional and highly skilled law enforcement agency, employing the most mod-ern technical methods. Moreover, he saw his people as one of the FBI's greatest assets, demanding high standards of competence and behavior. Yet there was a dark side to this, as his idea of an ideal agent was white, male, and college-educated. There was little place for women or minorities in Hoover's FBI, except perhaps as clerks for the former, and household servants (for African-Americans, at least) for the latter. In addition, while Hoover could be fulsome in his praise of local law enforcement, thus building alliances, he could be arbitrary and vindictive with his own agents, sometimes acting out of jealousy.

A prime example of the latter is that of Melvin Purvis, the special agent in charge of the Chicago office, and a man who achieved the Bureau's ideal of a gangbuster. Specifically, Purvis orchestrated the killing of John Dillinger in July 1934. However, Hoover felt threatened by the positive publicity that this act earned Purvis, as there was only room for one hero in the FBI—Hoover himself. The next year, he forced Purvis out of the Bureau; subsequently, Purvis practiced law until his death by apparent suicide in 1960.

Other agents suffered from the director's whims. Hoover had a tendency to transfer agents, under the guise of giving them additional experience. However, he did so with little or no regard for the hardships of these frequent moves, for the agents or their families.

One could view Hoover as simply a bad boss, and he certainly could be one.

There were aspects of Hoover's life that made him vulnerable to blackmail, or at least coercion. Most prominently, there have been consistent stories that the lifelong bachelor was gay, and had a long-term relationship with the Bureau's assistant director, Clyde Tolson. Holding power during a time when homosexuality was socially unacceptable at the least and criminal at worst, he was certainly more exposed to compromise than any of the family-oriented agents he liked to hire. Indeed, blackmailing closeted public figures was a favored tactic of the Mafia in New York; as America's top law enforcement official, Hoover certainly would have been an attractive target for extortion.

Whether or not he was blackmailed, Hoover stubbornly refused to direct the Bureau against organized crime for much of his time in office. He preferred to pursue outlaws like Dillinger, and subversives, such as the American Communist Party. Yet he would not even recognize the existence of La Cosa Nostra, and whatever attention he paid to urban organized crime was sporadic.

Hoover's inattention to the Mafia changed on November 14,

1957, when police raided a meeting of the highest-level mobsters from across America in the upstate New York town of Apalachin. This was uncovered, not by the FBI, but by an inquisitive state trooper doing basic police work. The arrest of more than sixty leading mafiosi was evidence of the mob's existence that even Hoover could not ignore.

In the years after Apalachin, Hoover became, if anything, more abusive of his powers. The FBI engaged in a long series of illegal wiretaps and "black-bag" burglaries, and not just against its new enemies in organized crime. In the sixties, Hoover sent the FBI after a new generation of domestic enemies, especially Martin Luther King Jr. In what may have been the Bureau's most insane abuse, Hoover tried to use audiotapes of King cheating on his wife in order to drive him to suicide. In addition, he undertrook an extended effort to ruin perceived enemies—the sixties-era Counterintelligence Program, or COINTELPRO. Here, those black-bag jobs and wiretaps flourished, usually extra-legally. Unlike MLK, many of the targets really were subversives and domestic terrorists, including the Weather Underground and the Black Panther Party.

Hoover was a methodical cataloger of the private lives of those whom he considered targets, such as MLK, and soon many members of Congress and Cabinet officials. Much of his effort to build political and popular protection involved managing image and publicity. Hoover influenced the portrayal of the FBI in the movies and on television, and also collected compromising information on those who could help or hurt the Bureau and its director. Even if he did not engage in direct extortion, potential victims' knowledge that Hoover possessed such information about them could be enough to protect him and the Bureau.

Keeping Hoover in office was an epic mistake made by every president from Coolidge to Nixon. Perhaps Silent Cal and his successor, Herbert Hoover, could be excused for not recognizing how manipulative, power-hungry, and ruthless Hoover was. The same could not be said for later chief executives. Then again, it would not have been easy to remove someone who so successfully cultivated an image of America's top cop, the head of a highly professional and incorruptible agency. It would have been even harder if the president had reason to believe that Hoover had evidence of embarrassing behavior. John F. Kennedy, for example, was a serial philanderer; public knowledge of his extramarital adventures would have undercut his image as a good Catholic family man, and of his White House as a latter-day Camelot. For his part, Lyndon Johnson was not always known for his own commitment to monogamy.

This is the core of the mistake: Hoover became bigger than his bosses. Presidents might come and go, but J. Edgar Hoover stayed, filling his file cases with the secrets, sexual and otherwise, of the powerful.

American history would have been much different had he been cashiered rather than allowed to die in office after almost five decades. To start with, presidents from at least Franklin Roosevelt to Richard Nixon would have been in positions to demand more accountability, as a chief executive should, from the FBI. Secondly, a Hoover-less FBI would almost certainly have demonstrated more respect for privacy and civil liberties. Had FBI directors been nominated and retained for specific terms, as they are now, there would have been no time or opportunity for them to build the kind of power base that Hoover had.

Specific investigations probably would have gone differently, and with more effectiveness, too. For one thing, the Mafia surely would have had a lot more reason to fear the FBI in the forties and fifties. There is no reason why the Bureau could not have gone after the Lucianos, Lanskys, and Gambinos of America as well as the Dillingers. Hoover might have had some excuse for not investigating La Cosa Nostra in the twenties, when the Bureau of Investigation was a fairly minor and weak agency, but when it became a premier law enforcement agency, the excuses should have vanished. The "Mafia? What Mafia?" approach was one of choice, not necessity.

There is one Mafia line of business that the FBI could have interdicted under a different leader: labor racketeering. With the end of Prohibition, organized crime looked to the labor movement for new revenue. The FBI was seriously inattentive to organized crime as it extended its power into organized labor. While men such as Jimmy Hoffa, Frank Fitzsimmons, and Anthony "Tony Pro" Provenzano, all Teamsters, were brought down by federal prosecution, the FBI did not interfere sufficiently with the Mafia's infiltration of the nation's biggest unions.

Plus, when the United States was faced by real domestic terrorism in the late sixties and early seventies, the FBI fell short, this time because of excessive zeal. COINTELPRO accumulated good intelligence, but unfortunately not enough of it could actually be used in court. Therefore, really dangerous characters were able to walk free, maybe most importantly the Weather Underground's married founders, Bill Ayers and Bernardine Dohrn. Rather than spending the rest of their lives in federal prison, these self-confessed serial bombers became college professors. Ultimately, COINTELPRO did not bring Ayers and Dohrn to justice so much as protect them by neutralizing the cases against them.

An America in which Hoover was removed after a decade at the top would have been a much better place. FBI effectiveness would have been increased by an earlier commitment to diversity. With the FBI stronger and getting an earlier start on investigations, it is highly possible that the Mafia would have been weakened sooner. Impeding the entry of criminal elements into the labor movement would have made unions cleaner and more accountable to their members. Perhaps, too, the Las Vegas hotel industry would not have been taken over by mob entrepreneurs funded with Teamsters Union retirement money.

Ultimately, J. Edgar Hoover did some good, leading the Bureau of Investigation into a new, stronger, professional agency. But he stayed far too long, and presidents lost control of the Bureau; indeed, it could be argued that the Bureau lost control of itself. If Hoover would not remove himself from his position, the president should have removed him. Yet none had the fortitude to do so.

|||||||||||||||||||||||||||||||||||||||||||||||||||||||||||||||||||||||||||||

# 51

# MY FAVORITE MISTAKE

### 1930

### By Bill Fawcett

|||||||||||||||||||||||||||||||||||||||||||||||||||||||||||||||||||||||||||||

Best when they are still warm.

In 1930, the owner of the Toll House Inn, a high-quality boardinghouse in Whitman, Massachusetts, had a problem. The inn always provided cookies as a snack for their guests. The owner and baker, Ruth Wakefield, had made sugar cookies several times that week and planned on a change. She hoped to make cocoa-flavored sugar cookies, which were always popular. But there was a problem. She was out of cocoa powder. Like most bakers, though, Ms. Wakefield was skilled at improvising with her recipes, and she did have some Nestlé chocolate bars on hand.

As she later explained, chocolate melted easily, and so if she broke up the bars and mixed them in the dough, she would have her chocolate sugar cookies. As it turned out, when the cookies came out of the oven, the chocolate had not fully melted. What she had were sugar cookies with small chunks of chocolate spread through them . . . and they were an instant hit. By mistake, she had invented the chocolate chip cookie.

The Toll House recipes were popular, and word quickly spread about this new and delicious cookie. Nestlé's sales in New England jumped as more and more bakers served chocolate chip cookies. When the company realized why their chocolate was suddenly so much more popular, they approached Ruth Wakefield about putting her Toll House chocolate chip recipe on every bag of their chocolate chips.

Now comes the reason why this is my favorite mistake ever. Ms. Wakefield agreed that the company could use her recipe, which, to this day, is still on every bag of Nestlé's chocolate chips. What, you may ask, was her price? It was ALL THE CHOCOLATE SHE WANTED FOR THE REST OF HER LIFE.

How did this mistake change the world? How many extra pounds have we added because of Ruth Wakefield's mistake? Aren't we glad it happened? Yumm.

# 52

# THE DUST BOWL

## 1930

### By Bill Fawcett

*Long-term planning, well, not really . . .*

The Dust Bowl happened because of a mistake, a confusion between a period of high rainfall in Oklahoma, the Texas Panhandle, and parts of Kansas, Colorado, and New Mexico, and the normal climate of this area. That and just plain greed. The United States was not only the source of weapons but also supplied much of the food for England and France during the world wars. So farmers were encouraged to occupy as much land as they could and plant as much of that land as possible. At first, this proved a great success. Then the realities of weather and soil ecology set in.

The soil in what later became known as the Dust Bowl was fertile but shallow. When it was held in place by the tough grasses native to the area, this was no problem. It provided excellent grazing for cattle and sheep. Farmers had always looked for cheap land and so had begun settling this area by the 1870s, many of them using irrigation in growing their crops. Around 1915, the government began encouraging them to use virtually all of this land for crops. It was a shortsighted policy, but it paid off in the short run. With the war on, by the end of 1915 grain prices had soared and the agriculture industry was highly profitable. Millions of acres of plains grasses were plowed up and wheat planted. Tons of food was produced for war-torn Europe.

But turning up the shallow soil had several negative effects.

First, it killed off most of the grasses that were needed to preserve the nutrients in the soil. Next, it meant that the earth was exposed to the dry air and high temperatures of the region.

When an extended period of dryness began around 1930, everything went wrong. First, the crops failed. It was costly to buy seed, plant it, and harvest crops every year. Farmers were paid once per year, and the money they had been earning had been spent on the purchase of more land and machines, not saved. And most farmland was mortgaged. With no crop, farmers couldn't pay their mortgages or their workers. This being the Depression, banks had few choices and no mercy. The loss of one crop normally meant the loss of the farm. Farms no one else wanted. So they sat empty.

By 1935, literally millions of acres were unoccupied. There had been no time for the slow-spreading plains grasses to reclaim the soil. And much of that shallow soil was already worn-out and unable to grow more than the heartiest weeds. Then came the wind.

A massive low-pressure zone, the first of many, blew down from Canada. Winds were gusting up to 65 mph on average, just short of hurricane levels, for hours or days. As this wind passed over the loose earth, it picked up particles. These particles moved and bumped into each other, building up a static charge. This charge meant that more and larger particles were picked up and shuffled against each other, increasing the charge and picking up even more dust. Eventually, this first dust cloud covered thousands of miles and carried dust up to as high as ten thousand feet. What few crops had survived were smothered as the dust storm passed over them. Animals left outside died, often with stomachs full of dust and clogged lungs. This first storm was often called Black Sunday, since the air literally turned black. Residents of the Dust Bowl had to block the bottom of their doors and windows with wet towels and rags to keep the dust out of their homes. To walk to your barn was dangerous, and many farmers strung ropes between buildings. This was not only to help them walk in the high winds, but because you could not see more than a few dozen feet—and to get lost was often fatal.

Storm followed storm as the static charge remained. Dust storms covered the nation, blanketing Chicago, St. Louis, and eventually

New York City. At one point, a Dust Bowl storm clogged New York Harbor so badly that ships were forced to wait miles out at sea for the air to clear. Even lighthouses and the sound of navigation buoys were obscured. What had been a regional problem became a national one.

In the Dust Bowl itself, most of the farms failed. It was simply impossible to grow crops or raise animals. Within a few years, over 60 percent of the population had fled. Many were impoverished and desperate.

Eventually, the dust settled and the storms ended. Some desperate attempts (and even one very foolish one) were made to ensure they didn't happen again. But at the start of WWII, the same mistake was made. As the price of grain skyrocketed, farmers began planting large fields of wheat again. Drought returned to Oklahoma and the Texas Panhandle, as it always does to that part of America, and for a while there looked to be a repeat of the Dust Bowl clouds in the making. This time—we're now in the 1950s—Congress reacted well, subsidizing the farmers so they could plant millions of acres that had been used for wheat—with grass. This worked and dust storms were not again a national problem.

The science of agriculture was advanced enough by WWI to see and predict the problems caused by farming such dry and marginal land. Had the government acted upon that knowledge, and protected the land, the area would be greener, more fertile, and more useful for grazing today. But then, there is the question of the millions of hungry and even starving people in war-torn Europe who ate the grain that had been raised there. *They* might say that it was worth the loss. Hunger does make you narrow your concerns.

## 53

|||||||||||||||||||||||||||||||||||||||||||||||||||||||||||||||||||||||||||||||||||

# HOOVERVILLES

### 1929

### By Bill Fawcett

|||||||||||||||||||||||||||||||||||||||||||||||||||||||||||||||||||||||||||||||||||

> With the best of intentions,
> he did nothing.

erbert Hoover was a national hero long before he was elected president. In his time, engineers who built skyscrapers, bridges, and mines were superstars like computer and software company founders are today. Hoover was an excellent mining engineer and very quickly became rich. When WWI erupted, America was neutral, but thousands of American citizens stranded in Europe were in real danger. A bomb or artillery shell does not check your passport. Hoover organized the evacuation of Americans, occasionally paying personally for their passage to the United States. His efforts likely saved thousands of lives. President Woodrow Wilson appointed him as head of the American Relief Administration, and he earned international recognition for the food and other aid provided to the war-torn countries of Europe. The packaged meals they provided were nicknamed "Hoover Lunches." Eventually, he became the secretary of commerce for President Harding and then his successor, Calvin Coolidge.

In 1928, Hoover won the presidency as a Republican, promising to maintain prosperity. This was not to be. By 1929, speculation and overleveraged investments ended the Roaring Twenties and brought on the Great Depression. Of course, as it began no one (including Herbert Hoover) realized just how bad things were going to get. All his life Hoover had believed in less government and in letting businesses and people do as they liked. In this he would have fit in with the modern Tea Party movement. He also had a strong faith in the ability of a free market to heal itself. So, as the Depression worsened and the stock market failed to recover, he took only limited action. While supporting recovery efforts, Hoover strongly opposed anything that resembled any handout that greatly increased the number of those dependent on the government. Unemployment went from 3 to 23 percent in less than two years. Banks failed and took with them people's savings. There was no FDIC back then—those losses are why it was created. A few of Hoover's efforts worked; some were even incorporated and expanded under the Democrats who followed. But, generally, his strict political philosophy made him deaf to more drastic and progressive actions.

Many of his fellow Republicans advised Hoover that the nation was demanding that he do more, but he refused. He publicly stated that he opposed any action that made Americans dependent on their government—a distinction lost on the millions who were straining to just feed their families. Working through American companies to bring about a recovery was only helping a little. They, too, were often in poor financial condition, and loans from banks were nearly impossible to get. Yet during the 1932 election, Hoover stood firm by his pure free enterprise philosophy. The public's reaction was to name the shantytowns filled with the unemployed "Hoovervilles." The election was a disaster and the Republican Party was stigmatized for years as being opposed to the common man and catering only to the rich—an image problem it retains almost a century later. More importantly, prior to 1932, Americans prided themselves on their independence. President Hoover's failure to recognize the desperation millions of Americans felt, and his unwillingness to compromise, earned him the enmity of the frightened and often impoverished public. When Franklin Delano Roosevelt ran for president, he offered a "new deal" that was just the opposite of what Hoover believed. Government would intervene, support, employ, and regulate the nation's way out of the Depression. The New Deal programs began an age, which we are still in, when people felt their nation owed *them*, not the other way around. Simply put, Hoover's inability to adjust his beliefs when the nation was in dire need led directly to the election of Franklin Roosevelt. Because Herbert Hoover stayed to the right, the nation took a strong turn to the left from which it has never completely recovered.

Had Hoover been more flexible when his policies were failing to alleviate the effects of the Depression, he would not have opened the way for the radically progressive turn the nation took. If he had not put philosophy over necessity, FDR would likely have run and won the presidency, but might not have been able to get Congress to accept his programs. Certainly there might have been a real challenge to Roosevelt's reelection had Hoover's intransigence not so stained the Republican Party. Had Hoover not been an ideologue when a practical statesman was needed, we might today have less government and more rights, and Americans might all share a greater sense of personal responsibility. Had someone just talked President Hoover into a compromise, there would have been no War on Poverty (we lost—the poverty rate remained about the same after billions were spent) and no continued erosion of personal liberties and an individual's rights in the name of providing for us all.

If President Hoover had been less intransigent, the direction America might have taken would be very different. The nation could, today, still be one that is closer to the traditional American values that thrived before the Great Depression and less inclined to look to the social contract mentality of Europe for guidance. Whether the resulting USA would have been better or worse is definitely a matter of opinion. That question is part of a discussion that continues even into the battles of today's elections. What is certain is that the attitudes of the American people, and the way our government acts a century later, would be very different if President Herbert Hoover, when faced with the Great Depression, had been more flexible.

# 54

# A CURE WORSE
# THAN THE PROBLEM

## 1934

**By Bill Fawcett**

Erosion was a serious problem, and a
drastic solution was found.

The United States was traumatized by the Dust Bowl. This had the beneficial effect of bringing conservation to the attention of every American. At the peak of the Dust Bowl storms, steps were taken to prevent erosion by using a decorative plant found originally in Japan. This plant was kudzu, a vine that is native to higher altitudes on mountainsides of Japan. With its deep roots and rapid growth, kudzu is able to survive in higher elevations and in rocky soil. It looked, at first, to be the ideal way to quickly cover areas of soil to prevent their being blown or washed away. But kudzu's strengths were also a danger. Still, the federal government got fully behind this miracle plant and pushed for it to be planted widely. This was a mistake that we are still paying for today.

The first kudzu to arrive in the United States was featured in the Japanese Pavilion at the 1876 Centennial Exhibition in Philadelphia. This was a celebration of the hundredth anniversary of the country and every world power competed to create a unique national exhibit. Japan's included one of its fabled gardens, filled with exotic plants—including kudzu. Kudzu has large leaves and sweet-smelling blossoms, and it grows almost overnight. It was particularly a hit in Florida, where it thrived in the wet, sandy soil. By the 1920s, with government encouragement, kudzu was being billed as a wonder plant. It was a fast-growing animal feed and could be made into medicines, a tea, even woven into baskets. Towns formed Kudzu Clubs to make more use of the plant and compete in growing it.

When the dust clouds came to the Dust Bowl, the federal government was concerned that erosion from wind and rain would continue until all the soil was lost. The Civilian Conservation Corps, one of Roosevelt's many Depression agencies, hired hundreds of unemployed men to go out and plant kudzu across the country. Farmers who volunteered were paid up to eight dollars an acre. That was as much as they could make planting and harvesting most crops. Through the 1930s and 1940s, pundits were regularly on the radio extolling the virtues of this wonder plant.

By the 1950s, though, even the government finally figured out that something was wrong. Kudzu grew too quickly and was too hard to eradicate. Fire, poisons, goats, chemicals, cutting—nothing would permanently destroy the deep-rooted plant. What was hearty enough to subsist in the dry, cold mountains of Japan turned into a Superman of plants in the warm, moist soil of certain parts of the US.

Kudzu grows as much as eight inches per day. It can creep up almost any surface. It will climb over any tree, smothering it, and even shinny up a metal light pole. Where kudzu grows, nothing else can. The large, thick leaves block all light and the deep, aggressive roots displace or destroy any competitors for the soil. To this day there is no real way to beat back kudzu on any scale. More than seven million acres of the southeastern USA is covered with the plant—seven million acres of, basically, green desert. And it continues to spread. The only saving grace is that kudzu cannot survive a hard frost. So those areas with a real winter are safe from it. Planting kudzu was a mistake—one that happened because bureaucrats and farmers saw a cheap and easy solution to a serious problem. But by their actions, they created a greater problem.

If planting kudzu had not been encouraged, it would today be a rare garden plant. Seven million acres of arable land, including many forests, would still exist. The soil of the Southern USA, where one mostly finds it, was never in danger of blowing away and water erosion could have been handled in other ways. Tens of millions of dollars in eradication costs would have been saved. There would be more farmland, more forests, and tens of thousands of farmers and homeowners in the Southern states would be able to stop battling this constant menace.

‖‖‖‖‖‖‖‖‖‖‖‖‖‖‖‖‖‖‖‖‖‖‖‖‖‖‖‖‖‖‖‖‖‖‖‖‖‖‖‖‖‖‖‖‖‖‖‖‖

# 55

# STALIN'S TERROR

## 1937

### By Bill Fawcett

‖‖‖‖‖‖‖‖‖‖‖‖‖‖‖‖‖‖‖‖‖‖‖‖‖‖‖‖‖‖‖‖‖‖‖‖‖‖‖‖‖‖‖‖‖‖‖‖‖‖‖‖

This is not the best way to make big
government smaller.

In Russia, the numerous purges committed by Joseph Stalin's secret police, the NKVD, are known as Stalin's Terror. It is an accurate name. One of the major goals of the purges was to instill terror in every Russian. There is no question they achieved this. Stalin's systematized purges, which began in 1930, mostly targeted people who might resist the forced industrialization of cities or the collectivization of farms. The Kulaks, farm owners in Ukraine, suffered greatly in these first purges. Hundreds of thousands were executed or banished to Siberia. The assassination of one of Stalin's political rivals, Sergey Kirov, provided Stalin with an excuse to purge anyone who might even potentially oppose his rule. Tens of thousands died or were worked to death in the camps. Stalin likely ordered Kirov's assassination personally, but that did not stop him from using it for his personal advantage. On the pretext they were involved in their leader's death, he purged Kirov's allies and even potential supporters.

By 1938, almost everyone in Russia feared the NKVD and Stalin. His control was total. The Russian dictator only had one potential worry. Even before the Nazis took power in Germany, he was acting on the assumption that Russia would have to defend itself from a Western invasion (again). Communist theory and Karl Marx specifically named the highly industrialized nations such as France,

Britain, and Germany as ideal places for communism to take root. So, he expected a massive invasion by Germany or the industrialized Western nations, bent on ending the threat of communism. In 1941, he was proven to be right.

Having spent a decade building up the Red Army, at some point Stalin realized that it was the only organization that was powerful and developed enough to threaten his absolute control. This he simply could not tolerate. So, in 1937, the NKVD conveniently discovered that many of the Red Army's commanders were plotting against the dictator. Although the records and statements of high-ranking officers offer no evidence for these allegations, and the real issue was simply that they represented a source of power potentially greater than Stalin's own, the NKVD was ordered to destroy the officer corps and bring the rank and file of the Red Army under his control. The commander in chief of the army and his seven top generals "confessed" to impossible plots at show trials and were shot. In 1938 and 1939, the purge spread. When the military purge ended, those executed, mostly by firing squad, included three marshals, 14 of the 16 men commanding armies, 65 of the 67 officers commanding corps, 136 of the 199 officers commanding divisions, and 221 of the 397 lower-ranked officers who commanded brigades. On all levels, nearly 35,000 trained officers were shot or imprisoned. To show any initiative, or even real competence, was enough to land an officer before a firing squad.

Stalin's Terror did not end with the destruction of his officer corps. All levels of society were subjected to it. The NKVD maintained their terror tactics, ordering executions or exile to work camps, even if no one was guilty. The important thing was to keep the masses fearful and subservient, not to impose justice. Its officers were actually given quotas of how many had to be killed and imprisoned. Everyone was encouraged to turn in their neighbors, friends, or even their parents. As the army was decimated, pressure on civilians rose until Stalin had to back down somewhat. But for the Red Army, the damage was done. Its poor showing against tiny Finland in 1939, and again in 1941, when Germany invaded, can be at least partly blamed on the lack of experience and the conditioned lack of initiative that resulted from the military purge. Only the least threatening, and so least competent, officers survived—not the kind of men who could have blunted the panzers in Operation Barbarossa.

Had Joseph Stalin left his army intact, it would have had the skill and flexibility to resist the Blitzkrieg. The later successes of the reconstituted Red Army, from 1942 on, demonstrate this. It might have helped prevent the loss of millions of civilian and military lives. Russia would have been less shattered by WWII. Then again, with an intact and well-trained Red Army, Communist Russia under the paranoid and sociopathic Joseph Stalin might have been a much greater threat in the early years of the Cold War—if that war had stayed cold. Or would a less desperate Russia have moderated its behavior much earlier, with democracy actually working, as was once hoped for in the 1990s, thus avoiding the current return to a strong-man dictatorship?

||||||||||||||||||||||||||||||||||||||||||||||||||||||||||||||||||||||||||||||

# 56

# SELLING OUT AN ALLY

### By Bill Fawcett

||||||||||||||||||||||||||||||||||||||||||||||||||||||||||||||||||||||||||||||

The consequence of not being
a dependable ally can be
the war you do not want.

World War I traumatized all of Europe and many of its leaders. The result was the leadership of France and England making a mistake that should stand as a lesson to all leaders who are dealing with politically strong thugs. The name of this mistake is the Munich Agreement. It was nothing less than the complete betrayal of an allied democracy. This did not happen overnight, but was the result of a steady progression of concessions, under pressure from Hitler.

It began after the Anschluss, in March 1938, when Austria was basically blackmailed into uniting with Nazi Germany. Hitler knew that many in Germany and in the German army did not yet support him. He looked to further enhance the Reich and discourage what internal opposition remained. The next large German-speaking population not under his control was in Czechoslovakia. Half or more of the residents of a region known as the Sudetenland spoke German. By May of 1938, the Western Allies were aware that Hitler had plans to occupy all of Czechoslovakia. Since that nation had a mutual defense treaty with France, England, and Russia, the Czechs resisted all of Hitler's threats.

Hitler continued to press. He made a series of speeches designed to inflame the German population and German-speaking Czechs. All this was covered in the world's press, and citizens everywhere began to prepare for another war, which neither Britain nor France wanted. In September, British prime minister Neville Chamberlain offered to meet Hitler at Berchtesgaden, his mountain retreat in the German Alps. Hitler agreed to hold off on any action until they met. This alone raised his status and quieted those members of the general staff who were still doubting him. At that meeting, it was agreed by Chamberlain that a vote would be taken in the German-speaking regions of Czechoslovakia regarding what country they wished to be part of. Since the referendum was being held only in the area where there was a German-speaking majority, and under pressure from the Nazis, the result was a given.

Yet even before the vote was taken, French foreign minister Georges Bonnet met with Chamberlain in London and proposed that all the parts of Czechoslovakia with a majority of German speakers, including the Sudetenland, just be given to Germany without a vote. The Czech government was not even invited to the meeting and, at first, resisted. Only when both Britain and France warned that they would not militarily support them against a German invasion did the Czechs accept.

Chamberlain then flew to Germany to meet Hitler again. This time, in the manner of all bullies, the Führer demanded not only that he get the regions, but that all non-Germans had to evacuate within a matter of days. The Czechs could not cooperate. France even began to mobilize its reserves. War seemed imminent. The French and British public saw their nations returning to the loss and deprivation that they faced in WWI. Sentiment against a new war was overwhelming.

Chamberlain arranged a four-sided meeting in Munich that included Hitler, himself, French prime minister Daladier, and Benito Mussolini. There they agreed to allow Hitler to annex the Czech territory at a slower pace. Not too strangely, the Russians remained passive and took no part in any of this. They signed a nonaggression pact with Hitler the following August. Chamberlain passed this new Munich Agreement on to the Czech leaders, who had not been at any of the meetings, but had no choice but to accept.

When Chamberlain returned to London, he was cheered by crowds happy that the war, which had seemed inevitable, had been avoided. In his now infamous speech, Chamberlain announced that this was "peace with honour. I believe it is peace for our time." The following March, Hitler invaded what remained of Czechoslovakia and, again, France and Britain did nothing. That September, Germany invaded Poland and the Allies finally had to act. When Chamberlain announced the Munich Agreement, his chief political opponent, Winston Churchill, reacted by saying to him, "You were given the choice between war and dishonour. You chose dishonour and you will have war." Churchill was shown to be correct within months—and WWII began.

After he'd sold out Austria and betrayed Czechoslovakia in the name of peace, Chamberlain's concession to Hitler reinforced the Führer's control of Germany and guaranteed an eventual war. Had he resisted, records now show that the Wehrmacht was prepared to withdraw from Czechoslovakia at the first sign of a French or British reaction. If the Allies had shown courage, Hitler, whose army was even less ready for a major war than France's, would have had to retreat. The Munich Agreement, instead, raised Germany's support and outright adoration of Adolf Hitler so high that any resistance to his wishes was impossible. If Chamberlain and Daladier had shown courage, WWII might not have happened. At a minimum, it would have been delayed and the Allies would have had time to modernize their armies—something France had just begun doing when the Sitzkrieg ended in the Blitzkrieg and the occupation of France. Hitler would have lost his total control over the general staff and there might have been no invasion of Poland. All history from then on would be different. There would likely have been no Total Solution, no Blitzkrieg of a better-prepared France, and no Barbarossa.

The lesson of the Munich Agreement should be clear. But how often have leaders with the best intentions (recently) conceded too much to thuggish enemies for the temporary illusion of "peace in our time"?

||||||||||||||||||||||||||||||||||||||||||||||||||||||||||||||||||||||||||||

# 57

## UNLEASH THE . . . FRENCH?

1939

### By Douglas Niles

||||||||||||||||||||||||||||||||||||||||||||||||||||||||||||||||||||||||||||

The army was ready, the leadership . . .

The brutal effectiveness of the new German military operational system called Blitzkrieg, in the first year of World War II, has caused people to regard that unprecedented success as inevitable, a force that the Western powers couldn't hope to resist until they learned to repeat the tactics themselves. In fact, however, there were several occasions when the Nazi government, under the uncontested decision-making power of Adolf Hitler, left itself ripe for a countermove that could have seriously disrupted or even derailed the progress of the German war machine.

The war in Europe began in earnest on September 1, 1939, when five powerful German armies smashed into Poland from the north, west, and south. The German general staff was not in any sense ready for a large and sustained war at the time, and had been assured by Hitler that no such conflict would commence until the economy was ready, perhaps in 1944. Yet the Nazi leader insisted on an invasion that his senior army commanders, all of whom remembered the humiliating defeat of 1918, considered irresponsible and rash. These influential staff officers only lacked a slight nudge before they would have been willing to unseat their dictator and arrange a hasty peace.

Yet little more than a month later, the Nazis occupied hapless Poland, dividing it with the USSR after a stunningly fast conquest, while the huge French army on Germany's western frontier essentially wrung its hands and waited to see what would happen. By the middle of October, Hitler's scheme had been vindicated, and Nazi forces were swiftly being railed back to the west to face France, the Low Countries, and the British Expeditionary Force that had been shipped across the English Channel.

At the start of the war, the German armed forces included nearly one hundred divisions, but only sixty-two of these were combat-ready. Of the latter, approximately forty-eight were infantry, and fourteen divisions were either armored (i.e., tank) divisions, or mechanized and/or motorized, meaning that half-tracks and trucks provided greater mobility than the foot march of standard infantry. Virtually *all* of the highly mobile divisions, as well as forty of the forty-eight combat-ready infantry, would be involved in the invasion of Poland, leaving just eight to guard against any response by France.

France, in turn, was mobilizing 110 divisions, of which about 6 were more or less ready for action when the war broke out. Though she needed some of these troops to protect her border with Italy and her North African colonies, France could still deploy 85 divisions to face Germany. Some may find it surprising to learn that France also had more tanks than her Nazi foe, and that the French tanks were equipped with bigger guns and heavier armor than the German panzers—though the latter were faster and more reliable. Unlike the new German organization, however, the French army was handicapped by the fact that its tanks were scattered in small groups throughout the vast army, with only one armored division designated—and *that* was not ready for action at the start of the war.

The real problem with France's lack of response was not in the capability of her army, but in the willingness of the general staff and political leadership to face the reality that had been thrust upon them. The scars of World War I marked them as much as, if not more than, they did the German commanders, who at least had a new doctrine to embrace. The hidebound generals of France remembered only the prime lesson of the last war: it was much easier and less costly to defend than to attack. They had not begun to recognize that tanks and aircraft allowed a new kind of war that rendered the deadly trenches of 1914 to 1918 obsolete. Also, there was a general sense of shock and dismay in both French military and civilian circles: Hadn't they just fought, and won—albeit at terrible cost—the "war to end all wars"? How could they be expected to do it again?

Yet all it would have taken was a cadre of aggressive and far-seeing officers, of high enough rank to influence French strategy. (The one officer who publicly preached such a doctrine, Charles de Gaulle, was too junior to influence policy.) But the truth remains: if French forces had made a concerted effort to move into the Rhineland while the Nazis were busy in Poland, there was very little Germany could have done to stop them. There is no telling with certainty what the effect of a solid push to the Rhine—and perhaps the threat of a crossing—might have had, but it could have been made against vastly outnumbered German border defenses.

The fact that leading German generals were very uncomfortable with their Führer's timetable is well-known. Such a surprising and aggressive move may well have been enough to trigger a revolt from the general staff, which could have led to Hitler's removal and an immediate end to the war. This would, in turn, have prevented a centrally organized Holocaust from even getting started. Though the USSR would still have held eastern Poland, an early end to the war almost certainly would have removed the Soviet influence from places like Czechoslovakia, Hungary, Romania, Bulgaria, and Yugoslavia—all countries that found themselves firmly on the wrong side of the Iron Curtain after the war.

The United States would not have gotten involved in the war in Europe, which would probably have given the empire of Japan pause as that fascist regime contemplated a plan to gain control of Asia and the Pacific. Certainly many, if not most, of the thirty-six million deaths attributed to the Second World War would have been prevented.

Of course, it is true that Hitler displayed an amazing ability to survive, managing to evade a number of coup (and assassination) attempts during his career, and there is no guarantee that the Germans could have overthrown their dictator in the fall of 1939. Even so, a French army that had **captured** much enemy territory at the outset of the war would of **necessity** have had a higher level of morale, self-confidence, and aggressiveness, not to mention combat experience, than the one that failed to put up much of a fight in May of 1940.

|||||||||||||||||||||||||||||||||||||||||||||||||||||||||||||||||||||||||

# 58

# LINE IN THE FOREST

### 1940

### By Bill Fawcett

|||||||||||||||||||||||||||||||||||||||||||||||||||||||||||||||||||||||||

*The enemy rarely acts as you expect,
much less as you want them to.*

Here is something that will surprise many readers: the Maginot Line worked exactly as planned. There was never an expectation that the German general staff would be stupid enough to attack it frontally. It was never intended to stop any attack completely, but to channel that attack to a location where it could be met and defeated. The Maginot Line was not a mistake—certainly not the mistake that cost France the war. This mistake, which doomed France to four long years of Nazi occupation, did not happen anywhere in France; it happened in Belgium.

There were a number of reasons why the Maginot Line stopped halfway to the Atlantic. One was cost. What had been built already had put a severe strain on France's military budget. Partially because of this, the French were slow to modernize in other areas, such as aircraft and antitank guns—a lack that cost them heavily when the Germans invaded. France simply could not afford more fortifications. Another reason was to not antagonize Belgium, which was expected to fight with them—although, in 1935, Belgium declared itself neutral in the vain hope of avoiding a German invasion. Perhaps more important was that, by the 1930s, the line was not expected to reach all the way to the Channel. The Maginot Line was designed to accomplish a few specific and important things, and these it did.

One of its purposes was to keep the industrial areas of northern France from being invaded as they had been in WWI. This it initially accomplished. In fact, a large part of the French army was concentrated in northeast France, with its back to the Maginot Line, when the nation surrendered. The Maginot Line was also supposed to free up troops for the defense of those areas it did not extend into. Again this it did accomplish.

Perhaps the main reason for the fortifications was to have the Wehrmacht do exactly what it did—attack through Belgium. Yes, the French general staff expected this and planned on it. The bulk of their army was in place and did move to cover an invasion through Belgium. The real war-losing mistake was that they moved to defend the wrong part of Belgium. This was because the French expected that the German attack would follow the same route as it had in WWI. After all, that had been a near-run thing, with "the miracle of the Marne" needed to save the country. Here you have a classic case of preparing to fight the last war instead of the current one.

The assumption that led to the disastrous deployment of the French army and British Expeditionary Force was that the area of southern Belgium known as the Ardennes Forest was so dense with trees and thinly crossed with roads that it was deemed an impossible route for any major invasion force. The area had been thoroughly surveyed, with this in mind, by the French, and all agreed it was impossible to launch a major attack through, or even for a major army to traverse, the Ardennes in less than several weeks. This gave plenty of time to react. That left only northern Belgium and the same route as Germany had taken in the last war. The historical reality is that it took the main German thrust much less than a week to cross through the Ardennes Forest.

Assuming that the Ardennes could basically "defend itself" and that the Maginot Line would do what it did, this left only an invasion route through northern Belgium. So, a large part of the French army and all of the BEF deployed in the north, ready to repel the enemy at the only place where the Allies felt the main German thrust could be made. This meant that when the Germans smashed through the lightly defended Ardennes to their southeast, the bulk of the Allied mobile forces were north and west of the breakthrough. This allowed the panzer divisions to turn west and cut off much of the French army, and the entire BEF, from France. The best units of the French and British armies were caught facing the wrong way and their lines of supply and communications severed in a matter of days. To modern armies, that situation is a disaster. Ammunition, gasoline, and food are consumed by the ton by a modern military unit. These could now be supplied only by sea, but the dominance of the Luftwaffe over the battlefield made this difficult as well. Combined with tactical mistakes, such as not concentrating their tanks effectively, a lack of antitank guns large enough to stop the panzers, and a failure to train their mobile infantry in modern tactics, it was enough to cause France to be completely defeated within a shockingly short time. The best of the French army and the entire BEF were caught out of position and effectively surrounded within days. All because of making an incorrect assumption about attacking through the Ardennes Forest.

Had there been sufficient forces facing the Ardennes Forest, or even if the bulk of the mobile French army and BEF had not surged into upper Belgium, WWII would have been fought very differently. If the attack in the Ardennes had been blunted, then once more the two sides would have been slugging it out. Had the Blitzkrieg not been aided by this major strategic mistake, Germany would not have been able to sweep across France and, perhaps, not even been able to knock that nation out of the war. With the French army intact and the BEF in a position to be used effectively, the price of a German victory would have been very high. This might have once more sparked a revolt by the German generals. A higher cost against a united Allied army would also have meant no invasion of Russia a year later. If France had managed to hold out, as it had in WWI, then trench warfare might have reappeared. With the Maginot Line, that would have favored the French. There could even have been a negotiated agreement, when the cost of a victory became apparent to the Nazis. Perversely, it might also have forced a peace, or at least a truce, that would have left Hitler in power.

# 59 and 60

|||||||||||||||||||||||||||||||||||||||||||||||||||||||||||||||||||||||||||||||||||||

## A VICTORY THAT
## GUARANTEED DEFEAT

### 1941

### By Bill Fawcett

|||||||||||||||||||||||||||||||||||||||||||||||||||||||||||||||||||||||||||||||||||||

*Know your enemy, know your enemy,
know your enemy.*

Two mistakes were made in December of 1941 that led directly to the defeat of both Japan and Germany in WWII. What is ironic about those mistaken decisions is that both were contrary to the actual needs of those nations. The decisions not only proved wrong over the long term, but were counterproductive at the time they were made.

It began with Japan. That nation was a modern industrial power that had been an ally of the British and Americans in WWI. Its problem was a lack of resources. Virtually everything that was needed to maintain a modern industrial state had to be imported. This included raw materials, from steel and oil to rubber and food. Virtually every decision and action the Japanese took up to 1941 was inspired by this need. Their first efforts to ensure the flow of materials they needed was the invasion of Manchuria. This helped provide minerals, but little else, as the country itself was a cold, forbidding waste. There was no chance for the Japanese to export excess population or to grow crops of significant yields. After absorbing Manchuria, now renamed Manchukuo, the next source of raw materials the Japanese eyed was China.

There was a long tradition of outside powers exploiting China. The European nations had maintained enclaves, such as Hong Kong, and forced trading concessions from the Chinese for more than a century. The Dutch and French held most of Indochina, and the Americans had grabbed the Philippines from the Spanish in 1898. Why should the Japanese not emulate what the other advanced nations had already done and grab what they wanted from the weaker nations around them? So Japan invaded China in 1931, quickly occupying much of northern China and most of its coast. But the Chinese resisted and this meant constant fighting on a large scale. Two million Japanese soldiers fought in China in the 1930s. This made the country a drain on, not a provider of, resources and put pressure on the Japanese leaders. For the next several years, the necessary raw materials could be imported from the largest Pacific Rim supplier of basic industrial materials, the United States. But the sheer brutality of the Japanese occupation of China eventually caused the USA to stop shipping it some strategic supplies.

So, to accomplish their goal of self-sufficiency in natural resources, the Japanese decided to seize the Dutch East Indies and French Indochina. These were resource-rich areas controlled by two colonial powers that had been conquered by Japan's ally, Nazi Germany. They were virtually defenseless and, when attacked, fell easily. What concerned the Japanese was not France or the Netherlands. Both nations were under the boot of Nazi Germany and there was little their governments in exile could do. The Japanese concern was for the British and Americans. So long as the USA held the Philippines and, thereby, the central Pacific Ocean, it could easily interdict from the air all the merchant shipping sailing from the Indies to Japan. The Japanese solution to this problem was their big mistake. That solution was to knock out the American Pacific fleet in Pearl Harbor and then occupy the Philippines themselves. Destroying the only other large fleet in the Pacific Ocean would ensure Japanese control of the sea-lanes and allow them to easily invade the Philippines. Once they occupied the Philippines, Japanese shipping would be safe from enemy aircraft.

It was short-term thinking, without consideration of all possible options. The plan also overlooked some important points about America and its Pacific navy. Simply put, there was no need to be in a war with the USA. Many Japanese leaders and commanders had worked and studied there. They knew the industrial potential of the nation. Contrary to the myth of foppish jazz lovers fostered by both their own and Nazi propaganda, they also knew that, if attacked, Americans could fight well. Nor would the loss of the Pacific fleet force America to accept any treaty the Japanese proposed. There was no chance Japan could actually attack the US mainland, or even hold on to Hawaii, for any significant period of time.

The political situation in America was such that, even though President Franklin Roosevelt was determined to fight against Hitler and feared what might happen if the Nazis were left to occupy all of Europe, the antiwar feeling limited American support of Britain and Russia. The president was so frustrated with the strong isolationist feelings of his country that the baseless rumor that he allowed the surprise attack on Pearl Harbor is still repeated. America did not want a European war. It certainly would not have been enthusiastic to fight an Asian war, whose purpose was to gain colonies lost by other countries. It seems unlikely that Roosevelt could have rallied a nation that was unwilling to fight to free France to instead fight a hard and distant war over Dutch possessions—on the far side of the world, in places most Americans had never heard of. Even if the Japanese had attacked the Philippines, the response would have been strong, but the USA would have been open to negotiations. But rather than try a diplomatic solution or attacking in the traditional manner, the Japanese leaders chose the one option guaranteed to change a reluctant participant into a devoted enemy. This was the surprise attack on Pearl Harbor, designed to knock out the Pacific fleet. It was just about the only way to *guarantee* that all Americans would rally behind the war effort. Yet the Japanese chose it.

On both a military and a political level, the attack on Pearl Harbor was pretty much the worst possible way to achieve their goal of controlling Indochina. The attack was not even needed to guarantee Japanese naval supremacy in the western Pacific. If the Pacific fleet had sailed to support MacArthur in the Philippines, it would likely have been a disaster. There were only three fleet carriers in the Pacific, compared to six for the Imperial Japanese Navy (IJN). There were eight American battleships and many smaller supporting ships, but most were of WWI vintage. The Japanese fleet was newer, better trained, and included two massive battle-ships armed with eighteen-inch guns, whose abilities were totally unknown to the Americans.

The American naval air doctrine was not yet refined and would also have left the US vulnerable. For example, it called for each carrier to operate independently at some distance from the others. What this meant was that all six Japanese carriers, working to-gether, with their more highly trained pilots and superior aircraft, would have defeated each American carrier, working alone. Nor would the American surface ships have done well. Even if most of Admiral Kimmel's ships had survived the multitude of waiting Japanese submarines (which were armed with the revolutionary Long Lance torpedoes) on their three-thousand-mile journey, they would have been outmatched by the main Japanese fleet when they met. With the USN force outranged, outgunned, and without con-trol of the air, a Tsushima-style defeat was possible, even likely.

The attack on Pearl Harbor was a complete mistake, one that was years in the planning and brilliantly executed, but unneces-sary. Diplomatically, the nature of the attack made certain that the desired treaty with the USA would never happen and that Roo-sevelt could rally a divided nation behind the war effort. Although militarily, the IJN was superior enough to badly punish the Pacific fleet, or worse, it was a victory that guaranteed eventual defeat.

The second decision made because of Pearl Harbor made even less sense. On December 11, 1941, Adolf Hitler declared war on an already-enraged United States. This was Hitler's decision and no one else's. At this point, having led Germany in successfully in-vading and defeating most of Europe, he personally controlled the nation. But Hitler had nothing to gain by formally going to war against the United States. President Roosevelt had long favored supporting the nations opposing the Nazis. But he had run into massive resistance in Congress and the idea of a new war in Europe was unpopular. Just a few days before the Pearl Harbor attack, there had been a massive antiwar rally, with thousands demanding that America stay out of Europe. Tons of goods and food were already crossing the Atlantic to England and newly attacked Russia. Declaring war would allow German U-boats to attack the eastern American coast, but this was not enough to even slow the shipments. The bottom line is that, viewed through the lens of history, Hitler gained virtually nothing by declaring war on the United States. So why did he do it? Perhaps he expected gratitude from the Japanese. He probably hoped they would attack Russia where it bordered Manchuria. Yet records and biographies show that the Japanese never had any interest in getting involved in another land war in Russia. Their army was already strained with occupying and suppressing much of China.

So, by declaring war on the United States four days after Pearl Harbor, the Nazis gained nothing but fewer restrictions on where their submarines could hunt. What Hitler lost was this: on December 6, 1941, a large number of American voters and Congress had opposed any involvement in Europe. So many that their president could do little even to assist Britain. On December 12, still angry over the sneak attack, all Americans actively supported war on both fronts. Roosevelt got to direct a great deal of the American war effort to Europe, as he desired. The flow of materials to Germany's enemies increased and soon tens of thousands of soldiers would follow. In the long run, forcing the entry of the USA into the war virtually guaranteed a resource-poor Germany that the largest industrial, food-producing, and financial power in the world would be its enemy.

So why did Hitler make the mistake of declaring war on an already enraged United States? Certainly the timing could not have been worse. It may just come down to that constant theme in any book about mistakes: Victory Disease. Germany had conquered France in weeks, and occupied Norway, Denmark, the Benelux countries, and Poland without taking significant losses. At this point, Operation Barbarossa, the invasion of Russia, was going magnificently. Entire Russian armies were being surrounded and destroyed by the Führer's panzers and the Red Army was falling back. Literally tens of thousands of square miles of Russian land had already been occupied. Expectations of a total victory within weeks were so high that no preparation was made for winter coats, because everyone in power was sure that the war would be over before it got cold.

The attack on Pearl Harbor was a mistake and Hitler's reaction to it was almost as great a blunder. Both had the opposite effect of what was expected. Had the Pearl Harbor attack not happened, it might have taken many more months or years before the United States joined WWII. Germany would have been tied up in Russia, but Japan could have been able to move on Australia, as the Japanese once hoped, or at least entrench itself on more islands and in Indochina. Had Roosevelt had his way, there might not even have been a war against Japan. He saw a Nazi Europe with manufacturing capability as great as the Americas united under the Nazis as the greatest threat. Even after Pearl Harbor, a much greater part of the American war effort was directed to Europe and Russia than to Japan.

So if the Japanese had not made the mistake of carrying out a sneak attack, American isolationist and antiwar factions might have given them months, or even years, before they had to fight against the US. If they had just done nothing, it was even possible that Roosevelt would have negotiated with them, in order to free himself to act against the Nazis. If Hitler had not reacted with his declaration of war, he might also have bought himself and the Third Reich many more months before the American people plunged into another world war. Neither the German nor the Japanese mistake was necessary. Both went about accomplishing their desires in the wrong way, and their actions had the opposite effect of that intended. The sneak attack on Pearl Harbor and the declaration of war it inspired in Adolf Hitler were mistakes that greatly contributed to both nations losing the war.

# 61

||||||||||||||||||||||||||||||||||||||||||||||||||||||||||||||||||||||||||||

# INVADING RUSSIA IS
# ALWAYS A MISTAKE

## 1941

### By William Terdoslavich

||||||||||||||||||||||||||||||||||||||||||||||||||||||||||||||||||||||||||||

Just 130 years after Napoleon tried,
Hitler should have known better.

Adolf Hitler had big dreams. But for the rest of Europe, they qualified as nightmares.

The Nazi dictator always wanted to send his armies east to acquire "living space" for the German people. Only, other people got in the way, namely Poles, Ukrainians, and Russians.

By June 1941, Hitler was ready to fulfill his "manifest destiny," a greatly enlarged Germany obtained at Russia's expense. When Operation Barbarossa got under way, 162 German divisions, of which 17 were armored, crashed into 158 Russian divisions, plus the equivalent of 11 tank divisions.

On paper, this looked like an even fight. On the ground, it was anything but. In six months, Hitler's panzer divisions spearheaded a series of sweeping attacks that destroyed much of the Russian army. And German troops were only twenty miles from Moscow.

Success was very close. Take the capital, and the Soviet Union will fall. So went the conventional thinking. That was when Soviet field marshal Georgy Zhukov unleashed his Siberian divisions, pushing the Germans back from the threshold of victory. It was the dead of winter, and those Germans not killed bullets and shells either died from the cold or wished they had.

Hitler's forces had, up to then, conquered Poland, Denmark, Norway, Belgium, the Netherlands, Luxembourg, France, Yugoslavia, and Greece. The diplomacy of victory netted Finland, Hungary, Romania, Bulgaria, and Italy as allies. German U-boats were sinking British cargo ships faster than Britain could replace them. The Luftwaffe, checked but not defeated, shrugged off its losses from the Battle of Britain. Even the sideshow in North Africa was paying off dividends as General Erwin Rommel's Afrika Korps routinely routed larger British formations.

Despite this record of victories why was the German army incapable of taking Moscow?

## Mighty Panzers, Humble Trucks

The answer may lie in the most overlooked area of warfare: logistics, which is the business of delivering supplies to the army in the field. Having it, or lacking it, can define the parameters of a campaign. In this regard, Germany's story goes back to the 1930s.

Militarily speaking, Germany lacked the industry to build an army en masse that could run on tires and treads. Only a fifth of the army, the initial invasion force Hitler fielded, could run on gasoline. Until supply could catch up to demand, the rest had to run on railway transport to the front and hay when they got near the fight—i.e., horses, not horsepower, propelled the infantry divisions. The horses towed the guns and supply wagons, just as they had for Napoleon and Frederick the Great. And they could move no faster than a man's march, maybe twenty miles a day, if they marched hard.

The panzer divisions could knife ahead up to fifty miles per day. No ground could be held, however, until the infantry caught up. The whole Russian campaign would have this awkward stop-start tempo.

Germany had some domestic car production, but only a fraction of that in the US. After successful campaigns in Western Europe, it stripped the conquered countries of anything with four wheels and a cargo bed. It assembled a truck force that could partially meet the needs of three army groups, if mechanics didn't mind maintaining over one hundred makes and models of trucks. The spare parts situation was hellish, to put it mildly.

Trucks could supply armies for about two hundred miles from the supply depot to the front. To move goods farther more economically, you needed railroads. Russian tracks were wider than the tracks back in Germany. Rail gangs had to narrow the gauge so German trains could use those lines, but Russian rails were still crappier and shorter. Going fast risked derailment.

Take all these factors together and you were stuck with an army that could probably fight its way from Poland to Smolensk—about three hundred miles—before running out of supplies and grinding to a halt. German war planners knew this going in.

## Shoestring Blitzkrieg

After seeing the Russians fight so badly against Finland in the "Winter War" of 1940, Hitler was convinced that Russia would be just as easy to conquer as Poland (four weeks) and France (six weeks). He was partially right. The Russian army suffered from a serious command deficit following Stalin's purges in the late 1930s. Green colonels are no substitute for able generals. The ill-handled Russian armies were easily encircled. Germany won many battles on the cheap between June and September.

You would not know that, though, from looking at the supply ledgers. Divisions were getting only half their supplies. Operations ground to a halt here and there for lack of fuel and ammo. Sometimes, supplies were off-loaded from trains and sent to the sectors with the greatest tactical need. This was no way to run a war.

German rail gangs gave up trying to change the gauge of hundreds of miles of track. Improvised depots became transfer points to move supplies from German boxcars to Russian boxcars, creating hideous bottlenecks and delays.

By fall, it was clear that there was no way the German army could keep three army groups on the move. To take Moscow, two of the army groups would have to be halted and the third would get all the supplies. It was only another 250 miles to Moscow.

Army group center was reinforced, pairing up three panzer armies with three infantry armies. One more encirclement battle pocketed Vyazma and more than five hundred thousand Russian troops. Then the rains came, turning roads into mud and immobilizing the attack.

It was not until November that the winter cold hardened the ground sufficiently for tanks and trucks to travel. Now different problems arose. Water pipes froze and burst on German steam locomotives. It was too cold for truck engines to start. Transmission oil froze in the panzers. And the troops lacked proper winter clothing.

By mid-December, the German army could no longer move forward. It could retreat, though, once the Russians attacked with masses of wide-tracked T-34 tanks backed by hordes of Siberian infantry dressed in warm winter uniforms. Hitler ordered troops to stay in place, regardless of the cost, to prevent a rout. That saved the German army, but it would never get that close to Moscow again.

## Mother Russia Is a Cruel Mistress

Invading Russia has never been a good idea, historically. France's Napoleon and Sweden's Charles XII failed miserably, losing their armies. Like his predecessors, Hitler was made overconfident by early victories.

The easier alternative is not invading. It is doubtful this would have been a sound strategy. Soviet dictator Joseph Stalin still allowed his staff to plan a possible attack on German-held Poland in the spring of 1942. Such a move was improbable, but not impossible.

Focusing on the German invasion itself, we can see that there were things that could have been done differently to better prepare for the campaign. Germany could have put more effort into expanding its auto industry, adding more trucks to its motor pool. Or it could have improved its rail capabilities, making them able to convert track from Russian to German gauge at a faster clip.

Operationally, Germany's generals could have narrowed the plan. As originally written, three army groups would have had to take Leningrad, Moscow, Ukraine, Crimea, and the Caucasus, all in one campaign season! And solidify their gains before the winter weather arrived! Planners could not seem to limit their goals to the attainable. While the German army captured some strategic objectives, German strength was stretched too thin in the attempt to take all of them.

Perhaps a better move was to forgo Leningrad and concentrate on Moscow and Ukraine. Or fight a slower campaign, moving all three army groups east by three hundred miles, stopping, then riding out the winter while managing a strained, but shorter supply line. The lull would have allowed rail lines to be converted to German gauge for their entire length; then the supply dumps could have been rebuilt.

By gambling, Hitler came within twenty miles of taking Moscow. Being less ambitious he could have reaped Moscow as the prize in 1942, avoiding Stalingrad and an overstretched campaign in the Caucasus. This would have been inconsistent with the way Germans fought their wars, favoring the attack and quick pursuit over deliberate advance and supply.

German determination and improvisation can only take an army so far when supplies are lacking.

# 62

## RONALD REAGAN
## STARS IN
## *CASABLANCA*

### 1942

### By Mike Resnick

What if this actor had not played on
the world stage?

The unproduced play was titled *Everyone Comes to Rick's*.
After it failed to find a Broadway producer, it was submitted
to Hollywood, where story editor Irene Diamond read it,
thought it had possibilities, and recommended that Hal B. Wallis
purchase the film rights, which he did for a less-than-munificent
$20,000.

The title was changed to *Casablanca*, where the action took place.
It starred Humphrey Bogart and Ingrid Bergman, it featured Claude
Rains and Paul Henreid, and it had a delicious supporting cast that
included Peter Lorre, Sydney Greenstreet, Conrad Veidt, S. Z. Sakall,
and Leonid Kinskey. It was rewritten on an almost day-by-day basis
by the team of Julius and Philip Epstein, with some additional help
from Howard E. Koch, and directed by Michael Curtiz.

The film was originally scheduled for release in mid-1943, but it
was rushed into distribution, with a world premiere on November
26, 1942, and an official release date of January 23, 1943, to capitalize on the Allies' landing in North Africa. No one at Warner Bros.
expected it to do much at the box office or in the awards, which just
goes to show how incredibly wrong people can be. *Casablanca* won
the Academy Award for Best Picture, became an instant classic, and
has always ranked among the top two or three films every time
the American Film Institute ranks its top one hundred films. It

made five-foot-seven-inch balding Bogart a romantic lead, as well as the most popular actor in America.

Okay, that's what happened.

But what might have happened is just as interesting.

Humphrey Bogart was not the first actor considered for the role of Rick Blaine. Jack Warner wanted George Raft or James Cagney, and after all, Bogart had only one big hit behind him—the recent *Maltese Falcon*—and he had never played a romantic lead.

But before they signed Bogart, they had in mind yet another Warner's contract player. There's every chance you may have heard of him. On January 7, 1942, Warner Bros.'s Hollywood News Press Service released the following statement: "Ann Sheridan and Ronald Reagan will be teamed by Warner Brothers for the third time in *Casablanca*."

Nothing came of it.

But what if Reagan *had* wound up with the role of Rick Blaine? Yes, he was in the army by then . . . but what if they'd held the movie for him? After all, not a single theatrical producer had been willing to put it onstage, and Bogart's name wasn't yet box office magic. What if the film, made in 1945, was every bit as popular with him in the lead as it was with Bogart? What logically follows?

Well, for starters, Reagan moves up the ladder to become Warner's number one romantic lead. But the wild popularity of *Casablanca* has created a huge demand for his screen services, and he finds himself overwhelmed with offers. His next appearance is the lead in *To Have and Have Not*, a role that would have gone to Bogart had Reagan not established himself as a romantic star in *Casablanca*.

The film is a hit, and suddenly Reagan has his choice of plum roles, roles that would never have been offered to him had *Kings Row* been the apex of his acting career. He beats out Gregory Peck for the lead in *Gentleman's Agreement*, actually wins an Oscar after beating relatively unknown Ernest Borgnine for *Marty*, makes thirty-five films—most of them big-budget, highly publicized ones—between 1946 and his retirement (after starring in his final film, a television remake of *The Last Hurrah*) in 1977.

At one time, during the war, he thought of working for the

Screen Actors Guild when he came home, perhaps even running for an office within the guild. But when he received literally two million accumulated fan letters and fourteen bona fide movie offers, he realized that he couldn't possibly take the time, at least not until he took some of these very choice acting jobs and put some money in the bank.

But of course, the more he performed, the more offers came his way, and the more the industry depended on him to keep performing, and he finally realized that no, he was not going to run for president (or any other office) of the Screen Actors Guild.

It was two decades later that the policies of Governor Pat Brown and other Democrats so outraged him that for the first time in his life he registered as a Republican. He was working constantly, as he had been since 1945, but he donated some $3 million to Republicans in state and national races.

It would be nice to say that he and Bogart traded places, but Bogart was an on-and-off liberal, and his chain-smoking caused his death in January of 1957.

So what *did* happen during the years that Reagan, under different circumstances, might have run for president, not of the Screen Actors Guild, but of the United States of America?

Well, there was quite a battle among Republicans, but George H. W. Bush emerged with the 1980 nomination, and beating Jimmy Carter when Iran was holding dozens of hostages and the prime rate topped 21 percent was even easier than it had looked, with the seated president winning only ten states.

Bush didn't scare the Ayatollah Khomeini the way a President Reagan would have, and in 1982, the United States invaded Iran, freeing all but five of the hostages (who were killed during the action) and replacing Khomeini with a pro-democracy, pro-America ruler.

Bush did not preside over the phenomenal economic recovery and job growth that Reagan would have brought about, but compared to the economy he inherited, he was soon labeled an economic wizard, and of course he won reelection in 1984.

It was said that he relaxed from the heavy pressures of his office by watching endless reruns of *Casablanca*.

# 63

## KURSK

1943

### By Harry Turtledove

"My stomach turns over."

After Field Marshal Friedrich Paulus surrendered the last ninety thousand starving, freezing Germans in Stalingrad at the end of January 1943, anyone with eyes to see should have understood that Hitler would never beat Stalin on the Eastern Front. (Paulus was promoted to field marshal just before the surrender, to persuade him to shoot himself instead of giving up—no German field marshal had ever surrendered. It didn't work. Only about five thousand of those Germans ever saw the Vaterland again. He was one of them.)

As the winter of 1942–1943 wore on, what wasn't obvious was whether the entire German position in the southern USSR would go to pieces. It didn't, thanks in large measure to some inspired generalship by Field Marshal Erich von Manstein. Hitler, perhaps feeling the hangover from Stalingrad, was uncommonly willing to let von Manstein give ground and lure the Red Army into overextending itself, in turn.

This the eager Soviet generals duly did, and the German field marshal chopped their columns to pieces one by one. The Germans even retook the key town of Kharkov (now Kharkiv, in Ukraine), which had fallen to the USSR not long before. Soon the Red Army, not the Wehrmacht, was the force eager for the spring thaw to glue both armies into position for several weeks.

When the snow melted and the mud came, the front was in about the same place it had been a year before. The major difference was that the Red Army held a large salient centered on Kursk, north of Kharkov. The Soviets had conducted successful operations during both the last two winters. The two previous summers, though, had belonged to Germany. Hitler was determined that the summer of 1943 should, as well.

A glance at the map showed that biting off the Kursk salient would be a good way to get back the strategic initiative. It would shorten the front the Germans had to hold and would free up several divisions to be used as a strategic reserve or—more likely—to go fight somewhere else. Thus, Operation Citadel was born, and scheduled by von Manstein for mid- to late April 1943—as soon as the ground dried out enough to let armor and men move freely.

There were two problems with this. One was that Stalin and Zhukov could also glance at a map. In case they couldn't, the Soviet spy ring code-named Lucy would have filled them in. Had the German attack gone in on April 15 or 25, none of that would have mattered much. But the attack didn't happen.

Delays were repeated. The Germans committed more and more to the assault. Hitler wanted to add the new Panther tank to the armored force . . . but the Panther had teething troubles. At one staff meeting, Guderian urged Hitler not to attack at all, but to build up resources for the big fight ahead in the west. Even the Führer had qualms. "When I think of this attack, my stomach turns over," he said. But he didn't call it off; he only postponed it again, this time to June 12. It ultimately began on July 5.

Meanwhile, Red Army soldiers and dragooned civilians dug mile upon mile of trenches and antitank ditches. They planted mines by the tens of thousands. The Soviets brought in guns and rocket launchers and tanks and men of their own. When the attack went in, it failed. On the northern flank, Model never got far. In the south, von Manstein came closer to success, but his armored thrust was stopped at Prokhorovka in the biggest tank battle the world had ever seen. The USSR could afford that kind of massive losses far better than Germany could. The Wehrmacht never regained the strategic initiative. After Kursk, the end of the war was still almost two years away, but it was all downhill from then on.

Even if the Germans weren't going to win in the east, could they have husbanded men and matériel well enough to force a draw there? Could they have killed enough Red Army soldiers and destroyed enough Red Army T-34s to make even a cold-blooded butcher like Stalin decide peace was a better bargain than more slaughter? If they could, how?

Besides biting off the Kursk salient early, while it still could have been pretty easy, another way was to let the Soviets charge ahead, temporarily yield some ground, and then counterattack, taking advantage of superior German technical ability. That was what von Manstein had done when he rescued the situation after Stalingrad. He wanted to try it again.

This time, though, Hitler rejected his plan. Hitler always hated retreat, even temporary retreat for military reasons. This was almost certainly a mistake, and a bad one. Germany needed to conserve what soldiers and machines it could. The third largest economy in the world, it was fighting number one (the USA), number two (the USSR), and number four (the UK). Under any circumstances, those were bad odds. The colossal expenditures of Operation Citadel—one historian has termed it "panzer hara-kiri"—only made them worse than they would have been otherwise.

Had the Führer handed the military reins to von Manstein and the other high-ranking officers, who actually knew what they were doing, could they have inflicted enough casualties on the Red Army to knock it out of the war? It seems unlikely. The USSR had two and a half times Germany's population, and far more than two and a half times Germany's natural resources. It had powerful allies. And Soviet generals, while perhaps not up to von Manstein's exacting standards, got steadily better at their trade throughout the war. Once the Wehrmacht failed to knock the Soviet Union out in the early rounds, it was going to lose the fight.

Given a more intelligent conduct of the war from 1943 on, could Germany have lasted longer than it did? Yes, probably. Hitler's refusal to retreat, no matter what, and his fortress cities that trapped and destroyed the garrisons condemned to hold them, wasted manpower and threw away tanks and guns. A more mobile defense would have been harder for the Red Army to smash.

Such a defense might well have kept the Nazi regime fighting into the summer of 1945, instead of collapsing in the spring. And that would have gotten Hitler and his cronies exactly what they deserved, for who can doubt that atomic fire would have incinerated Berlin and, as necessary, other German cities with it? And who can doubt that a world with the Nazis literally seared out of existence would have been a better place?

||||||||||||||||||||||||||||||||||||||||||||||||||||||||||||||||||||

# 64

# PROPAGANDA COUP, FOR THE WRONG SIDE

## 1943

### By Bill Fawcett

||||||||||||||||||||||||||||||||||||||||||||||||||||||||||||||||||||

How many thousands of lives was an
unthinking comment worth?

The Casablanca Conference was a meeting between US president Franklin D. Roosevelt and British prime minister Winston Churchill in Casablanca. It took place for ten days, beginning on January 14, 1943. Stalin had been invited, but stayed in Moscow because the Red Army was engaged in a series of offensives. The location was symbolic. The city had been held only two months before by the Afrika Korps and was freed after the American Operation Torch landings in North Africa. The purpose of the meeting was to craft long-range plans against the Nazis. At this point, they still controlled most of Europe and were still allied with Italy. So it was not as if the Allies were looking for the war to end anytime soon. Most of the ten days were spent in planning. Churchill and Roosevelt got along well and, when it was over, both gave speeches that appeared in all the world's newspapers.

President Roosevelt gave a powerful speech and in it he demanded the "unconditional surrender" of Germany. This had neither been discussed nor planned by the two leaders. It likely came as a surprise to Churchill. When the American press caught the phrase, it headlined every newspaper: "Roosevelt Demands Unconditional Surrender."

By 1943, things were not going well on the Eastern Front. That offensive Stalin had stayed to supervise would drive the Wehrmacht out of Russia and Ukraine. Morale among civilians and soldiers was failing. But with this slip of the tongue, Roosevelt did more to harden German resistance than anything Goebbels had ever said. To the Germans, still remembering how the nation was embarrassed and economically destroyed by the Treaty of Versailles after WWI, unconditional surrender meant complete devastation or even the end of their relatively new nation. (Germany had not been unified until 1871.) Immediately the Nazi propaganda machine took this demand and told the German people they would all be enslaved or even forced to labor in Russia. Stalin made no secret of his plans to avenge Russian losses on Germany. As it advanced, the Soviet army engaged in rape, destruction, and pillaging, without limit. Also, the carpet bombing, by the USAF, of German cities was intended to break the will of the Germans, with indiscriminate bombing causing massive civilian casualties. This showed there were few limits on what the Allies would do to the German population. So the Germans were already afraid of what might come and had no reason to doubt that the worst would happen.

Others tried to take back the phrase. But the damage was done. Not only did it ensure that the German people had no alternative to fighting to the last, but it also solidified Hitler's position, just as the bad news from the Eastern Front was spreading. This was followed by the release, but not adoption, of the Morgenthau Plan created by the American secretary of the treasury, according to which, after the war, the Allies would destroy all of Germany's heavy industry and turn the entire nation into a land of farmers. Millions would have starved, but since nearly a million Germans had been killed by the carpet bombing, they had no reason to doubt that the Americans meant what they said. After being told by President Roosevelt that their only choice was unconditional surrender, all Germans felt they had no choice but to resist. There was no alternative.

Had Roosevelt not made this speech and thereby handed Goebbels the means to solidify the German people's resistance, the last days of the war might have come sooner and been less bloody. Hitler's power might have been curtailed after news of the many Eastern Front defeats spread. That would have allowed for open support for those who wanted to work out a deal, or even an honorable surrender, in 1944. The war could have ended earlier, with tens of thousands of lives saved, and the fanatical resistance that continued even as Germany collapsed could have been avoided.

## UNHAPPY BIRTHDAY
## AND GOOD NIGHT

### 1944

### By Bill Fawcett

||||||||||||||||||||||||||||||||||||||||||||||||||||||||||||||||||||||||

D-Day Normandy could have
been a disaster.

There were a number of reasons why the Allied landing in Normandy succeeded. Two of them were mistakes that in any other context would be considered trivial. One was made by the commander of the defending German forces on the Atlantic Wall. Erwin Rommel had worked for months improving and expanding the beach defenses all along the French coast. Millions of mines had been laid, bunkers had been prepared to protect cannon and machine guns from naval bombardment, and Rommel had coaxed additional panzer units from Hitler. If the Allied landing could be crushed, it would be at least another year before they could try again. Logistics and weather guaranteed a long delay after any failure. This would free up strong forces to be shifted to the Eastern Front, and the Germans hoped a loss would lead to a negotiated peace.

The Germans knew that the Allies were preparing to land, but they didn't know where. A brilliant series of deceptions convinced many of the German generals that the attack would cross the English Channel at its narrowest and land at Pas de Calais. A fake army was created, and perhaps the only armor commander capable of matching Rommel was put in command. This was General George S. Patton. False orders were planted on a body that would wash ashore and be found by the Germans. These deceptions succeeded in tying up two panzer divisions in the first hours of the landings. Despite this, D-Day Normandy was several times so close to failing that Eisenhower considered pulling everyone back. But what really allowed D-Day Normandy to succeed were two mistakes in judgment about what appeared to be trivial matters.

Because Hitler fell for the subterfuge used by the Allies, two panzer divisions were held near Pas de Calais. Being fooled was a mistake but not an irretrievable one. The first mistake that guaranteed the Allies' success happened because Hitler had gotten tired of Gerd von Rundstedt and Rommel arguing over tactics. Von Runstedt wanted to gather all the panzers and infantry divisions first and then strike at the beachhead with the maximum force possible. Rommel wanted to attack immediately with whatever was at hand against what would be disorganized and hard-to-supply beachheads. Rather than choose one strategy or the other, an irritated Hitler tried to choose both. So the mobile divisions in France were split under three commanders. Rommel got three panzer divisions, but two were required to remain north of the Seine River so they could turn toward either Normandy or Pas de Calais as needed. This meant they were near the landing beaches. Von Runstedt got direct command of everything in France and Denmark, but was hesitant to act without the Führer's approval. Finally, Hitler had his personal military headquarters, OKW, take overall command of four elite divisions, 1st SS, 12th SS, 17th SS Panzergrenadier, and Panzer Lehr. They could have made a difference, but they didn't.

The first trivial but war-changing mistake was one of timing and temerity. The four elite SS divisions Hitler personally controlled were supposed to join in the counterattack if the Allies landed, but could not act without orders from OKW. OKW acted on everything only after they had Hitler's personal approval. No one wanted to challenge the Führer's authority. It had not been long since an assassination attempt had led to the execution of a large number of officers. No one wanted to be the next one shot.

Hitler was not healthy, and he had been sleeping erratically. There is some evidence that he was getting juiced with narcotics. He often stayed up talking most of the night and did not go to bed until dawn. When the news came and OKW received the request for the four powerful formations to move toward Normandy, the Führer was asleep. Once asleep, Hitler reacted badly to being awakened. And when Hitler reacted badly, the Gestapo tended to make people disappear. So no one in OKW was willing to wake the Führer, and four of the most powerful and best-equipped divisions in France sat idle. Much of a day was lost. This was a day when the Allied landing turned aggressive, a day when tens of thousands of men, tanks, and guns landed on the Normandy beachhead—one day that made all the difference.

The second mistake in judgment denied the German defenders their best general. This was the man Hitler had brought in to ensure that the landing failed. He was the Führer's favorite general, one who had shown in North Africa that he could defeat the Allies—Field Marshal Erwin Rommel. Rommel had definite ideas about delaying the landing and about using panzers to divide and overwhelm each of the beachheads.

The weather was blustery and the seas rough on June 5, 1944. There were only a few moments in the day when the tide would be right for the invasion. All of the Allied commanders had concerns about the weather. Just how close Eisenhower was to delaying the landing is a matter of record. Then the weathermen in England saw a break long enough for D-Day to succeed. Seeing the same weather while at his headquarters in France, Erwin Rommel decided that any Allied landing would be impossible. That meant he could take advantage of the break to fly back to Germany. The sixth of June was his wife's birthday, and he could be home to celebrate it. The next morning, Rommel woke in his home to the news that the Allies had landed. His first comment was "How stupid of me." He had made the classic mistake of expecting the enemy to act as he thought they should. Field Marshal Rommel rushed back to Normandy, but he arrived too late to drive the Allies back into the Channel, as he had planned to do.

Had the Desert Fox been at his HQ in command of Army Group B, the 21st Panzer could have attacked sooner. The two other panzer divisions he had direct command of, the 2nd and the 116th, might have rushed over the Seine River and arrived much sooner than they actually did. Under Rommel's dynamic leadership, and according to his plan, significant counterattacks would have begun just hours after the first landings. The American landings on two of their beaches were going so badly that the troops on them were almost withdrawn. Had those beaches been hit by the 2nd SS or the 21st Panzer divisions, it would have been a slaughter. During the first hours of the landing, the beachhead the Americans held was only yards wide. The entire invasion could have ended badly.

It is always tough to confront the boss with bad news when he is in a bad mood. Had someone woken Hitler when news of the D-Day landings arrived, he would have had only a few hours' sleep, but fifty thousand veteran soldiers and two panzer divisions could have arrived near Normandy much sooner. By adding those divisions to his, Rommel would have had an attack force that was strong enough to drive in the beachheads, even a day later.

So, two seemingly minor decisions changed the war. If Rommel had not assumed that Eisenhower would not order the landing because *he*, personally, would not have, history might read very differently. The Desert Fox could have used Hitler's four divisions, and his own seven mobile divisions, to counterattack the Normandy beachhead sooner and in greater force. All those who were in charge of D-Day have written how it was a near thing, at first. So, how would it have been if the Desert Fox had thrown five panzer and two panzer grenadier divisions at an Allied landing while the men were still struggling to get ashore, land sufficient supplies, and move clear of the beaches?

If D-Day had failed, there would have been no chance that the Allies could try again before the winter weather made the Channel impossible to cross. Russia, already feeling it was being forced to do all the fighting, might well have balked at carrying the load another year. A separate peace was possible. Certainly, Stalin had no loyalty to his Western allies. Without a Russian front, the Reich would have been impregnable and no more landings would have been feasible. The Nazis, at least until the truce with Russia unraveled, would control virtually all of Europe. If they had managed to revive and use the industrial strength of the continent, the Third Reich would likely have grown proportionally stronger than Russia. We could be dealing with a Nazi Germany even today.

Many things contributed to the Allied success in Normandy. Brave men, heroic sacrifices, air superiority, and amazing improvisation, from the Mulberry harbour to the flail tanks. These and tens of thousands of brave men all made vital contributions. But if it was not for a birthday party and an unwillingness to wake a grouchy boss, the Allies would have suffered more significantly and might even have been trapped on the beachheads. If those two mistakes had not been made and the D-Day landing had failed, the Nazi Party might still rule Europe today.

||||||||||||||||||||||||||||||||||||||||||||||||||||||||||||||||||||||||||||

# 67

# BATTLE OF THE BULGE—ALLIED MISTAKES

## 1944

### By Bill Fawcett

||||||||||||||||||||||||||||||||||||||||||||||||||||||||||||||||||||||||||||

But I thought we were winning?

The Battle of the Bulge was really the result of two major mistakes. The first was that, despite the massive German buildup and plenty of warning signs, the Allied command was completely surprised. This was the result of several smaller mistakes, and a number of smart moves by the Wehrmacht.

To begin, many American officers were told that the attack was coming. A number of German prisoners were taken, or deserted to the American lines, many of whom told their captors what they had been trained to do. Reports included this information, but it was completely ignored at higher administrative levels. A German counterattack simply did not fit with the view the top commanders had of the war. A number of reports of increased German activity in the Ardennes sector were also written off as being the work of nervous new units, or simply judged to be impossible. The Americans and British had been rolling back the Germans for months. Each attack had ended in a German retreat. There had not been a German counterattack of any size since D-Day Normandy. Even those who acknowledged that there was increased activity were sure that the terrain of the Ardennes Forest was too difficult for any major offensive to take place there. That assumption was common, but rather amazing since, in 1940, the initial German flanking attack that rolled up the French army came though that same forested terrain. The Wehrmacht went to great lengths to disguise the buildup. Even the code name of the operation was designed to fool the Allies, Operation Watch on the Rhine.

The American reaction to or, rather, disregard of evidence was a product of that all-too-common Victory Disease. The war was all but over. Everyone would be home before the end of the next summer, maybe sooner. The Germans were losing and the Allies advancing, and the vast majority of commanders from Eisenhower down saw no reason for this to change. Further, intelligence sources told them that Germany was virtually out of gasoline. Without fuel, the panzers could not run. This was close to true. The Wehrmacht actually began their offensive without enough fuel to reach their full objectives. The panzer commanders were told to capture the abundant American supply depots and use the Allied fuel stored in them. So the Allies were sure that the Germans would not, and could not, counterattack in December of 1944. This opinion was reinforced by the lack of decrypted German radio transmissions mentioning anything like an attack. The top brass had become too dependent on the Ultra decryption team. When the British intelligence unit reported no activity, the generals all took this as meaning that there was none, despite other warnings.

The other intelligence source that the Allied generals had great confidence in was air-force surveillance. The Germans did an exceptional job of hiding during the day and moving at night, and obscuring signs that they had passed. It helped that, out of sheer desperation and a lack of fuel, the Wehrmacht had reverted to WWI transport methods. Rather than a swarm of easily spotted trucks, many of the supplies were brought forward by fifty thousand horses pulling wagons.

The result was that the carefully gathered reserves of the Wehrmacht were able to strike with complete surprise. The portion of the front they attacked was a "quiet sector," in which new and recovering units were stationed. It was considered a safe position, where new units could gain experience without much risk and replacements could be integrated into veteran units. So, when the mass of armor and elite infantry hit, they not only seriously outnumbered the defenders; they also outclassed them. Thousands of American soldiers were captured in the first few days. After a communications mix-up, two entire regiments, the 422nd and 423rd Infantry, were surrounded and captured while trying to hold a line when their flanking units had retreated. There, alone, 6,500 men surrendered, the largest surrender of US soldiers in the entire war.

The German offensive continued to roll forward, protected from air attack by a severe storm center and benefiting from the chaos that ensued as the Allies scrambled to stop them short of the Meuse River. Had the Germans successfully crossed the Meuse in strength, they would have had a good chance of capturing Antwerp, the only large port and source of supply for two army groups. Finally, a combination of clearing weather, the solidification of the Allied line, the resistance of Bastogne, and the arrival of Patton's 3rd Army broke the offensive.

Tens of thousands of Allied soldiers were killed or wounded, the entire front thrown into chaos. Patton's order to rescue Bastogne made him unable to carry out his planned offensive south into the Saar. All the Allied generals had to do was listen to their intelligence reports. There were more than enough units to strengthen the line in Ardennes. Nothing the Germans did, other than attacking at all, was new or unusual. There should never have been a Bulge at all, much less a battle to recover it and free Bastogne. If the Allies had trusted their own field intelligence and not looked for reasons to continue to believe what they wanted to believe—that the war was almost over—there would not have been a Bulge formed to battle over. Perhaps the only real value the Wacht am Rhein operation had for Germany was that it distracted and wore down Patton's 3rd Army. If this mechanized corps had not had to make its brilliant change of facing and rush toward Bastogne, it would have remained free to attack into Germany as Patton had planned. There would have been no mobile reserves to stop the advance into the Saar and beyond. Patton's attack could have been a decisive breakthrough. The war might have ended sooner or the Allied armies might well have been able to be first to Berlin.

||||||||||||||||||||||||||||||||||||||||||||||||||||||||||||||||||||

# 68

# BATTLE OF THE BULGE—GERMAN MISTAKES

## 1944

### By Bill Fawcett

||||||||||||||||||||||||||||||||||||||||||||||||||||||||||||||||||||

Unrealistic expectations doomed this offensive from the start.

The Battle of the Bulge lasted two weeks, from December 16, 1944, until the end of the month. The war against Russia was going badly for the Nazis. A diminishing number of defenders were being pushed back across Poland toward Germany. The Allied forces were literally across the river from western Germany and her industrial heart, and the Germans lacked the men, weapons, and fuel to defend the Reich in a two-front war. If things continued this way, it was only a matter of time until total defeat. Hitler realized that a masterstroke was needed, something that might enable him to reach a favorable agreement with one side or the other. The Russians were implacable and could never forgive the virtual destruction of half their nation and twenty million dead. The democracies, whom Hitler always saw as morally deficient, seemed a possible weak link. So it was against the Allies, poised to enter Germany on a broad front, that he ordered a surprise attack through the Ardennes. After all, an attack there had worked very well against France, but the situation in 1944 was very different from that of 1940. This was Operation Watch on the Rhine, which was later known as the Battle of the Bulge.

The problem was that the entire Nazi operation was based on inaccurate assumptions. The Führer had always underestimated the will and the leadership of the Western Allies. He believed, accurately, that the strain of the war was testing those nations' resolve. What he did not realize was that they became more, not less determined the longer the war lasted. Based on his selective reading of British and American newspapers, Hitler also thought that the leaders of England and the United States were often in conflict. This, again, was simply not true. So his goal to put enough stress on the British and American armies that their alliance would fail, or they would seek a separate peace, was unrealistic, at best. To accomplish this, he felt he needed to do two things: greatly disrupt the military situation of the Allied forces, preferably by isolating the British from the bulk of their allies, as had happened in 1914 and 1940, and then offer a separate peace, when the cost to England or America for continuing the war seemed too high.

Thus Hitler called in reserves and reinforcements from all of Germany. This not only weakened those units not planned to be part of the attack, but also limited how much support could be given to those who were trying to resist the Red Army on the Eastern Front. This was a desperate bid, using the very last dregs of manpower that were capable of fighting at all. Many of the infantry divisions used in the Battle of the Bulge were composed almost entirely of clerks, the slightly disabled, navy and Luftwaffe personnel, such as mechanics who no longer had any airplanes to work on, and whoever else could be found. Anyone not in uniform already, and capable of firing a weapon, was enlisted. Children as young as sixteen were given a few weeks' training—and armed.

The spearhead of the Watch on the Rhine attack was veteran panzer divisions. Many were SS divisions that were well equipped and highly trained. Once the attack started, the panzers surged forward against the thin American line. The inexperience of the German infantry divisions that were supposed to be supporting these tanks was so great that they often clogged, and even blocked, key roads. Divisions meant to follow up and push through the gaps created by the panzers were more often stranded miles behind them, in gigantic traffic jams of their own making. They lurched, not surged in to occupy their objectives, after the SS and other armored divisions initially pushed the Americans back. This lack of infantry support allowed the American forces to maintain a continual line even as they were driven back toward the Meuse and the Bulge was formed.

The near-term objective of the Nazi attack was to cross the Meuse River and retake the port of Antwerp. This was the only still-functioning port near the fighting that the Allies controlled. Most of the larger ports farther south in France had been destroyed before being retaken, and were still unusable. Antwerp was the source of the majority of supplies for both the British and American armies that were beginning to push into Germany. If the Nazi armored divisions could capture and hold, or even just destroy, Antwerp, the Allied logistics would collapse. That, Hitler expected, would cause a split between the Brits and the Americans, and the war-weary British would accept a separate peace. America, he believed, would have no choice but to follow. The plan also required that the Allies react to the attack as Hitler expected, which, of course, they did not.

Based on incorrect assumptions, Hitler's attack plan had stripped the nation of its last reserves of manpower and fuel. As the battle unfolded, other mistaken assumptions were revealed. To succeed, the German formations had to move quickly and punch through the Allied line. Then the Allies had to react slowly, allowing the Germany infantry to keep up with the advance. This would permit the panzers to continue to push forward. The key assumption was that the Americans would panic and pull back, without forming a solid line or retaining any strong positions behind the advancing panzers. This did not happen. In fact, it never could have happened—if for no other reason than that the panzer divisions did not have enough fuel to reach Antwerp, much less fight multiple battles and then move on to the port. Nor was there enough fuel for the trucks carrying the infantry to follow them. This flaw was painted over by a belief that the panzers would be able to complete their advance by capturing American supply dumps and using the fuel they found there.

Hitler and his staff's objective was for the first panzers to reach the Meuse River by the end of the first day. This was beyond unrealistic, even if they had enough fuel. The Americans were pushed

back, but not broken. The American 82nd and 101st Airborne occupied two key towns that controlled most of the roadways and,
even when surrounded, refused to be driven out or surrender. They
bogged down the German advance, as did stiffening resistance.
Artillery and tanks that were intended for the breakout over the
Meuse River were instead expended in unsuccessfully attacking
Bastogne.

Another basic assumption was that the attack would happen in
stormy, overcast weather. The Luftwaffe could no longer contest the
air, even over a limited battlefield. So the battle was to be fought in
weather so foul that airpower was not a factor. As things turned
out, the iced-over roads and snow-blocked fields only further hampered the already hesitant infantry advance.

The farthest forward any panzer reached was when Kampf-
gruppe von Böhm got to within a few miles of the Meuse River. This
was the 2nd Panzer Division and elements of Panzer Lehr. There
they ran into General Lawton Collins's VII Corps, were stopped,
and then driven back. Then General Patton's 3rd Army, which had
been attacking south when the Bulge began, smashed through the
9th Panzer on the Bulge's southern flank. On December 22, the sky
cleared and the Allied air forces returned with a vengeance. The
Germans were attacked relentlessly from the air. Tanks and artillery were bombed—any movement during the day inevitably drew
a strafing or bombing. By Christmas, Patton had relieved Bastogne.
Outnumbered, out of fuel, and with failing morale, those who could
tried to retreat. By New Year's Day, all the ground lost by the Americans had been recaptured.

The force that attacked and created the Bulge was, in reality,
Germany's last reserve. For months before the attack, most of the
production of tanks, automatic weapons, and artillery was diverted
to the Ardennes. The Wacht am Rhine offensive was made with
640 tanks, over a thousand pieces of artillery, and nearly 150,000
soldiers. This is as many men and nearly as many tanks as took
part in the attack on the Kursk salient in 1942. Gathering these
resources was done at the expense of the existing fronts. Virtually
all of the panzers and much of the artillery involved were lost. Be-

fore the battle began, its commander, Gerd von Rundstedt, issued a message that correctly reflected the importance of the attack:

"Soldiers of the Western Front! Your great hour has arrived. Large attacking armies have started against the Anglo-Americans. I do not have to tell you more than that. You feel it yourself. WE GAMBLE EVERYTHING!"

Von Rundstedt was correct. Hitler gambled everything on his attack through the Ardennes. It appears he hoped to repeat the success he'd had there in 1940. But this time the odds were very different, the Allied response firmer, and the German resources simply not there. Due to surprise and the Allies' overconfidence, the Germans wreaked terrible havoc in the first days, but never had a chance to reach their objectives. And even if they had reached Antwerp, they would have been an inconvenience and no more. There was no real chance that they could bring about the desired Anglo-American split.

What if Hitler had listened to his field commanders and used his last reserves to support them rather than in a doomed offensive? Germany had no chance to win WWII, or even survive, at this point. So the question is, how would the war have progressed if Hitler had not wasted this last reserve? Had the soldiers remained on the Western Front, the battle for the Saar and then the heart of Germany would have become a slow grind, at best. Eight additional panzer divisions in the field and another 150,000 (even poorly trained) infantry fighting from defensive positions would have slowed the Allies, if not stopped them. This would have allowed the Russians to advance farther into Germany and the Balkans than they did. Munich, not Berlin, might have been a divided city, and nearly all of Germany and Austria might have ended up under Communist control. The Cold War would have been different, and the wealth and power of Soviet Russia greater.

If instead of wasting the men in the Bulge, Hitler had sent them to the Eastern Front, it might have made a dramatic difference. Russian tactics, such as mass charges, were costly. The Red Army had suffered literally millions of dead and disabled. Even their pool of recruits was drastically reduced. Older and younger Russian soldiers had begun appearing in the front lines. If Germany's last reserve had been sent east, the commanders there might have made great use of such a force. The front might well have stabilized somewhere in Poland or at the German border. With his army halted and punished, Stalin might have been unable to grab so much of Eastern Europe and certainly the Anglo-American forces would have occupied most of Germany. Undoubtedly, the millions oppressed by the Communists in East Germany and Eastern Europe would have preferred that Hitler not waste his last reserves on a futile attack. The Cold War would have been very different, and a poorer and weaker Russia would have been likely.

# 69

# MISPLACING AUDACITY

## 1944

**By William Terdoslavich**

There are old soldiers and there are
bold soldiers, but there are no old,
bold soldiers.

Operation Market Garden was supposed to end the war in a single bold stroke.

Just drop three airborne divisions into the Netherlands to take and hold a corridor for a rapid Allied advance. That will require seizing several key bridges, the last one sixty miles behind enemy lines. Now run a corps up the connecting roadway to relieve the paratroopers. Upon crossing the last bridge over the Lower Rhine, make a right turn and attack eastward to take out the Ruhr—Germany's industrial heartland.

And who was the author of this daring operation? Field Marshal Bernard Law Montgomery, renowned for his thorough planning and *caution*.

This operation went beyond the boundaries of calculated risk. It was a gamble. Failure of any one part could jeopardize the success of the entire operation. Montgomery depended on nothing going wrong.

But in war, things go wrong all the time. It's called *friction*. Carl von Clausewitz first defined it in his masterwork, *On War*, as the accumulation of small difficulties. "Everything is very simple in war, but the simplest thing is difficult," he wrote. That is what friction is like.

## Jumping into the Unknown

On September 17, 1944, almost two thousand C-47s and gliders all over southeastern England loaded up their human cargoes, bound for the Netherlands. The 101st Airborne concentrated its drop around Eindhoven. The 82nd Airborne dropped farther north, near Nijmegen. The drop zones were close to their objectives.

The greatest task was entrusted to the British 1st Airborne Division. Dropping near Arnhem, it had to seize one of three crossings over the Lower Rhine. Just take one and Montgomery can then cross his troops to outflank the entire German army.

Sounds great. If the task was so important, why were the British only sending two brigades of their division? The third brigade was slated to arrive the next day, while a Polish airborne brigade was scheduled to arrive two days later.

Friction began eating away at Montgomery's plan a week before the paradrop. Reconnaissance photos showed the presence of German tanks in the Arnhem area. No one on the British 2nd Army's staff that was overseeing the operation saw the photos. The radios to be used also lacked the needed range to communicate with all units in 1st Airborne's designated area of operations, from the drop zone in Oosterbeek to the bridge at Arnhem seven to eight miles away, the division's farthest objective.

Friction only got worse once the British 1st Airborne was on the ground. Most of the radios stopped working. Close air support could not be called, which was especially bad since two depleted German panzer divisions were in the area. The division's final brigade arrived, but had to fight its way to Oosterbeek from its drop zone to the north—and that took a day or two.

And of those three battalions that would fight their way into Arnhem? Only one made it. The first two crossings were destroyed, but the third was still standing—the bridge that was farthest away. And that lone battalion held only the northern end of the bridge. And forget about that Polish airborne brigade—it never arrived. Fog in Britain grounded the aircraft.

Now, British XXX Corps had forty-eight hours to run up sixty miles of road to relieve all three airborne divisions, provided all the bridges were captured. But there was more friction. The 101st Airborne seized most of the bridges in its area, but the retreating Germans blew one of them up. It had to be replaced by a pontoon bridge—that took time. Friction.

That lone battalion holding half of the Arnhem Bridge held out until the fourth day—forty-eight hours after it was supposed to be relieved. It ran out of ammo and surrendered after suffering heavy casualties, a victim of friction.

The 82nd Airborne also seized most of its objectives, except for the rail bridge over the Waal at Nijmegen, well defended by the SS panzer troops. Taking the bridge was not possible until XXX Corps' tanks appeared. They were late. More friction. The 82nd then had to wait for boats to aid a battalion crossing to seize the bridge from the north while attacking it from the south. It was done successfully, but that was more friction.

On the operation's fifth day, that Polish airborne brigade finally showed up, flying into a hot DZ and losing a quarter of its strength as German ground units shot up the gliders. More friction.

The Poles managed to secure a perimeter on the Lower Rhine's south bank, opposite Oosterbeek, with help from XXX Corps. By now Operation Market Garden was in its seventh day. Capturing any bridge across the Rhine was hopeless as the British and Poles concentrated their efforts on saving what was left of 1st Airborne. It took two days to pull this off, all the while suffering German gunfire.

By the time the battle was done, British 1st Airborne, which jumped with more than ten thousand men, barely had more than two thousand left. Worse, no crossing over the Rhine was seized. The war would not be over by Christmas.

## Grease Beats Friction

There is nothing you can do about friction. Things go wrong. It is the nature of war. You can't eliminate friction. Simplifying a plan can cut down on the number of things that can go wrong, reducing friction from a decisive drag to a chronic, but manageable, inconvenience.

Perhaps the simplest solution would have been to move 1st Airborne's drop zone from Oosterbeek to the polder country south of Arnhem. This was where the Poles were landing, even though British planners thought the waterlogged ground would be a poor choice for a DZ.

That would have placed the division closer to one of its three main objectives—the bridge at Arnhem. Taking the bridge from one end, however, would still be problematic. The best suggestion came from the division's glider regiment commander, Colonel George Chatterton: land the gliders close to or on the bridge approaches. That could have put a battalion on the spot. Surprise and daring would do the rest. His idea was rejected by his higher-ups.

Had the glider coup de main been successful, close to two brigades could have reinforced that bridge capture, taking up positions in the town of Arnhem. Urban warfare favors infantry and would have lessened the Germans' meager advantage in tanks. They, and not the British, would have likely suffered the massive casualties that came from fighting their way into town. The division DZ would be held for resupply, instead of watching it all fall into German hands, as it did during the actual battle.

Not all the problems belonged to the 1st Airborne. Spearheading British XXX Corps' drive was the Guards Armored Division, advancing down a single road. It would have been nice if the British were able to move another corps beside it to lend some breadth and depth to the attack, but all were hamstrung by the lack of supplies. Montgomery only had enough to supply one corps on the attack. About 1,400 trucks that could have supplied two more divisions were sidelined in late August due to faulty pistons.

Then there is sequencing. Montgomery could have shortened his supply line by capturing the major port of Antwerp—*after* securing the sixty-mile-long Scheldt Estuary leading up to the port. (Montgomery later wrote in his diary that he regretted this oversight, which is a lot coming from a general who claimed never to have made a mistake.)

Taking the Scheldt, then Antwerp, might have freed up trucks to support an additional corps to support XXX Corps, perhaps protecting its flanks from the many company- and battalion-sized attacks on the British flank that slowed down the British advance. (Friction, friction, friction!)

Friction did its worst. Only good planning and wild improvisation can get around that. Montgomery, for all his paper daring, could not do both.

# 70

||||||||||||||||||||||||||||||||||||||||||||||||||||||||||||||||||||||||

## THE GOOD COMMUNIST

### 1945

### By Teresa Patterson

||||||||||||||||||||||||||||||||||||||||||||||||||||||||||||||||||||||||

Did the USA create its own disaster?

September 2, 1945, Vietnam. It was the end of World War II. Bright red pennants ruffled in the breeze of the crowded Ba Dinh Square in Hanoi. The Japanese, who had taken Vietnam from the French, had just surrendered, and the mood in the square was festive and excited. People in bright-colored traditional dress banged drums and blew whistles. Amid the tumult, a slender Vietnamese man stepped onto the stage erected on the edge of the square. American OSS officer Archimedes Patti watched from a nearby platform as the crowd quieted and the wiry, intense man began to speak, captivating his audience. Patti did not speak Vietnamese, but even without his interpreter, he knew the words well.

*"All men are created equal; they are endowed by their Creator with certain inalienable Rights; among these are Life, Liberty, and the pursuit of Happiness."*

He himself had helped advise the speaker on the correct order of the words only hours before. Most of the crowd had never read or even heard of the original document, but it was obvious from their fervent reaction that the words connected with them. The speaker was Nguyen Sinh Cung, better known as Ho Chi Minh—on that day, the self-declared president of the provisional government of the Democratic Republic of Vietnam.

The French, during years of colonial control, had raped the

country, impoverished the people, and plundered Indochina for the profit of France. The end of World War II had left the French colonists in disarrayed exile, most driven out when the Japanese overran Vietnam. Now defeated, the Japanese were leaving. The official ruler of Vietnam, Bao Dai, a French puppet, had just abdicated. Ho Chi Minh, believing the moment was ripe for the people of Vietnam to gain their freedom as an independent country, had stepped quickly into the resulting power vacuum. Patti, there as an OSS (precursor to the CIA) agent on a mercy mission to liberate POWs, noticed that the takeover had been peaceful and efficient. No weapons were fired, and even the hated French remaining in Hanoi were unharmed.

Ho Chi Minh had spent his whole life preparing for that moment— the moment when he could promise his people a free and independent future. And the people in the square that day loved him for it. He lacked only one thing to make his dream a reality: official recognition from the US and the world.

Even Patti, watching from the sidelines, saw the opportunity. He had spent time with the enigmatic Ho Chi Minh and believed it was in the best interest of the US to support him, or at least recognize his government. Ho was officially a Communist, but he was a "good Communist." He had been a staunch ally against the Japanese during the war. When the French failed to provide needed intelligence, Ho's people had come through with extremely accurate and actionable intelligence. When the French refused to supply fighters, Ho supplied his own Viet Minh fighters to assist and participate in the Deer Mission to cut Japanese supply lines, an action that infuriated Ho's supposed Soviet masters. The Soviets insisted that all Communists refrain from aiding the US against Japan. Ho ignored them. The French and other informants insisted on being paid for their intelligence, bad as it was. Ho refused. He asked only that the US live up to its promise of self-determination for all peoples, as outlined in the Atlantic Charter of 1941.

Unfortunately, lacking any real authority, Archimedes Patti could do no more than tell Ho that the US took the charter seriously, and send positive reports back to his superiors. He hoped they would realize that this unusual man, who valued democracy and hated the Chinese, was a "good Communist" and could provide a stable government, as well as a path toward a democratic future for Vietnam. He sent *lots* of reports, detailing his observations and recommendations.

Unfortunately, whether by design or incompetence, no one ever read those reports. They were never even opened. Years later, Patti found them filed away, still carefully wrapped with their seals intact.

But Patti was not alone in his opinion. Many people in the State Department's Southeast Asia Division also believed that an independent Vietnam would be good for US interests, that it would support the promise of self-determination, and that Ho Chi Minh was the best choice to lead it. They realized that "Uncle Ho," despite being a confirmed Communist, was first and foremost a patriot. He himself said that when the socialists and Communists had split, he only opted to join the Communists because he realized their more powerful Soviet patrons had the potential might to liberate Vietnam from the French. "It was patriotism and not communism that originally inspired me." Unfortunately, he discovered that the Soviets had little interest in Vietnam.

Even President Roosevelt had been no fan of French colonialism. He was against anything that would "further France's imperialistic ambitions" and stated that France had "milked [Vietnam] for one hundred years." He had made it clear to many in his administration that he had no intention of handing Indochina back to the French.

But somehow, after Roosevelt's death, President Truman never got the memo. As far as the Truman administration was concerned, there was no such thing as a good Communist. They felt that any Communist presence in Southeast Asia would simply create an invitation to the Chinese. He believed the struggle in Indochina was a struggle against global communism. It didn't matter that Vietnam and China had been enemies for two thousand years.

The State Department as a whole backed the administration and ignored the Southeast Asia Division, believing that it was much more important to keep France as a friend than to support a commie in any way—no matter what the indigenous people wanted. So the US gave Vietnam back to the French. Twice.

When Ho Chi Minh realized the US not only refused to recognize his government, but also intended to give the country he and his people had fought for back to their former oppressors, he felt betrayed. At this point, Ho was willing to do anything to save his country from the clutches of the French. So when his traditional enemy, the Chinese, offered to back him in the quest to take back his country, he was desperate enough to agree.

By not realizing the difference between a pro-Western "good Communist" and the Communists of China, and failing to embrace the chance to create a much-needed ally in Ho Chi Minh, the US made a catastrophic mistake that led to one of the bloodiest wars in its history.

If the Democratic Republic of Vietnam had been granted autonomy—or even just been given the promise that the French would not return to oppress them—Ho would have felt obligated to maintain a strong alliance with the US, if only to keep the French from returning. His Communist leanings would have soothed the Chinese and prevented their expansion—so long as he did not threaten them by pressing for additional territory. If the Chinese tried to move in, Ho's forces would have met them with the same ferocity used against the French and their allies—but this time the US would be covertly supporting *him*.

The French, pouting over the loss of their cash-cow colonies, would have refused to support the rearming of Germany. This would have made the Cold War more difficult, but with the entire military power of the US free to focus on Russia, not all that difficult. The French probably would have tried to retake Vietnam. And been soundly defeated—as happened at Dien Bien Phu. But without US intervention, prevented by our alliance with Ho's government, the French would have been forced to leave Vietnam once and for all.

A peaceful Vietnam would have supported and promoted stability throughout Indochina. Cambodia's prince Norodom Sihanouk would never have been caught in the vise between the North Vietnamese and the US that led to his overthrow. The resulting falling dominoes that led to the despotism of Pol Pot and the massacre of at least two million Cambodians would never have happened. Both Vietnam and Cambodia would have become tourist destinations, renowned for their natural beauty and ancient art and culture.

In the US, the $120 billion spent on Vietnam would have been invested in the modernization of the nation's defenses. These defenses would have dramatically shortened the Cold War, as Russia would have been forced to realize it was militarily outmatched. Ho Chi Minh, as a former Soviet ally and now friend of the US, could even have assisted in negotiations.

There would have been no runaway inflation, and probably no Arab oil embargo. President Lyndon Johnson would have had two strong terms in office, solidifying pet projects such as civil rights. There would still have been protests, but only on racial issues. War protests would never have existed—though the music scene would probably have been a lot less interesting.

Most importantly, fifty-eight thousand Americans, seven hundred thousand Vietnamese, and two million Cambodians would not have lost their lives to war and its atrocities.

# 71

||||||||||||||||||||||||||||||||||||||||||||||||||||||||||||||||||||||||||||

## MacArthur's Folly

### 1950

### By Douglas Niles

||||||||||||||||||||||||||||||||||||||||||||||||||||||||||||||||||||||||||||

*Hubris* is derived from the Greek
*hybris*, which denotes insolence
and violence.

General Douglas MacArthur was a larger-than-life figure, a man who invariably did things in a big way, and one who left an indelible mark upon his country and, eventually, the entire world. The son of a Medal of Honor winner, he would be awarded that exalted medal himself. On the way, he left his imprint on the United States Army, with remarkable terms both as student and commandant at West Point, as a division-level officer during World War I, as a stalwart defender of the status quo against Depression-era protesters in Washington, DC, and as an army commander (of both Filipino and American armies) during World War II in the Pacific. His last great act was to be the United Nations supreme commander during the Korean War.

MacArthur presided over some notable successes, displaying remarkable courage under fire during both world wars, presiding over the army's half of the island-hopping strategy that took his forces the length of New Guinea and the Philippines during World War II. He had been appointed to command the massive armies gathering to invade the Japanese homeland in 1945 and 1946; when that invasion was rendered unnecessary by the atomic bombs dropped in August of 1945, it was MacArthur who famously accepted the Japanese surrender aboard the battleship *Missouri*, anchored in Tokyo Bay.

But his record was not without blemish. His violent routing of the Bonus Marchers—a band of penniless World War I vets and their families who had gathered peacefully in Washington during 1932 to seek help from the government—was regarded by many as a brutal act of oppression. In command of all the armed forces of the Philippines by December of 1941, he allowed his own troops to be hit by a surprise attack a full day *after* Pearl Harbor had been bombed. Neither did his personality make him easy to admire: a tremendously vain and insecure man, he never allowed his subordinates to share in "his" glory, and he constantly and publicly criticized and complained about his superiors, both in the Pentagon and in the White House.

After the Japanese surrender in 1945, he served as the de facto ruler of that island nation as it struggled to recover from a devastating war. By all accounts, he made generous and wise decisions that hastened the Japanese recovery—and also, naturally, kept MacArthur's name in the headlines. His area of responsibility also included the virtually unknown backwater of Korea, a mountainous nation occupying a large peninsula jutting south from the Chinese mainland. At the end of the Second World War, Korea had been divided, almost haphazardly, along the 38th Parallel of latitude, so that Soviet armies north of that line and American forces to the south could accept the capitulation of the Japanese soldiers garrisoning the peninsula.

The division was intended to be purely temporary, as it was taken for granted that Korea, freed of Nippon occupation, would have its liberty restored as a single country. However, as the fault lines between the Western Allies and the Soviet Union hardened in the immediate aftermath of the war, the division of convenience in Korea became a political boundary. The Americans helped to install Syngman Rhee as president of a capitalist democracy (albeit a repressive one) in the south, while the Soviets installed Kim Il Sung as the dictator of a harsh Communist regime in the north. North Korea became the Democratic People's Republic of Korea, a name coined without any apparent attempt at irony, with a capital at Pyongyang; South Korea would officially be known as the Republic of Korea (ROK) and had as its capital the soon-to-be-thriving commercial center of Seoul.

Korea's bifurcation became more pronounced when Mao Zedong's revolutionary Chinese Communists defeated Chiang Kai-Shek's Nationalists in 1949. With Chiang's surviving forces exiled to the island of Formosa (which they renamed Taiwan), a powerful and militant Communist state occupied the border directly to the north of North Korea. Kim Il Sung's confidence was bolstered by this powerful and nearby ally, while his army was strengthened by tanks, combat aircraft, and other equipment from his original benefactor, Soviet chairman Joseph Stalin. Kim skillfully played Mao and Stalin against each other as he curried favor with both.

When Kim's North Korean Army (NKA) launched a surprise invasion of South Korea on June 25, 1950, he embarked upon a gambit to unite the two Koreas under the banner of world communism. He also provided Douglas MacArthur the opportunity to preside over his most strategically brilliant military operation, one he would unfortunately follow with one of the most catastrophic and far-reaching mistakes of the nascent Cold War.

Immediately after receiving news of the invasion, MacArthur flew to Korea and visited the battlefield south of Seoul, the capital city that had fallen on the second day of the war. He informed President Truman that the ROK was doomed without stout American support—and that support was quickly supplied. American air and naval forces were immediately rushed to Korea, hampering the NKA's drive to the south, while ground forces arrived more gradually. The enemy's offensive finally ground to a halt with only one South Korean port, Pusan, in the far southeast corner of the country, remaining free of North Korean control.

Holding the perimeter around Pusan with a thin screen of forces, MacArthur mustered a division of United States Marines and another from the army, together with enough sealift capacity to land these troops on an enemy shore. The shore he chose was Inchon, a port located on a notoriously capricious waterway—but it was the port in South Korea that was closest to Seoul, in the northwest corner of the nation. The landings went off without a hitch beginning on September 15, and less than two weeks later, Seoul had been liberated and the entire NKA—which was still arrayed along the Pusan perimeter, far to the south—had been cut off from support and mostly surrounded. Surviving enemy soldiers either were captured or made their way northward as refugees, leaving their equipment behind. Kim's invasion had been not just stopped, but obliterated, and the Korean War seemed to be, for all intents and purposes, won.

Except that Douglas MacArthur wasn't finished. He was determined to occupy North Korea, and to eliminate Kim's regime once and for all. At the time, this seemed like a sensible goal, and Presidents Rhee and Truman, as well as the Joint Chiefs of Staff (JCS) in the Pentagon, all supported the move to the north, which began at once. In short order, Pyongyang and a succession of North Korean ports on the east coast were occupied by the United Nations forces. If MacArthur had halted there, he would have gained an immense victory, and utterly broken the power of North Korea.

And stopping in North Korea while still more than a hundred miles from the Chinese border was an idea that was starting to make sense to President Truman and the JCS. Concerned about China's ability to intervene in a war they had thus far remained aloof from, they encouraged MacArthur to halt. But the general was out for ultimate blood and glory, and just as he had not allowed himself to believe the Japanese would attack the Philippines in 1941, he convinced himself that the Chinese would not interfere with his move right up to their border. Perhaps he assumed that the atomic bomb—which Truman was unwilling to use against China—would intimidate Mao. MacArthur continued his northward advance, shrugging off the concerns of his superiors.

The Korean peninsula widens in the north, with many ridges of rugged mountains across the center. The two wings of the UN forces, 8th Army in the west and X Corps in the east, inevitably moved farther apart, and closer to Communist China, as they advanced northward. A vast swath of unknown, unscouted ground lay between the two prongs of the advancing army, which, by now, were far out of mutual support distance.

MacArthur steadfastly ignored rumors and reports of potential Chinese intervention, as if he believed such a thing to be completely out of the question. Even as Chinese soldiers were captured, intelligence sources warned of a massive threat in increasingly strident terms and, on November 1, a Chinese assault broke up a US Army regiment. And yet, when some three hundred thousand Chinese soldiers struck on the twenty-fifth of November, the attack came as a complete surprise to General MacArthur.

Many of the far-flung UN spearheads were hammered by assailants on three sides, while several others were surrounded and wiped out. The 1st Marine Division, encircled and besieged, fought an epic thirteen-day battle southward from the Chosin Reservoir to claw its way out of the trap down a single, serpentine mountain road. Many thousands of American fighting men died, and most of their hard-won gains—including the city of Seoul—were yielded to the advancing Chinese before the UN army's position was stabilized.

Douglas MacArthur, meanwhile, seemed to remain out of touch with the reality of his war. He pleaded with Truman to bomb China proper, and when the president refused to yield, he blamed his commander in chief for the disaster into which *he* had led his army. More than once he made the ludicrous argument that the Nationalist Chinese, trapped on their tiny island nation of Taiwan, be "unleashed" against the massive Communist-controlled mainland. With his public criticism of the president, including a letter the general wrote that was read aloud to Congress by a Republican House leader, Truman felt that he had no choice but to remove General MacArthur from command, thus bringing the old soldier's career to a close in April 1951.

Following MacArthur's removal, the Korean War lingered for two more years, costing many thousands of lives. When it ended, the border between the two Koreas lay in just about the same place it was when North Korea invaded the south. The Kim Dynasty in North Korea has lasted to this day, and represents one of the most brutal and repressive governments in the world. Yet, if MacArthur had shown a little more restraint in fall of 1950—or President Truman had exerted stern control of his willful general—the war could have ended with a victory for the United Nations, and a North Korean regime greatly reduced in population and territory.

A solid United Nations victory in Korea would not have destroyed the Communist bloc or ended the Cold War, but it is possible to imagine that the lingering showdown between East and West might have been less fraught with nuclear peril. A unified Korea, even if it did not include the entire peninsula, would have spared that nation's population the legacy of division and distrust that still lingers today, and the majority of the north's population would likely have benefited from the vibrant economic and social growth that happened in the south. The portion of unoccupied Korea north of Pyongyang may well have been annexed by China, and for those people that would have been preferable to the corruption, instability, and brutality that have been the hallmarks of North Korea's three-generation dynasty of ruthless dictators.

And it is even possible that, following a stinging and humiliating military setback in 1950, the Communist world would have been less willing to support the rebels in the civil war that racked Vietnam, making America's tragic involvement there completely unnecessary.

# 72

# THE BATTLE AND COLONY LOST

## 1953

**By Douglas Niles**

Hubris knows no nation. . . .

One of the most significant, yet underrecognized, effects of the Second World War was the sundering of the great empires that several European powers had established on the continents of Africa and Asia. The overseas holdings of the Netherlands and Belgium bent beneath these winds of change and gradually broke away, while the vast territories of France and England convulsed more quickly under the nationalist independence movements heralding the advance of the modern age.

Although the latter two nations counted themselves among the victors in the largest war in human history, both had suffered terrible losses in personnel, property, and prestige. England, although physically battered by bombing, was mostly intact. But France had been ravaged by more than four years of Nazi occupation, and deeply scarred by combat, as much of the nation became a battleground during the summer of 1944.

After the war, England retained some control over her most important colony, India, but the inevitability of independence was written on the wall. In fact, there had been a growing independence movement in that South Asian nation even before the Second World War. India, like other British colonies in the Middle East and Africa, would move gradually, but inexorably, toward nationhood.

France, which, in addition to physical losses, had suffered severe insults to her legendary Gallic pride, was more reluctant to part ways with her overseas territories, and chose to wage war in an attempt to restore imperial power. The nation's colonial power was split between several territories around the Mediterranean Sea (including Algeria, Tunisia, and Lebanon) and the valuable Southeast Asian realm of French Indochina. The latter was a trove of wealth, especially valuable for its natural resources, most notably rubber and timber.

French Indochina encompassed the countries that would come to be known as Vietnam, Laos, and Cambodia. French rule of these colonies had ended, for all practical purposes, in the summer of 1940, when the Nazi conquest of the home country left Indochina open to exploitation by Germany's Asian ally, Japan. The armed forces of Nippon wasted no time in occupying and garrisoning Indochina, and made most profitable use of Vietnam, which, with its large cities, long coastline, and excellent ports, would prove to be a significant power base for the massive war of conquest that Japan would launch at the end of 1941. It was also a key source of rubber, necessary for any nation to wage modern war.

After the war, and the utter defeat of Japan, France moved swiftly to reassert control of her former colonies. But the population of Indochina—and especially the Vietnamese—was tired of being dominated by foreigners and eager to assert their independence. After French intervention in 1946 crushed a nascent local government in a matter of weeks—as the Europeans used their naval power to bombard coastal cities, killing thousands of Vietnamese civilians—an organized resistance group called the Viet Minh, who had previously fought the Japanese, took up arms against the French.

The Viet Minh was composed of a mixture of Vietnamese nationalists and dedicated Communists, united mostly by their determination to create a free nation. These fighters willingly battled the French Far East Expeditionary Force, which had been dispatched to seize control of Indochina. Under the charismatic leadership of Ho Chi Minh, and the military skill of his chief military commander, Vo Nguyen Giap—and with steadily increasing support from Communist China and the Soviet Union—the Viet

Minh gradually progressed from an irregular force of guerrillas into a veteran, highly motivated army. They were bolstered by a sense of national identity and had inherited a history of resistance to foreign oppression against the Chinese, the French, and the Japanese.

From 1946 to 1953, the war was waged at a stage of low intensity highlighted by many small but bloody encounters. The French seized control of the cities and other population centers and, with superior artillery and armor, were able to hold off a succession of enemy attacks, gradually driving the Viet Minh into the country's interior. The guerrillas had no air force and began the war with no artillery arm, but the French were slow to recognize their enemy's growing capabilities in both guns and tactical ability. This failure would eventually prove catastrophic.

A succession of French commanders, supported only by lukewarm enthusiasm from the home country, tried to lure the Viet Minh into open battle. When they did so, they often inflicted heavy casualties on Giap's troops. The Vietnamese general continued to rely upon guerrilla tactics, even as he was being increasingly supplied by his Communist allies. After the Chinese Communists took control of China's border with North Vietnam in 1949, the shipments to the Viet Minh increased substantially, thus aiding the rebels considerably in their attempt to forge a modern army.

Even so, the French were no strangers to warfare, and had a long history of military accomplishment. After the humiliation of WWII, they were desperate to return to the status of an international power. Yet it is hard to reconcile that pride, and the desire to regain the status of empire, with the laundry list of poor decisions that were made during what became known as the First Indochina War.

For one thing, the war suffered from a lack of popular support in France, which banned the use of conscripted troops in colonial campaigns. Thus, it was fought by professional soldiers, colonial troops, and units of the legendary French Foreign Legion; even in combination, this was too small an army for the mission assigned. The effort was also poorly funded, as the main threat to French security was readily recognized to be a rearmed Germany, closely followed by the threat of Soviet aggression. By 1953, dissatisfaction on the home front had grown into a political force and it began to look as though the war would simply be abandoned.

The supreme commander of French forces in Vietnam at that time was General Henri Navarre, and he decided that the time had come to try to force a decisive engagement. Though he was not at all convinced that the war could be won, he was determined to risk a significant number of his best troops on an important operation. He made the decision to establish a strongpoint deep in the territory held by the Viet Minh, blocking a key supply route between Vietnam and Laos. The intent was to force General Giap to attack the French position. At that point, Navarre believed, French artillery and airpower would deliver a smashing defeat to the rebellion and an honorable peace could be arranged.

Unfortunately for France, and especially for the men Navarre dispatched on his ill-fated campaign, the general seemed to ignore virtually every standard rule of warfare as he went about planning this crucial battle. The French plan would be a spectacular failure on all three levels of war: strategic, operational, and tactical. Before it began, it was opposed by virtually every ranking officer under Navarre's command, but the general stubbornly insisted on going ahead. As the target, he selected a valley with an old airstrip, in a place called Dien Bien Phu. The location was far beyond reach of reinforcements or gunnery support, except from the air.

Next, Navarre made a terrible choice of commander for the operation, selecting a dashing cavalryman, Colonel Christian de Castries—a skilled proponent of mobile warfare—to lead a static force holding an entrenched, defensive position. Then he ignored a time-honored military maxim—"hold the high ground"—by placing his forces in a deep valley, leaving the rugged and forested heights surrounding Dien Bien Phu to the enemy. Finally, he drastically underestimated his enemy's capabilities.

In November of 1953, nearly two thousand elite French paratroopers parachuted into Dien Bien Phu, quickly taking control of the objective, seizing the airstrip, and commencing to prepare defensive positions. Over the next few months, the garrison would increase to some sixteen thousand men, supplied only by air. Seven fortified strongpoints were established around the airfield, but none of these occupied any of the significant points of high ground.

The one principle of warfare the French successfully employed was surprise, as General Giap was quite unprepared for their tactics. Once he figured out what was going on, however, he was delighted by Navarre's operation. Giap quickly ordered multiple divisions into the hills around Dien Bien Phu, and his dedicated men hauled many pieces of heavy artillery and antiaircraft guns with them through the mountainous jungle. Once they approached the French base, the Vietnamese tunneled through the mountain crests, bringing their guns into firing positions that would be essentially invulnerable to French return fire.

On March 13, 1954, the Viet Minh opened with an attack on the first French strongpoint, supporting their soldiers with a devastating artillery barrage. By the end of the first day of battle, Castries was forced to acknowledge that his own guns were completely unable to counter the enemy cannons. (In fact, on the third day of the battle, artillery commander Colonel Charles Piroth committed suicide, humiliated by this utter failure of French gunnery.) Meanwhile, Viet Minh antiaircraft gunnery took a heavy toll on French aircraft trying to support or resupply the garrison.

The battle would rage with varying levels of violence for nearly two months, but the outcome was preordained by the first day's combat. The Vietnamese attacked French entrenchments in waves, suffering many casualties but gradually shrinking the defensive perimeter. The airstrip, in range and line of sight of attacking guns, was soon rendered unusable, and attempts to supply the garrison by parachute were completely insufficient.

Colonel de Castries himself withdrew to his bunker and seemed paralyzed by indecision—perhaps because he had no good options. His men fought bravely, but it was a hopeless fight. When the French surrendered on May 7, they had suffered a decisive, even historic, defeat. For the first time, an army of former colonials had used modern weapons and tactics to defeat their conquerors.

A peace conference in Geneva commenced the next day, and Ho Chi Minh arrived with news of Giap's epic victory. As a result, France withdrew from Indochina and Vietnam was divided into north and south. Thus the seeds of the next, even bloodier, Indochina War were inevitably planted.

But what if the French had been willing to allow the Vietnamese to gradually obtain independence, as the British had with India? The country could well have remained a valuable trading partner of France, and would have stood a better chance of withstanding the all-consuming brand of communism that would eventually grip the nation with such deadly, divisive, and long-lasting consequences.

And the United States would never have had to send a single combat unit to Vietnam.

# THE PERSIAN MUDDLE

### 1953

### By Dr. Paul A. Thomsen

‖‖‖‖‖‖‖‖‖‖‖‖‖‖‖‖‖‖‖‖‖‖‖‖‖‖‖‖‖‖‖‖‖‖‖‖‖‖‖‖‖‖‖‖‖‖‖‖‖‖‖

Gifts for our friends in Iran . . . er . . .
Iraq . . . ah . . . Oh, never mind.

Diplomacy has always been a quid pro quo world of keeping one's friends happy to ensure your own happiness. There is also something to be said for nerfing an adversary's ability to hurt by turning his potential weapons of death into humanitarian gifts. In 1953, President Dwight Eisenhower attempted to accomplish both with his "Atoms for Peace" program. His altruistic plans, however, were built on the mistaken belief that friends always stayed friends. Instead of fostering peace and lasting friendships, Eisenhower's gifts bore poisoned fruit for America's allies and plunged the Middle East into an unprecedented arms race, involving nuclear, chemical, and even biological weapons.

In the Cold War, President Eisenhower planned to turn the destructive energy of the atom toward positive ends. Since assuming office in 1953, Eisenhower, hero of the Second World War and former NATO commander, had struggled to blunt Soviet nuclear weapons capabilities and create an advantage for America's allies. To this end, in a 1953 speech in New York, he proposed an "Atoms for Peace" program, in which all nuclear states would contribute radioactive fuel to a general pool for study, and financial aid to applicant developing countries, with the United Nations overseeing the program. It would, he thought, limit the material available for nuclear weapons creation and inspire a revolution in medicine, clean energy, and scientific advancement for friendly nations.

The president was wrong on both counts. Putting aside the technology and supervision issues that existed with ensuring the Soviet compliance, the rapid pace of innovations in nuclear weapons warheads and delivery systems guaranteed that the plan of a general pool of donated nuclear material would not hamper Soviet nuclear weapons production. In short, a series of scientific discoveries shrank both the mass and the delivery requirements for the creation of nuclear weapons, while simultaneously increasing the yield. The idea of stockpiling nuclear material was to limit the production of nuclear weapons. Instead, it *encouraged* weapons to be made more lethal with less.

Moreover, despite Eisenhower's altruistic motives, the program actually bred instability in the Middle East. With the United Nations' blessing, in 1956, Iraq undertook nuclear research under the Atoms for Peace program by establishing the Iraqi Atomic Energy Commission. In 1962, it bought a two-megawatt research reactor from America's adversary, the Soviet Union. In response to Iraq's moves, Iran (Iraq's neighbor and longtime rival) also received United Nations nuclear support with the founding of the Tehran Nuclear Research Center in 1957. In the early 1970s, Iraq violated the precepts of Non-Proliferation of Nuclear Weapons by proudly announcing that it would be making "the first Arab attempt at nuclear arming." In response, all the United Nations or the United States could do was impose sanctions for the foreseeable, but still unforeseen event.

Iran's shah, who had been receiving diplomatic gifts and concessions from the United States for years, balked at the development, but he had even worse problems. Instead of putting his oil money into bettering his people's lives, he spent extravagantly on luxury goods, military equipment, and various violent means to ensure his people's compliance. Bad choice. With Iraq waving the nuclear trump card, Iranians, feeling threatened from without and within, demanded their own nuclear weapons, better living conditions, and, failing those, the head of the shah. In January 1978, a reformist movement took to the streets of Iran and, a year later, turned into a bloody revolution, which toppled the shah and left his donated nuclear technology in the hands of an anti-American revolutionary government—right next door to another angry nuclear power. So much for peace!

If Eisenhower had been more realistic, many of the bloody consequences of his initiative could have been prevented in the twentieth century, and mitigated in the early twenty-first. Like biological weapons in modern times, or the secrets of gunpowder and Greek fire in antiquity, nuclear research was out of reach for most twentieth-century countries. Anyone can reasonably figure out the scientific steps to build a nuclear bomb, but it takes a lot of time, money, practical engineering experimentation, and access to rare elements to produce a single working city-killing nuclear weapon. Eisenhower could have demanded strict conditions for applicant/ personnel management, research facility locations, and materials and tools used in the nuclear research, beyond just the fissile material. The products could have then been shared without the fear of someone, such as A. Q. Khan, selling both his knowledge and stolen plans. Like firearm laws, these changes would have made monitoring individuals and designated facilities involved in nuclear research relatively free of Iraq's lies, the threat against its neighbor, and the deadly aftermath of the Iranian revolution. Furthermore, the program should have called on NATO's seminal defense—that an attack on one member of the nuclear club would be an attack on all nations—limiting the potential for rival neighbors like Iran and Iraq to get ideas about mushroom clouds over each other's cities.

By limiting the nuclear option, Eisenhower would have ensured a far safer Middle East than America faced over the next fifty years. While it is likely that the shah's excesses would have eventually triggered a revolution, a nonnuclear Iraq would have been less of a threat to Iran and would not have been attacked by Israel. Everything would have proceeded in a conventional expression of war, as it already had for millennia. Consequently, there would have also been less reason for America to twice invade Iraq, since Iraq would not have "needed" money from the southern oil fields, and there would have been no grounds for a Bush administration fear of a nuclear mushroom cloud over an American city. If there had been an Iraq-Iran war, Iran would have likely responded as it did, but the end of the conflict would not have seen them able to achieve the nuclear option A. Q. Khan gave them.

Instead of keeping the nuclear Pandora's box shut, Eisenhower's designs brought nuclear proliferation and bloody mayhem to the Middle East. In the late 1970s, Iraq built an enriched uranium breeder reactor near Baghdad. As they neared completion, feeling strong and in need of cash, Iraq invaded Iran with conventional forces in 1980. Although caught by surprise, Iran quickly counter-attacked with everything at their disposal. Rapidly outgunned and outgeneraled, Iraq was on the verge of being swallowed by Iran. Secretly aided by supplies from America, Saddam Hussein was able to drive back the invasion by the "almost daily" deployment of chemical weapons attacks. Unable to absorb the casualties, Iran de-escalated the conflict to a Cold War stalemate. Over a million lives were lost in that conflict alone. In June 1981, Israel, another "Atoms for Peace" beneficiary, declared the Iraq reactor a mortal danger to its national security and destroyed the complex in an air strike. In 1990, Iraq invaded Kuwait and Saudi Arabia in an attempt to stabilize the economic problems caused by their atomic dream-built wars, costing millions more in damages, approximately 22,000 Iraqi deaths, and the loss of 383 American lives. Now fearing for its security, Iran bought the services of another "Atoms for Peace" recipient, Pakistan's Abdul Qadeer Khan (who also reportedly sold secrets to North Korea, Libya, and others), kicking off a crash clandestine nuclear program in a country constitutionally committed to the "death" of the United States and Israel. As a result, it could be said that the road to hell in the twenty-first century truly was paved with good nuclear intentions.

Without Eisenhower's blanket "Atoms for Peace" policy, the world would be far colder. There would be far fewer nuclear scientists and nuclear power plants. There would also, therefore, be less advancement in practical nuclear medicine, heavy restrictions on body scans, and more tightly controlled radiation therapy for cancer patients. There are also several trade-offs. A full-scale Iran-Iraq war would have been far less likely. There would have been no need for America to invade Iraq in 1990 or 2003. Many of today's nuclear nations, such as Iran, Pakistan, Israel, North Korea, and China, would likely have failed to emerge as dominant global players. In short, had Eisenhower never ventured to propose the plan, the world would be a safer place and America's rivals far less capable of mass destruction.

# 74

# DO NOT DISTURB

### By Bill Fawcett

*This is enough to make you believe in poetic justice.*

This is a tale that includes a mistaken order that gave the world just a little touch of justice. It is generally a good idea, if you are a paranoid and irrational absolute dictator, that you be feared. Quite possibly, the dictator who was feared the most, barring maybe Genghis Khan, was Joseph Stalin. The Russian dictator personally ordered millions of deaths. He executed or banished to labor camps several million kulaks, small farmers who lived in Ukraine, for no other reason than that some of them might resist collectivization. Of about ninety thousand German soldiers captured at Stalingrad, fewer than six thousand ever returned to Germany. Stalin held on to power with an iron grip and his willingness to execute anyone, even his highest officials, was made apparent time after time.

By the early 1950s, Stalin was not in the best of health. Years of heavy drinking and long hours were taking their toll. He suffered from arteriosclerosis, which can manifest itself with constant pain. His personal physician of several years, Vladimir Vinogradov, made the mistake of suggesting that the dictator try to relax and maybe delegate some of his duties to others. Stalin flew into a rage and had the doctor arrested. For the rest of his life, he seems to have reacted to that suggestion by ordering a purge of certain (mostly Jewish) doctors. Lavrenty Beria later stated that Stalin considered ordering every Jew in Russia (and there were millions) to Siberia, just because most of the doctors in Russia were Jewish.

Failing health made the murderous dictator, already irrational, far more difficult to be around. Even Beria, head of the secret police, feared him and never contradicted anything Stalin said. Being a heavy drinker means you do not like being disturbed. Having personally ordered the death of entire peoples, the Communist Party leader was justifiably fearful of being assassinated himself. Since he trusted no one, Stalin's guards were under orders to never let anyone, including themselves, enter his office or even knock on its door until he, personally, came out and told them they could. Now, the imposition of absolute orders has a tendency to backfire, since exceptions tend to arise. The exception to Stalin's order turned out to be a mistake that effectively accomplished what assassins and Nazi bombers had failed to do—kill him.

One day, in the middle of February 1953, Stalin had been up most of the night drinking, as was his habit. He was in his dacha at Kuntsevo, near Moscow. He retired to his suite, which included an office and a bedroom. And sometime during that day, it appears that he suffered a stroke. He needed immediate medical care, but he was alone at the time and no one was allowed to enter or disturb him. An entire day and night passed, but Stalin did not appear. His guards were afraid to do anything; disobedience was fatal. Finally, a maid ventured in. She found the Russian dictator sprawled on the floor of his bedroom. He was conscious, but unable to speak, and he had lost bladder control. There is no way to be sure how long he had been in this condition, but it was likely many long, painful, and frightening hours. Joseph Stalin's absolute order and paranoia doomed him to hours of suffering and helplessness.

The guards called the four closest of his associates. These were Nikita Khrushchev, Malenkov, Beria, and Bulganin, who hurried to the dacha. By the time they got there, Stalin had been cleaned up, put to bed, and was asleep. The next morning, the Russian leader woke, but was barely able to move and could not speak. Untreated for more than a day, the stroke had taken its fullest effect. He never recovered and, on March 5, died. There were many competent doctors in Russia, and if Stalin had been found within a short time after he was stricken, some recovery might have been possible. He might have lived, debilitated, but alive and able to communicate. But everyone feared for their life and he lay stricken too long. Stalin basically ordered the method, if not the time, of his own death.

# 75

# GOOD NIGHT, VIETNAM

1956

## By William Terdoslavich

Perception can trump
reality every time.

Americans view war as a contest between good and evil, with the US being the good guys, of course. It worked in World War II. It did not work with the Vietnam War. Public support started high, but slowly waned as the war dragged on. Failing to win left Americans mistrustful of their leaders, their government, and any institution that had authority.

So what went wrong?

## Hot Fight in a Cold War

The Vietnam War was a violent chapter in the larger Cold War, the five-decade-long standoff between the democratic USA and Communist USSR. Direct confrontations between the two nations were frequent in the 1940s and 1950s, but died down after a near-nuclear exchange during the Cuban Missile Crisis of 1962. After that, all confrontations were indirect, usually between client states, or between a superpower and an enemy client.

The Cold War was also a zero-sum game. Any gain made by one side was a loss for the other. Trouble spots that could be ignored in the past became crucial and had to be dealt with. Win and you looked more powerful. Lose and you appeared weak.

The Vietnam War was fought in that context. The US bankrolled the French, who lost in 1954, after eight years of fighting the Communist Viet Minh. Peace talks saw a division of the former French colony. The Viet Minh took control of the government of North Vietnam, and sought to conquer South Vietnam for the sake of "national unification." But that would mean a win for communism, so the US had to back South Vietnam. In the conventional thinking of the time, there was no other choice.

The American part of the Vietnam War began in the summer of 1964. North Vietnamese PT boats attacked the destroyer USS *Maddox* on patrol in the Gulf of Tonkin. A second night attack on two destroyers probably did not happen. Nevertheless, President Lyndon Johnson decided to commit to an air war against North Vietnam. It was an election year and he had to look tougher than his opponent, Senator Barry Goldwater (R-AZ). Johnson obtained a resolution from Congress authorizing the use of military force. A subsequent Viet Cong attack in early 1965 against a US air base in South Vietnam prompted escalation.

Between February and December of 1965, the US sent 180,000 troops to South Vietnam, at first to protect air bases, then to take the war to the enemy. Likewise, North Vietnam, one of the poorest nations in the world at that time, sent 100,000 troops down the Ho Chi Minh Trail through "neutral" Laos and Cambodia to infiltrate into South Vietnam. The North Vietnamese were bankrolled and equipped increasingly by the USSR.

And so this went on through 1966, 1967, and 1968. Between conscripts and professionals, the US deployed about five hundred thousand men, while South Vietnam raised another one million men, with roughly half assigned to frontline units. And every year, North Vietnam sent another hundred thousand men down the Ho Chi Minh Trail, losing most of them in battle against the Americans.

President Johnson was unmindful of one thing: Americans expect to see some results after three or four years of fighting. In a democracy, political support for a war declines the longer it goes on, and drops even faster if results are lacking, or negative. The message Johnson gave to the American people in 1968 was simple: "We are winning." General William Westmoreland, our guy in command in South Vietnam, said so, too. But he always asked for more men every year—and got them. However, there was no Gettysburg or D-Day in Vietnam to show the public we were winning. The war was mostly a counterinsurgency campaign, with American forces chasing guerrillas and winning every firefight, but leaving the enemy in control of any territory when US forces moved on.

## A Surprise Attack Yields Surprise Results

For many, the breaking point came on January 30, 1968. During the lunar New Year holiday (known as Tet in Vietnam), NVA and Viet Cong units simultaneously attacked five major cities and forty-four provincial capitals in South Vietnam. US forces had a rough time of it, but eventually destroyed most of the Communist forces.

The attacks were supposed to trigger a massive uprising of South Vietnamese peasants against the corrupt South Vietnamese government. Instead, the peasants fled the fighting wherever they could. The Communist government in North Vietnam was staring at a massive defeat.

Or were they?

Back in the United States, support for the war drained away. After being told for three years that the US was winning, Americans watching the TV news saw Communist forces attacking everywhere in South Vietnam. If we were winning, why were the bad guys still fighting as if nothing had happened?

Student protests exploded on college campuses nationwide. Antiwar presidential candidate Senator Eugene McCarthy scored 40 percent of the vote in the New Hampshire primary against Lyndon Johnson, who should have won by a much higher margin. Even CBS News anchorman Walter Cronkite called the war a "stalemate" in an on-air editorial. On the advice of many current and former foreign policy experts, a weary President Johnson went on national TV to announce a halt to the US bombing of North Vietnam. He offered North Vietnam peace talks. And he tossed in that he would no longer seek reelection.

North Vietnam's Communist leadership was totally clueless about American politics and culture. That ignorance did not stop them from spinning the story in their favor. Yes, the destruction of America's political will was the real objective, they claimed, even though North Vietnam lost every battle fought in the Tet Offensive. That peasant uprising in South Vietnam never came close to happening.

## Winning in 1964 Cancels 1968?

One problem that hobbled any Democrat serving as president, or running for the presidency, was the suspicion that he was "soft on communism." This stemmed from the "loss of China" to communism in 1948, while Truman was president. This triggered a witch hunt for Communists in the State Department conducted by Senator Joe McCarthy (R-WI), which caused more damage than it repaired.

Johnson's predecessor, President John F. Kennedy, ran as a hard-line anti-Communist in 1960. Johnson, feeling boxed in by his lack of foreign policy expertise, felt compelled to fight for South Vietnam, even though he would much rather have passed civil rights laws and created a massive welfare state to eliminate poverty in the US.

In truth, Johnson did have political capital. He had won in 1964 with over 60 percent of the popular vote, carrying forty-four states. Johnson was now president in his own right. He could have passed on Vietnam, limiting US involvement to the existing advisory mission (about fifteen thousand troops) plus air units. More hawkish Republicans would have objected, but that's about it.

Burying the ghost of Joe McCarthy would have been a hundred times better than appeasing it. The US might have still "lost" Vietnam, but it would have been a marginal defeat, suffered in 1965 or 1966, instead of 1975. Despite defeat, the US grew more powerful. A unified Vietnam simply became poorer, exporting refugees rather than revolution.

Where the US suffered its greatest setback was right here at home. The nation literally tore itself in half. Antiwar protests became violent. Love of country was replaced with scorn. People stopped trusting their government—and any other institution that held authority. Social norms weakened and a counterculture took root that was the total opposite of the hardworking, clean-cut patriotism of the WWII generation. And it made the US reluctant to deploy force where needed for fear of repeating defeat.

Perhaps skipping the Vietnam War and avoiding the domestic turmoil would have been a hundred times better. But that would have required the United States to take a dive during another fight in the Cold War. That may have been asking for too much.

||||||||||||||||||||||||||||||||||||||||||||||||||||||||||||||||||||||||||||

# 76

# THE HUNGARIAN
# REVOLUTION

### 1956

### By Jim Werbaneth

||||||||||||||||||||||||||||||||||||||||||||||||||||||||||||||||||||||||||||

Rollback and massive retaliation fail.

The Cold War was the dominant foreign policy issue for the United States from the end of World War II to the final days of the Soviet Union in 1991. It split the world in two, divided between the United States and its allies, on the one hand, and the USSR and its supporters, on the other. There was the emergence of the Third World out of the ruins of Europe's colonial empires, but that just created a new set of venues for Soviet-American competition. In retrospect, the "third way" between them, pioneered by India and Yugoslavia in particular, amounted to an attempt to thread the needle between the superpowers.

It was a time that created plenty of opportunities for mistakes. The invasion of Afghanistan was one of the key events leading to the Soviet Union's demise, and escalation of America's presence in Vietnam helped tear American society apart. There were others as well: the Soviet suppression of the "Prague Spring" in 1968 and the support of the Polish army's coup against both Solidarity and the Polish Communist Party twelve years later. These incidents revealed the moral bankruptcy of Marxism-Leninism to a degree not seen since the Nazi-Soviet nonaggression pact. On the other side, the United States supported some absolutely terrible dictatorships—opposition to communism was more important than any commitment to human rights, let alone the ideals that America claimed to uphold.

Perhaps lost in the glare of later events was a major mistake on the part of the United States, one that began early in the Cold War. This was a tendency by the Eisenhower administration, and its secretary of state especially, to transform the policy of containing Soviet communism into one of rolling back its gains. This emphasis on liberation might have sounded good, and lent a sort of moral clarity to American foreign policy. It demonstrated, too, that the United States was unwilling to simply sit by in the face of tyranny.

Unfortunately, it was a major mistake in the 1950s. John Foster Dulles might have been more premature than entirely wrong, but this would have been cold comfort to those who ended up being hurt by his policies.

Coupled with this was a strategy of massive retaliation against Soviet threats, first announced in a speech by Dulles in 1954. This was not just a brand of impressive-sounding rhetoric; it was also rooted in Eisenhower's "New Look" defense policy. The New Look downgraded support for conventional forces and operations in favor of strategic nuclear weapons, which offered much more cost-effective firepower. Therefore, there was a close connection between massive retaliation through nuclear warfare and a quest to acquire "more bang for the buck" by investing in it.

The shortcomings of the fatal combination of rollback, massive retaliation, and an undue faith in nuclear weapons were revealed in 1956. Hungary's Communist dictator, Mátyás Rákosi, was removed from power on July 18. Rákosi was one of the "Little Stalins" installed in power in the wake of the Soviet Union's overrunning of Eastern Europe at the end of World War II, and was a worthy protégé of the Soviet dictator. He was servile toward Moscow and oppressive toward his own nation, all while mismanaging the Hungarian economy. In addition, though born a Jew, he adopted a tone of anti-Semitism himself. However, in the changing environment of the Communist world following the death of Stalin and the rise to power of Nikita Khrushchev, Rákosi fell out of favor with the Soviets as well as with his own people.

This unleashed a season of turmoil in Hungary. Rákosi was succeeded as chairman of the Council of Ministers of the People's Republic of Hungary by the more moderate Imre Nagy, an advocate of a "new course" of socialism. With the lid of repression lifted somewhat, popular expectations rose, even with the Communist Nagy in power. In October, a combination of frustration and expectation flared into open revolution, with the approval of the new leader. Hungary rejected communism, the Soviet Union, and its Eastern European military alliance, the Warsaw Pact. Supportive crowds eliminated the secret police, tore down statues of Stalin, and even drove the Soviet military out of Budapest as the forces of revolution spread from the capital. The banner of the Hungarian Revolution became the Communist-era flag, only with the Communist coat of arms cut out of the center. Then the Soviets quickly returned in overwhelming force and put down the revolution. Nagy was removed from power, imprisoned, and, after a secret trial, executed in 1958.

The American response revealed the inadequacies of the policies of rollback and massive retaliation. There was no significant diplomatic response, in part because the United States found it difficult to credibly condemn Soviet actions in Hungary even as its own British and French allies were invading Egypt during the Suez Crisis. At the root of it all, though, the United States simply did not have either the means or the compelling national interest to intervene in Hungary. It did not have an ally that shared a border with Hungary, and therefore had no land access to the country. Nor did it have sufficient ground forces in Europe, even if they could have gotten to Budapest; after all, West Germany still had to be defended.

Finally, the policy of massive retaliation did not allow for much of a graduated response, something between doing nothing and initiating a nuclear war. Also, aiding Hungary simply was not worth the risk of starting World War III and a nuclear exchange between the superpowers. Therefore, when the Hungarian people rose up in order to roll back communism, as Dulles had called for, they did so without concrete American support.

The United States might have paid a price, but it was in terms of damaged credibility and the exposure of shortcomings in its foreign and military policies. The cost to the Hungarians was the invasion of their country and the attendant large-scale destruction, a scant eleven years after World War II. Already suffering from the economic policies of Rákosi, Hungary had little chance to recover from that conflict.

Ironically, the reimposition of communism upon Hungary was a process that could have gone worse, while the American search for policies less extreme than rollback and massive retaliation could have gone better. Nagy's Soviet-chosen replacement was János Kádár. While less of a democrat than Nagy, he was more competent as a manager of a national economy. Kádár maintained a foreign policy that was faithful to the Soviet Union and the Warsaw Pact, while, over the long term, instituting a mixed socialist and free-market economy that raised the national standard of living. Like all Communist Eastern European leaders, he had to walk a razor's edge between the Soviets and his own people, forestalling another invasion by the USSR while keeping domestic elements from becoming restive. Kádár was able to manage both more or less effectively, and when he resigned in 1988, it was as much due to ill health as to anything else. He died the next year, three months before the end of communism in his country.

By the end of the 1950s, the United States was in search of a replacement for the policy of massive retaliation, and found it in a new doctrine termed "Flexible Response." Particularly embraced by John F. Kennedy and pioneered by Professor Henry Kissinger and General Maxwell Taylor, this reemphasized conventional military power, everything from special forces to new airmobile units, and advocated options short of outright nuclear war. There was an underlying principle that every foreign policy problem and military challenge was a nail when the only tool available was a hammer. The Kennedy-era approach was to put more tools into the toolbox.

Unfortunately, this policy was quickly put to the test in Vietnam, both by Kennedy and his successor, Lyndon Johnson. That war involved a whole range of catastrophically bad decisions by the United States. Thus, the search for a more nuanced, flexible approach to foreign policy resulted in a series of awful choices.

Had the United States used a less belligerent, less confrontational approach to containing the Soviet Union in the 1950s, it might have emerged from 1956 with more credibility. Embracing rollback was no more practical than addressing every challenge with nuclear saber rattling; preventing the spread of Soviet-aligned communism, especially in Europe, was actually working quite well at the time. It would continue to do so, at least until the Vietnam War. Certainly, too, a foreign policy without rollback would have been more in line with real, rather than imagined, American power. In the process, it would not have offered false hope to the peoples of Eastern Europe.

# 77

# THE SUEZ CRISIS

## 1956

**By Jim Werbaneth**

Britain and France defy
their new reality.

There are decisions that render those who made them weaker and decisions that reveal an already existing weakness. The first includes Hitler's brainstorm to invade the Soviet Union in 1941. An example of the second occurred fifteen years later, when Britain and France, in concert with France's ally Israel, invaded Egypt in order to undo President Gamal Abdel Nasser's nationalization of the Suez Canal. It all seemed like a good idea at the time, but collapsed in failure, revealing the death throes of the European colonial empires. With the end of the colonialist era, the nations of the continent were not the independent forces that they once were.

The reasons go back to the Second World War. Britain might have won the war, but it was a loser of the peace. Its finances and manpower were stretched to the limit, and a little beyond, by six years of conflict. Moreover, with Germany defeated and peace in the Pacific on the horizon, the British people, in 1945, elected a Labour government under Clement Attlee. Winston Churchill, the wartime leader and champion of the old British Empire, was cast out in favor of a government promising a redirection of resources from the overseas empire to the country itself, and a welfare state. In effect, the people of a devastated Britain opted to change into another sort of country, one more concerned with internal social equity than with external dominance.

Along the way, too, subject peoples tried to go their separate ways. India achieved independence in 1947. As the jewel in the crown, it was both the British Empire's centerpiece and even its reason for being. By 1956, Britain faced insurgencies in Malaya and Kenya (the "Mau Mau"), and among the Greeks of Cyprus, the island that would be the base of operations for Suez.

France was even worse off. Its place as a "winner" of World War II was something of a matter of charity from the United States. The country was invaded and quickly defeated by Germany in 1940, and was divided in its loyalty between the Vichy government of Marshal Philippe Pétain and the Free French, the latter marred by the prickly, proud demeanor of its leader, General Charles de Gaulle. Thus, while Britain suffered from bombing, high casualties, economic strain, and all the attendant costs of global war, France was defeated, divided, and occupied. Finally, it became a bombing target and battleground for others.

France was facing crises in its colonies that would almost wrench the country apart. First, there was its war to keep control of Vietnam, ending with a decisive defeat at Dien Bien Phu in 1954. Even with the United States largely footing the bill, France was beaten by the Communist Viet Minh. Then came the war in Algeria, on France's very doorstep, which would end with that country's independence in 1962. France would face violent division, too, as a new breed of bitter-enders in the French military turned on de Gaulle and his government.

While Britain and France faded, power migrated to the east and across the Atlantic, to the Soviet Union and the United States. These countries became the superpowers of the postwar era, despite wartime destruction to the USSR that was even worse than that of France. Yet the British and French governments insisted on acting as though they were still first-rate powers. Further, the new United Nations replaced the moribund League of Nations, and collective security was much more *en vogue* than gunboat diplomacy. Simply put, the world had changed by 1956, and the leaders of France and Britain did not fully realize it.

The Suez Crisis started soon after Britain withdrew its last soldiers from the Canal Zone in June 1956. President Nasser, a dynamic, charismatic soldier politician with aspirations of leading the entire Arab world, took control. British prime minister Anthony Eden was incensed, and forged a partnership with France to regain control of the canal. Ideally, they would remove Nasser from power, especially as Eden saw him as an aggressor dictator of the sort that his country had failed to contain in the thirties.

The operation to retake the Suez Canal could be described as one of "good cop/bad cop." The part of the bad cop was taken by France's close ally at the time Israel. Reluctantly, the Israelis accepted their role as aggressor; they would invade the Gaza Strip and the Sinai, and drive toward Suez. The British and French would then step in, ostensibly to separate the combatants, but actually to occupy the canal.

Israel duly launched its Operation Kadesh on October 29, 1956. Then on November 5 and 6, France and Britain struck Egypt from the Mediterranean. Militarily, it was something of a flawed success, with the Israelis performing the best, followed by the French, and last by an indifferently commanded Britain. But politically, it was a disaster. The coalition had almost no international support, the chief exception being West Germany. The United States was hostile and the United Nations refused support. After all, the Soviet invasion of Hungary was going on at the same time, and President Eisenhower did not feel that the US could condemn the Soviets while giving a pass to the British and French. In addition, he did not support the return of what he saw as colonialism in the post–World War II world.

The United Nations, with Canada as a major player, mediated a cease-fire, and the British and French retreated from Egypt on December 22. Israel continued to occupy the Sinai until March of the next year.

The winners were Egypt and Israel. Nasser faced down two fading great powers and remained in power. Plus, he got to keep the canal. Israel's performance was the first step toward establishing itself as a regional superpower. Furthermore, it managed to lift the Egyptian closure of the Straits of Tiran, instituted before the crisis. This opened Israel's Red Sea port of Elat to shipping in the Indian Ocean, an economic boon to the Jewish state.

Another winner was Canada. Secretary of State for External Affairs Lester Pearson won the Nobel Peace Prize for his efforts in mediating the war. In the process, the UN was strengthened, and Pearson proved that the international organization could send peacekeeping forces to help end a conflict. Naturally, these included Canadians.

Had Britain and France not made the decision to resolve the Suez Crisis militarily, the world would have ended up differently. First, they would have been able to retain the illusion of being superpowers, however briefly. Second, by negotiating for compensation instead of demanding the return of the canal, they would have had a better chance of achieving a foreign policy goal that was more within their diminished means. A partial victory would have been better than a complete defeat, especially as a total military and political win was out of the question.

For Egypt and Israel, the military option led to peace over the long term, though this could not have been anticipated at the time. In 1970, Nasser died of a heart attack and was replaced by Anwar Sadat. Though he fought his own war with Israel in 1973, Sadat flew to Jerusalem in 1977 and made peace with Israel. Thus, by retaining power, Nasser set the stage for his designated successor to achieve peace with his bitterest enemy. Whether Nasser would have approved is open to question. Still, had he been driven from power in 1956, it is far from certain that a Sadat presidency would have happened at all.

In Canada, Pearson became prime minister from 1963 to 1968; without his diplomatic success in 1956, this, too, would not have been a sure thing. Further, upon his retirement, his protégé, Pierre Trudeau, became leader of the Liberal Party and prime minister. Though his legacy is more controversial today, in 1968, the young prime minister was the beneficiary of "Trudeaumania." Love him or hate him—and Canada remains sharply divided on that—he was a dominant force in Canadian politics until 1984. Without the Suez conflict, both Pearson and Trudeau would have had a harder climb to the top.

For the people of Britain, any effects from Suez were short-term. Eden resigned his office the next year and was replaced by

Harold Macmillan. The new prime minister had a much better standing with the Americans, going back to World War II, and quickly repaired the "special relationship." Moreover, Macmillan was able to convince Britons that they had never had it so good. His government restored a confidence that never should have been shaken by Suez. For Frenchmen and -women, the angst that began in World War II continued. Suez faded, but was replaced by the longer-term strife in Algeria, where conscripts fought Arab fighters in an increasingly brutal war. France continued to attempt an independent course, but without the credibility of a top-rank power.

For ordinary Israelis and Egyptians, war came again in 1967 with a resounding Israeli victory in the Sinai, and in 1973, Arab armies came close to destroying Israel. Then, four years later, Egypt and Israel were able to achieve peace. Israel would still call reservists to the colors from civilian life, but never again would it fight the Egyptians. Twenty-one years after Suez, peace would be generally elusive in much of the Middle East, but it was a reality between two of its most persistent combatants.

The historical ripples from Suez did not last long, outside of Egypt, perhaps. Without a political victory over the two fading empires, it is possible that Nasser might not have survived long enough to leave his country to Sadat, and therefore open the door to peace with Egypt. Also, the French Fourth Republic fell two years after Suez, bringing de Gaulle to power with the Fifth Republic. While the direct cause of the change was a crisis in Algeria, it is possible that without the damage of Suez, the transition would have come later. As France is still under the Fifth Republic, with its strong presidential system, one can speculate that current French political life might be different today without the mistake of Suez in 1956.

||||||||||||||||||||||||||||||||||||||||||||||||||||||||||||||||||||||||||||

# 78

# HAVE A HEART

## 1958

### By Bill Fawcett

||||||||||||||||||||||||||||||||||||||||||||||||||||||||||||||||||||||||||||

A few million lives were saved by
using a mistaken resistor.

Writing a book on mistakes and how they changed history can be depressing. But there have been beneficial mistakes as well. Perhaps the best known, though more of an accident than a mistake, is the discovery of penicillin, since antibiotics were discovered only because, in 1928, Alexander Fleming spilled crumbs into a petri dish and didn't clean them up. Here is another accident that has saved the lives of a lot of people.

Wilson Greatbatch left the navy for a career in medical research in the 1950s. One of his experiments involved a small oscillator, weighing only a few ounces, that would record each beat of a human heart. This was to assist in diagnosing heart problems and irregular heartbeats. During its construction, Greatbatch mistakenly inserted the wrong resistor. Silicon technology was still new and such mistakes were easy to make. When he attached the "recorder" to the patient, instead of recording heartbeats, it sent out a small electric charge every few seconds. The charge was barely noticeable by the patient, but did cause his heart to beat whenever the device sent out a pulse of electricity.

Like Fleming and his bread crumbs, the brilliance of this scientist lies not in the mistake, but in his recognition of the potential the mistake offered. Until this fortunate slipup, there were machines used to change heartbeat. They involved a painful jolt, used a lot of power, and weighed several pounds—hence, most definitely not portable or practical. They were used in hospitals, and only in extreme cases. Within months, Wilson Greatbatch refined his oscillator until it weighed even less than before and could be easily implanted. The first modern pacemaker was implanted in 1958, and helped the patient live for eighteen months. He continued to improve his pacemakers until the 1970s, when, frustrated by the need to change their batteries so often, Greatbatch turned his attention to lithium batteries. His greatly improved battery was soon used almost universally.

The National Society of Professional Engineers lists the pacemaker as one of the top ten engineering accomplishments of the twentieth century. The world would likely be a darker place without Greatbatch's grabbing that wrong resistor. Pacemakers can add decades to the lives of those who need them. Now there are even special pacemakers for athletes that allow them to prolong their years of competition. More than a million people worldwide are alive today because of this mistake—more than two hundred thousand in the USA alone, because of their pacemakers. Among the many people who have gained years of life because of Greatbatch's mistake are Mother Teresa, Kirk Douglas, Pope Benedict, Ted Williams, and Elton John.

# 79

# HISTORY MAKES A WRONG TURN IN DALLAS

## 1963

### By Douglas Niles

*A lot of bad luck made this mistake
worse, no matter how many shooters.*

The assassination of President John F. Kennedy on November 22, 1963, is arguably the greatest national trauma modern Americans have suffered. All Americans who were at least of grade-school age when it happened still remember where they were and what they were doing when they learned the news.

That trauma differed substantially from the two other events of modern US history that might also merit this dubious distinction: the Japanese surprise attack on Pearl Harbor on December 7, 1941, and the al-Qaeda terrorist attack on September 11, 2001. These latter left the nation roused and angry, ready to seek vengeance against an identifiable and almost universally hated foe. In both cases, the nation united under the incumbent president in a shared desire for retribution.

The perpetrator of the trauma in Dallas, however, was a miserable loser, a man so abject that his attempts to defect to the Communist world had been rebuffed by both the Soviet Union and Cuba. He was dead two days after he committed his monstrous crime, so there was no opportunity for explanation or closure. Tragically, about the only positive thing that could be said about Lee Harvey Oswald is that he was a reasonably competent marksman with a cheap rifle. Also, perhaps, that he was lucky.

Many of the mistakes of history, including most of those discussed in this book, involve a powerful person making a foolish decision that has dramatic and far-reaching effects. Some of the world's greatest "mistakes," however, resulted only from bad luck. There was nothing foolish or rash about President Kennedy's decision to include Dallas on his trip to Texas. Nor was it the least bit unprecedented for him to ride in an open car, along a route that had been made public in advance. But the decisions that led him to sit in an open car as it crossed Dealey Plaza that November day would turn out to be the worst, and the last, of John Kennedy's life.

It is maddening to imagine all the alternate scenarios. What if the date of the trip had been changed? There had, in fact, been a warning sent to the White House by a leader of the Democratic Party in Texas, pointing out that a notorious right-wing firebrand, disgraced and retired General Edwin Walker of Dallas, had labeled the president a "liability to the free world." The warning was disregarded, not even shown to JFK, because a presidential adviser believed Kennedy never would have taken it seriously.

Fate played an even more whimsical role in this tragedy: the perpetual loser and chronically unemployed Lee Harvey Oswald happened to get a job in mid-October 1963 sorting deliveries at the Texas School Book Depository; and less than six weeks later, the president's motorcade would take him past that very building! Even if JFK was determined to visit Dallas, what if a minor change in route had taken him down a different street? Oswald would not even have had the chance to take his shot.

Before 1963, three United States presidents—Abraham Lincoln (1865), James Garfield (1881), and William McKinley (1901)—had been killed by gunshots during a bloody thirty-six-year stretch in American history. After McKinley's death, the Secret Service, which had been created to protect against counterfeiting, was assigned the important task of protecting the nation's chief executive. Since then, though would-be assassins had targeted Presidents Taft, Teddy Roosevelt, Hoover, Franklin Roosevelt, and Truman, none succeeded. Only one chief executive was wounded: Teddy Roosevelt, out of office for several years and campaigning to return to the presidency, famously survived because a pistol bullet was slowed by the many folded pages of a speech, as well as a metal glasses case. (He went on to finish his speech with the slug embedded in his chest.)

In any event, Fate played her cruel joke in Dallas, and the nation's young, vibrant leader was cut down only thirty-four months—less than three years!—into his first term. But how might history have unfolded if Kennedy had lived? How much of the fractious sixties would have been altered, even improved? It is one of the great questions of speculative history in the modern age. Would JFK have gone on to become one of our greatest presidents?

Of course, there are a few scenarios besides untimely death that could have damaged Kennedy's legacy. If his serial philandering had been brought to light, there is little doubt that public opinion would have turned against him. But the media in the 1960s was not inclined to report such matters, and even if a political opponent uncovered enough dirt to make charges, it was no sure thing that such an attack would have gained traction. Perhaps even more serious, of course, is the question of JFK's health. Despite the president's projecting an image of youth and vigor, his body was a wreck. Any one of his laundry list of physical ailments could have landed him in a wheelchair, or rendered him incapable of governing in his familiar, strong style.

Yet, if those dangerous waters could have been navigated—as he had navigated them, very successfully, so far—there is little doubt that Kennedy would have been elected to a second term in 1964. After all, his much-less-charismatic successor, Lyndon Johnson, beat Republican Barry Goldwater in a historic landslide during that election, which also delivered solid Democratic majorities to both houses of Congress.

And how might JFK's second term have proceeded? His proposed initiatives included tax cuts and increased federal support for education and medical coverage for the poor and elderly. These programs would almost certainly have been enacted. Would America's mood of confidence and optimism have maintained itself, instead of dissolving into the chaotic polarization of the historical sixties?

Of course the two biggest questions need to be asked: What would JFK have done about the American involvement in Vietnam, and how would he have dealt with the fractious and increasingly violent civil rights movement?

Jack Kennedy did, in fact, send the first American troops to Vietnam—special forces soldiers with a mission to train the South Vietnamese Army. Would he, like Johnson, have responded to the Communist insurgency by committing massive numbers of American soldiers and marines? Quite possibly, he would have. There is evidence from his handling of the Cuban Missile Crisis that JFK had the moral fiber to stand up to a whole array of advisers who were encouraging him to take military action. Perhaps, emboldened by the security provided a president by a second term, he might have refused to commence the American buildup that began in 1965.

It is even more challenging to consider JFK's role in the civil rights movement. It was not an issue that was as near and dear to his heart as it was to LBJ's, and, as a Northerner, Kennedy would have had a harder time rallying the support of those Southern Democrats who begrudgingly lent their support to the Texan. Yet Kennedy was also a man with a sense of justice, and it may well have turned out that he would have decided to come down on the right side of history.

Sadly, even tragically, we never had the chance to find out.

III

# WHEN THE SHUTTLE GOES THE WAY OF THE DYNA-SOAR

## 1963

### By William Terdoslavich

IIIIIIIIIIIIIIIIIIIIIIIIIIIIIIIIIIIIIIIIIIIIIIIIIIIIIIIIIIIIIIIIIIIIIIIIIIIIIIIIIIIIIIIIIII

To not go where no man has
gone before.

The Space Shuttle was the most amazing, most advanced spacecraft that ever flew. It was also a white elephant. There was a cheaper alternative that could have flown twenty-five years sooner, had the right people made the right decisions.

In the 1950s and 1960s, aerospace engineers were tinkering with a reusable space plane called the X-20. The concept was called Dynamic Soaring, shortened to Dyna-Soar. It was a delta-winged craft with rudders at the wing tips and an onboard rocket engine, capable of transporting a single pilot.

Later designs showed configurations carrying a few astronauts in a passenger compartment. This would have been useful to support a planned low-earth-orbit space station, based on a Gemini capsule mated to an upper rocket stage for the station's casing.

Yet all this advanced thinking did not add up to a program. With Projects Mercury and Gemini using space capsules to put astronauts into orbit, and uncertainty over what Dyna-Soar would be used for, the need for a space plane seemed expensive and redundant. The program got chopped.

## Advanced Thinking, Advanced Design

Dyna-Soar was born amid conflicting visions. NASA wanted to test the boundaries of hypersonic flight. The air force wanted a piloted spacecraft that could nuke Russia from orbit, snatch Russian satellites, and do high-level reconnaissance. And all this was going to happen in 1966!

The cockpit would have life support for the pilot, while the central section remained isolated, but pressurized with a 100 percent nitrogen atmosphere. Into that compartment would go up to 990 pounds of equipment for instrumentation and data recorders to measure up to 750 variables affecting the space plane. The two unpressurized equipment bays just aft would house propellant tanks and a single rocket engine.

Sketches of Dyna-Soar showed a space vehicle roughly one-third the size of the Space Shuttle. The onboard rocket engine could kick out seventy-two thousand pounds of thrust. The space plane could ride into orbit on top of a Titan IIIC booster, a much simpler configuration than the shuttle's.

In orbit, the Dyna-Soar would retain the Titan's third stage for the needed burns to change orbit or altitude. Flight plans called for the pilot to jettison the third stage over the Indian Ocean before lining up for approach on Edwards Air Force Base in California. The plane would then land on a set of wire brushes instead of wheels.

"Coming in hot" would have been an understatement for the Dyna-Soar. Plans called for a molybdenum coating of the underbelly and wing leading edges, expected to withstand temperatures of up to 1,500 degrees Celsius. The zirconium nose cone had to withstand reentry heat of 2,000 degrees Celsius as well.

By the end of 1962, the project looked like it was coming together. Critical subsystems were tested. Advances in metallurgy made the structure of the Dyna-Soar feasible. And a full-sized mock-up was rolled out, making the Mercury space capsule look . . . *dull*.

Dyna-Soar was going to be an honest-to-God flying machine, giving the pilot full control over yaw, pitch, and roll. He would even have to fly the thing by hand during reentry. *We even had the test pilots who could do this.*

## The Bean Counter Strikes Back

Defense Secretary Robert McNamara was not impressed. He could see that Dyna-Soar lacked direction. And that spawned questions: Is it an air-force space plane ready to take on the Soviets? Is it a NASA research vehicle that could do what no one had ever done before? If no one could say what Dyna-Soar was for, then how could anyone plan missions for it?

The Dyna-Soar did not make it past 1963 when McNamara killed it after a series of project reviews. It was a cruel death. Dyna-Soar was just months away from being flight-tested. Uncle Sam had just spent $530 million and the program was more than halfway done.

Maybe Dyna-Soar did not die in vain. Six years later, its data would be reused on another design: the Space Shuttle.

## Same Problem, Different Program

NASA needed a replacement program for the Apollo program while it was under way. As Neil Armstrong planted the American flag on the moon, others worried about what came next.

Thus the shuttle was born on paper, concurrent with a manned space station called Skylab. Once again, interagency wants screwed around with NASA's needs. Money was no object in putting a man on the moon, but the shuttle would have to come in on a limited budget. And in the inflationary 1970s, those budget dollars would lose value very quickly.

The air force wanted to launch the shuttle from Vandenberg Air Force Base in California to achieve circumpolar orbits, ideal for space-based reconnaissance and spying. The NRO wanted an extra-large cargo bay to launch its next generation of spy satellites, each one the size of a school bus.

If NASA wanted to achieve budget priority, it would need to cut the other agencies in for a piece of the action, making the shuttle program harder to kill. But the political compromises were affecting design, making the shuttle larger than originally intended, and more expensive.

In the end, NASA got a space truck, with a cargo bay measuring fifteen by sixty feet. The agency wanted the shuttle to be the DC-3 of spaceflight, capable of flying fifty times per year. The best NASA did was nine missions in 1985. Other years saw four to six flights. And it took about ten thousand people to prepare and launch the shuttle, at a cost of about $450 million per mission. The loss of *Challenger* (1986) and *Columbia* (2003) set the program back several years.

The air force did get to use the shuttle for some classified missions, which proved to be of marginal value. Along with the NRO, it still found it more convenient to use conventional boosters to put its satellites into orbit. If taking astronauts up to the International Space Station was all the shuttle did, wouldn't a cheaper space capsule do just fine instead?

Once the program reached its 135th flight in 2011, the loss of another orbiter became statistically certain. The shuttle was grounded. The total program cost was more than $200 billion.

## The Better Course of Action

The Apollo program was a Cold War effort to beat the Russians to the moon. It cost $20 billion in 1960s dollars—well over $100 billion today, adjusting dollar value for inflation. To skip Apollo would have been *daring*. So let's look at how things would have turned out if Dyna-Soar had gotten funded.

When Dyna-Soar was canceled, it was less than three years away from spaceflight, with only another $300 to $400 million to be spent to get there. That first flight in July 1966 would have seen test pilot James Wood become the seventeenth American to go to space, at the controls of a true space plane.

From there, assume a number of orbital missions in the next four years to fully develop the program's capabilities. The Dyna-Soar would have been a frequent flier, with less crew support needed to ready the craft for the next mission, compared to the shuttle.

NASA was already tinkering with space station design concurrent with the Apollo program. One scheme, called the Manned Orbital Laboratory, would have relied on a Gemini capsule mated to a Titan third stage containing the station. First flight was expected in 1971. With Dyna-Soar acting as the crew shuttle, the Gemini capsule would have been downgraded to a lifeboat.

In real life, we got things backward. Our first space station, Skylab, went into orbit *before* the shuttle *Columbia* was flight-ready. Skylab burned up on reentry in 1979, several years before *Columbia*'s first flight.

The Dyna-Soar/MOL combination would have gotten the program order right—shuttle first, space station second. A supported base in low earth orbit could have been the construction site for a reusable lunar lander. The first man—or woman—could have set foot on the Sea of Tranquility in 1979. And the first moon base would have followed, all the while tracing supply and support to MOL.

Eventually, all this space hardware would have been replaced with better stuff. Having made history, Dyna-Soar would have ended up hanging from the ceiling of the Smithsonian Air and Space Museum, alongside the *Spirit of St. Louis* and above the Mercury capsule.

*If only things had turned out differently.*

‖‖‖‖‖‖‖‖‖‖‖‖‖‖‖‖‖‖‖‖‖‖‖‖‖‖‖‖‖‖‖‖‖‖‖‖‖‖‖‖‖‖‖‖‖‖‖‖‖‖‖‖‖‖

# 81

# GULF OF TONKIN: THE BATTLE THAT WASN'T

## 1964

### By Douglas Niles

‖‖‖‖‖‖‖‖‖‖‖‖‖‖‖‖‖‖‖‖‖‖‖‖‖‖‖‖‖‖‖‖‖‖‖‖‖‖‖‖‖‖‖‖‖‖‖‖‖‖‖‖‖‖

Since they brought Captain Robert Jenkins's ear into Parliament in 1739, has there been a valid provocation for war?

The end of World War II brought the beginning of the Cold War, the glowering showdown between the Communist bloc (represented by the Soviet Union and, after 1949, China) and the Western democracies allied with the United States. Between 1950 and 1953, violence erupted between the two factions in Korea, but the war was limited to that embattled peninsula and eventually ended with a cease-fire. The primary front for potential war seemed to be the "Iron Curtain" that Winston Churchill so eloquently described as slicing across Europe. The divided city of Berlin was also a potential flashpoint, and Fidel Castro's revolution in Cuba established a Communist domain in the western hemisphere. But actual combat between the two sides, each armed to the teeth with nuclear weapons, remained mercifully infrequent.

Against this backdrop, however, a conflict had long simmered between North and South Vietnam, ever since the French had withdrawn from their former Asian colonies in 1954. The end of the First Indochina War brought the fateful dissection of Vietnam into the Communist north and the capitalist south—two nations almost guaranteed to be enemies destined to fight a war. Throughout the late fifties and early sixties, Communist rebels sought to overthrow the ostensibly democratic, and inarguably corrupt, regime ruling South Vietnam. These rebels became known as the Viet Cong, and received weapons, training, and supplies not just from North Vietnam, but from the Communist regimes in China and the USSR as well.

The United States had a strong, vested interest in the survival of the South Vietnamese regime. Presidents Dwight Eisenhower and John Kennedy felt compelled to support the south against the threat presented by "world communism." Yet by 1964, with President Lyndon Baines Johnson in the Oval Office, the Viet Cong insurgency in South Vietnam had grown into a significant threat to that nation's very survival. Heavily supported by Communist North Vietnam, the Viet Cong made regular attacks against isolated South Vietnamese army installations, and had wrested control of large parts of the country, notably rural areas covered by heavy forests and rough terrain, from the Saigon government.

In the early 1960s, the American role on the ground was limited to small, elite units—notably the legendary Green Berets of the US Army—who trained and helped to lead South Vietnamese military units. Many of these national units consisted of soldiers drawn from ethnic minorities and occupying outposts in the hinterland of the rugged, forested countryside. At the same time, the United States Navy maintained a robust presence in the South China Sea off the coast of South and, to a certain extent, North Vietnam. A strategic headquarters, the Military Assistance Command, Vietnam (MACV), was established in Saigon in 1962, and early in 1964, General William Westmoreland arrived to take command.

In August of 1964, the United States Navy off the coast of North Vietnam created a confrontation that provided the impetus for one of America's most tragic military adventures. The clash was minor and—at least for the United States—bloodless, but against the backdrop of the Cold War, it would be exaggerated into a catastrophic misjudgment that paved the way for the Vietnam War.

The destroyer USS *Maddox* was part of the United States Navy fleet patrolling the South China Sea. The ship was outfitted for a specialized collection of electronic data, intelligence that could be used to help understand the capabilities and locations of North Vietnam's military assets. In late July, *Maddox* was ordered to probe close to the Communist shoreline, testing Hanoi's resolve in a blatant challenge. Under the command of Captain John Herrick, the ship would close to within ten miles of the coast, which became a point of controversy. The United States recognized an eight-mile limit to North Vietnam's territorial waters, while North Vietnam claimed the waters out as far as twelve miles.

As usual in history, there were other factors in play. On August 1, South Vietnamese commandos landed on North Vietnamese islands, very close to the mainland, and conducted reconnaissance and sabotage operations. In other locations, a team of agents was dropped into North Vietnamese territory (where they were immediately captured), while Laotian aircraft pilots under CIA direction launched attacks against installations within the Communist country.

At the same time, *Maddox* patrolled offshore, bristling with electronic gear, a little more than a hundred miles from the site of the raid. Naturally, the Communists believed that the US warship was controlling, or at least supporting, the activities of the South Vietnamese special forces. North Vietnam responded on August 2 by sending several PT boats toward the American destroyer. A minor clash, involving gunfire from the American destroyer and torpedoes from the PT boats, resulted. Several American bombers were launched from a nearby aircraft carrier and attacked the North Vietnamese craft; the PT boats, some of them suffering damage, retired.

Captain Herrick initially reported that *Maddox* had been subjected to an aggressive torpedo attack that his ship had evaded before returning fire. This was the information that Defense Secretary Robert McNamara passed to the president that day. Herrick corrected his report a short time later, acknowledging that his ship opened fire first. When McNamara learned, a few hours after receiving the initial report, that the first report was inaccurate, he neglected to inform LBJ of the fact.

It would be years later before the true sequence of events became publicly known. In fact, *Maddox* had fired at the PT boats when they approached to within about ten thousand yards of the American warship. Only *after* they were fired upon did the North Vietnamese vessels move in and launch torpedoes, all of which the destroyer evaded. One of the boats was struck by a shell from *Maddox*, while others suffered damage from American aircraft that flew in support of the ship.

Word of the engagement reached Washington, DC, almost immediately, but some details—such as the fact that the Americans had fired first—did not reach the president's desk until much later. Meanwhile, tensions in Vietnam, and offshore, continued to run high. On August 4, amid stormy weather, *Maddox*—now accompanied by the destroyer USS *Turner Joy*—picked up radar and sonar signals suggesting more enemy PT boats in the area. Both American ships blazed away at unseen targets for nearly four hours. Initial reports claimed that two enemy vessels had been sunk, though no wreckage or other confirmation could be obtained. Within hours, Captain Herrick was reporting his doubts that any enemy vessels had been involved, suggesting that an inexperienced sonar man had possibly been reacting to the sounds of the destroyer's own propellers.

Nevertheless, LBJ wasted no time in deciding that firm action was called for. He was engaged in a presidential campaign against the Republican hard-line anti-Communist Barry Goldwater and believed that a show of strength was imperative. And indeed, Johnson was sincerely worried about Communist aggression, in Vietnam or anywhere. Thus he addressed the American people in a broadcast late in the day of August 4, emphasizing North Vietnam's aggression in the Gulf of Tonkin.

While a few members of Congress asked for more details, they were in the minority. For the most part, the media and the population—lacking many of the facts—embraced the vigor and tone of the speech. On August 7, Congress passed the Southeast Asia Resolution, giving the president the power to dispatch whatever forces he deemed necessary to confront the Communist menace in Vietnam.

By 1965, only a year later, it was clear that South Vietnam would be doomed within a few months without robust American intervention, so LBJ dispatched a force of United States Marines that summer, and quickly followed up with regular US Army forces. Within a few years, the American military presence would exceed a half million troops, but the president also insisted on crippling restrictions for combat operations based on a not unreasonable concern about Chinese intervention. So the unwinnable war continued and, by 1972, would cause some fifty-eight thousand Americans—and countless hundreds of thousands of Vietnamese—to perish.

By 1973, the US had grown weary of the war in Vietnam, and the next president, Richard Nixon, withdrew the last American combat troops at the beginning of his second term. Just as it would have been in 1965, without American intervention, South Vietnam was doomed, falling to the north in 1975—ten years after the arrival of America's initial combat forces.

If Congress, and LBJ, had considered a more measured response in 1965, and had more carefully sought out the facts instead of rushing to condemn Communist aggression, all those lost lives could have been spared. South Vietnam would have inevitably been absorbed by the north, but there would have been less time for a generation's worth of hatred to grow, and a united Vietnam in the mid-1960s would not have automatically become an implacable enemy of the United States. With Vietnam united in 1965 instead of 1975, the road to the country's current prosperity would have begun that much sooner, and been paved with much less human blood and suffering.

Perhaps the most appropriate epitaph for the entire incident, which led to a decade of tragedy for both America and Vietnam, came from LBJ himself in 1965, when he commented to his press secretary about the incident in the Gulf of Tonkin:

"For all I know, our navy was shooting at whales out there."

||||||||||||||||||||||||||||||||||||||||||||||||||||||||||||||||||||||||||||||||

# 82

# MISSISSIPPI BURNING

## 1964

### By Jim Werbaneth

||||||||||||||||||||||||||||||||||||||||||||||||||||||||||||||||||||||||||||||||

The beginning of the end of
the Ku Klux Klan.

Sometimes bad people make bad mistakes and the innocent suffer, but out of the horror comes a better world. This was definitely the case with the Ku Klux Klan murders of civil rights workers Michael Schwerner, Andrew Goodman, and James Chaney on June 21, 1964. Before the murders, the Klan was a powerful force in the South and beyond, with military historian Max Boot describing it as one of the most effective insurgencies in history. While segregationist politicians worked openly within the system, the KKK provided an armed wing in the shadows. But after the killing of Schwerner, Goodman, and Chaney, all that changed, and today the Klan is little more than an easily mocked cliché.

Klan groups had been terrorizing people, especially black people, since the days of Reconstruction. Over time, the white robe and flaming cross became the symbol of a true grassroots movement, one that vented its wrath toward immigrants, Catholics, and Jews along with its traditional African-American targets. President Woodrow Wilson vocally approved of the glamorizd portrayal of the KKK in D. W. Griffith's *Birth of a Nation*. Yet underneath the robes always lurked terrorists.

In the early sixties, Mississippi was the center of a conflict between segregationists and those determined to extend civil rights, especially the right to vote, to the state's black population. Not only did Klansmen participate in this conflict as a private group, but they counted law enforcement officers as members. The murders of Schwerner, Goodman, and Chaney were committed by a Klan group alleged to have been led by Neshoba County sheriff Lawrence A. Rainey.

These murders were hardly the only Klan outrages of the time, but they were critical in mobilizing the federal government to prosecute segregationist offenders whom the state of Mississippi was either unable, or unwilling, to bring to trial. Though FBI director J. Edgar Hoover was suspicious of civil rights groups as Communist fronts, he and President Lyndon Johnson were moved to muster federal assets to solve the triple murder. Johnson mobilized sailors to search for the bodies and Hoover personally went to Mississippi to lead the investigation.

The federal government stepped in, named twenty-one conspirators, and arrested most of them, on December 4, 1964, for violating the victims' civil rights. Seven were convicted in 1967, but none served more than six years in prison.

Nonetheless, the murder of three men was a turning point in the history of the civil rights movement. Johnson was able to use the crime to muster support for his Civil Rights Act and Voting Rights Act, thus making the goals of Goodman, Schwerner, and Chaney federal law. Further, national media attention was not healthy for the "Invisible Empire" of Klan organizations. Along with the coverage of other murders and violence, this exposure helped make membership in the KKK shameful.

This does not mean that the federal government was always on the side of the angels. For example, the FBI solved the 1965 murder of Detroit housewife and civil rights activist Viola Liuzzo, again by Mississippi Klansmen. However, in order to cover up the fact that one of the four killers was a longtime paid Bureau informant, Hoover allegedly attempted to smear Liuzzo as a drug user who had an extramarital affair with a black man, dynamite allegations in the midsixties. Yet federal power remained largely on the side of the civil rights movement. Even with Hoover's sometimes ambivalent attitude toward the KKK's victims and his suspicions of their Communist ties, enforcement of Johnson's keystone civil rights legislation was a boon for integration and a body blow to its opponents.

All of these acts of violence amounted to a major mistake by the Ku Klux Klan. The Neshoba County murders were crucial, possibly because the killing of idealistic young Northern activists along with a local black colleague made the story national in scope.

The Klansmen overplayed their hand, misreading the political culture of America, its media, and the attitude of the federal government. Had they not made the mistake of murdering Schwerner, Goodman, and Chaney, expecting to get away with it, American life would have been much different. To start with, Johnson might not have been able to get his Civil Rights and Voting Rights Acts through Congress, at least in their historical form. He faced strong opposition from pro-segregation conservatives in his own Democratic Party and required a coalition with Republicans to succeed. Without the sympathy generated by the murders, it is probable that his opponents would have been more difficult to defeat.

Second, without federal action against the Klan, however erratic, and public rejection of its goals and methods, the KKK would certainly have remained a force in American life. It might have been an effective covert movement for much of its existence, but from 1964 onward it went into a steep decline. Today it is a fringe movement and the butt of numerous jokes. Minus the mistakes made in Mississippi fifty years ago, one could have expected more actions, more support, and a more powerful Klan. Thus our world owes much to the sacrifices of those activists—and the miscalculations of their killers.

# 83

## *STAR TREK* IS
## CANCELED

### 1969

**By Jim Werbaneth**

> NBC is shortsighted about a
> farsighted TV show.

Perhaps no other television show had the long-term cultural impact of *Star Trek*. Yet the original series ran for just three years, seventy-nine episodes, and was canceled by NBC in 1969. It had started with excellent ratings, but they had fallen and become more erratic, a situation not made any better by NBC's tendency to bounce the show from one time slot to another. Thus, by far the most important science-fiction show of all time passed from the network lineup into syndicated reruns.

Though it probably would have taken a clairvoyant to see it at the time, this was one of the worst decisions made by any broadcast network. In its short life, and with a budget so low that saltshakers were pressed into service as medical tricorders, the show acquired a hold on the imagination of millions that would make it a cultural mainstay, and eventually a highly profitable franchise of new series and films. But in 1969, unloved by network management, *Star Trek* was cut loose by NBC.

The show was a phenomenon in syndication, especially among independent UHF stations. Not only did the small *Star Trek* oeuvre exert its hold on millions of viewers; it provided a quick and easy route for independent stations to compete with network affiliates, especially during weekday afternoons, when the show, with its legions of primarily young male fans, competed against soap operas, with their older, primarily female viewers. And the competition was not only among viewers but also among advertisers; think of toy companies going against detergent. There was something supremely disruptive about coming home from grade school or junior high and insisting on watching *Star Trek*.

Then everyone grew up.

NBC seemed to recognize its mistake right away. Its response was to run two seasons of a new animated *Star Trek* in 1973 and 1974, featuring many of the original cast members. However, like the original series, it suffered from low budgets and production values to match. It was short-lived, in part because it did not appeal to the younger children who were the prime viewers of animation. Further, *Star Trek* creator Gene Roddenberry seemed almost ashamed of it, demanding that it not be considered part of the overall canon.

The real return of *Star Trek* to larger audiences came with the franchise's first movie, unimaginatively entitled *Star Trek: The Motion Picture*, in 1979. This reunited the original cast in a live-action setting. Of lasting impact on the future of the franchise was the transformation of the Klingons; originally resembling humans with Attila the Hun's facial hair, they became more alien-looking humanoids, sporting distinctive brow ridges, speaking their own language, and possessing their own samurai-like culture. Their evolution would continue as they became allies instead of enemies of the Federation. The movie was a commercial but not a critical success.

As *Star Trek* movies continued to be produced, a pattern seemed to emerge: the odd-numbered ones were less than impressive, while the even-numbered ones were worthwhile. This started with *Star Trek II: The Wrath of Khan*, which resurrected the character of an exiled superhuman from the original series, again played by Ricardo Montalban.

Then came a new series, appropriately entitled *Star Trek: The Next Generation*. This took place a hundred years after the original, with a new, larger, improved *Enterprise* and, of course, a new crew. Running from 1987 to 1994, it spawned a new generation not just of *Star Trek* fans, but also disputes, such as who was a better captain, the original (James T. Kirk) or the new (Jean-Luc Picard). More series followed, with *Star Trek: Deep Space Nine* and *Star*

*Trek: Voyager* set in the *Next Generation* era, and *Enterprise*, set at the dawn of human interstellar flight.

Finally, the characters and starship *Enterprise* of the original series were the subjects of a reboot by J. J. Abrams, with new movies, entitled simply *Star Trek* and *Star Trek into Darkness*, in 2009 and 2013 respectively.

Where was NBC in all of this, and how did it benefit? With the end of the animated series in 1974, the network's affiliation with the franchise was over. Paramount Pictures produced the motion pictures and the *Next Generation*–era series, and syndicated *The Next Generation* and *Deep Space Nine*. *Voyager* and *Enterprise* were carried by the UPN network. But at no time after the animated series did NBC benefit from the success of the franchise. And so the network's cancellation of the show turns out to have been one of the biggest mistakes in entertainment history.

One might argue that no one could foresee the enduring appeal of *Star Trek*. But there is evidence that it should have stayed on the air longer than three years. One story, told by Nichelle Nichols, is key. She was planning on leaving the role of Uhura in the original series to pursue her first love: music. Attending an NAACP convention, she was confronted by Dr. Martin Luther King Jr., who insisted that she remain on *Star Trek* as a role model to young girls of color. She changed her mind and stayed. It is sad that the network suits could not see what Dr. King saw.

In order to become a commercial success, the original *Star Trek* needed time and money to grow. This would have been more likely if NBC had found a good time slot and stuck to it. Had this happened, the network would have been in on the franchise and the profits. For the viewers and all of those devotees, whether they are called Trekkies or Trekkers, there would have been a lot more *Star Trek* to go around, a lot earlier.

In addition, the show would have probably motivated even more young people to raise their aspirations. *Star Trek* inspired students to explore science and technology as careers, even become astronauts. For example, the character of Scotty inspired some to become engineers in real life, and as Dr. King so emphatically stated, Uhura showed a future in which black girls could grow up to be technicians and leaders. Maybe the NBC bean counters could justify their decision at the time, but history tells a different story. They had their chance to be part of a constructive, inspiring phenomenon lasting generations, and they blew it.

‖‖‖‖‖‖‖‖‖‖‖‖‖‖‖‖‖‖‖‖‖‖‖‖‖‖‖‖‖‖‖‖‖‖‖‖‖‖‖‖‖‖‖‖‖‖‖‖‖‖‖

# 84

# RICHARD NIXON GUTS THE MANNED SPACE PROGRAM

## 1971

### By Jim Werbaneth

‖‖‖‖‖‖‖‖‖‖‖‖‖‖‖‖‖‖‖‖‖‖‖‖‖‖‖‖‖‖‖‖‖‖‖‖‖‖‖‖‖‖‖‖‖‖‖‖‖‖‖

History may judge this as his
greatest mistake.

When it comes to presidential mistakes, Richard Nixon made some of the biggest. After all, he was the only president forced to resign in disgrace. The Watergate scandal was a third-rate burglary compounded by a first-rate failure of a cover-up and fraught with mistakes, starting with the formation of the "Plumbers" unit that carried out the break-in.

Yet Watergate was not Nixon's only major mistake. As the scandal was playing out on American televisions, he attempted to assert his power through a process called impoundment; that is, he refused to spend funds allocated by Congress to certain projects. In this sense, it was a kind of takeover of the budget process—after the fact. Impoundment was not a new power, as it dated back to Thomas Jefferson's refusal to pay for new gunboats that he judged to be unnecessary for the common defense. But Nixon's use of it proved costly, both to important scientific ventures and to the presidency itself.

The American space program had to overcome an early lead by the Soviet Union to beat the Russians to the moon. In 1957, the Soviets put the first satellites into orbit, beating the hapless American Project Vanguard to this crucial milestone. Adding to the humiliation were jokes about the astronauts being little better than "Spam in a can." Yet in July 1969, it was Americans who were making that one small step for a man, while the Soviet space program remained in earth orbit.

There is no doubt that soon after Apollo 11, the American program had hit its own doldrums, with public support and even interest fading fast. John F. Kennedy had challenged America to go to the moon, saying that "we do these things not because they are easy, but because they are hard." By contrast, Nixon took out his pen and cut the space budget. Rather than lead America toward new goals in space, he basically killed what was left of Apollo and dimmed America's chances of ever returning to the moon.

Several additional missions to the moon were planned but never got off the ground. Some, such as the Apollo-Soyuz Test Project, were retasked as earth orbital missions, for political reasons. Others were canceled and their parts were cannibalized for use in lower-cost experiments like Skylab. Thank the budget-minded Richard Nixon, who thought he could reap political capital by denying humanity its destiny in the stars and denying certain companies of jobs.

One has to consider what might have happened had Richard Nixon fought for the space program, as JFK had done a decade before. Apollo and Saturn technology could have been developed further, into a new generation of spacecraft capable of extended missions on the moon; as it was, two later missions used a new model of the Lunar Excursion Module (LEM), capable of supporting astronauts for extended stays on the lunar surface. Second, new generations of post-Apollo and Saturn launch vehicles could have been developed for manned ventures reaching even farther, even to Mars. Thus Nixon's tightfisted stance toward space programs forestalled manned exploration of the planets, perhaps permanently.

What programs did survive were of a lesser nature. Skylab was a promising part of the Saturn booster program, building an orbital space station around the third stage of the Saturn V rocket. Due to the failed deployment of a solar energy array, it had to be jury-rigged into functionality by its first crew. Thus the execution did not live up to its concept. Some smaller Saturn IBs were retained for launching astronauts aboard Apollo command and service modules to Skylab, and the last carried three Americans on the Apollo-Soyuz mission of 1975. While this first joint American-Russian flight was of significant political value, it was of limited scientific value.

What really kept astronauts from going beyond earth orbit was the Space Shuttle, the most significant program to survive Nixon's budgetary agenda. The technology was impressive when it first flew in 1981, and this spacecraft was not only huge, but reusable—a first. Further, it was the primary launch vehicle for the International Space Station, another successful project. However, the shuttle proved more expensive and less efficient to operate than projected, and the loss of the *Challenger* and *Columbia*, with their crews, was devastating to NASA.

In effect, the American manned spaceflight program was put on a low-earth-orbit leash. Then, when the shuttle stopped flying in 2011, the United States lost its ability to put astronauts into space. Now NASA relies on Russian equipment to carry its people to the International Space Station. As tensions mount because of Vladimir Putin's adventures in the Crimea and eastern Ukraine, there is the possibility that the escalation of a new Cold War will ground American astronauts altogether.

As an embattled and increasingly unpopular president, Richard Nixon lost the power of impoundment, which was never to be regained by his successors. In 1974, Congress passed the Impoundment Control Act, stripping the president of the right to exercise this power unilaterally. As evidence of just how embattled Nixon was at the time, he signed it, albeit reluctantly. Because of the loss of impoundment, presidents also lost some of the leverage once employed to act against excessive federal spending.

There was one positive result of Nixon's mistake in impounding funds, and that was the creation of the Congressional Budget Office in 1974, through the same law that ended impoundment. Besides stripping the chief executive of the power of impoundment, Congress created its own agency for budgetary study. Unlike the White House's Office of Management and Budget, the CBO is truly bipartisan, and offers analysis without advocacy.

Despite the achievements of NASA in the era of the Space Shuttle, and the political benefits of the CBO, Nixon's undermining of the American manned space program was an enormous mistake. The road not taken leads to improved booster and spacecraft technologies, taking Americans back to the moon, and almost certainly beyond. It is also one that leaves the president with a tool against real overspending and budgetary irresponsibility. Thus, while we might remember Richard Milhous Nixon chiefly for the grand mistakes of Watergate, they were not the only major miscues of his presidency. The effects of his gutting of the space program still linger forty years later.

# 85

# NIXON NOW, NIXON FOREVER

## 1972

### By Dr. Paul A. Thomsen

Were we really this close to
dystopia or utopia?

On June 17, 1972, five men were arrested breaking into Democratic National Committee headquarters at the Watergate Hotel in Washington, DC. According to Nixon's White House press secretary, Ron Ziegler, it was nothing more than a "third-rate burglary," but the act was really a presidential campaign mistake. Although the "Nixon Now" campaign later went on to win the election without the burglars, the act, ordered by the Nixon Administration, doomed his presidency and radically altered the American political landscape.

Richard M. Nixon built his political career in bruising right-vs.-left campaign fights by doing the unexpected. Born in 1913 in Yorba Linda, California, to devout pacifist American Friends Service Committee parents, he abandoned a safe job in the Washington, DC, Office of Price Administration to enlist in the navy in 1942, serving in various administrative positions in the Pacific War. In 1946, he defeated the five-term liberal Democratic House representative Jerry Voorhis through allegations that the incumbent had secret Communist leadings. Later, Nixon rode political shotgun for Congressman Joseph McCarthy, investigating Alger Hiss's alleged Communist sympathies. By deftly abandoning McCarthy early, Nixon rode the Hiss-won public fame to election to the United States Senate in 1950. In 1952, he was chosen Dwight Eisenhower's vice-presidential running mate without suffering the stain of the McCarthy controversy.

Whether by poor timing or a rival's superior political maneuvering, Richard Nixon spent much of the 1950s and 1960s doing political damage control. In September 1952, he was forced to defend himself against accusations of illicit campaign donations, which included a dog given to his children—named Checkers. The controversy didn't sink Nixon, but it did tarnish his role in the Eisenhower White House. In the 1960 presidential election, he was unable to overcome the more popular political lightweight John F. Kennedy. In 1964, he failed to gain the Republican Party presidential nomination. Even his 1968 presidential primary victory was marred by the showing of Nelson Rockefeller and newcomer Ronald Reagan. For Nixon, it seemed that every campaign held a potentially crippling X-factor.

Throughout his first administration, Richard Nixon was preoccupied with the fear of losing the next election. By drawing from a narrow pool of Democratic and Republican voters, he was forced to become a master centrist. Unable to rely on either party for support in Congress, he built coalitions of issue-oriented groups, such as environmentalists, some antiwar protesters, and a "law and order" constituency. He also gave little ground to his competition. For example, in 1972, Nixon trumpeted the signing of campaign finance reform legislation into law, but he also conveniently failed to ensure the legislation's enforcement. In another example, in 1969, he publicly celebrated the moon landing, but privately cut much of the space program's budget. He was also known for withholding funding for congressionally authorized federal programs of which he did not approve.

In the 1972 presidential election, Richard Nixon really didn't have that much to fear, but his past electoral woes had twisted the president's perceptions. Nixon managed to win the support of those who wanted America to wind down its commitment to Vietnam. His foreign policy achievements in China and Russia deflected perceptions that he might be too militant. Funding for the Equal Opportunity Employment Commission, the Environmental Protection Agency, and the proposed creation of the Occupational Safety and Health

Administration ensured solid support from the vital center of American politics. By contrast, his Democratic opposition, George McGovern, stood solidly on the left of American politics (thus alienating the other two-thirds), offering a weak national security platform and a weak presidential campaign in which he was forced to switch vice-presidential running mates. Still, Nixon feared wild cards like the leaks surrounding his bombing of Cambodia and the unauthorized publishing of the *Pentagon Papers*. To alleviate his fears, he had five men, called the Plumbers, arm his reelection campaign with dirt on the competition.

Had he not acted on his fears, the American political landscape of the time would have been fundamentally different. His past political successes offer some clues. First, the president, an adept marketer, had already successfully reframed the failure of the American military to defeat the Vietnamese Communists as an attempt to bring about "peace with honor." It's likely that he would have tried to spin the end of the Vietnam War as a completion of the US commitment to Vietnam, dispelling the Ford administration's defeatist rhetoric and the perception of a failure of the American military. Second, his centrist approach to politics, as well as his personal indignation, would have precluded "his" Republican Party from running a right- or left-leaning candidate. Hence it is probable that his onetime competitor Ronald Reagan would not have found national backing in a Nixon-run party.

It is also likely that political issues would have been marginally different. The Democratic reformers who swept into Congress in 1974, such as Chris Dodd and Henry Waxman, would have found as little purchase as their predecessors against the president's deft hand, making the prospective campaign finance successes in 1974 effectively stillborn. Although a Carter candidacy could have succeeded on an anti-Washington candidacy, Carter and Walter Mondale, or another Democrat, would have spent most of their time undoing Nixon's layered bureaucratic infrastructure. Lastly, the "Moral Majority" neoconservative movement might not have arisen in the late seventies if the last dregs of the sixties protest movements hadn't been emboldened by the failure of a presidency.

Instead, the president succumbed to his fears, and someone in the White House ordered the break-in at the Watergate and ended Nixon's political career. It took considerable time, political blood, and legal fighting, but eventually Nixon realized that he could not win a Watergate fight against a polarized Congress. On August 8, 1974, he resigned from the presidency, having won the 1972 presidential election and forever lost his center.

Without Watergate, there would have been no end to a Nixon legacy. Ford would never have been president. Reagan would likely not have run again for high office. "Deep Throat" would have remained a reference exclusively to the porn industry. No one would have heard of reporters Woodward and Bernstein. Public policy in the United States would also likely have continued to be largely issue-oriented and far less polarized into liberal and conservative extremes. The age of the "Imperial Presidency" would also have continued well into the 1980s. A stronger national security agenda would have precluded minor skirmishes in favor of stronger resistance to the Soviet invasion of Afghanistan and, should the Iranian revolutionary government have proven aggressive, we might have seen a full military commitment in 1980 to restore the shah and free the Iran hostages. Tensions would have skyrocketed between the West and the Soviet Union, now divided from China. And, sadly, Alan Moore and Dave Gibbons's blockbuster dystopian comic-book-series-turned-blockbuster-movie, *Watchmen*, would have been considered far too controversial to film. In a sense, a less fearful Nixon would have overseen a political world in which America's "we are one" sentiment would have overshadowed the "many voices" culture.

||||||||||||||||||||||||||||||||||||||||||||||||||||||||||||||||||

# 86

# THAT KODAK MOMENT

1973

**By William Terdoslavich**

||||||||||||||||||||||||||||||||||||||||||||||||||||||||||||||||||

Too narrow a focus.

Once upon a time in America, every photograph ever taken had something to do with the Eastman Kodak Company, popularly called Kodak. It was a company so well-known that it could stand beside motherhood, apple pie, and Coca-Cola.

Chances were good that every family photo was taken with a simple Kodak point-and-shoot camera, loaded with Kodak film, processed with Kodak chemicals, and printed on Kodak paper.

Kodak lasted over a century. It had a brand name once as recognizable as McDonald's. It was once a Fortune 500 company. Its stock was one of thirty that made up the Dow Jones Industrial Average. But now Kodak is just a footnote in business history, a name hardly anyone has ever heard of.

What happened?

## Just Press the Button and Leave the Rest to Us

In America, an inventor is usually some guy who looks for a better way of doing something, because the present way sucks. George Eastman was one of those guys.

He wanted to take pictures of his vacation trip to the Dominican Republic—back in the 1870s. That meant lugging a huge single-shot camera that used glass plates instead of film. Everything was heavy.

Eastman thought this was stupid. So, like anyone inconvenienced by current technology, he looked for a better way. He started by replacing that glass plate with a sheet coated in light-sensitive gelatin. When somebody else invented film, Eastman coated it with his patented goo and camera film became a product.

In 1888, Eastman changed the name of his company to Kodak. He just liked the distinctiveness of the letter K and made up a name that sounded right, but meant nothing.

Eastman turned out several cameras that used his film, but really struck gold when he went to market with the "Box Brownie" in 1900. The camera came preloaded with a hundred-shot roll of film. You sent the camera back to Kodak for processing, and your developed pictures came back with your camera, reloaded with another hundred-shot roll of film.

"Just press the button and leave the rest to us," Kodak once advertised.

It worked.

## Betting on a Chip

Kodak spent the rest of the twentieth century coming out with new film formats and new products—personal movie cameras (and film), color slides (and slide projectors), film packed in preloaded cartridges that went into cheap point-and-shoot cameras (the Instamatic).

By 1976, Kodak sold *90 percent* of all camera film in the United States, as well as *85 percent* of all cameras. It was taking in $10 billion a year by 1981. By 1988, Kodak employed over 145,000 people. The company even made X-ray film and cornered the market for that, too!

But Kodak was the mighty dinosaur that took no notice of the little mouse nibbling at its toes. That mouse was the Charge-Coupled Device (CCD), a light-sensitive chip invented in 1969 by George Smith and Willard Sterling Boyle at AT&T Bell Labs.

By 1973, the CCD found its way to Kodak's lab at corporate headquarters in Rochester, New York. A young twentysomething engineer named Steve Sasson was told by his boss to find a practical use for the chip.

Sasson scrounged a lens from a Kodak Super 8 movie camera,

with the CCD mounted right behind it. He slapped together six circuit boards for the electronics, linked to a digital/analog converter. The portable cassette tape recorder would store the data. Sixteen nickel-cadmium batteries powered the system.

When Sasson demonstrated the first digital camera, it snapped an image in less than a second. But it took twenty-three seconds to record the digitized image to the tape cassette, and another thirty seconds to play back the data and display a 100x100-pixel image on a black-and-white television.

The executives at Kodak were not impressed.

## Film Works

Kodak practically owned the American market. Close to 100 percent of its revenues came from camera film and everything that revolved around it. Why stop a machine that is printing money?

Vince Barabba, head of Kodak's market research unit, glimpsed the future in 1981. He studied the existing film business and knew that the digital camera could only improve with time. So he told his bosses he had good news and bad news. The bad news first: digital will replace film. The good news: Kodak had about ten years to figure out how to make the transition to digital and stay in business.

Barabba left Kodak in 1985. Kodak executives stuck to film.

Not all was lost—yet. Change always comes from the top. If you hired the right CEO, he could demand change—*and get it!* That moment came in 1989, when CEO Colby Chandler retired. Kodak's board could choose a digital future by picking Phil Samper, or stick to film by tapping Kay R. Whitmore. The board chose Whitmore. He lasted three years.

Kodak's board then turned to George Fisher, bringing him over from Motorola, where he was also CEO. Fisher plowed $500 million into the Advantix Preview film and camera system. This was a digital camera that relied on *film*. It previewed the shot you took; then you used it to order the number of prints you wanted. The product flopped. Fisher was out by 1999.

While Fisher pursued folly, Kodak finally brought out its first true digital camera, the DC20, in 1996—*fifteen years* after Sony brought the first digital camera to market. It was a start, nonetheless. By 2001, Kodak was number two in the US digital camera market, behind Sony. But Kodak was also losing sixty dollars on every camera sold. Worse, every digital camera sold subtracted from Kodak's revenues from film, chemicals, and paper.

The last blow came from cell phones, which Sharp and Samsung managed to outfit with small digital cameras. They were good enough for snapshots. Then Apple came out with its iPhone in 2007, packing a simple two-megapixel camera. No one needed to carry a point-and-shoot camera anymore.

## Developing a Slow Death

Kodak financed its decline the hard way: by failing in its attempt to diversify, and by selling off existing units to pay for its doomed digital camera division.

Diversification failed when Kodak bought Sterling Drug in 1988, only to sell it six years later, after realizing that film chemistry and drugs made a poor fit. Kodak then sold off its Eastman Chemical Company.

The cash helped improve Kodak's digital camera effort. Kodak reached 27 percent market share in 1999. But competition from Nikon, Canon, and Apple eventually took that market share away. Kodak doubled down on consumer cameras again, selling off its X-ray equipment unit for $2.35 billion in 2007. (Officially, it did not want to invest the needed funds to migrate X-ray from film to digital.) Despite the added cash, Kodak's digital camera market share fell to just 7 percent by 2010.

By the end, Kodak was selling off its patents, just to keep the camera business going. The final straw came shortly before 2012, when Kodak closed all of its processing facilities and laid off more than a hundred thousand employees. Over $6 billion in debt outweighed $5 billion in assets. Kodak filed for Chapter 11 bankruptcy.

## Taking a Different Picture

When a major company goes down, it takes many livelihoods with it. Kodak once employed more than 145,000 people. Each one took home a paycheck that supported a family and kept a roof overhead. It would have been a hundred times better for them if Kodak never went out of business. Ditto for the stockholders who invested in Kodak, and the scientists who developed its new products.

To survive, Kodak would need to kill film, which was its sacred cash cow. It could have been done, if Kodak's board had been far-sighted enough to heed the Barabba report and hire Phil Samper to drive its digital transition.

Underneath that veneer of a red brand name on a bright yellow box, Kodak was a technology company. It had over 1,700 patents, including those needed for digital photography. If it could not compete in cameras, it could still collect royalties from those patents. Kodak would still have the scientists on its payroll to develop new products.

Kodak's rival, Fujifilm, showed how it could be done. It had a near monopoly on film in Japan, where the company obtained 60 percent of its profits. Once executives saw the digital handwriting on the wall, they decided to take that figure down to *zero*. They would milk as much cash out of film as possible while that market existed, prepare to switch to digital, and diversify. Kodak made the same choices, albeit haphazardly, with little regard for sequence and planning.

Fujifilm applied its chemical expertise to cosmetics, since skin care products and camera film both rely on antioxidants. It also applied its film expertise to optical films for LCD flat panels, now used in smartphones, tablets, digital cameras, and computer screens. Restructuring and layoffs freed up cash to buy other companies in markets where Fujifilm could make a yen.

Kodak was too wedded to existing lines of business that produced tons of cash. Marketing outweighed technology. Management vetoed innovation.

And so Kodak was done in by the very technology it invented— the digital camera.

# 87

# THE LIFE OF MAYOR LINDSAY

### 1974

### By William Terdoslavich

The death of traditional liberalism.

t is hard to believe, but the prosperous and relatively safe city of today was once the worst place to live. That is what New York City was like when Mayor John V. Lindsay left office on the morning of January 1, 1974.

The best that can be said of Lindsay was that he was a good man who did a bad job. He was not evil, but much of the good he tried to do was easily outweighed by the bad it produced.

## "He Is Fresh and Everyone Else Is Tired"

Robert F. Wagner Jr. was finishing his third term when Lindsay saw his opportunity to run for mayor. He had already put in several terms in Congress, representing Manhattan's posh Upper East Side. In the House, he was a staunch supporter of civil rights and wanted very much to improve the lot of the poor. Although he was a Republican, his liberalism was very much in sync with local political sentiments.

The election of 1965 pitted Lindsay against Comptroller Abe Beame, a clubhouse Democrat running to win, and conservative William F. Buckley Jr., who was running to make a point.

Good-looking, in his early forties, and very telegenic, Lindsay projected an image of confidence and competence. "He is fresh and everyone else is tired," wrote columnist Murray Kempton. The description stuck.

Lindsay cruised to a clear victory, snaring 44 percent to Beame's 41 percent of more than two million votes cast. Lindsay made it very clear that he would govern by principle, not politics.

Just as Lindsay was taking his oath of office on January 1, 1966, he faced his first crisis. Michael Quill, head of the Transport Workers Union of America, called for a walkout. All subways and buses in New York City ground to a halt.

Lindsay handled the crisis by lecturing, not dealing. That did not sway Quill. Lindsay caved after thirteen days. He approved a $52 million pay raise over two years. But more importantly, Quill showed that Lindsay could be pushed around. The mayor was nothing more than a pretty face.

## All Hell Breaks Loose, Again and Again and Again

Mayors have to do two things to succeed in office. The first is crisis management. The second is everyday management. Lindsay proved he was no good at either.

Imagewise, Lindsay successfully promoted New York as "fun city," an exciting place to live, where something was happening every day. It wasn't much fun for the average New Yorker.

Crisis management and everyday management collided badly in 1968. Lindsay wanted to decentralize the school system, putting an experimental local school board in the largely black neighborhoods of Ocean Hill and Brownsville in Brooklyn. He expected parents to have greater say in how their neighborhood schools were run. Instead, the district supervisor transferred thirteen teachers and six administrators, without cause. What worsened the crisis was that all of the people transferred were white and Jewish.

The United Federation of Teachers cried foul, pointing out that the transfers violated their contract. To underscore this point, all the teachers went on strike—*for fifty-five days*. One million children went unschooled.

The crisis was finally sorted out by New York State, which found cause to remove the administrators. Thirty-two local school boards were set up, each one with contracting power, but no say in which teachers got hired and fired.

Other unions lined up to take their shots at Lindsay. The cops staged a slowdown. The firefighters made threats. The sanitation men walked off the job for two weeks, allowing garbage to pile up. And then came the snow.

New York got hit with a massive blizzard in February 1969. Manhattan got plowed out pretty quickly. The snowplows were never seen in Queens or Brooklyn. Lindsay was puzzled about why people were complaining, as he had no trouble getting around. Five days later, he took a trip into Queens and was greeted with jeers and boos wherever he went. And he didn't get far, despite using a four-wheel-drive truck, *because the streets were still buried under fifteen inches of snow.*

## Bronx Cheer

To Lindsay's credit, he did one good thing. Shortly after Martin Luther King's assassination in 1968, as many American cities succumbed to rioting, Lindsay went straight to Harlem to walk the streets, maintaining calm in the black community.

Lindsay tried to do good during the civil rights era. He really believed that the city should take an active roll in empowering the black and Hispanic population, just as it had done for the Irish, Italians, and Jews in previous decades. Only, in those days, patronage and civil service, in addition to welfare, were the tools New York City used to give newcomers a stake.

Lindsay turned his back on his Republican and middle-class supporters, openly courting the black and Latino vote. He did away with the eligibility requirements and time limits for welfare. Cases soared from 500,000 to 1.2 million in just four years, finally reaching a budget cost of $1.2 billion.

Lindsay ran for reelection in 1969. Many wished he hadn't. He lost the Republican nomination to John Marchi, a little-known state legislator from Staten Island. Drab and colorless, Marchi represented the values of solid, ethnic middle-class New Yorkers who'd had enough of the glamorous Lindsay. Fun city wasn't much fun for them, as crime and taxes went up.

Mario Procaccino, a Bronx clubhouse politician, secured the Democratic nomination. Procaccino also tried to rally those white, ethnic middle-class New Yorkers. He even derided Lindsay as a "limousine liberal."

Lindsay ran a "mea culpa" campaign, admitting his faults to his well-to-do liberal supporters and reaching out to the black and Puerto Rican communities for their votes.

It worked. Running on the Liberal Party line, Lindsay snared 42 percent of the vote, with Procaccino getting 34 percent and Marchi 22 percent. The opposition split the remaining votes, allowing Lindsay another four years in office.

Times Square sank into decay. Crime doubled. The white middle class fled to the suburbs. City unemployment shot up. Unions got generous raises. The City University of New York (CUNY) went to open admissions, flooding the campuses with tuition-free students unready to learn. Welfare rolls remained high.

Lindsay tried to deal with all these problems by running for president as a Democrat in 1972. He bombed in the Florida primary and placed sixth in Wisconsin. Back home, many New Yorkers felt he was ignoring his day job as things only worsened. Brooklyn Democratic party boss Meade Esposito summed it up best: "I think the handwriting is on the wall; Little Sheba better come home."

## Lindsay Leaves a Mess

Crime, taxes, economic decline, and budget problems only accelerated as Lindsay prepared to leave office. He was tired and no one else was fresh.

From 1966 to 1973, murder shot up 137 percent and robbery skyrocketed by 209 percent. Lindsay tried to head off the problem by hiring four thousand more cops and issuing walkie-talkies, but all the cops did was chase 911 calls. And they did nothing to control "quality of life" crimes, like graffiti vandalism or the destruction of city infrastructure.

Government spending shot up 133 percent during Lindsay's years in office. Even when adjusted for inflation, city spending was up 61 percent, while the city's economy *declined*. By the time Lindsay left office, welfare, hospitals, and the City University of New York consumed $4 billion per year. And free hospitals and universities were not benefits other cities even bothered to offer.

To pay for all this, Lindsay passed a commuter tax and a city income tax. It was not enough. He borrowed to make up the difference, with short-term debt hitting $3.4 billion. There were no new parks or bridges to show for it. New York City shed 610,000 jobs by the time Lindsay left office. And each lost paycheck meant that much less income that could be taxed.

## Low Beame

It would have been a hundred times better if Lindsay had never run for mayor. Born rich, he had no sense of money. Sincerely liberal, he wanted to help the black and Hispanic poor, long disadvantaged before the civil rights era. The result was no real advancement for blacks and Hispanics, abandonment of an increasingly dangerous city by the white middle class, and near bankruptcy.

Had Lindsay not been mayor, the most likely winner would have been Abe Beame. He would have been mayor eight years sooner than he actually was, governing a city in better financial shape than the one he presided over in 1973.

Beame was no less a liberal than Lindsay. He believed a city job was the ticket into the middle class. (It had worked for him.) He probably would have used civil service, not welfare, as the ladder to get blacks and Latinos "into the game," And he would have worked through the existing network of black and Hispanic elected officials to deliver patronage and services, instead of appeasing the worst radicals in New York's civil rights movement, as Lindsay did.

That's how the city used to work before Lindsay was mayor. Beame knew how to run it that way. Instead, the Lindsay legacy sputtered on until it nearly bankrupted New York City. A bailout and budget cuts only made things worse. Voters blamed Beame, who came in fourth in the 1977 mayoral primary.

The voters might as well have been voting out Lindsay, whose legacy ended with that election.

# 88

# THE DEVELOPMENT AND SORTA DEPLOYMENT OF THE B-2 BOMBER

## 1977

### By William Terdoslavich

B-2 or no B-2? That is the question.

Everything about the B-52 is awesome. It can fly twelve thousand miles on a tank of gas. It is capable of striking anywhere in the world. It can carry up to seventy thousand pounds of bombs. And it can speed along at more than 500 mph at fifty thousand feet.

The B-52 is also mortal, like any warplane. The rule of thumb is simple: as soon as the first production model takes to the sky, begin designing its replacement. This will take years. As soon as the last B-52 comes off the assembly line, the prototype for the new bomber should roll out of the hangar.

The air force bought about 750 B-52 bombers in the 1950s and 1960s without suffering much of a budget overrun. In fact, some 76 B-52s remain with the bomber fleet, these being the last models delivered in the early 1960s.

*And ever since then, the air force has been designing the B-52's replacement.*

## Higher, Faster . . .

The first replacement was the six-engine XB-70 Valkyrie, a humongous delta-winged monster that could break the sound barrier by brute force alone. The downing of the U-2 over the USSR by a SAM missile in 1960 rendered the XB-70 program moot. President John F. Kennedy canceled the program while the air force changed the B-52's nuclear mission to low-altitude penetration.

*But the air force still needed a replacement for the B-52.*

The B-52 added conventional bombing to its mission list during the Vietnam War. And throughout the war years, older B-52s were retired. So where is this promised replacement bomber?

Well, there is the B-1 Lancer. The design was born from the desire to merge a supersonic bomber like the old B-58 Hustler with the dependable, high-payload B-52. And it had to be capable of flying a low-altitude penetration mission to nuke the Soviet Union.

Designers gave the B-1 a "swing wing." Fully extended forward, it gave the B-1 a lot of lift. Swept back, it gave the B-1 the ability to go to Mach 2 without a lot of drag. Dropping the purchase of limited-range F-111s freed up some budget dollars to pay for the more able B-1.

Several B-1A prototypes were delivered for testing in the early 1970s. Defense officials were estimating a program buy of about 200 to 250 aircraft. Program costs were hitting $100 million per B-1 as President Gerald Ford pondered keeping the plane—or killing it. The 1975 defection of a Soviet fighter pilot—along with his MiG-25—revealed that the plane had a "look down/shoot down" radar that made life hazardous for any low-altitude penetration bomber.

By 1976, the B-1 was becoming a campaign issue. Governor Jimmy Carter (D-GA), running for president, promised to kill the B-1 because the plane was too expensive, overdue for replacement, and obsolete. He made good his promise in early 1977, shortly after taking office. Rockwell International made sure the B-1 had at least one subcontractor in every state and congressional district. Carter took a lot of political heat for ending the program, but was he killing an eagle or a turkey?

## Swing Wing Gives Way to Wing Thing

*The B-52 still needed a replacement.* If the B-1 won't do, don't worry. We have the B-2! Carter made the decision to go ahead with the B-2 in 1978. Only the public did not know about it. The program was top secret.

The Northrop B-2 Spirit was revolutionary in design. Designer Jack Northrop had experimented with "flying wings" during the post-WWII years. The all-wing design got rid of drag since there was no fuselage or tail, and every square foot of the plane created lift. The older flying wings—the XB-35 and jet-powered YB-49— were hard to fly. The B-2 relied on computers to make the control changes needed to eliminate that problem.

The flying wing was also hard to spot on radar, which was a good starting point to give the B-2 "stealth" technology. The airframe was "sculpted" to deflect radar beams. What could not be deflected could be absorbed by the B-2's special paint and the composite materials used for the plane's skin and leading edges. Landing gear, bombs, and engines were fully recessed, again leaving radar nothing to bounce off of.

By 1981, Jack Northrop was already in failing health, confined to a wheelchair and unable to speak. The air force briefed him on the B-2, noting how much of the plane's design came from Northrop's previous work. In a feeble hand, Northrop wrote his reply: "Now I know why God kept me alive for 25 years." He passed away ten months later.

## Lancer or Spirit?

The B-1 came back from the dead anyway, becoming a campaign issue in 1980. Governor Ronald Reagan (R-CA) charged the Carter administration with weakening US military strength at a time when the USSR was probably drawing ahead.

Reagan won the 1980 election. Upon assuming office, he had two choices: leave the B-1 dead and put all his chips on the B-2, or build the B-1 and skip the B-2. Reagan was backing a five-year, $1-trillion rearmament program, less grounded in thoughtful strategy and more reliant on throwing money at problems. He decided to buy both planes.

The B-1B went into production in the early 1980s, with a hundred-plane buy at $200 million per plane. Likewise, the B-2 went into development, with the first plane rolling out in 1989, about a year after the air force took delivery of its last B-1.

The B-2 Spirit was the better plane. But it faced a bigger problem in 1991. The Soviet Union collapsed, taking away its raison d'être. The 134-plane buy was knocked down to 20 planes. And the program cost had to be spread among those remaining airframes, boosting the per-plane cost to *$2 billion each.*

Today the US Air Force is stuck with three different bombers—20 B-2s, 67 B-1s, and 74 B-52s. That yields a total bomber fleet of 161 aircraft, but spread out over three different types, yielding no economies of scale but plenty of expense. And there are programs afoot to overhaul and modify the B-1 and B-52 to keep them flying until 2040.

*The XB-70, B-1, and B-2 were all supposed to replace the B-52. But the B-52 is still flying.*

## Paper Airplanes

Had Reagan stuck with killing the B-1, the B-2 could have gotten a full build-out of 134 planes. The B-2 would still be very pricey, but spreading out 134 planes over $40 billion would have cut per-plane costs down to around $300 million each. Maintenance crews would have to maintain only one bomber type, not three.

Stealth makes it possible for the B-2 to operate in "nonpermissive" environments where the B-1 and B-52 would be shot down. This becomes an issue as countries like China and Iran focus on Anti-Access/Area Denial (A2/D2), a strategy using low-cost sensors, computer networks, and precision-guided missiles to sink any approaching US warship or shoot down any incoming US warplane.

The B-2's stealthy features would challenge A2/D2, but with only 20 aircraft, there is some question whether there is enough "force" to make it so. This would take on a different complexion if the US had the full 134-plane fleet to mount its challenge.

Add to this the B-3, now on the drawing board as the next replacement bomber. The US Air Force is hoping to score $55–$70 billion to fund a hundred-plane purchase. With no B-1s or B-52s around, the stealthy B-3 could gain uncontested funding, either replacing the B-2 or adding to the bomber fleet.

A twenty-first-century bomber force would be a nice thing to have.

*But we are still flying the B-52.*

# 89

||||||||||||||||||||||||||||||||||||||||||||||||||||||||||||||||||||||

# WHAT MASSACHUSETTS MIRACLE?

## 1977

### By William Terdoslavich

||||||||||||||||||||||||||||||||||||||||||||||||||||||||||||||||||||||

Silicon Valley once had a competitor.

The computer industry as we know it was not always based in California's Silicon Valley. Along the outer rings of the Boston metro area, there was another concentration of high-tech companies every bit as competitive.

Digital Equipment Corporation (DEC) and Wang Laboratories were once as well-known as Apple or Microsoft. How did they disappear?

Being located in a high-tax state wasn't the cause. Nor were government regulations a hindrance. Wang and DEC collapsed because they could not change as their industry changed. And no amount of government intervention could have altered that.

## In the Beginning . . .

The stories of Wang and DEC begin with their respective founders, An Wang and Ken Olsen. Despite different starting points, they pursued similar paths to success.

An Wang began in 1936 by attending Shanghai's Chiao Tung University to study electrical engineering. He was sixteen. He left China for good in 1945 to pursue a doctorate in physics at Harvard.

In 1948, while at Harvard, Wang invented the computer memory core, the predecessor of the memory chips used today. In 1951, Wang Laboratories began business above a garage in Boston's South End, with just a $600 investment. The company started by making special-purpose data entry equipment, paper tape readers, and digital logic modules.

That $600 investment turned into $15,000 in revenue in Wang's first year in business. And the company would keep growing on an average of 40 percent per year *for the next thirty-three years*. Wang himself would go on to log another thirty-nine patents, all laying down the initial building blocks of the modern computer industry.

Wang's success blossomed in the 1960s when the company went to market with a desktop calculator, the LOCI-2. It then developed LINASEC, a special-purpose computer used by typesetters to justify newspaper columns.

The next step up was office computing, with the Wang 1200. It was a Wang 500 calculator hooked up to a keyboard from an IBM Selectric typewriter and a dual tape cassette deck for data storage. Each tape cassette could hold twenty pages of text. Because one could edit text on this system, there was no need to retype entire documents.

## Meanwhile, in Another Part of Massachusetts . . .

Olsen came to computing by way of the Massachusetts Institute of Technology, where he earned a BS and an MS in electrical engineering; following this, in 1950, he was hired at MIT's Lincoln Laboratory.

While at MIT, Olsen and his pal Harlan Anderson noticed students shunning share time on faster IBM computers to tinker with a smaller computer called a TX-0, an eighteen-bit machine built to test circuitry. The TX-0's programming could accept programming input from a user.

Anderson and Olsen sought to commercialize the TX-0, so in 1957 they founded Digital Equipment Corporation, with the help of $70,000 from Harvard Business School professor Georges Doriot.

Anderson left the company shortly after it was founded, leaving it all to Olsen.

DEC entered the market by making lab test modules, racking up $57,000 in revenue in its first year. But Olsen's ambition was to make a programmable, interactive computer that was smaller than a refrigerator-sized IBM mainframe. In 1960, DEC launched its PDP-1, a true minicomputer. Prices ran from $100,000 to $900,000, depending on configuration. But more importantly, the minicomputer became a lower-cost programmable alternative to the big IBM mainframe.

## Big Trends Come in Small Packages

It was in the 1970s that the fortunes of DEC and Wang skyrocketed.

Wang got there in 1977, with its Office Information System. At that time, the klutzy mash-up between a desktop calculator, typewriter, and tape cassette deck was replaced by a networked terminal with its own processor, feeding text files into a common disk storage unit via coaxial cable. Up to twenty-four users could share a system, which required no special training to administer.

That utility translated into massive success. Of the 2,000 largest companies in the United States, about 1,600 were buying and using products from Wang Laboratories. No one used a typewriter anymore, except to write an address on an envelope.

DEC was doing fine, finally reaching a plateau with its sixteen-bit PDP-11 minicomputer in the mid-1970s. At this point, Olsen switched gears as his design gurus developed a thirty-two-bit architecture, known as Virtual Address Extension, shortened to VAX. Combining the right feature sets with good prices and attractive marketing, the VAX minicomputer was so successful that in five years Olsen scrapped DEC's effort to design its own mainframe computer. The best part about the VAX system was that it could be upgraded instead of replaced.

In the 1980s, DEC would go on to become the largest computer company in the world—after IBM. Meanwhile, Wang grew bigger than this California upstart company called Apple, which was also enjoying high growth.

But Apple was doing something different. In the late 1970s, it began selling "personal computers"—basically, stand-alone units that fit on a desktop and ran prepackaged programs.

IBM also noticed this trend early, and set up a "skunk works" to develop its own PC, unhindered by company bureaucracy. Other companies jumped in to develop an operating system for the IBM PC, as well as applications and, most importantly, network systems.

The whole setup was standardized and interoperable. But most importantly, *no one owned the standard.* If you bought a PC by another maker and an application from some third company, it would all work just fine with IBM's stuff.

Olsen and Wang didn't see that coming.

## The Higher the Peak, the Deeper the Fall

By 1989–1990, DEC hit over $11 billion in revenues, with profits close to $1.3 billion. Olsen's company was so hot it might as well have been printing money. *Fortune* magazine had singled out Olsen as the most successful entrepreneur in the United States.

An Wang retired from an active role running his company in 1986, turning over the reins to his son, Frederick. By this point, Wang had diversified into personal computers and minicomputers. An Wang's personal fortune hit about $1.6 billion, making him the fifth richest man in the United States. His company now ranked 227 on the Fortune 500 list, with revenues reaching $2 billion.

But DEC and Wang had one common weakness. They both relied on proprietary software and systems. A company using either Wang or DEC equipment could not add on computer hardware, software, networking gear made by another vendor.

IBM Multimate, WordPerfect, XyWrite, and Microsoft Word were all word processing programs that worked the same on any IBM-compatible PC. And they cost less than Wang's proprietary solution.

DEC's fumble was even more embarrassing. It missed the boat on personal computers, operating systems, open systems, and networking, *and* failed to freshen up its VAX product line. Olsen was too insistent on maintaining DEC's proprietary product lines, instead of ditching them to exploit changes that were under way in the marketplace.

DEC's sales fell. The company's board gave Olsen a pink slip in 1992, replacing him with Robert Palmer. But even he could not stop Digital's decline. By 1998, DEC was sold to Compaq for over $9 billion.

Wang's decline was far bloodier. Frederick Wang only lasted three years as president. Wang Laboratories financed its expansion with debt, not by additional stock offerings. When sales went down, those loan repayments became harder to make. An Wang eventually fired his son, replacing him with Richard Miller. Wang passed away the following year.

Under Miller, Wang Laboratories shifted to open systems, eliminated the company's debt, and restructured as well. But Wang Labs still lost money. By 1992, Miller threw in the towel. Wang filed for Chapter 11 bankruptcy.

## The Path Not Taken

It is always a hundred times better for a company to make the right choices to stay competitive. People don't get laid off. Stockholders don't get burned. Lenders see their loans repaid. And the towns where the companies are located do not suffer downturns.

DEC and Wang needed to be willing to "eat their young" in order to survive. Proprietary systems fueled their growth by holding customers captive to their computer systems. Open systems proved just as good, but cheaper and easier to integrate. Corporate customers switched to IBM, Compaq, Hewlett-Packard, 3Com, and Microsoft instead of sticking with DEC and Wang.

If DEC and Wang had revealed the source codes for their proprietary systems early enough, they could have become industry standards that others would have had to follow. That did not happen, so failure followed. The Massachusetts Miracle that then-governor Michael Dukakis loved to talk about turned into the Massachusetts Mirage instead.

Finally, the fall of DEC and Wang served as a harsh warning to other high-tech companies. Beware of disruptive change. When it comes, embrace it. Don't worry about what it does to existing products and services.

Now IBM is faltering. It has undertaken a crash effort to embrace cloud computing and cognitive computing, as these areas offer the promise of future growth. Hewlett-Packard is splitting itself in half, with the better portion focused on services and cloud computing. Even Microsoft is trying to reinvent itself while it has the money to do so, following thirty years of dominance in office applications and operating systems.

No high-tech company wants to be the last dodo bird holding the buggy whip. No company wants to be the next DEC or Wang.

# 90

# BACK WHEN THE COLD WAR WAS HOT

### 1979

### By William Terdoslavich

> East is East and West is West,
> And never the twain shall meet.
> —RUDYARD KIPLING

Life was so much simpler during the Cold War. It was us vs. them, with no shades of gray.

The world was unnaturally divided between democratic free-market states and Communist kleptocracies with controlled economies. Dictators were free agents who allied with the side offering the best deal.

Any nation, no matter how poor or small, was significant. If the US picked one up as an ally, it was a loss for the Soviets, and vice versa. South Vietnam, Nicaragua, Mozambique, Somalia—all acquired outsized importance because of this.

That zero-sum game would be played to the death in Afghanistan.

## What Brezhnev Wants, Brezhnev Gets

Soviet Communist Party chairman Leonid Brezhnev was on his last legs in the late 1970s. A lifetime of vodka and cigarettes was finally catching up to him. The other old men in the Politburo were in better shape—*barely*.

These old men were not like the Russian Communists of old. They were more rigid and bureaucratic than revolutionary and ruthless. Despite this, the Soviet Union was having a good decade in the 1970s. Communism picked up South Vietnam, Cambodia, Laos, Angola, Mozambique, Ethiopia, Somalia, and Nicaragua. The US got nada.

The SALT II treaty locked in another decade of nuclear parity with the US. The Helsinki Accords recognized Soviet spheres of influence while making empty promises about human rights. President Jimmy Carter was a pushover.

But there was one problem: Afghanistan. Fighting between two factions in the Communist Party there got out of hand in 1979. Red rule was imperiled. The US had a chance to overthrow the government. There was only one solution for the Soviets: stage a coup, invade Afghanistan, and take full control.

All this was cloaked as "the Brezhnev doctrine." Wherever communism had advanced to, it shall not retreat from. This rule automatically committed the Soviets to backing any Communist regime anywhere in the world, at any cost. The Soviets had plenty of guns, but weren't exactly rolling in money. Their flimsy economy was a poor foundation for an evil empire.

## You Break It, You Buy It

The 40th Motor Rifle Army was tapped to do the dirty work of invading Afghanistan. It numbered fifty-two thousand men. More soldiers would come later to double the size of the deployment.

A quick assault by airborne and special forces decapitated the incumbent Soviet-backed government and installed a replacement regime. Armored forces traveled down Afghanistan's national ring road, taking control of every city. It was just like Hungary in 1956, or Czechoslovakia in 1968.

Afghanistan turned out differently, though. Once the invasion was completed, the new regime in Kabul tried to impose its atheistic, secular values on the rural Muslim Afghans. The Afghans took up arms to fight back.

The Red Army would conduct operations in groups of ten thousand to fifteen thousand, trying to maneuver entire brigades to surround, then overrun, guerrilla-held areas. This never worked. The Afghans never stood their ground if they could help it. When confronted by superior forces, they retreated into the mountains. When they could mass against isolated Soviet garrisons or convoys, they attacked. Fighting at close range negated Soviet advantages in artillery and airpower.

Politically, the enemy proved to be a hydra-headed monster. There were thirteen major factions fighting the Soviets to one degree or another. Some groups were ethnic-based, formed of Uzbeks, Tajiks, Hazaras, or Pashtuns. About seven groups based out of Pakistan were the prime recipients of American CIA aid, channeled by Pakistan's Inter-Services Intelligence agency (ISI). Saudi Arabia and the rich Gulf states also funneled in cash and arms. And Afghanistan was a good place to send Arab extremists who would be a threat to ruling governments back home. Let them fight for Islam elsewhere.

The Russians found they could not "kill" their way to victory. They generated six million Afghan refugees, who sheltered either in Iran or Pakistan, becoming recruitment pools for the resistance. The Soviets could not invade these sanctuaries, unless they wanted to fight a bigger war that was beyond their means. The CIA's covert supply of American Stinger antiaircraft missiles only added to their misery by negating the Soviet airpower advantage.

## No Country for Old Men

This strategic stalemate continued until the mid-1980s, as Soviet search-and-destroy missions could not pry the grip of the mujahideen from their land. Strategic thinking at the top changed with Mikhail Gorbachev's rise to power in 1985. (This followed the death of Brezhnev and two other successors in the preceding three years.)

Gorbachev understood the deteriorating position of the Soviet Union. American rearmament was outstripping the Soviets' ability to keep pace. The war in Afghanistan was draining his country's strength, as were the smaller ancillary wars in Ethiopia and Angola. Gorbachev had to cut his losses. Afghanistan was the best place to start.

The Russians equipped and financed the Afghans to fight their own war against the mujahideen. By 1988, the last Russian unit crossed the Amu Dar'ya River to Termez, marking the end of the Soviet War in Afghanistan. (A civil war continued for another six years.)

The Soviets lost about 15,000 men, with another 40,000 or so wounded. Mujahideen losses were around 140,000 to 200,000 killed or wounded. Soviet forces may have peaked at around 100,000 or so combatants, compared to 90,000 for the Afghan resistance. And the mujahideen had no trouble maintaining force size.

More worrisome were the thousands of Arab volunteers who fought in Afghanistan. The rise of Islam did not fit the "us vs. them" Cold War worldview, so it did not draw much notice. An entire covert network of Arab recruitment and funding still existed, waiting to find another purpose. One such organization was al-Qaeda (the Base), run by an obscure person named Osama bin Laden. What would he do next?

## Skipping Afghanistan

Would things have turned out better if the Soviets had not invaded Afghanistan? The political necessities of the Cold War did not allow a Soviet client state to switch sides. That would have made it look like the US was winning.

It would have taken a major change of thinking for Brezhnev and his wheezy old men to handle Afghanistan adroitly. The Afghan Communist Party was racked by infighting, but eventually one faction would win out. The Russians could have supported the winners, but more importantly, they could have restrained them from imposing atheistic Communist rule on the countryside.

This would have required foreigners to understand Afghanistan and accept it for what it is: a country divided between many tribes and factions, none of whom are obedient to any central authority. *Just leave them alone.*

The Soviet Union was still in decline, but without an Afghan War, the downward pressure against the "evil empire" would have lessened. There would have been no multifaction Afghan guerrilla uprising, no CIA interference, and no Arab volunteers bringing radical Islam into the region. The rebirth of Islam would still have happened. But that historical current would have followed different channels.

The post-Soviet Afghan Civil War would not have happened. Therefore, the Taliban never would have come into existence to seize the country in 1994. And no invitation for al-Qaeda to take up residence in 1996 would have been forthcoming.

It was from Afghanistan that bin Laden approved the 2001 attacks on the United States. But without the chain of events that brought him to Afghanistan, what would have happened? His path to infamy would have taken a different route, with perhaps a different outcome. What that path would have been is too hard to say.

There would have been one definite side effect, though: 9/11 never would have happened. New York's World Trade Center would still be standing. The Pentagon would have been spared a jet hit. And Shanksville would still be just another small town in Pennsylvania.

||||||||||||||||||||||||||||||||||||||||||||||||||||||||||||||||||||||||||||||||||

# 91

## THE IRAN HOSTAGE
## RESCUE ATTEMPT

### 1980

### By William Terdoslavich

||||||||||||||||||||||||||||||||||||||||||||||||||||||||||||||||||||||||||||||||||

Desert one, America zero.

The limits of American power are drawn in failure. It can make the United States look weak and hapless. That was the kind of nation President Jimmy Carter was leading in the late 1970s. His well-meant decency and his indecision only made things worse.

Carter was plagued with problems beyond his control. The economy was in recession and inflation was rampant—a combination economists said was impossible. The Shah of Iran was overthrown in a revolution. Iranian oil exports ceased. The price of gas doubled. Americans waited in long lines to refuel their cars for the second time in six years.

And on November 4, 1979, protesting Iranian students overran the US embassy in Tehran, taking more than fifty State Department employees hostage. At first, this seemed like just another crisis.

The media didn't see it that way. Beginning in January 1980, CBS News anchorman Walter Cronkite signed off every night by reminding Americans how many days had passed since the hostages were first taken. And those days added up . . . 60 . . . 65 . . . 72 . . . 84 . . . 90 . . . 100 . . . 120 . . .

Americans rallied around the flag, united by their outrage. They also noticed that no one seemed to be doing anything about the hostage crisis. And that sucked.

## Taking America Hostage

What triggered the embassy seizure? The deposed Shah of Iran, despised by Iranians for his tyrannical rule, wanted to enter the US for cancer treatment. Carter at first refused. But Chase Manhattan chairman David Rockefeller and former foreign policy top gun John J. McCloy pressured the president to change his mind, as the US had to stand by its allies for better or worse.

US chargé d'affaires L. Bruce Laingen in Tehran warned higher-ups in the State Department that it would be a bad idea to let the shah into the US. Iranians feared that the United States would try to reinstall him as Iran's ruler. When Carter did allow the shah in for "humanitarian reasons," the Iranian government did not see it that way. Protesting Iranian students had no trouble penetrating the flimsy perimeter of the US embassy compound. They took the personnel inside captive.

Carter appeared decisive at first, expelling all Iranian students studying in the US, freezing Iranian assets, and placing an embargo on Iranian oil imports. But three sets of talks in five months failed to obtain the release of the hostages. As soon as US negotiators had a deal, Ayatollah Khomeini, Iran's real leader, would veto it.

All this was happening while Carter was running for reelection, facing a very stiff primary challenge from Senator Ted Kennedy (D-MA). On April 11, 1980, the mild-mannered Carter decided a rescue mission was a better option than talking to the Iranians. He needed results. Now.

## A Reach Too Far

Colonel Charlie Beckwith had a plan.

Beckwith created the US Army's Delta Force, tasked with high-risk rescue when terrorists took hostages. But the plan was not simple.

Delta Force commandos would be flown into Iran on C-130 transports, landing at a remote, abandoned airstrip, and board a flight of US Navy RH-53 helicopters. The refueled choppers would then fly to a hide spot, where the Deltas would switch over to trucks for the drive into downtown Tehran.

Upon their arrival at the embassy, one Delta team would storm the walls while a second team set up a perimeter. A smaller third team would seek out the senior American diplomats, including Laingen, held at another location. The teams would round up the hostages and board the RH-53s that were scheduled to arrive as the raid concluded. They would fly to another airstrip to join the C-130s, then fly out of the country.

The plan faced some politically necessary alterations. Interservice rivalry required that all four services participate. The plan could be practiced in parts, but never as a whole.

In spite of this, Operation Eagle Claw was on. The mistakes could come later.

## Eagle Claw, Turkey Flight

Any plan on paper changes the moment it comes into contact with reality. For Beckwith and the Deltas, that came on April 24. The inbound flight of C-130s arrived at the airstrip, known as Desert One, on time.

Then things began to go wrong. A truck and a bus drove by Desert One just as the C-130s were taxiing in. The truck was shot at. The bus passengers were detained.

A dust storm played havoc with the navy's inbound flight of eight RH-53s. One turned back. A second suffered mechanical failure en route and was abandoned, its crew picked up by the other choppers. The helicopters arrived late, not all at once, and low on fuel. Next, a third helicopter developed a hydraulic problem and could not fly. Beckwith did the math. He needed to move about 178 hostages and commandos out of Tehran. Six helicopters were the mission's minimum and he was down to five, risking further losses if he proceeded.

Beckwith called it off.

As planes and choppers departed, an RH-53 clipped a C-130 carrying a fuel bladder. Both aircraft went up in a single fireball, killing eight. The survivors, some burned, fled to the other C-130s, which took off without further incident.

## For Want of a Helicopter, a Presidency Was Lost

The raid to free the hostages and Carter's bid for reelection were tied together. He needed one to succeed in order to achieve the other. Instead, his hopes for reelection went up in smoke at Desert One.

The hostages were finally released on January 20, 1981, as Reagan took his oath of office. The fifty-two Americans were flown to Germany, where ex-president Carter welcomed them back to freedom.

But could this story have ended differently?

Carter could have avoided the entire hostage crisis by telling the Shah of Iran to go someplace else for cancer treatment. The president would have caught hell from foreign policy elites, but keeping the shah out would have dampened the spark that set off the embassy seizure in Tehran.

Relations with Iran would have remained fraught, since the US was instrumental in overthrowing Iran's government in 1953. As Laingen recalled, the US was willing to improve relations with revolutionary Iran before the hostage crisis and had no interest in restoring the dying shah to power.

Maintaining an embassy in the following years would have made it easier to monitor Iran. Terrorism? Nuclear program? It is easier to find these things out if you are on the scene. The US would have more leverage in Iran today if it had a relationship to build on, making it easier to negotiate a more thorough nuclear treaty than the one under consideration as of mid-2015.

Keeping the shah out would not have guaranteed Carter's reelection. He was presiding over a wrecked economy. But lack of a hostage crisis would have robbed Reagan of his best issue to challenge Carter. The election would have been closer, the outcome still uncertain.

The other possibility is more implausible. Say the hostage rescue actually worked. Carter would have crushed Kennedy in the primaries and vanquished Reagan in the fall election. America's tilt toward conservatism would have received a sharp check.

Carter and his associates knew that it was the hostage crisis that sank Carter's presidency. "I wish I'd sent one more helicopter to get the hostages and we would have rescued them and I would have been reelected," said Carter at a 2015 press conference.

Then again, Carter getting reelected would have ended Ronald Reagan's political career. For many Americans, history without Reagan would be *unthinkable*.

‖‖‖‖‖‖‖‖‖‖‖‖‖‖‖‖‖‖‖‖‖‖‖‖‖‖‖‖‖‖‖‖‖‖‖‖‖‖‖‖‖‖‖‖‖‖‖‖‖‖‖‖‖‖‖‖

# 92

# SADDAM HUSSEIN TAKES ON THE WORLD!

### 1980

**By William Terdoslavich**

‖‖‖‖‖‖‖‖‖‖‖‖‖‖‖‖‖‖‖‖‖‖‖‖‖‖‖‖‖‖‖‖‖‖‖‖‖‖‖‖‖‖‖‖‖‖‖‖‖‖‖‖‖‖‖‖

It's not easy being a megalomaniac
with delusions of grandeur.

In the 1970s, Saddam was a street-smart thug who had clawed his way up the ranks in the Iraqi Ba'ath Party. Now number two, he served President Ahmed Hassan al-Bakr faithfully, being an especially ruthless go-to guy who got things done. Of course, this talent came in handy when Saddam got rid of Hassan al-Bakr in 1979, along with his followers.

Now Saddam Hussein was number one. He wanted to be a great man leading a great nation. But Iraq could not be great if its access to the sea remained constricted. Geography was Iraq's first enemy. It's only port, Umm Qasr, is connected to the nation's second city, Basra, by a single waterway, the Shatt al-Arab. This waterway also demarcated the Iraq-Iran border. Throughout history, either Iran or one of Iraq's predecessor states (Ottoman Empire, "Arabistan," and others) might claim the entire waterway up to the farther shore, instead of sharing it.

Iraq claimed the Shatt al-Arab all the way to the Iranian shore, a claim Iran never recognized. While the Shah of Iran was in power in the 1970s, he successfully bankrolled Iraqi Kurds into rebelling against Iraq, and thwarted an Iraqi armored thrust into Iran. The 1975 settlement of this war called for the Iraq-Iran border to run straight down the Shatt al-Arab. This provided no cushion protecting access between Basra and Umm Qasr.

Four years later, Iran was being convulsed by a revolution that ousted the shah and saw his eventual replacement by Ayatollah Khomeini. Iranian revolutionaries had already seized the US embassy in Tehran, holding about fifty Americans hostage. The Iranian army was being purged of its pro-American elements. And Iran's main oil fields were just across the Shatt al-Arab in Khuzistan province, which had a largely Arab population that was not too keen on Iranian rule. The Iranian theocracy was all chaos and probably incompetent. The time looked good to steal Khuzistan, fair and square.

Saddam Hussein then ordered his army to attack. The date was September 17, 1980.

## Bad Guys vs. Bad Guys

The resulting Iran-Iraq War did not go off exactly as planned. Instead of collapsing, Iran rallied. Instead of taking Khuzistan, the Iraqi army got stuck. Though the Iraqi army was decently equipped, it was poorly trained and had some problems executing operational plans. It was hard to say what bogged down the Iraqis first, the swampy ground or their lack of initiative.

The five-division Iraqi attack was further blunted by hordes of untrained Revolutionary Guards, backed by depleted Iranian army units. The Revolutionary Guards made good cannon fodder, staging frontal assaults on Iraqi positions, World War I–style. Any penetrations would then be exploited by what few tanks and APCs the Iranian army could field.

And so the Iranians pushed the Iraqis out of Khuzistan to the very threshold of Basra, Iraq's second city. The modest Iranian navy wiped out the even more modest Iraqi navy. Iran now controlled the Persian Gulf, cutting off Iraq's ability to export oil to pay for its war.

By 1982, Iraq was on the ropes. The Iranians regained Khuzistan and now were close to taking Basra. The Iraqi army managed to put up a good defense, keeping the Iranians at bay. The stalemate lasted until 1986, when the Iranians launched a surprise attack across the mouth of the Shatt al-Arab, taking the swampy Al Faw Peninsula. Iraq's access to the Persian Gulf was now cutoff.

Saddam Hussein finally had to trust his generals and allow them to fight the war as they saw fit. The generals resorted to "scripting" operations, basically giving very detailed orders to units that had to be followed to the letter in order to complete an operation. Once the end of the script was reached, attacks ceased and a new script was drawn up.

By 1988, Iran finally shot its bolt trying to take Basra for the last time. In a series of five scripted attacks, the Iraqi army expelled the Iranians from the Al Faw Peninsula (flanking the Shatt al-Arab), the area around Basra, and the hill country to the north along the border. The Iraqis also fired salvos of Scud missiles on Tehran to demoralize the Iranian people and "persuade" Ayatollah Khomeini to seek peace, which he did. The result: the same border as before the war, plus a small sliver of Iranian territory. You might as well have given Saddam Hussein a free T-shirt for "winning."

## The Eagle Is No Chicken

The eight-year war left Iraq with a one-million-man army, thousands of tanks, hundreds of combat aircraft, and an experienced officer corps. Okay, so maybe fighting a bigger nation was not the way to go, but how about picking on a smaller one? Kuwait was right next door. It had a tiny army and air force. It sat on a lot of oil. And Bubiyan Island flanked Umm Qasr to the west. Seizing this island would gain some buffer territory to protect Iraq's only outlet to the sea.

So in August 1990, Saddam Hussein attacked again! The well-scripted invasion sent all eight divisions of Iraq's Republican Guard into Kuwait, overrunning the tiny nation in hours. The plan was to stick the world with a fait accompli. Just hunker down and wait for the West to come crawling to the negotiating table. Saddam Hussein would dictate terms, keep Kuwait, and double his share of the world's oil supply. The resulting higher price of oil should help pay for more arms purchases and an upgraded nuclear weapons program.

But Iraq's army was now just north of Saudi Arabia's oil fields, in fact too close for comfort. And this provoked a response from the United States. Hussein committed about five-sixths of his army to holding Kuwait. US president George H. W. Bush worked the phones to cobble together a global alliance against Iraq. It took six months for the US to ship two mechanized corps, plus two marine divisions, to Saudi Arabia. Add to that the division-sized contributions from France, Britain, Syria, and Egypt. The Saudi army was all in. Six US aircraft carriers deployed to the region. The USAF showed up with more than 1,100 aircraft.

In January 1991, the US and allied warplanes began bombing Iraqi frontline units and destroyed Iraq's air defense system. Baghdad was bombed. Roads and bridges leading to Kuwait were slammed. The Iraqi air force barely resisted. This was followed in February by a four-day-long ground offensive that punched northward into Kuwait while swinging two corps west into the desert, north into Iraq, then east to cut off retreating Iraqi units. This plan was partially successful, destroying about half the Iraqi army.

US war plans were limited to liberating Kuwait. That kept the alliance intact, but also left Saddam Hussein in power as a frustrated dictator who excelled at starting wars he could not win.

## What Could Have Been Better?

Not having Saddam Hussein around would have been a hundred times better, period. But that would still have left Iraq constrained by geography, its only port always vulnerable.

The more rational strategy would have been to avoid the Iran-Iraq War entirely. If Iran was crippled by revolution, it would probably stay that way. Hussein could have resorted to covert means to stir up the Arabs of Khuzistan against Iran, and maybe they would have asked Iraq for protection. An invitation to stay is far more politically effective than an invasion. And he would still have gotten his protective buffer for Umm Qasr.

Let's say that did not happen. What alternative could Saddam have pursued? Iraq did have a slow-moving nuclear weapons program, replacing the one lost to an Israeli air strike back in 1981.

Had Saddam waited until he'd had an atomic bomb in hand, he could have taken Kuwait anyway and been more likely to keep it. The US is very cautious about militarily confronting nuclear states. Containment and/or economic sanctions would have resulted, and sanctions don't last forever . . . unless you keep making mistakes.

Then again, maybe the actual outcome was a hundred times better than what could have been. Saddam Hussein was a dictator strongly influenced by his ego and his yes-men, more likely to act before thinking. Maybe that incompetence was a hundred times better than a *rational* ruthless dictator commanding a nuclear-armed Iraq, eventually taking over the Middle East.

# 93

||||||||||||||||||||||||||||||||||||||||||||||||||||||||||||||||||||||||||||||||||||

# TANDY CORPORATION

## 1985

### By K. B. Bogen

||||||||||||||||||||||||||||||||||||||||||||||||||||||||||||||||||||||||||||||||||||

The beginning of the end.

## The Beginning

Computers come and computers go. TRS-80, CoCo, Model 1, Model 4, Model 16, Model 100, Tandy Model 1000. Does anyone remember these? Tandy Corporation/RadioShack was once one of the biggest names in home computing. So what happened?

Tandy started out as a family-owned leather store in 1919. They carried leather and leather-crafting supplies. In time, they added wall decorations and flooring to the list, selling such items as picture frames, mirrors, wall art, and wall and floor tiles. In 1963, Tandy Corporation bought the Boston-based electronics store called—you guessed it—RadioShack. And, thanks to the marketing talent of Charles Tandy, it became a giant in the electronic retail business. They sold parts, wire, small appliances, electronic toys, and more. But it didn't stop there. In 1975, the leather and the wall- and flooring-related items were spun off into different companies (Tandy Leather/Tandycrafts and Color Tile), and Tandy Corporation began focusing on the electronics market.

In 1957, John Roach joined the Tandy team as manager of Tandy Data Processing. A few years later, he became vice president of distribution for RadioShack. In 1975, he rose to vice president of manufacturing. After Charles Tandy's death in 1980, Roach was appointed executive vice president. Next, he was RadioShack's president and chief operating officer. Then CEO in 1981. And chairman in 1982.

Roach focused his attention on the computer market. And, as he rose up the corporate ladder, RadioShack's computer sales rose with him. Until they didn't anymore.

The Model 4 and Model 16, mentioned above, were some of the earliest home computers sold by RadioShack. There were others. They had everything a neo–computer wizard might need. A word processor, BASIC, and other useful software were included. Additional software was available, such as C compilers, Database Management software, and more.

Released in 1983, the Model 100 was one of the early netbook-sized portable computers. Its small size (300 x 215 x 50 mm or approximately 12 x 8.5 x 2 inches) made it perfect to slip into a briefcase or purse. It had a full keyboard, a built-in modem, and up to 32K static RAM. Yes, computer geeks, that's 32*K*.

Unfortunately, all of the TRS-80 computers used proprietary software. If it wasn't written exclusively for the destination machine, it didn't run. But then, all of the other computers on the market at the time were like that. If it wasn't IBM-PC software, it didn't run on an IBM-PC. If it wasn't Apple software—well, some things never change.

Then, wonder of wonders, IBM's proprietary software shell was cracked. Computer companies raced to see how fast they could crank out computers that were PC-compatible. And so did Tandy. The SQC group spent many hours making certain that the Tandy Model 1000 (then known only as "Project 557") was 100 percent compatible with IBM shelf software. Then there was Model 2000, which was (is it possible?) *too* fast. It couldn't run IBM's software. At first. And there was the Model 3000, 4000, etc. RadioShack continued producing newer, faster PCs until the end of the 486.

Tandy Corporation/RadioShack sat at or near the top of the heap for decades. What happened?

## The Beginning of the End

Tandy jumped into the PC-compatible market with both feet. And they did it really, *really* well. But, as so often happens, they made a few mistakes along the way.

In 1985, they pulled the Model 600 out of mothballs. It had been sitting in the warehouse, unwanted and unloved, for who knows how long? Years, maybe. Up until the Model 600, Tandy had been fairly competitive, even aggressive, in the computer race, holding its own with the likes of Epson, IBM, and others. But not with the 600.

The Model 600 was a laptop computer, complete with hinged display, modem, floppy drive—a TRS-80 home computer in a size that fit into a briefcase, with room to spare. They dragged it out of the warehouse, dusted it off, and asked SQC to perform the usual testing on it. But in secret.

One member of the SQC team was asked to take the 600 home and check it out. So, the tester smuggled the computer and documentation out in two briefcases. One for the computer and one for the documentation, which outweighed the computer. This went on for a week. Every night after work, the tester took the briefcases home, then spent the evening checking the operating system, software, and documentation for errors. And every morning, the two briefcases had to be lugged back to the office, to be kept under lock and key.

The good news was there were no problems discovered in the testing. The bad news was that it was a TRSDOS machine, using the famed Tandy proprietary software. The *really* bad news was that, by the time the Model 600 was being tested, there were already several similar machines on the market. The Osborne 1, the Epson HX-20, and more. It was a case of letting the horse out of the barn *after* it had burned down. Or, in this case, after someone had built three other barns and filled them with horses.

Tandy *could* have released the 600 earlier, after it was first built. And that *could* have been a major building block for them. But they didn't. They released it too late, and other companies beat them to market. They kept its existence a secret and they kept the testing a secret. The upper management didn't seem to want anyone to know about the 600—not their customers, not their employees, and especially not their competitors. And, apparently, not the marketing department. Sales were poor and it was dropped from inventory shortly after its release.

Then, a short time after the testing and release of the Model 600, the SQC department was disbanded, leaving only a handful of employees to tidy up. The reason? The company was switching to "vendor support" for the third-party software. And since SQC's main function was to test the third-party software, they weren't needed anymore. Unfortunately, "vendor support" is virtually synonymous with "no support."

If Tandy had tested and released the 600 soon after it was *originally* developed, marketed it properly, migrated the concept to the PC-compatible era, *and* (and this is a very important *and*) continued to develop and test their own software and hardware products, perhaps they would have remained at the top of the heap. By eliminating the thing that made them famous (computers and related electronics), they were eliminating their future.

And that was only the *beginning* of the end.

||||||||||||||||||||||||||||||||||||||||||||||||||||||||||||||||||||||||||||||||||

# 94

# THE EVIL EMPIRE DISAPPEARS

### 1987

## By William Terdoslavich

||||||||||||||||||||||||||||||||||||||||||||||||||||||||||||||||||||||||||||||||||

Then Gorbachev tore down
that wall. . . .

For more than forty years, the United States and the Soviet Union stared each other down. It was a strategic stalemate between ideologies: democracy vs. communism, free-market capitalism against Marxist central planning.

Both sides had massive armies, air forces, and fleets ready to fight a war that did not happen. Nuclear missiles were always ready to destroy the other side in twenty minutes. The red button was never pushed.

Americans are very familiar with their side of the story, from the Berlin Airlift to the presidency of Ronald Reagan. We thought the Soviets were acting from strength, but we never saw their weakness. Their side of the story was a mystery, which is why the fall of the Soviet Union was a surprise.

No one saw it coming. How did it happen?

The answer rests with one man: Mikhail Gorbachev, the last leader of the Soviet Union. In the US and Europe, he is admired for having the courage to change his country, even though the result was a noble failure. In Russia today, he is despised for giving away the Soviet Empire.

## Communism Reaches Its Limits

The Soviets looked like they were winning the Cold War in 1980. They had invaded Afghanistan and were backing newly won red regimes in Ethiopia, Mozambique, Angola, and Nicaragua. Wherever communism advances, it shall not retreat, proclaimed Soviet leader Leonid Brezhnev.

The US was in disarray. The Americans lost the war in Vietnam, screwed up the Mayaguez Rescue, saw its pet dictators overthrown everywhere, and was now paralyzed by the hostage crisis in Iran. The US even accepted nuclear parity with the Soviet Union in two successive arms control treaties. American power was either checked or clearly in retreat, depending how you looked at it.

But appearances were deceiving. The Soviet economy had stopped growing. It had gotten this far by ripping economic growth out of the people through threats, weak incentives, and finally mass deception. "They pretend to pay us, so we pretend to work," was how one joke described it.

The capstone of this rickety structure was the Politburo of the Communist Party, headed by Brezhnev. The cronies and hacks running the ministries were either old or ill. And they were dropping like flies.

Brezhnev kicked the bucket in 1982. Yuri Andropov followed him to the office, and eventually to the grave in 1984. Next came party hack Konstantin Chernenko, who became general secretary of the party while already in ill health, then shuffled off this mortal coil in 1985.

Mikhail Gorbachev, then a youthful fifty-four, won the game of musical chairs that typified Soviet succession. Gorbachev knew he was being dealt a bad hand. To revive the economy, he had to stage a revolution from above.

When the United States hits a bad patch like this, it usually reinvents itself, like it did after the Civil War and the Depression. That was not the case in the Soviet Union. Its last big change was the Russian Revolution of 1917. Gorbachev wanted to change a system that was built to stay the same.

## Appearances and Buzzwords

Gorbachev began his premiership by trying to renew workplace discipline. This went nowhere. His decision to quit the unwinnable war in Afghanistan made sense, but could not be implemented until an Afghan army was trained to take the place of Russian soldiers. A summit conference with Reagan in Reykjavík, Iceland, proved fruitless, as neither leader could find a way to cut nuclear arsenals. The massive Soviet defense budget would continue dragging down the economy.

Gorbachev changed course in 1987 by announcing a policy of *glasnost*, or openness. No longer would the Soviet Union control the media and the press. Gorbachev was banking on the media's exposure of the Soviet Union's flaws to set up the climate for his next policy, *perestroika*, or restructuring. Some kind of limited free-market reforms would be instituted to jump-start the moribund economy.

But Gorbachev, a lifelong Communist, hadn't a clue as to what a free-market economy looked like or how it would work. The Communist Party was filled with conservative deadwood, and they resisted change. The reforms did nothing to alleviate the shortages of just about everything. Russians still lined up to get milk and bread. The Communist Party maintained its monopoly on everything.

To bypass Communist resistance at home, Gorbachev put in place a parliament and allowed people to elect candidates from multiple parties. To remove the American threat, he pursued a policy of acquiescence with the West. He even signed a treaty with Reagan to zero nuclear arsenals in Europe.

*Don't threaten anybody.* This policy would soon be put to a brutal test.

## The Year That Changed Everything

Poland, Hungary, East Germany, Bulgaria, Romania, and Czechoslovakia were the captive states of the Soviet Union. They acted as a buffer, keeping NATO away from Russia while the latter based multiple-tank armies there—aimed at Western Europe's core.

The people living in these countries were not fond of the Soviet "presence." Russian troops brutally suppressed the Hungarian uprising of 1956. They occupied Czechoslovakia in 1968. They almost invaded Poland in the early 1980s, backing off when the Polish army staged a coup d'état to suppress a trade union movement.

These peoples of Eastern Europe noticed Gorbachev loosening the Communist grip on the Soviet Union. So in 1989, they made their move. One by one, mass gatherings in public squares and mass movements of people over the border to the West happened. The Berlin Wall finally came down, chipped to pieces by protesters as border guards watched, awaiting orders that never came.

Gorbachev did not call out the Red Army to stop any of it. By year's end, all six nations had non-Communist governments. East Germany reunified with West Germany, with US president George H. W. Bush brokering the deal.

Gorbachev had the Soviet parliament elect him as president of the USSR, diminishing his role as chairman of the Communist Party. He then worked on loosening the relationship between the Soviet Union and its component "republics." A Russian federated republic would be created. The subordinate republics would be free to do as they wished, but Russia would retain control over the military and foreign policy. The Communist Party's monopoly on power would end.

The true Communists had finally had enough.

## Coup de Blah

In August 1991, Vice President Gennady Yanayev, Prime Minister Valentin Pavlov, Defense Minister Dmitry Yazov, and KGB Chief Vladimir Kryuchkov staged a coup d'état to overthrow the Gorbachev regime. They decreed that all political activity was to cease and all newspapers were to be shut down. Gorbachev was placed under house arrest while vacationing in the Crimea.

The plotters hoped the Russian people would rise up and join their cause. And the masses did rise to form a ring around the Russian White House, Russia's parliament building—to protect their democratically elected government. Special forces dispatched to take the building chose not to. Russian Federation president Boris Yeltsin stood atop a tank, speaking to the crowd, encouraging resistance.

In three days, the coup collapsed due to popular indifference. The plotters were arrested. Gorbachev returned to Moscow, his grip on power gravely weakened. The coup proved Gorbachev was in charge of nothing.

The recently elected Yeltsin was now the de facto leader of Russia. By year's end, the component republics of the Soviet Union, like Ukraine and Kazakhstan, declared independence. Their agreement with Yeltsin, known as the Belavezha Accords, was ratified by Russia's soviet (council), declaring the foundation of the Commonwealth of Independent States on December 8, 1991, as the Soviet Union's legal successor state. But it would not control the military or foreign policies of the former Soviet republics.

All Gorbachev could do was resign from his meaningless presidency on December 25. The red banner of the Soviet Union that flew over Lenin's tomb was hauled down. A tricolor Russian flag was raised.

And with that final whimper, the Soviet Union *disappeared*.

## Say You Want a Revolution . . .

For the United States, seeing the Soviet Union vanquished without a fight was *great*! This was a hundred times better than fighting World War III. And it left the US as the world's sole superpower.

What followed next was a hundred times worse.

Yeltsin captained an unsteady Russia from crisis to crisis. It was another "Time of Troubles" for Russia, much like the lost decades before the Romanov Dynasty came to power in the early 1600s. Only this time, Russia was not being invaded by foreign hordes.

Russia lost a war to insurgents in Chechnya. A currency crisis in 1998 gutted the nascent capitalist economy, now run by former Communist hacks. Corruption and chaos were common. An ill Yeltsin chose a former KGB unknown named Vladimir Putin to succeed him as president in 1999.

Putin understood how to steal and use power. It took a while, but he turned Russia from a democracy back into a dictatorship, and has vexed the West with armed interventions in Georgia (2008), Ukraine (2014), and Syria (2015).

Now it becomes clear that Gorbachev's failure was not such a good thing after all. If Gorbachev had successfully rebuilt the Soviet Union as a decentralized state with a market economy, Russia could have staged a stable, successful comeback. Gorbachev's re-election, followed by orderly succession, would have cemented democracy as Russia's form of government.

Putin would have remained obscure, more a victim of history, when the Berlin Wall came down and communism disappeared. Instead, those events shaped the man now running Russia. And that sore loser wants to make Russia great again—at our expense.

|||||||||||||||||||||||||||||||||||||||||||||||||||||||||||||||||||||||||||||||||||

# 95

## NOT NOW, SAYS ZHAO

### 1989

### By William Terdoslavich

|||||||||||||||||||||||||||||||||||||||||||||||||||||||||||||||||||||||||||||||||||

No more Mr. Nice Guy.

Freedom. Good people like it. Bad people hate it. That's pretty much how Americans size things up.

Whenever people take to the streets to protest oppression by some dictator, they have our sympathy. We root for these underdogs. We want the good guys to win.

Sometimes they don't.

In China, in 1989, tens of thousands of people crowded into Beijing's Tiananmen Square, demanding that government be accountable to them. The government responded by sending in the army to contain the protesters, and hopefully suppress their perceived "bourgeois liberalism." When suppression failed, the army shot at the unarmed crowds.

More than twenty-five years later, we still remember. Only the Chinese government wants to make people forget the story, especially as it revolved around one forgotten man: Zhao Ziyang.

## May You Live in Interesting Times

China was wrecked and weakened by the practices of Chairman Mao Zedong's "Cultural Revolution" in the 1960s. The revolution was supposed to purge the last bits of pre-Communist China. A reign of terror resulted.

Radicalized cadres of students flooded into Beijing and other cities. Professors, professionals, and party members were swept out of their offices, forcibly demoted, and forced to work in menial jobs on collective farms and in factories. One of those swept away was Deng Xiaoping. Another was Zhao Ziyang.

As things broke down for lack of experienced managers to run them, many technocrats and former party leaders were "rehabilitated" in order to run things again. Mao died in 1976. Many of his radical cronies were still in power. Returned from disgrace, Deng moved carefully, consolidating his own power base and, when strong enough, purging the party of its radicals.

By the 1980s, Deng began the economic reforms needed to shift China from a collective to a market economy. He picked Hu Yaobang as general secretary to oversee change. Reform was causing a lot of social unrest, without getting results. Deng removed Hu in 1986 and next reached out to Zhao to help fix things.

This would not be easy. State-owned industries were shut down. People lost jobs. Official corruption was systemic. The government limited families to having only one child. People were not free to move to cities to seek work, but they did. The government did not seem to be in charge.

In the middle of all this, Hu keeled over from a heart attack in April 1989. Only in China would the death of a Politburo member become a political problem.

## Appearances Can Be Deceiving

In China, the Communist Party must have a monopoly on politics. Any approved event that draws a crowd can have an outward appearance, but acquire a hidden meaning.

The late Hu favored government reforms, was against corruption, and wanted to see a government more accountable to the people. Showing up at Hu's funeral was a "vote" for this agenda.

Tens of thousands of Chinese did show up. The college students began protesting, at first in small crowds. They tried to present a list of grievances to the government, asking that Hu's reputation be rehabilitated, as well as granting freedom of speech, press, and assembly. They also wanted increased funding for colleges and research. And they wanted this reported fairly in state media.

The "April 18 Petition" was pretty much ignored. Government security forces did nothing to arrest the students behind the petition. The government looked weak to the students, who kept marching. Student protests spearheaded the Cultural Revolution. Should the Politburo decide to crack down on the protests or conciliate?

Here Zhao Ziyang stood out. He called on the government to urge the students to return to classes, and to open a wide-ranging dialogue with them and the intellectuals—and for the police to refrain from violence.

With that said, Zhao boarded a train and headed off for a state visit to North Korea.

That was his biggest mistake.

## Only One Vote Matters

While Zhao was away, Li Peng began to play. The hard-liner had direct access to the only person whose decision mattered, the semi-retired Deng Xiaoping. And he kept it that way.

Li used his temporary powers during Zhao's North Korea trip to call a standing committee meeting. Zhao would not be present to argue for a kinder, gentler approach to the perceived disorder. Instead, the committee members concluded that the crowds of protesters were staging a carefully plotted attempt to overthrow the government. This information was presented to Deng. Already burned by the Cultural Revolution, he did not sympathize with protesters. He sided with the hard-liners. That was all that mattered.

Then Li Peng took liberties with Deng's statements. He published them in the official party newspaper, the *People's Daily*. There, party members read Deng's remarks, in which he accused the protesters of having "anti-Party and anti-socialist motives."

Now the students were angry. The protests spread throughout China. Zhao returned from North Korea only to find he had no pull with his fellow Politburo members.

By mid-May, students had encamped in Tiananmen Square in the very heart of Beijing, near Mao's tomb, the Great Hall of the

People, and the Forbidden City. If this happened in Washington, it would be like having protesters all over the Mall between the Capitol, the White House, and the Lincoln Memorial.

Soviet Union chairman Mikhail Gorbachev was expected to pay a visit, ending a thirty-year breach with China. He had to be greeted at the airport, with restricted public and press access. Tiananmen Square was already occupied.

On May 17, Zhao finally got his meeting at Deng's home. Waiting there for him was the entire Politburo. Zhao realized that the deck was stacked against him. He made his presentation anyway, calling on his colleagues to revoke the *People's Daily* editorial labeling the students as a threat. This would allow the government to regain political control of the situation. Using violence to restore order would only make things worse.

No one spoke in favor of Zhao's remarks. Li Peng responded by criticizing him. Finally, Deng spoke. Backing down would only make things worse. He called for martial law to be imposed on Beijing. The People's Liberation Army was mobilized for the task.

Zhao made a speech to the students two days later in Tiananmen Square. His show of solidarity was his swan song.

## Tanks for the Memory

Starting on May 20, approximately 250,000 troops were brought into Beijing, taking up positions around the city. Outside the main protest area, many of the city's residents successfully encouraged the troops to briefly withdraw from the area. Soldiers were ordered back into Beijing, timing their moves with other military operations against similar protests, spreading throughout other Chinese cities. Then, on the night of June 3–4, two divisions were tasked with clearing Tiananmen Square of all protesters. The soldiers were from outlying parts of China. They had no sympathy for the protesters. *They would follow orders.*

International media was thick in the square. They went live on TV or filed news reports describing how truck-borne troops fired into unarmed crowds, and how the military cordon kept ambulances from picking up wounded protesters. Bystanders commandeered bike-rickshaws to rush the wounded to nearby hospitals, which were already swamped. The sound of gunfire continued through the night. By six a.m., Tiananmen Square was cleared of people, leaving the square covered with litter, wreckage, and blood. To this day, we have no sure information as to how many protesters were killed. Maybe three hundred? Maybe a thousand?

Deng appeared on state television several days later, with the Politburo members and their semiretired elder sponsors, thanking the army's generals for saving the nation. Heavily edited footage showed troops arriving in Tiananmen Square, facing down retreating protesters, *nonviolently*.

Zhao faced the Politburo several weeks afterward. If he made a statement of "self-correction," admitting his doctrinal errors, he would obtain some forgiveness. Zhao refused. Stripped of his office, he was condemned to house arrest, which lasted the remainder of his life, until 2005. Zhao was proof that nice guys finish last.

## No More Mr. Nice Guy

Shanghai Communist Party boss Jiang Zemin was called up to replace Zhao. Jiang managed to disperse protesters in his city without using force, upholding Deng's policy of law and order.

Once Deng fully retired from behind-the-scenes control, Jiang was free to steer China on a course of ultranationalism. The Communist Party retained its monopoly on political power, but allowed private enterprise to take root. The economy improved, raising the standard of living for ordinary Chinese. So long as life got better, the government was good. *But it is illegal to mention the Tiananmen Square Massacre.*

That is how China works. Back when emperors ran the country, their legitimacy as rulers without question depended on maintaining peace and prosperity. As soon as the people suffered from flood, famine, corrupt officials, or civil war, the ruling dynasty lost that legitimacy and either fell or was overthrown. A new emperor would take the throne. Times would be good again. And the cycle would repeat itself.

So how was the "Communist Dynasty" supposed to handle

China's bad times? It would have been a hundred times better if Zhao had had his way. And it would have been consistent with Chinese culture. Peasants had long brought petitions to their emperors, asking that problems be fixed. The situation in Tiananmen Square was no different.

Zhao would only have been able to keep his top job for another six or seven years. But during that time, he could have steered China on a course that balanced economic change with social justice. China would be less of a military threat to its neighbors, who would be more eager to trade with Asia's largest state. China would have naturally secured regional dominance without threatening anyone.

Instead, the ultranationalist course has been policy for more than twenty-five years. China has built military forces and wants to annex the South China Sea at the expense of neighboring states and international law. And it relies on its cyber-warfare capabilities to steal intellectual property from American corporations to further advantage its own companies.

Had Zhao prevailed, China would still be great, but as a friend, not as an adversary.

||||||||||||||||||||||||||||||||||||||||||||||||||||||||||||||||||||||||||

# 96

# THE PEACE DIVIDEND

### 1992

### By Dr. Paul A. Thomsen

||||||||||||||||||||||||||||||||||||||||||||||||||||||||||||||||||||||||||

For one brief shining moment,
Camelot . . . almost.

When the Soviet Union disintegrated in 1990, the United States breathed a sigh of relief that the Cold War had ended finally and peacefully through economic war. The Soviet state literally fell apart, because it could no longer afford to maintain defense and intelligence budgetary parity with America's and NATO's combined high fiscal commitments. Lost in their revels, the American public, however, mistakenly believed they could now safely reroute money from the nation's physical defense to pay for assorted domestic projects. The move did not accurately anticipate future needs and hollowed out the wrong budgetary lines. As a result, the domestic avarice of American leaders left the military vulnerable in battle and the intelligence community incapable of stopping future threats.

While padding the defense budget was popular in the Cold War, 1990s American leaders found austerity to be voter friendly. In 1989, defense spending sat at $303.5 billion. In the 1992 presidential election, Democratic nominee Bill Clinton won the popular vote partially by promising to shrink military spending by $60 billion over five years to fuel domestic growth. After all, everyone likes job growth and affordable housing. To this end, Clinton cut the visible military, including troop size, equipment, soldier benefits packages, and the resulting "nonessential" bases. In 1994, he also proposed cutting Pentagon civilian and military workers by 181,000, gaining a further $4 billion budget reduction. A 1996 defense budget of $265.7 billion made voters elated with their newfound domestic prosperity, and the American military a pale non-battle-ready shadow of its Cold War–era self. Besides, why would you need military administrators to write new manuals or strategize future war fighting when the country was never again supposed to go to war? As a result, there was no one left inside the military to watch or plan for the rise of another enemy like the Soviets or some new nightmare.

Similar cuts were also made to Intelligence Community (IC) budgets with equally deleterious results. Initially, Clinton had promised to cut intelligence spending by $7 billion over four years. Some Democrats, such as Congressman Bernie Sanders in 1992, strongly advocated deeper cuts, including defunding the CIA for even more peace dividend gains. Instead, congressional Democrats in 1993 settled for an additional $1 billion cut from the intelligence budget and further quiet cuts in subsequent years.

For the Central Intelligence Agency alone, this meant a reported 18 percent overall budgetary loss and a 16 percent loss in personnel. Quicker than a Soviet strike, CIA Cold War heroes of human intelligence collection, analysis, and personnel recruitment were left crippled. Silenced by national security confidentiality orders, IC employees were unable to defend themselves. Thereafter, many IC employees retired in disgust. The few who remained were reduced to using outdated PCs and unable to afford secure Internet access. By the end of the decade, the IC stood malnourished, half blind, and in fear they might not be able to detect America's next rising enemy.

Initially unnoticed during these budgetary bloodlettings, America's new "nightmare," a collection of Muslim militant extremists called al-Qaeda, watched and studied the nation's new defense reality. Some had helped the CIA defeat the Soviets in Afghanistan years earlier. Others had tried to bring down the Saudi and Egyptian governments. Together, they saw America's struggle to contain Iraqi aggression and maintain a peace dividend in the 1990s as an exploitable sign of weakness with which they could drive America from the Middle East. First, in October 1993, al-Qaeda quietly supported a Somali ambush of an understrength special forces task force during a humanitarian mission, resulting in mission failure, American casualties, and international humiliation when the Americans had to be rescued by a better-armored nearby United Nations relief force. Later, in 1998 and 1999, a few small al-Qaeda suicide teams managed to destroy two multimillion-dollar American embassies in Africa and nearly destroyed the USS *Cole* while it was refueling in Yemen.

Subsequent CIA and military efforts to find and kill the group's leader, Osama bin Laden, also failed. Although the group was considered a highly credible threat to the American homeland, the resource-poor CIA was also unable to convince American policy makers that al-Qaeda was more than just a bunch of lucky cave-dwelling fanatics. And remember those Pentagon administrators Clinton cut at the end of the Cold War? Well, they never had a chance to create a new attack response protocol for the post–Cold War era. Hence, when the military was alerted of an attack on the American homeland, the ready alert fighter pilots who hit the sky within minutes of the first attack did not immediately look for hijacked aircraft. Instead, they followed the still-unchanged Cold War protocol for responding to an incoming attack. Until they were told otherwise, they went looking for Soviet nuclear submarines, which the manuals indicated would be the greatest threat to the nation. As a result, on September 11, 2001, three hijacked planes went into three buildings, another was forced down by the heroic action of its civilian passengers, and approximately three thousand Americans paid the ultimate price for the Cold War peace dividend.

Instead of cutting the physical military and IC infrastructure, American policy makers could have achieved the same goals by making targeted defense cuts against big-ticket items. For example, Clinton's budget promise could have been achieved by cutting two defense research programs, antiballistic missile (ABM) technology and the V-22 Osprey, along with a minor bit of force redundancy reduction. In 1993, Clinton had pushed for a $5.4 billion ABM budget. By 2001, it carried an $8-billion-a-year budget and still didn't work. Similarly, in 1981 the V-22 tilt-rotor-controlled Osprey air-craft was granted a $39 billion development budget. Many rede-signs and fatal accidents later, it finally entered battle in 2007 at a final cost of $56 billion and a production cost of $100 million per aircraft. These two projects' budgets alone would have funded Clinton's promised peace dividend.

In the early 1990s, America could have reaped the benefits of a still-strong national security capability, literally changing the world by this shift in funding cuts. The new peace dividend would have afforded the 1993 American Somali task force their budget line for air support and armored transports, which would have minimized casualties and, likely, turned the tide of the Mogadishu ambush. It would have supplemented, not undercut, the IC's abili-ties to see and stop emergent threats with better equipment. More-over, the CIA would have been able to track and kill al-Qaeda with new recruits, PCs, and hired assets in advance of the 9/11 plot's conception, ending bin Laden and precluding the more than de-cadelong wars in Afghanistan and Iraq. Globally, instead of react-ing to brush fires with overused token forces, America could have actively engaged the world supported by the judicious use of smarts and will. The still-intact national security infrastructure could even have changed from domestic introspection into a Pax Americana, generating economic development abroad and profits at home. It was an idea Clinton, nearing the end of his second term, eventually came to appreciate.

The world would have been different. The 1993 Battle of Moga-dishu would not have ended in disaster. The 1994 Rwandan geno-cide could have been stopped. When Slobodan Milošević and other participants realized the combined potency of American military and NATO might, the Kosovo War would have been considered a bad idea. The al-Qaeda nightmare would have died stillborn in the 1990s. Without the fear factor of bin Laden, a well-staffed IC would have also been equipped to counter Dick Cheney's flawed WMD argument for the invasion of Iraq with hard facts, saving one mil-lion Iraqi lives, 6,800 American soldiers, and 6,900 contractors from duty and death. Pat Tillman would still be playing football. Neil Young's "Let's Roll" would never have been recorded. Instead,

Congresswoman Gabby Giffords and many others would have died from gunshot wounds to the head without the crucial medical experience gained in the Second Iraq War. A few big-ticket defense contractors might have gone hungry for a while, but they would have likely eventually found work designing software to replace the dwindling number of lower-class workers with automation. Even more Americans would have found jobs, bought houses, and prospered free of fear under a sustainable peace dividend.

‖‖‖‖‖‖‖‖‖‖‖‖‖‖‖‖‖‖‖‖‖‖‖‖‖‖‖‖‖‖‖‖‖‖‖‖‖‖‖‖‖‖‖‖‖‖‖‖‖‖‖‖‖‖‖‖

# 97

# BLOCKBUSTING DECISION

## 2000

**By Bill Fawcett**

‖‖‖‖‖‖‖‖‖‖‖‖‖‖‖‖‖‖‖‖‖‖‖‖‖‖‖‖‖‖‖‖‖‖‖‖‖‖‖‖‖‖‖‖‖‖‖‖‖‖‖‖‖‖‖‖

After all, the Internet is just a trend.

In the 1980s, movies on videotape were perhaps the main form of home entertainment. Video recorder technology had taken the entertainment world by storm and many movies made more money in the VHS version than in the theaters. The king of videotape sales was the Blockbuster store chain. Founded in 1985, the chain expanded greatly in 1988 to more than four hundred stores and opened its one thousandth by 1991. Media giant Viacom bought the company in 1994. The company changed direction in the mid-1990s and rental DVDs began to dominate its stores' shelves. Their success was so great that other companies saw an opportunity—and took it. In 1997, Amazon began offering DVDs along with books and other merchandise; it and other new competitors cut deeply into Blockbuster's DVD sales, but did not compete with their core business of DVD rental. The same year, a company whose focus was limited to renting DVDs through the mail was started. This was Netflix. The mail-order company grew, though not so fast or so large as to really challenge Blockbuster's dominance in the DVD rental market.

In the year 2000, the management of Netflix arranged a meeting with Blockbuster. They spoke at length about the online market and its possibilities. The Netflix executives proposed to work with Blockbuster and handle all of their online activities. Blockbuster was offered a partnership, or the chance to purchase Netflix for what was, to them, pocket change. The Blockbuster management's reaction was less than farsighted. According to Netflix CFO Barry McCarthy, "They just about laughed us out of their office."

By 2008, Blockbuster had eight thousand stores and sixty thousand employees worldwide, with sales of more than $5 billion a year. Netflix had also begun to grow without any connection to the company. As the Internet became faster and more efficient, Netflix added to their online DVD rental program a movie-download service. Blockbuster stores continued to sell DVDs.

By 2014, Blockbuster had gone bust. Today, the chain is essentially gone and the company they laughed out of their office now has revenues of over a billion dollars a quarter. The derided Netflix has become a multibillion-dollar corporation and is even doing original programming.

The mistake Blockbuster made was not to look into the future, and to assume the business model they were using would last forever. If the (formerly) very successful management of Blockbuster had seen and accepted the potential of Netflix, you might still be able to find a Blockbuster store today.

# 98

SANDRA DAY
O'CONNOR
CHANGES HER MIND

2000

By Mike Resnick

One vote, a single opinion, determined
the next US president.

The closest presidential election in United States history occurred in the year 2000, between George W. Bush and Al
Gore. At eleven p.m. Eastern, some networks projected that
Bush was the winner. At two thirty a.m. Eastern, they changed that,
either proclaiming Gore the winner or placing the race back in the
undecided column. By four a.m. Eastern, the networks had agreed
on only one thing: the race was too close to call.

Eventually it boiled down to the state of Florida. They counted,
and recounted, and recounted again. When the dust cleared, Bush
had a 327-vote lead. But Florida law gave Gore a chance to demand
hand recounts in districts of his own choosing. Bush's people went
to court over that, and the Supreme Court ruled seven to two that
Gore couldn't cherry-pick the districts for a recount, that *that* put
a different weight on votes from different districts.

Gore's people sued again, Bush's countersued, and the entire
nation waited to find out who their next president would be. After
the Supreme Court heard all the arguments, it decided five to four
in Bush's favor and Bush, the son of the forty-first president of the
United States, became the forty-third.

Bush was very aware of his tissue-thin margin, and went out of
his way to be conciliatory, even joining with Teddy Kennedy to

push the "No Child Left Behind" act. He moved very carefully, very cautiously, for the first nine months of his term.

Then came September 11, the destruction of the World Trade Center, the attempted destruction of the Pentagon, and the deaths of more than three thousand Americans as the US was invaded by a hostile power, one hardly anyone had heard of prior to that day.

Bush instantly mobilized the armed forces and prepared them for action, and indeed in a few months they invaded Afghanistan, destroyed Osama bin Laden's headquarters, and defeated al-Qaeda. It was a quick, efficient operation with very few American casualties. The only negative was that bin Laden himself escaped and went into hiding, and for the rest of his presidency Bush had teams searching the Middle East, and the world, for him.

Then, little more than a year later, the intelligence services of the United States, Great Britain, and Israel, among others, believed that it was likely Iraq's Saddam Hussein had a stockpile of nuclear weapons. After all, he was an avowed enemy of the United States, Bush's father had already won a brief, humiliating war with him a dozen years earlier when he drove him out of Kuwait, and he had blocked inspection teams from doing their job. Since we now had a battle-hardened army, it made sense to invade and unseat Hussein and free his people from the yoke of tyranny before he could use those nukes on the United States.

Well, we won the war and executed Saddam, but to this day no one has found any weapons of mass destruction in Iraq that were produced when we thought they were being made. For better or worse, our strife in the Middle East became George W. Bush's lasting legacy.

But it became his legacy because of a single person. Which one? It had to be a Supreme Court justice, one of the five who ruled in favor of Bush over Gore.

What if Sandra Day O'Connor had changed her mind, if Clarence Thomas's, Anthony Scalia's, and William Rehnquist's arguments hadn't swayed her, but Ruth Bader Ginsburg's had? There were tens of millions of votes cast, but that one single vote could have changed history.

Let us say that she did, indeed, change her vote, and Al Gore became our forty-third president.

Not much different would have happened at first. Wanting to get bin Laden since the early nineties, Gore would have been more receptive than Bush to warnings and plans to remove the al-Qaeda threat from Afghanistan upon entering office, but luck would have played a big role in getting the terrorist head, discovering the plan to attack America, and stopping the nineteen hijackers before the 9/11 attack was under way.

Perhaps.

More notably, Gore, a left-leaning liberal, would have been far less inclined to take on Iraq. He would have wanted to try diplomacy first, going to the UN for stiffer sanctions in retaliation for the regime's continued flagrant peace treaty violations. Failing there, he would have likely returned to Clinton's policy of cruise missile attacks and Persian Gulf naval patrols, limiting Iraq's ability to make money off of black-market oil, continuing to kick the can down the road with containment strategies. It is therefore likely that Saddam Hussein and his Ba'athist regime would still be in power today.

But as more people the world over are learning from ISIS every day, you cannot reason with committed fanatics. There would almost certainly have been more attacks, and when Gore finally yielded to public pressure to go after bin Laden, the situation in Iraq would have been placed on a back burner.

Gore would have tried for the kind of quick, clean, limited war that George H. W. Bush had fought against Iraq in 1991 . . . but Iraq was a country with definite boundaries and no allies (or at least none willing to go to war with the United States on Saddam's behalf). Al-Qaeda had no national boundaries, and its leadership was in hiding, presumably (but not definitely) in the Middle East.

As this was going on, Gore would have latched on to the notion of global warming, a notion that was made to seem more likely than it actually was due to a number of alleged forged e-mails uncovered at the University of East Anglia and elsewhere. Believing in it totally, Gore might have begun investing huge amounts of federal funds in companies that were trying to capitalize on it.

Because he would have been publicly committed to the destruction of al-Qaeda, and because the economy wouldn't start tanking for another couple of years, Gore would win a narrow re-election in 2004. Between the war and the huge push for alternate power sources, the economy would begin tanking in 2006, and Gore would spend his final two years trying to turn it around with eco-safe technology. When he left office in 2008, it would be generally acknowledged that Saddam Hussein was the most powerful military foe the United States had faced—and was still facing—since Adolf Hitler.

For want of a nail, a war was lost—and for want of one judge's vote, another war was much further from victory than it might have been.

‖‖‖‖‖‖‖‖‖‖‖‖‖‖‖‖‖‖‖‖‖‖‖‖‖‖‖‖‖‖‖‖‖‖‖‖‖‖‖‖‖‖‖‖‖‖‖‖‖‖‖‖‖‖‖‖‖‖‖‖‖

# FALL OF THE AZTEK'S EMPIRE

2001

**By William Terdoslavich**

‖‖‖‖‖‖‖‖‖‖‖‖‖‖‖‖‖‖‖‖‖‖‖‖‖‖‖‖‖‖‖‖‖‖‖‖‖‖‖‖‖‖‖‖‖‖‖‖‖‖‖‖‖‖‖‖‖‖‖‖‖

Recently the US Supreme Court said
that corporations are people. Maybe
they have a point. Even the biggest
can make mistakes as efficiently
as any person.

The Pontiac Aztek was ugly since birth. It did not have to be that way.

The Aztek was supposed to be a "crossover" vehicle—half minivan, half SUV. Preliminary sketches showed a concept car with a sleek, sloping hood and a rakish roof that slanted downward to the rear. Somewhere between design and construction, the Aztek got pushed in from both ends, yielding a bug-eyed bucket on four wheels.

On one level, this is a story about making a car the wrong way. But the Aztek was something more than that. It symbolized everything that was wrong with its parent, General Motors, a company so choked by bureaucracy that it could not do anything original quickly and efficiently.

And in the competitive auto industry, failure to innovate is the kiss of death.

## Pontiac Used to Be Sexy

Pontiac was once the car preferred by grandmothers. It was plain, cheap, reliable, and totally unremarkable. That changed in the late

1950s, when Semon Knudsen became Pontiac's division chief, with John DeLorean on board as chief engineer. They made Pontiac bad, sexy, and fun to drive.

The first move was to push the wheels farther apart by five inches. The "wide track" improved the car's handling. Stock-car drivers began racking up wins in Pontiacs. And the car looked meaner and a little lower to the ground.

It was DeLorean who took Pontiac to the next level. GM executives imposed a limit on engine size. DeLorean bent the rule by offering a massive 389-cubic-inch eight-cylinder monster as an "option" for his GTO. Pontiac sold five thousand GTOs before GM executives were told of the deception. By then, it was too late. DeLorean had invented the classic American muscle car, and it was literally driving itself out of the showroom.

In the following decade, one out of ten cars on the road was a Pontiac. And it wasn't just the GTO. The Bonneville, the Firebird, and the Tempest followed. BMW sent engineers to Pontiac, just to learn how DeLorean did it.

By the early 1970s, the world changed, and not for the better. The Arab oil embargo of 1973 doubled the price of gas. The great American muscle car could give you four hundred horsepower, but only at 8 mpg. And this became a real kick in the wallet with every fuel fill, assuming you could buy enough gas after waiting in line for two hours.

DeLorean was gone. Pontiac's star faded. The brand went into decline. And GM was still clueless.

## Back to Boring

General Motors reverted to its classic default strategy—making average cars that they thought people wanted to drive. How could it do anything else? GM's infamous corporate culture rewarded conformity, amplified caution, cut costs, and placed process before product.

No matter how hard GM tried to be different, it always ended up the same. GM acquired Hughes Aircraft for its electronic expertise, and Electronic Data Systems to computerize design, engineering, and manufacturing. A joint venture with Toyota running an auto plant, known as the NUMMI project, gave GM a chance to learn about Toyota's superior assembly methods. GM's Saturn division would be the test bed for new engineering and manufacturing techniques that could be applied systemwide.

Some of these projects were ignored. Others lagged.

A frustrated executive at GM, Elmer Johnson, wrote a twenty-five-page memo back in 1988, describing an insular, bureaucratic culture that stifled innovation. This was back when it took as many as seventy executives two months to make a change in a product—much too long to react to changes in the market. Johnson wanted to streamline the hideous bureaucracy, identify proven leaders inside GM and promote them on merit, and restore the connection between making cars and making money.

The memo was binned. So was Johnson.

The Pontiac Aztek was not even a gleam in the eye of its producer, and it was already doomed.

## And Now for Something Completely Different

By the mid-1990s, GM tried to reinvigorate from within. Then-chairman John Smale, formerly of Procter & Gamble, saw the need for sexy, unique-looking cars and trucks that could turn heads. Sadly, this was lost to the process of design-by-committee, guided by focus groups, *with no one clearly in charge.*

By the late 1990s, GM market research finally saw the need for "something different"—the crossover. This would look like an SUV, but combined with the smaller virtues of the minivan. The concept sketches for the Aztek showed something smaller than a full-sized SUV, with its long front end proportional to a boxy but slanted back end that still looked good, but provided a lot of cubic space for hauling stuff.

The whole point of the Aztek was to not look like a dorky minivan that dads and moms used to shuttle the kids around the suburbs. No, this Aztek was for people to go camping! It had an optional tent that was fitted to the rear hatch, and a removable center console between the front and back seats that doubled as a twelve-can cooler. *This car had good ideas built in.*

The bad ideas triumphed. The "car guys" wanted to put the Aztek on a truck frame. The cost-cutting bean counters insisted the Aztek be fitted on a minivan platform—the very thing the Aztek was trying to get away from. This squeezed the front end in. The back end was shoved in and upward. What once looked like adventure on four wheels now looked like a large, ugly bug. *And there was no one who could stop this from happening.*

GM launched the Aztek with great fanfare for the 2001 model year, but the fans were not impressed. Only twenty thousand were sold instead of seventy thousand. The sticker price was too high for younger buyers—higher if you included all-wheel drive as an option.

The audience of *Car Talk*, an NPR-syndicated radio show, voted the Aztek the ugliest car in America back in 2005. The two Boston wise guys who hosted the show, Ray and Tom Magliozzi, cackled with glee as they read the cutting remarks on the air.

"Looked like it went to the crusher before the showroom."

"Was Pontiac taken over by a high school shop class?"

"Ever see this car from behind? It's like getting behind a horse that's ready to drop a load."

Despite repeated attempts to prettify a hopeless design, Pontiac pulled the plug on the Aztek after four years. It never came close to making its sales goals.

### What If It Worked?

The Pontiac Aztek and GM's corporate culture are inseparable. What if the Aztek had come out right? That would have required a forceful personality, another DeLorean. GM vice chairman Bob Lutz provided that kind of force, but he came on board *after* the Aztek's launch. As Lutz once quipped, he would fire the guy who made that car, *if only he could find him.*

Lutz did pull off the Pontiac Solstice, a sexy two-seater that sold well. For Pontiac to have really succeeded, it would have needed a pipeline of designers willing to go out on a limb to create the new, next big thing. Talent can be cultivated.

The bigger "what if" is what the world would be like if GM had re-formed itself, following Elmer Johnson's epic 1988 memo. The biggest gain would be a deep bench of competent middle managers and executives who would rebuild the link between making cars and making money. Again, Lutz pointed out the "Harvard Business School" mentality that stressed constant cost cutting as a fault. It destroyed the connection between product and profit.

With real managerial strength, GM could have maintained market share against Japanese imports. It could have changed production from SUVs to small cars once gas prices went up. (Instead it kept on making Escalades and Hummers. No one wants to buy a gas guzzler when gas hits $4.85 a gallon.)

Saturn, Oldsmobile, and Pontiac would still be around. GM would have been a competitive, creative car company. It would have had the institutional expertise to weather the "Great Recession" of 2008 without the need of a federal bailout or Chapter 11 bankruptcy filing. Pension funds and investors holding GM stock or bonds would not have gotten burned. And many GM retirees would still have their pension and health benefits. A lot more GM assembly-line workers would still have paychecks—and homes.

And if the Aztek had turned out cool, then maybe Walter White of *Breaking Bad* would have driven something else, like a Dodge Caravan?

III

# SADDAM HUSSEIN: AL-QAEDA AND WMDS!

## 2003

### By Douglas Niles

IIIIIIIIIIIIIIIIIIIIIIIIIIIIIIIIIIIIIIIIIIIIIIIIIIIIIIIIIIIIIIIIIIIIIIIIIIIIIII

Now you see it. . . .

T he suicide attacks perpetrated by al-Qaeda terrorists on September 11, 2001, cost thousands of lives, destroyed the World Trade Center, damaged the Pentagon—and changed the political dynamic of the United States and the world. With solid knowledge that the fanatical jihadist organization had training camps and support from the Taliban government of Afghanistan, the American military wasted little time, beginning retaliation against that country in the first weeks after 9/11. Spearheading a brilliant offensive with airpower, special forces, and light infantry—while CIA agents were already effectively recruiting and directing anti-Taliban factions among the Afghans to corral the enemy—the US went to war against that fundamentalist Islamic regime.

Within a matter of months, the Taliban had been removed from control of the landlocked country. The fanatical Islamic group was reduced to the status of a fugitive guerrilla organization straddling the border of Afghanistan and Pakistan. A steady influx of American army and marine units began to try to establish a government in one of the most historically remote and ungovernable places in the world—and this was a task that would clearly take a long time and require a lot of attention and investment.

Still, it seemed to many that the terrible damage inflicted on 9/11 called for further retribution. The question was: Where should

America strike next? One answer was obvious to President George W. Bush and Vice President Dick Cheney, and it was based in history from decades earlier.

Long before 2001, the United States had recognized brutal Iraqi dictator Saddam Hussein as a Very Bad Man. During the 1980s, Saddam had exhausted and bankrupted his country with a bloody, but futile, eight-year war against Iran. Then, in 1990, he had tried to restore his nation's financial health by invading his biggest creditor, Kuwait. While that small but wealthy country was immediately declared to be a new Iraqi province, the rest of the world—under the leadership of President George H. W. Bush and the United States—had gathered a powerful army, including units from a large coalition of nations, along the southern borders of Iraq and Kuwait.

Operation Desert Storm commenced on January 17, 1991, with a five-week air campaign involving an unprecedented level of precision bombing. The Iraqi air force, air defenses, and many fixed targets on the ground were bombed into oblivion. On February 24, the Allied ground forces attacked and immediately swept forward across the entire front. In only one hundred hours, they had captured or destroyed a huge portion of the Iraqi army, and completely evicted the Iraqis from Kuwait.

Operation Desert Storm was over. It had been an unqualified success, achieving its objective with remarkably few Coalition casualties and obvious tactical brilliance. However, since his removal had not been a goal of the operation, it did leave Saddam in control of Iraq. Furthermore, Desert Storm had the unintended consequence of convincing American political leadership that US military forces could accomplish any task quickly, and with little cost.

In the decade after the war, the dictator cemented his power, and continued to bluster against his primary enemy, Iran. While his people and his armed forces suffered under economic sanctions and a "no-fly" zone imposed by the Desert Storm victors, Saddam himself weathered the years in fine style, continuing to oppress his people and rail against Iran.

This remained the status quo in Iraq on 9/11, 2001. As the administration of the new President Bush—son of the chief executive who had initiated Desert Storm—continued to look for potential

9/11 accomplices, Saddam Hussein seemed to be a very likely suspect. And he represented a potential future threat as well. The damage on 9/11 had been inflicted by terrorists using airliners as weapons; but how dangerous would it be if fanatics got access to military-grade weapons of mass destruction (WMDs), such as chemical or nuclear materials?

Indeed, Saddam had been known to use poison gas against both the Iranians and ethnic minorities, such as the Kurds, in his own country. If the US could gather enough evidence to suggest that Hussein still had the potential to manufacture WMDs, the administration believed it would have sufficient justification to launch an invasion of Iraq that would topple Saddam from power. And if Saddam could be linked to al-Qaeda and 9/11, that fact would cement the case for war.

With this goal in mind, the Bush administration, through the office of Vice President Cheney, demanded that its intelligence sources, including the CIA, NSA, FBI, and branches of the military, come up with "intel" that would support an invasion. Although the intelligence community failed to find Cheney's proof, a privately funded group of analysts, housed inside the Pentagon and granted access to only unclassified intelligence reports, made several logical leaps based on circumstantial data. Virtually any source that claimed to have such evidence was accepted by Cheney's people and the White House, while sources that brought forth information disagreeing with or contradicting the desired conclusion were suppressed or discredited. In almost a parody of Adlai Stevenson's memorable presentation to the United Nations, when he displayed surveillance photos proving the existence of Soviet nuclear missiles in Cuba in 1962, Secretary of State Colin Powell took "artist's concept" drawings—essentially, cartoons—before the UN to show the array of installations Saddam was allegedly using to manufacture and deploy WMDs. (The testimony, whether knowingly or not, ignored the fact that the source behind these drawings was an Iraqi exile who desperately wanted to return to power in a post-Saddam Iraq.)

It is clear, in retrospect, that the proponents of the Iraq War, a group of conservatives known as "neocons," were convinced that the invasion and its aftermath would be an easy triumph for the United States, and a validation of their aggressive policies. It is worth noting that all of these advocates of war, including Bush and Cheney, and also Defense Secretary Donald Rumsfeld, Deputy Secretary of Defense Paul Wolfowitz, and the esteemed political adviser Richard Perle, had been busy doing other things while so many American men of their generation had been called to the war in Vietnam. That is, *none* of them had any combat experience (though the president had in fact been a pilot in the National Guard). The one influential administration member who had a stellar battlefield record in Vietnam, Colin Powell, was notably less enthusiastic about invading Iraq than were the neocon "armchair generals."

Eventually, of course, the Bush administration and its one-sided collection of evidence, supported by an American population still desiring retribution for 9/11, convinced a large majority of Congress that war with Iraq was justified. Though the link between Saddam and al-Qaeda had never been supported by a shred of evidence—and in fact, defied logic, since the fanatically religious jihadists had no reason to support a secular dictator—such a connection continued to be hinted at, especially by the vice president.

Since the justification for war was so tenuous, the second Bush administration was much less successful than the first in developing a coalition of allies. When Iraq was invaded in March of 2003, American forces did almost all of the fighting; only Great Britain provided more than token support. At the same time, the very-much-unfinished campaign to pacify Afghanistan languished, inevitably moving to the back burner. It would continue to lag in resources and attention as American military and political leadership directed a laserlike focus on Iraq.

Of course, Saddam's government was toppled in short order, but a catastrophic failure to plan for control of the country after the dictator was removed meant that the fighting, the occupation, and the casualties would continue for many years. Iraq would be torn by a virtual civil war, with American forces caught between Sunni and Shi'a factions, and a strong al-Qaeda presence—which had not existed in Iraq under Saddam, but moved in quickly after the dictator's fall—maintaining a steady stream of terrorist attacks against both Americans and the fledgling Iraqi government.

When President Bush left office in 2008, a "surge" of American military forces had finally begun to exert some measure of control. However, the surge was never intended to be a permanent occupation force, and when President Obama—with the support of the majority of American voters, who had grown tired of the long war—continued the postsurge withdrawal of US troops from Iraq, the civil war resumed with a vengeance. By 2014, al-Qaeda had been replaced by an equally vicious and fanatical group of jihadists, often known as ISIS, who controlled even more territory and exerted more military power than the original terrorists had ever imagined.

Some 4,500 Americans lost their lives in the Iraq War, and $2 *trillion* was spent by 2013, in a campaign to eliminate weapons that were not being manufactured as the White House had articulated. Fourteen years after 9/11, both Afghanistan and Iraq remain ravaged by violence, and the legacy of President George W. Bush has been permanently marred by one of the greatest mistakes in American military history.

Yet if America's leaders had focused the nation's might on creating stability and some level of freedom in Afghanistan, and maintained the status quo in Iraq, both countries—and the entire Middle East—would almost inevitably be in better shape today. There was no chance that al-Qaeda would gain a foothold in Saddam's Iraq, nor would ISIS even exist. Sometimes it can be better to confront an enemy you know, rather than to eliminate that enemy and open the way for an even more broadly based and insidious threat.

# CREATING THE ENEMY

### By Bill Fawcett

> The last stumble is just a case of being overzealous in cleaning house. It shows once more the danger of ideology trumping common sense.

In 2003, the USA had just fought a war to displace Saddam Hussein. Just a few days after the occupation of Baghdad, on May 23, 2003, Paul Bremer, who ran the civilian team that was to administrate post-Saddam Iraq, announced that he was disbanding the Iraqi army. As of his announcement, the entire army, the Republican Guard, and all the employees of the Defense and Information Bureaus were out of a job. Bremer's idea was to quickly erase all trace of influence by those who had any loyalty to the displaced dictator. Anyone above the rank of colonel and any civilian administrators who held decision-making positions were further banned from any employment by the new government or with the occupying American forces. Those of lesser ranks could reenlist, but their former ranks were not to be recognized. This mistake immediately took four hundred thousand skilled and trained leaders, administrators, and soldiers and left them without any way to make a living or support their families. The Iraqi army, which had eighty years of proud history and tradition and had fought Iran to a standstill a decade earlier, was gone in a day. All their skills and tradition were discarded for political reasons. Clearly, there was no thought as to where so many men with their specialized skills would go.

The result was immediate. A shortage of people able to maintain order plus the incomplete occupation of the country led to an increase in lawlessness and violence. More importantly, the dismissals meant that tens of thousands of highly trained and experienced military officers were both in need of employment and embittered. For a range of reasons, including tribal rivalries, corruption, and distrust, the new Iraqi Defense Force never jelled. When it was called upon to face up to ISIS, it was found that half the soldiers who were on the rolls, and had been paid for years, didn't even exist. Their pay had been going to bureaucrats and the unit's commanders. And despite the billions that had been spent on it, the defense force soldiers had not been trained well enough to be effective in combat. The Iraqi Defense Force literally dissolved when challenged by a fraction of their number of determined Islamic fundamentalists. Guess who was commanding those victorious ISIS fighters. Of the forty top commanders of ISIS in 2014, at least twenty-five were former Iraqi army officers.

"We could have done a lot better job of sorting through that and keeping the Iraqi army together," stated General Ray Odierno in a *Time* magazine interview. "We struggled for years to try to put it back together again."

If President Bush and the victorious Coalition forces had followed the example of the British in 1941, and retrained and selectively cleansed the Iraqi army, there likely would never have been an ISIS. Certainly, its success would have been greatly limited. Nor would the officers of an army that had fought a bitter war against the Iranian mullahs be as likely to have turned to Iran for support and military leadership (as Iraq has now). Finally, with a strong army with a tradition of nationalism, there might have been a counterforce to the corrupt government that followed Saddam's defeat. Iraq almost certainly would today be a better place, a more peaceful place, and a balance to Iran. But through fear, revenge, or unthinking reaction, the well-trained Iraqi army was jettisoned and that nation is still paying the price—and may continue to do so for generations.

# AFTERTHOUGHT

There were many mistakes made all through history that are not in this book. You can find many of them in two equally irreverent books, *100 Mistakes That Changed History* and *Trust Me, I Know What I'm Doing*. There have been many miscalculations made since 2003. There will always be new mistakes for historians to view with 20/20 hindsight. But those recent errors both large and small are too new to be viewed as history. Defining what have been the most recent mistakes and who is to blame for them is called politics. And a few of those blunders are also maybe just a bit too painful to include . . . yet. On the brighter side, despite three books full of mistakes spread all across history, civilization still marches on. I find that very reassuring.

# ABOUT THE AUTHOR

**Bill Fawcett** has been a professor, teacher, corporate executive, and college dean, and written or coauthored over a dozen books, including *100 Mistakes That Changed History* and *Trust Me, I Know What I'm Doing*. His company, Bill Fawcett & Associates, has packaged more than 250 titles for virtually every major publisher. He is also one of the founders of Mayfair Games, a board and role-play gaming company.